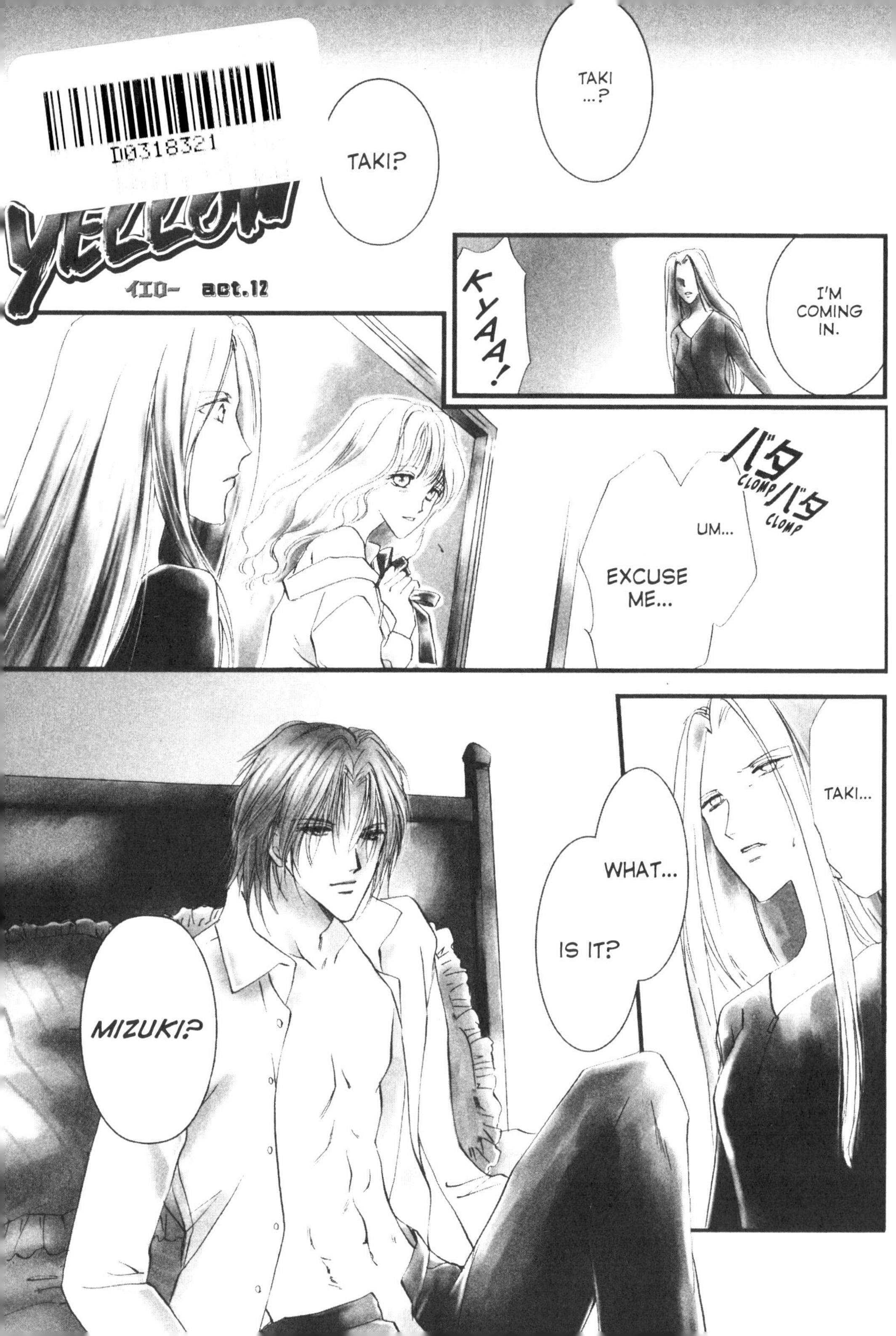
YELLOW
イエロー act.12
TAKI …?
TAKI?
I'M COMING IN.
KYAA!
バタバタ
CLOMP CLOMP
UM…
EXCUSE ME…
TAKI…
WHAT… IS IT?
MIZUKI?

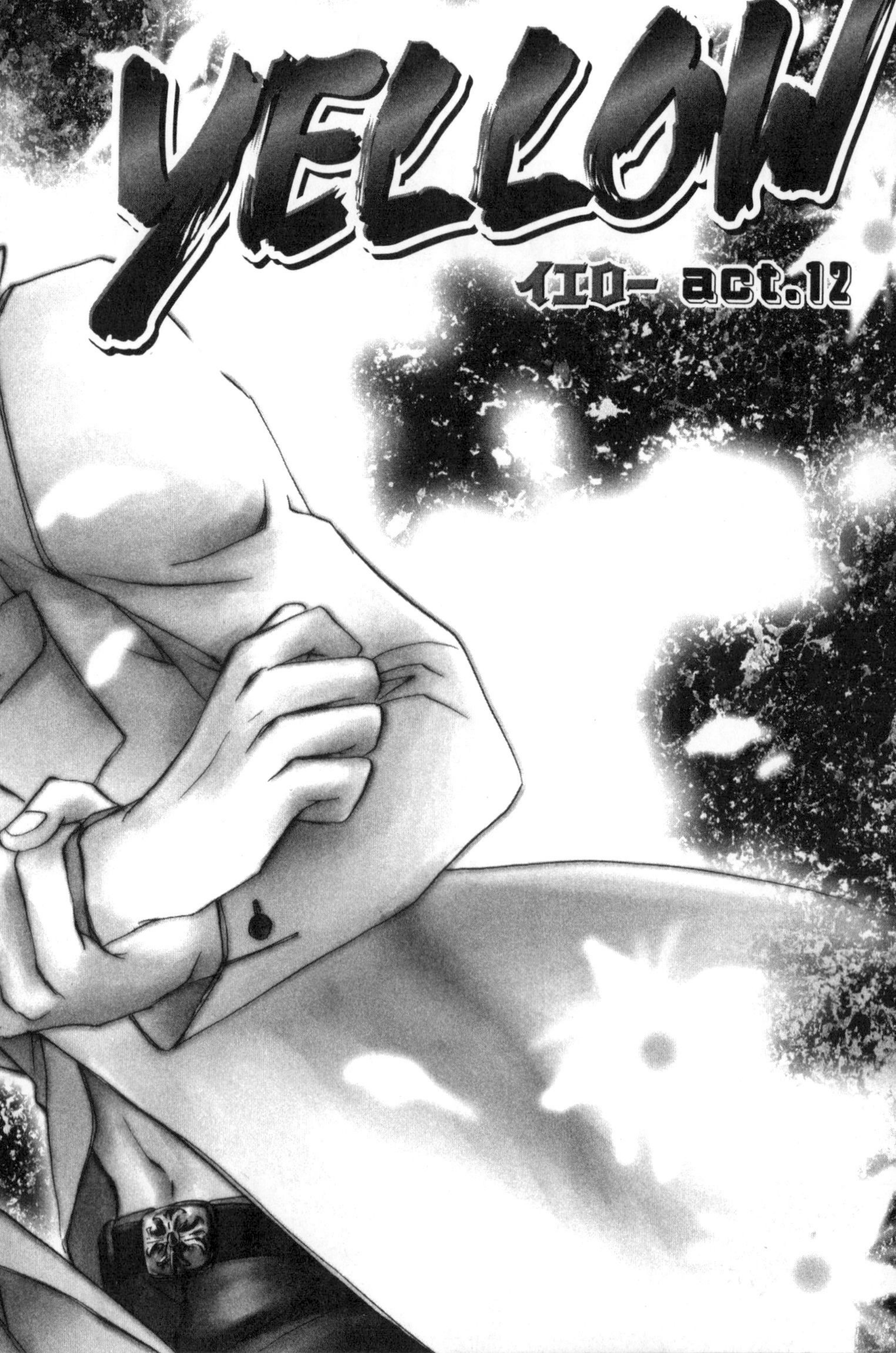
YELLOW
イエロー act.12

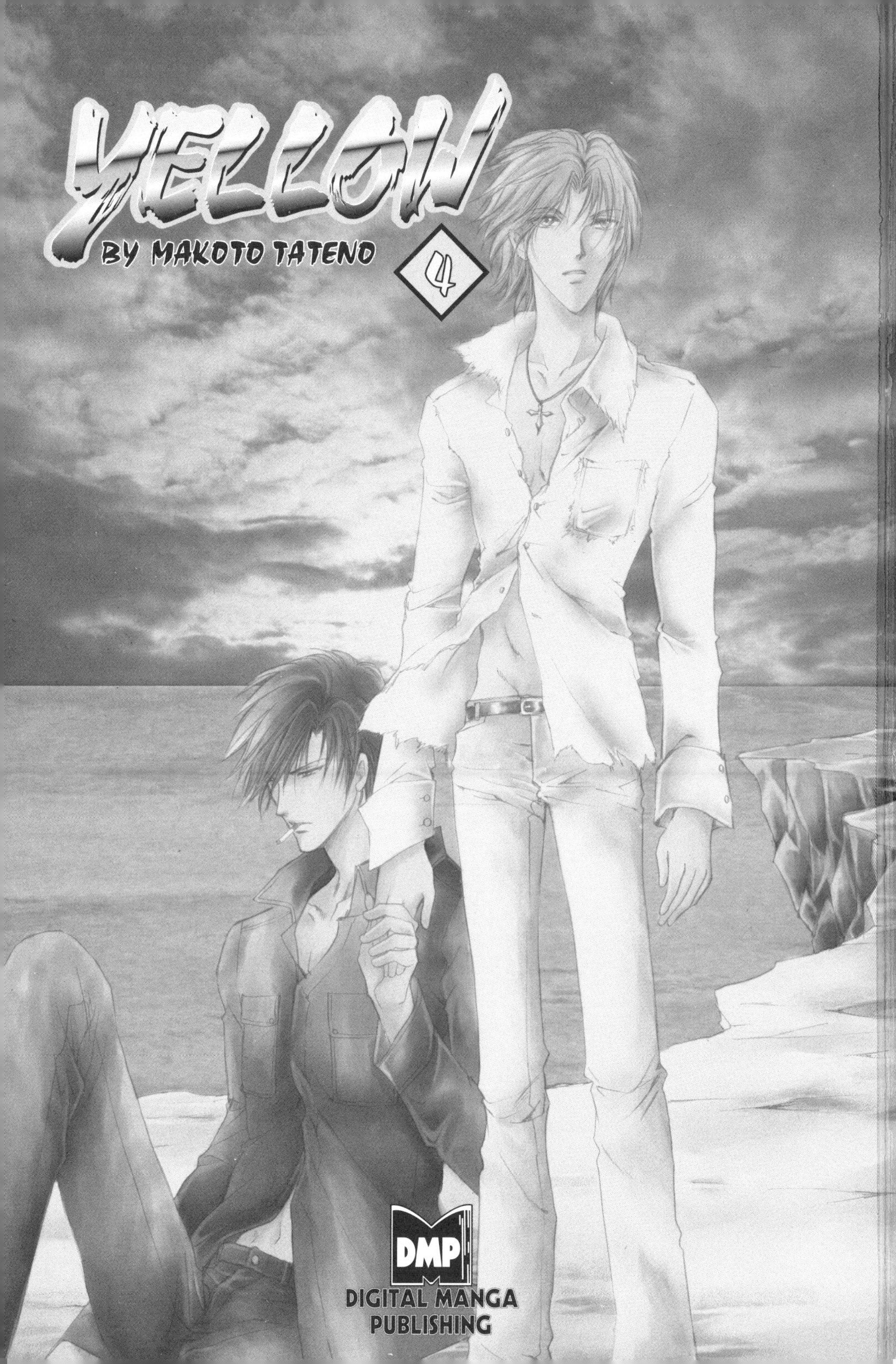
YELLOW
BY MAKOTO TATENO
4
DMP
DIGITAL MANGA
PUBLISHING

YELLOW 4

Translation & Editing	Studio Cutie
Lettering	Studio Cutie
Graphic Design	Eric Rosenberger
	Wendy Lee
Editor in Chief	Fred Lui
Publisher	Hikaru Sasahara

English Edition Published by
DIGITAL MANGA PUBLISHING
A division of DIGITAL MANGA, Inc.
1487 W 178th Street, Suite 300
Gardena, CA 90248

www.dmpbooks.com

First Edition: April 2006
ISBN: 1-56970-895-9

3 5 7 9 10 8 6 4 2

Printed in China

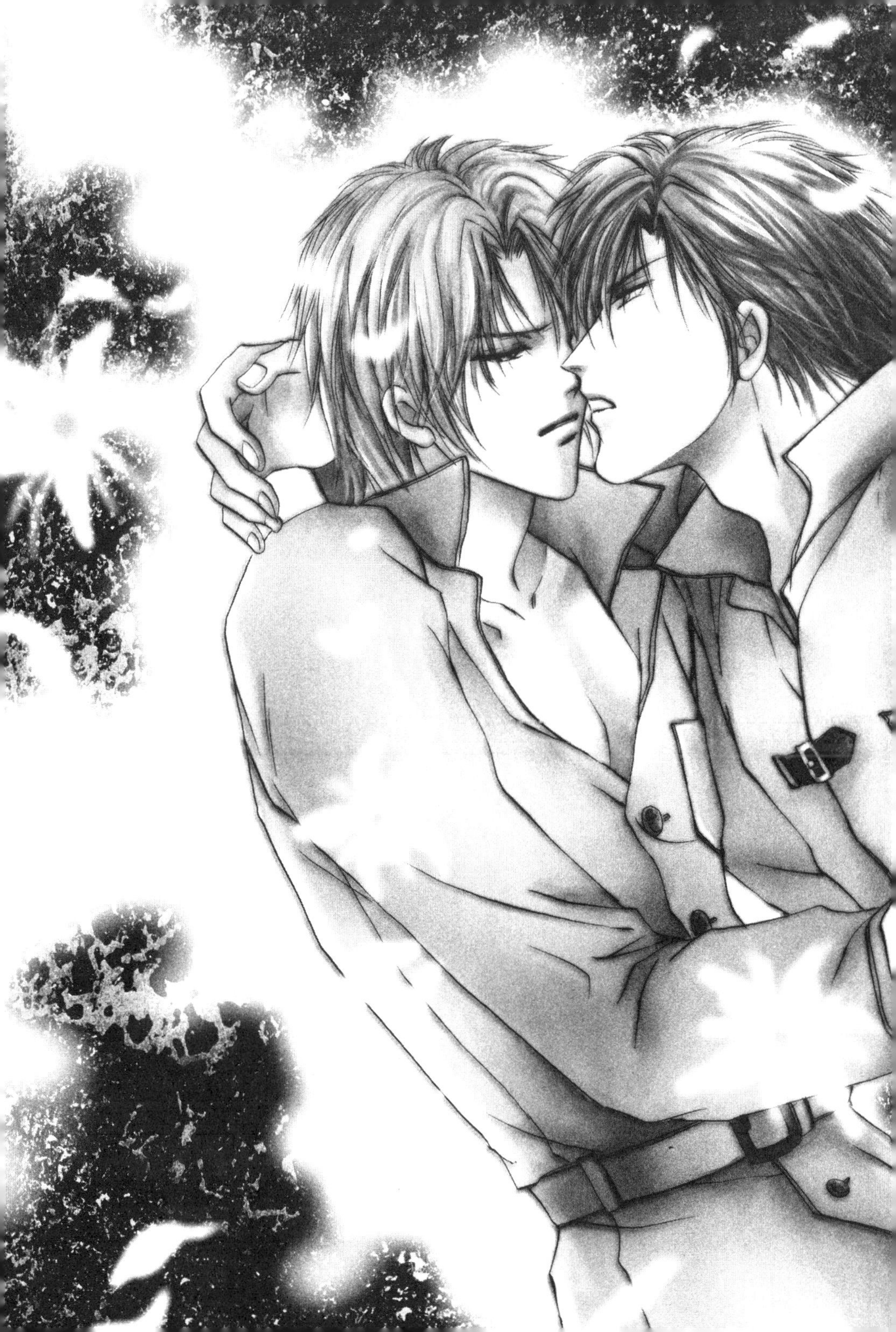

YELLOW

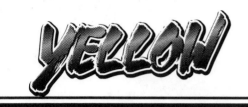

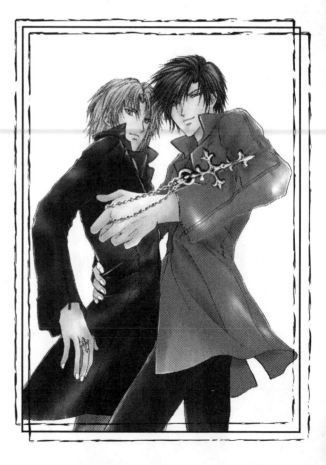

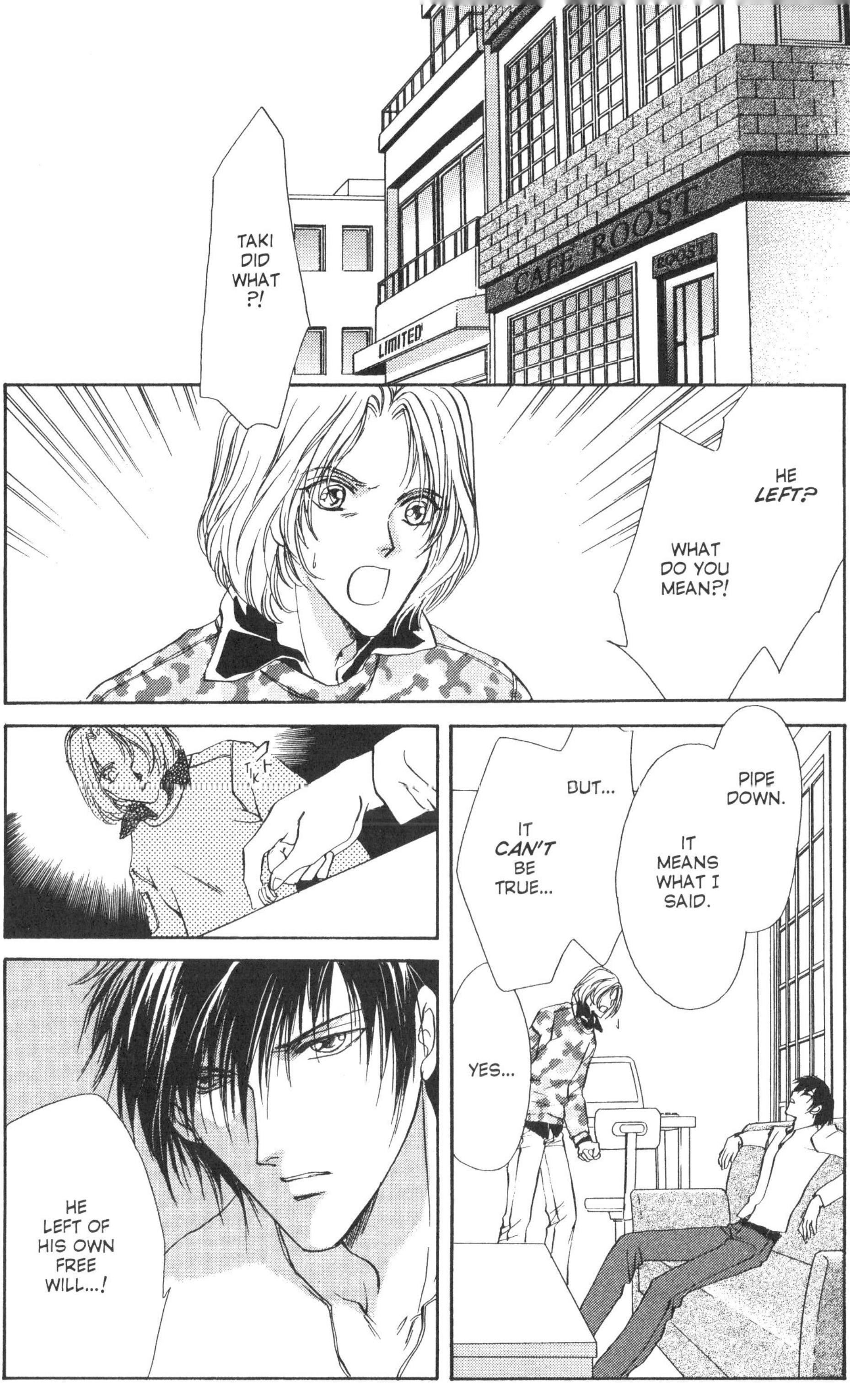
TAKI DID WHAT?!
HE *LEFT?*
WHAT DO YOU MEAN?!
PIPE DOWN.
IT MEANS WHAT I SAID.
BUT...
IT *CAN'T* BE TRUE...
YES...
HE LEFT OF HIS OWN FREE WILL...!

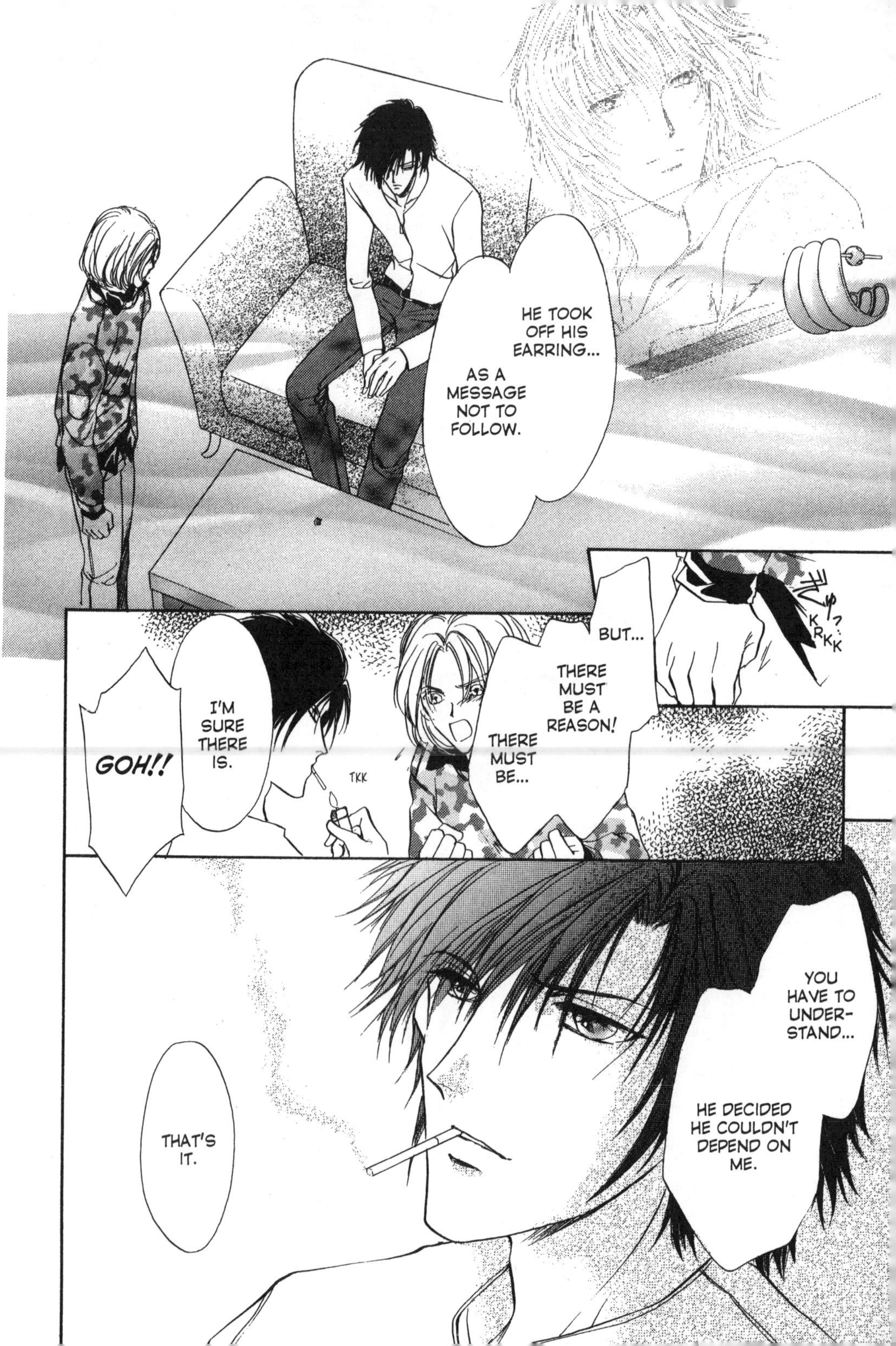
HE TOOK OFF HIS EARRING...
AS A MESSAGE NOT TO FOLLOW.
BUT...
KRKK
THERE MUST BE A REASON!
THERE MUST BE...
I'M SURE THERE IS.
TKK
GOH!!
YOU HAVE TO UNDER-STAND...
HE DECIDED HE COULDN'T DEPEND ON ME.
THAT'S IT.

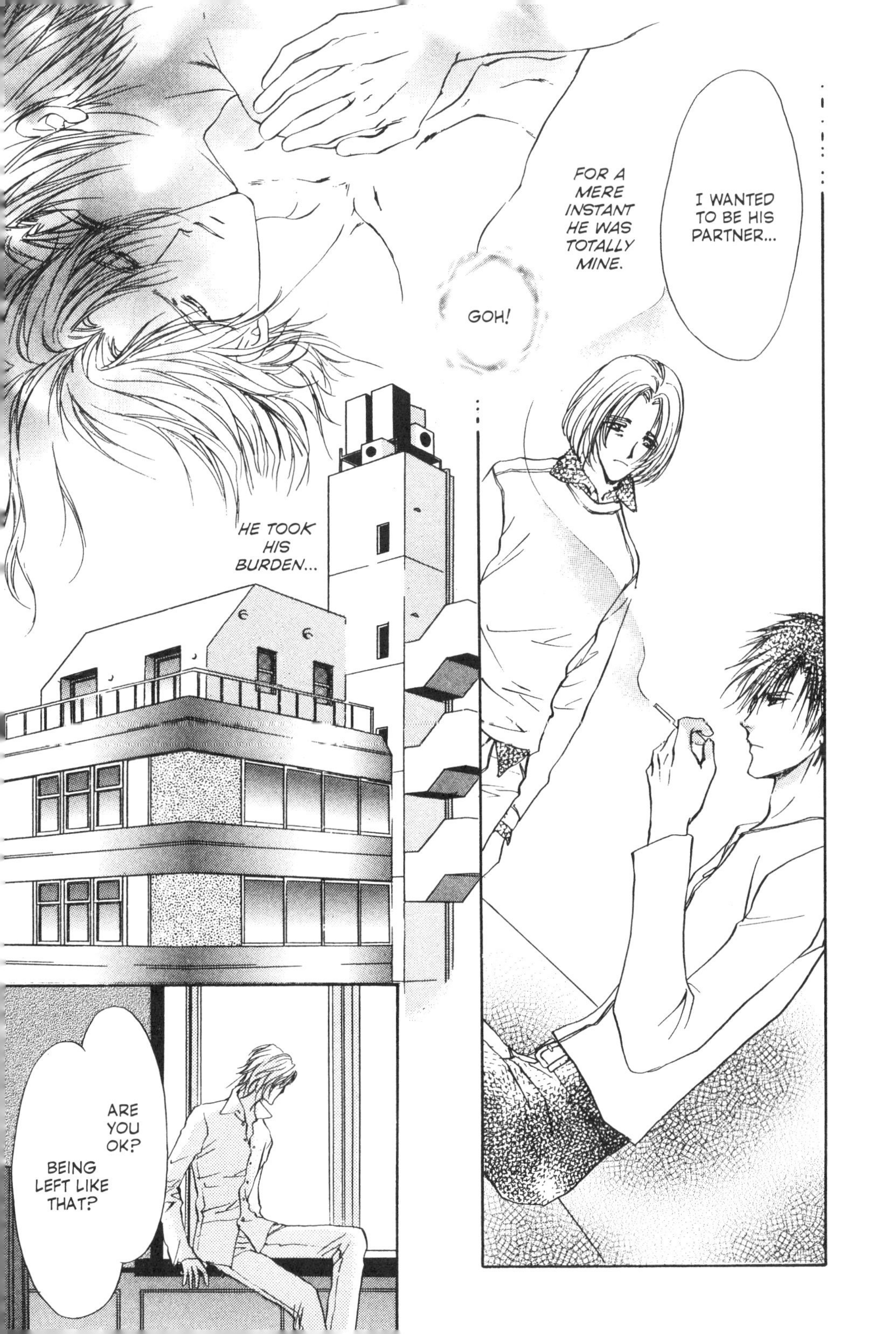
I WANTED TO BE HIS PARTNER...
FOR A MERE INSTANT HE WAS TOTALLY MINE.
GOH!
HE TOOK HIS BURDEN...
ARE YOU OK?
BEING LEFT LIKE THAT?

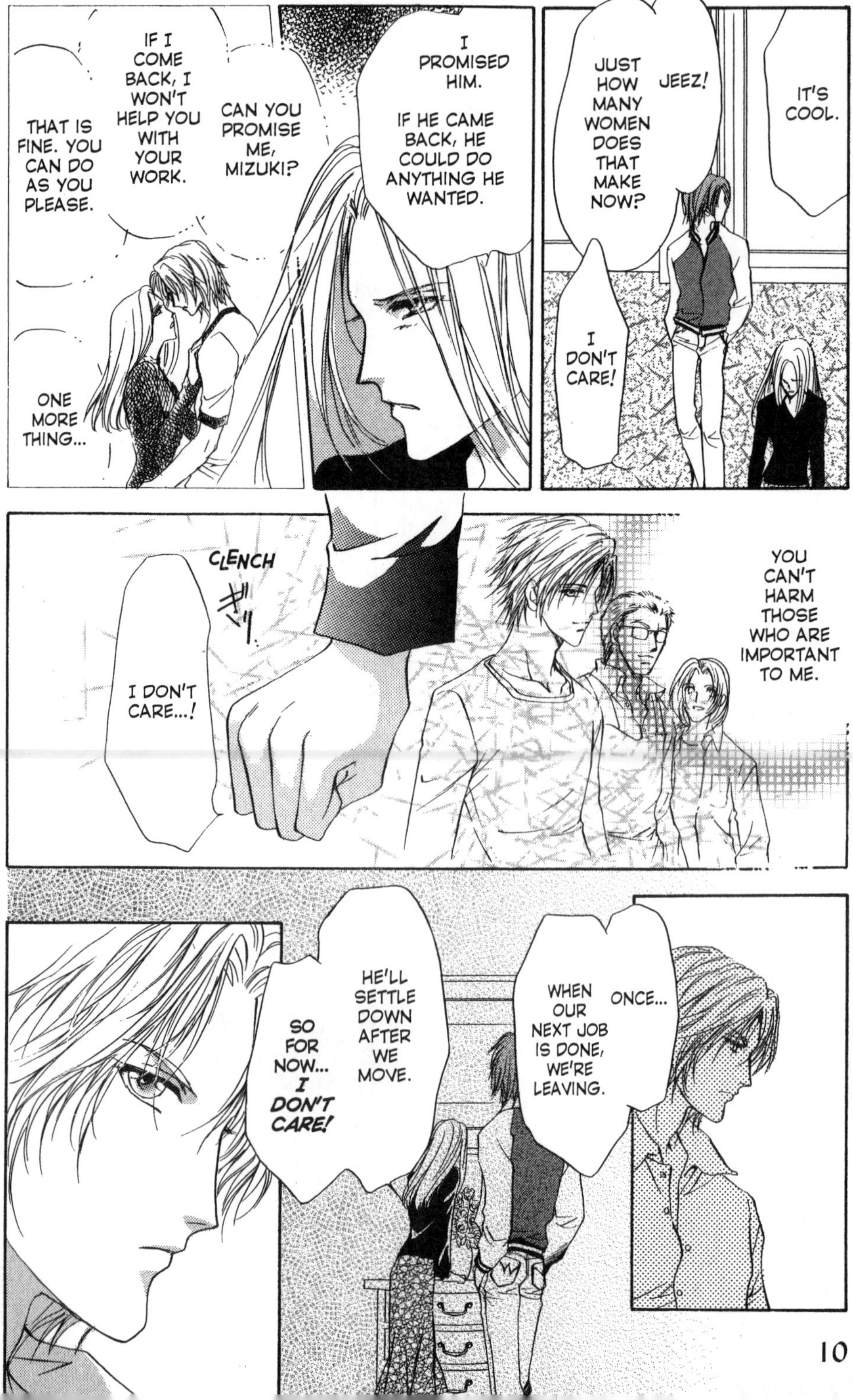
IT'S COOL.
JEEZ! JUST HOW MANY WOMEN DOES THAT MAKE NOW?
I DON'T CARE!
I PROMISED HIM.
IF HE CAME BACK, HE COULD DO ANYTHING HE WANTED.
CAN YOU PROMISE ME, MIZUKI?
IF I COME BACK, I WON'T HELP YOU WITH YOUR WORK.
THAT IS FINE. YOU CAN DO AS YOU PLEASE.
ONE MORE THING...
YOU CAN'T HARM THOSE WHO ARE IMPORTANT TO ME.
CLENCH
I DON'T CARE...!
ONCE...
WHEN OUR NEXT JOB IS DONE, WE'RE LEAVING.
HE'LL SETTLE DOWN AFTER WE MOVE.
SO FOR NOW... ***I DON'T CARE!***

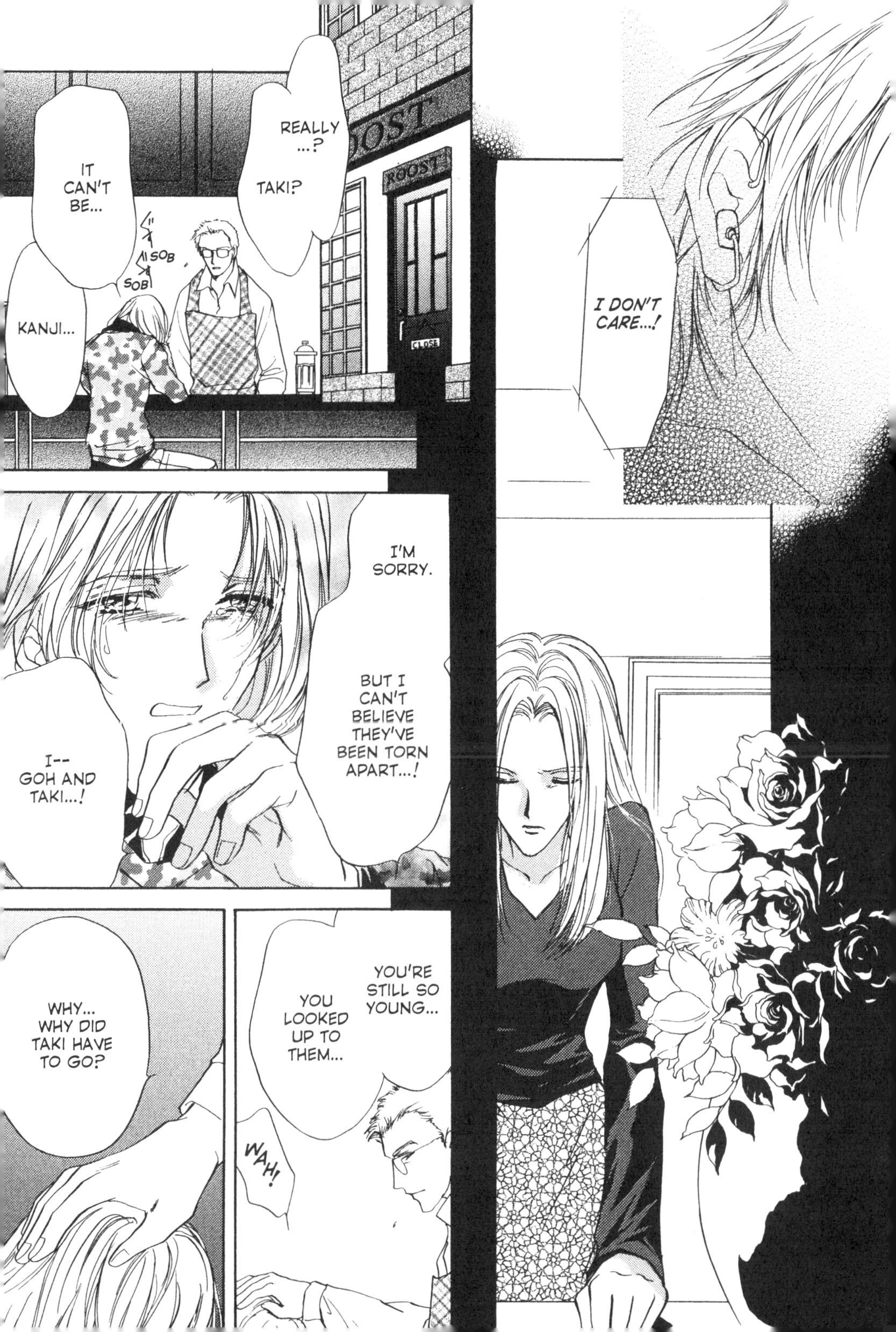
I DON'T CARE...!
ROOST
ROOST
CLOSE
REALLY ...?
TAKI?
IT CAN'T BE...
SOB
SOB
KANJI...
I'M SORRY.
BUT I CAN'T BELIEVE THEY'VE BEEN TORN APART...!
I-- GOH AND TAKI...!
YOU'RE STILL SO YOUNG...
YOU LOOKED UP TO THEM...
WAH!
WHY... WHY DID TAKI HAVE TO GO?

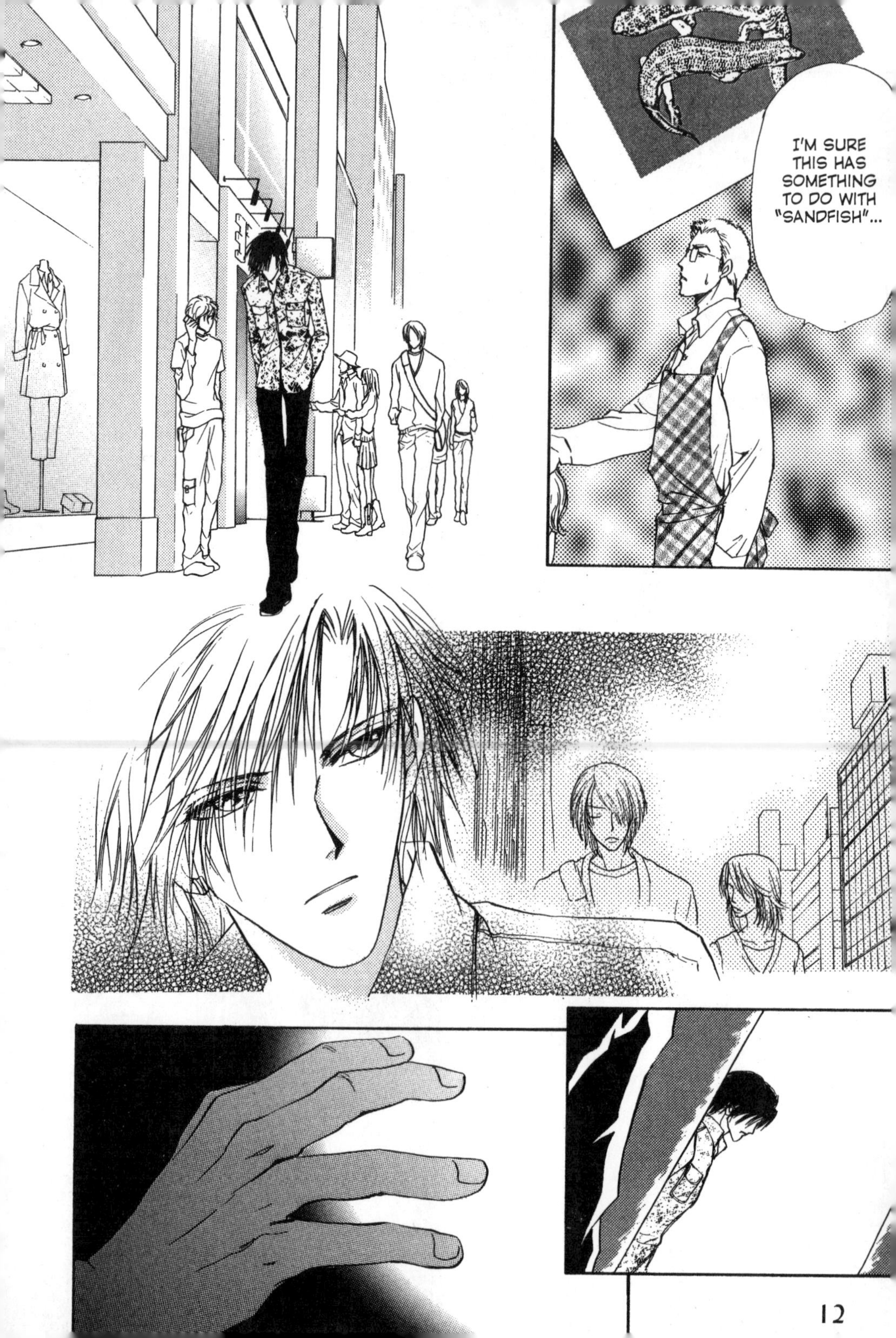
I'M SURE THIS HAS SOMETHING TO DO WITH "SANDFISH"...

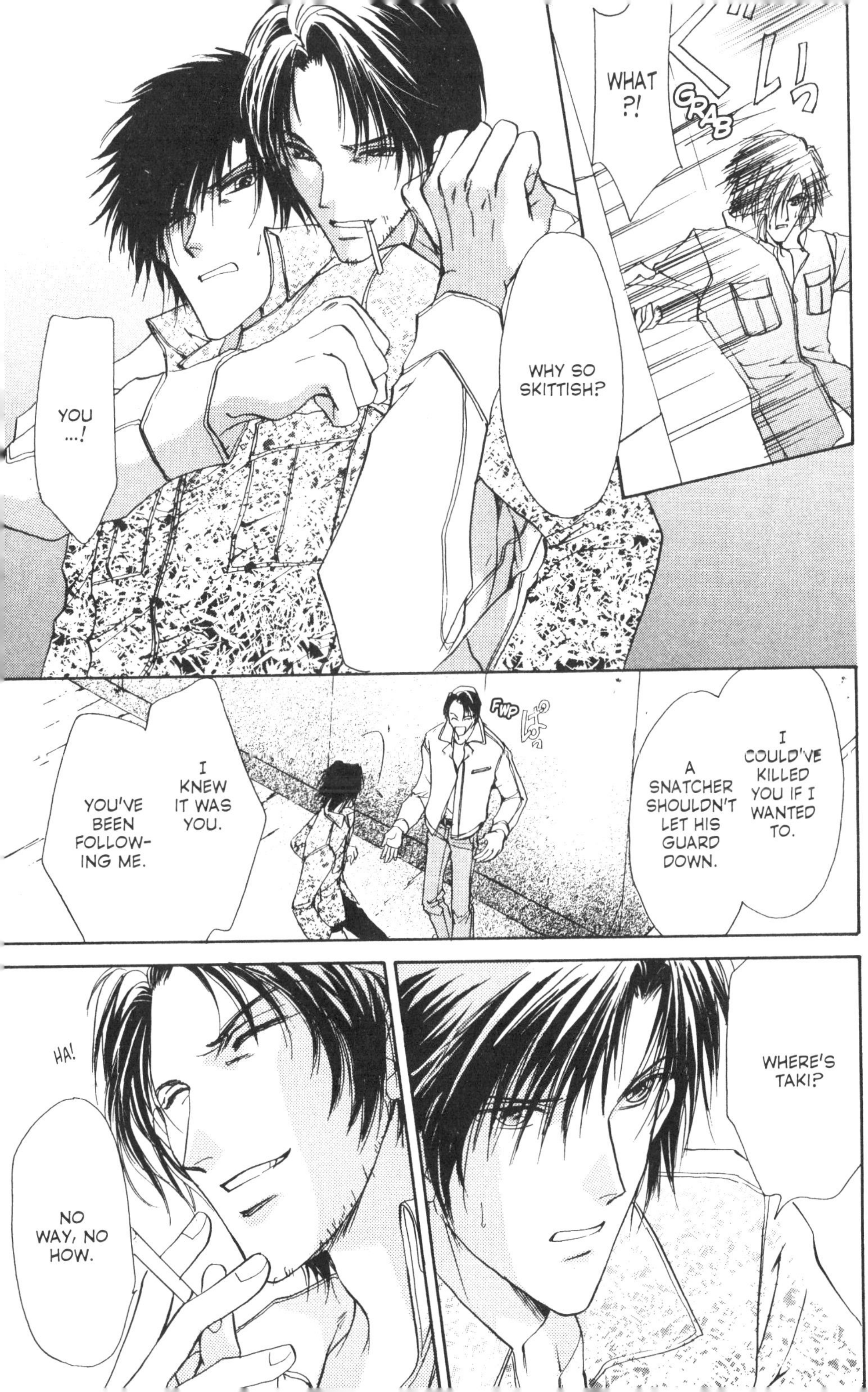
WHAT?!
GRAB
WHY SO SKITTISH?
YOU ...!
I COULD'VE KILLED YOU IF I WANTED TO.
A SNATCHER SHOULDN'T LET HIS GUARD DOWN.
FWP
I KNEW IT WAS YOU.
YOU'VE BEEN FOLLOW-ING ME.
WHERE'S TAKI?
HA!
NO WAY, NO HOW.

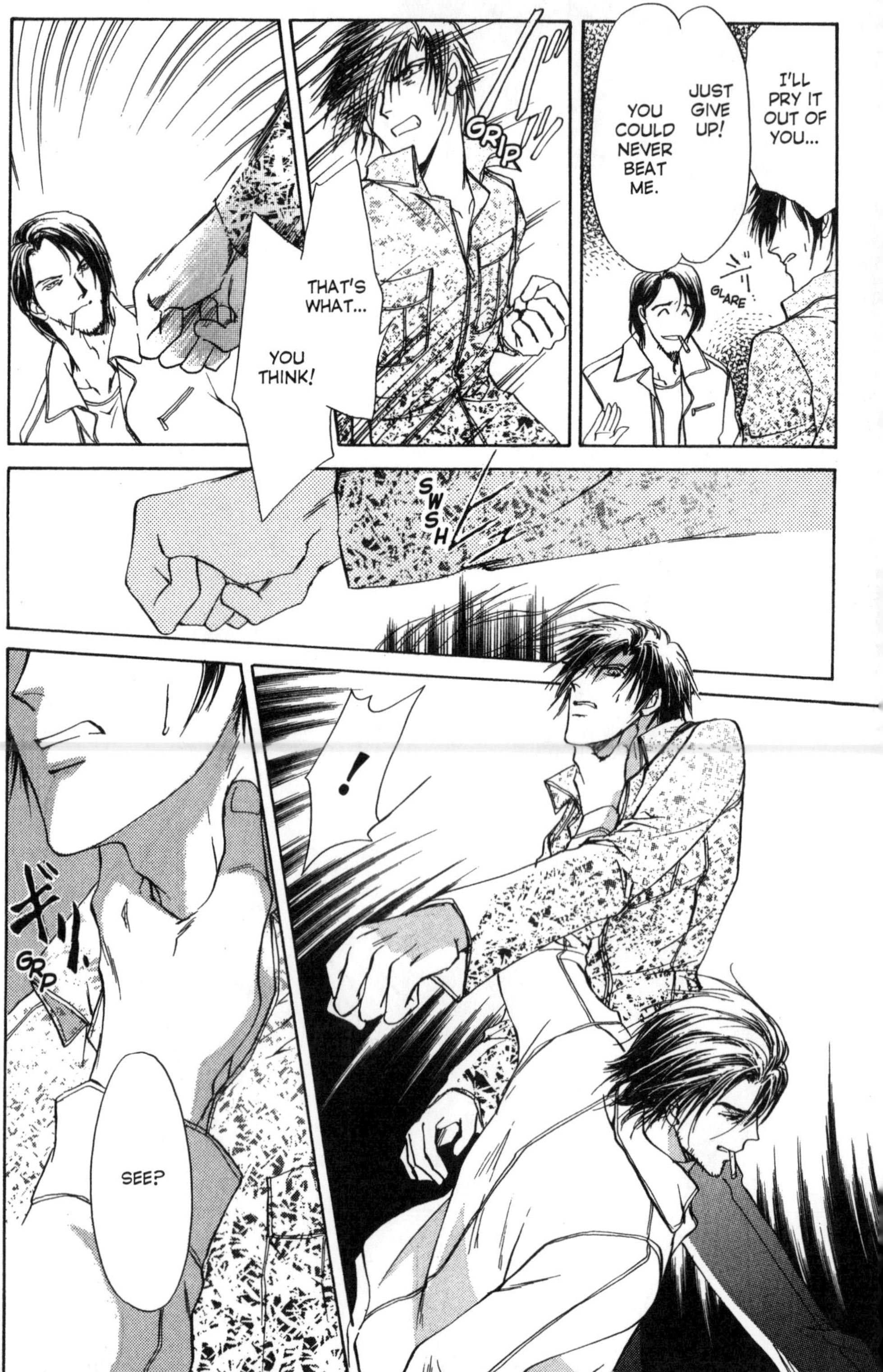
I'LL PRY IT OUT OF YOU...
JUST GIVE UP!
YOU COULD NEVER BEAT ME.
GLARE
GRIP
THAT'S WHAT...
YOU THINK!
SWSH
!
ギリ
GRP
SEE?

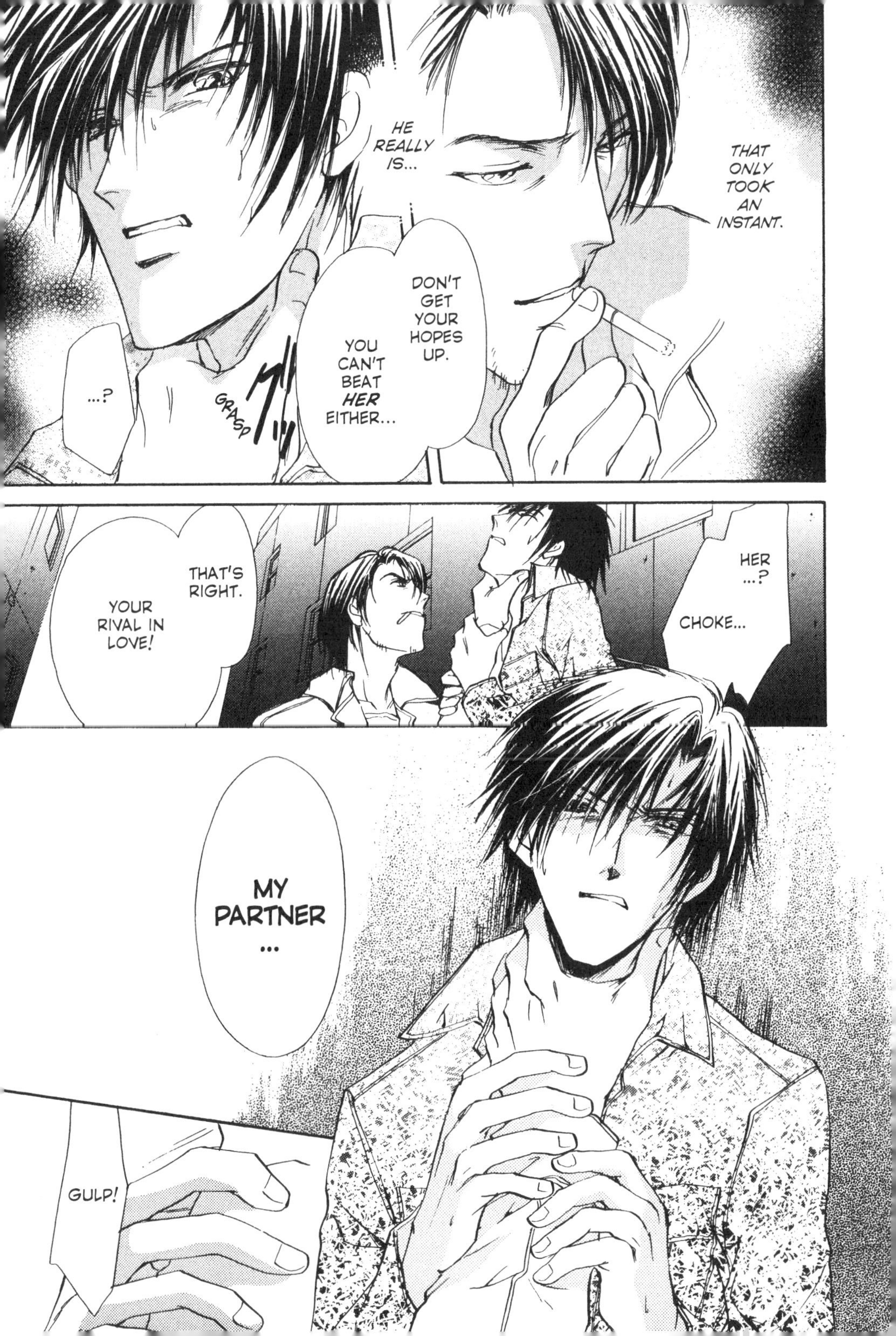
THAT ONLY TOOK AN INSTANT.
HE REALLY IS...
DON'T GET YOUR HOPES UP.
YOU CAN'T BEAT **HER** EITHER...
GRASP
...?
HER ...?
CHOKE...
THAT'S RIGHT.
YOUR RIVAL IN LOVE!
MY PARTNER ...
GULP!

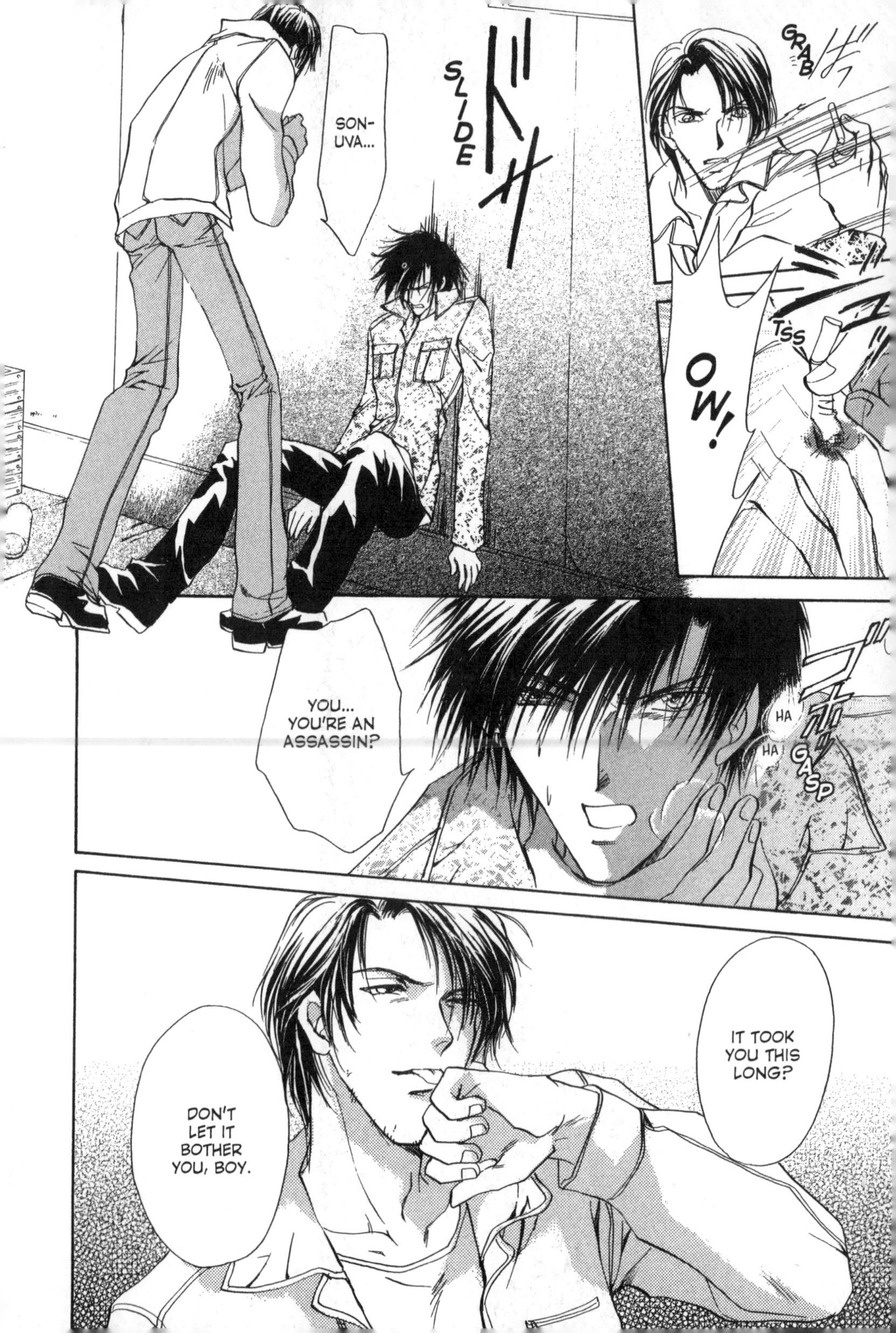
GRAB
TSS
OW!
SLIDE
SON-UVA...
YOU... YOU'RE AN ASSASSIN?
HA
HA
GASP
IT TOOK YOU THIS LONG?
DON'T LET IT BOTHER YOU, BOY.

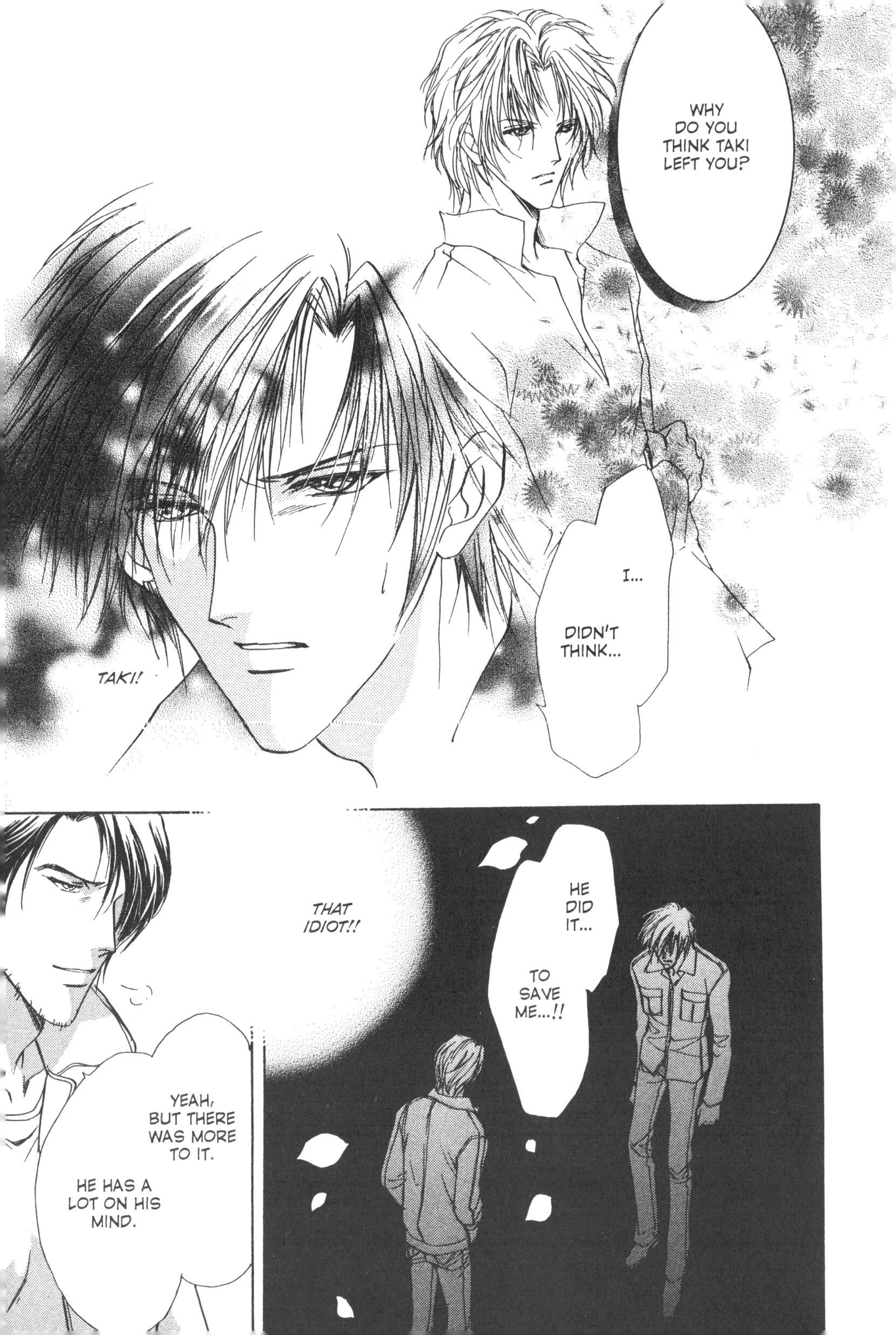
WHY DO YOU THINK TAKI LEFT YOU?
I...
DIDN'T THINK...
TAKI!
HE DID IT...
TO SAVE ME...!!
THAT IDIOT!!
YEAH, BUT THERE WAS MORE TO IT.
HE HAS A LOT ON HIS MIND.

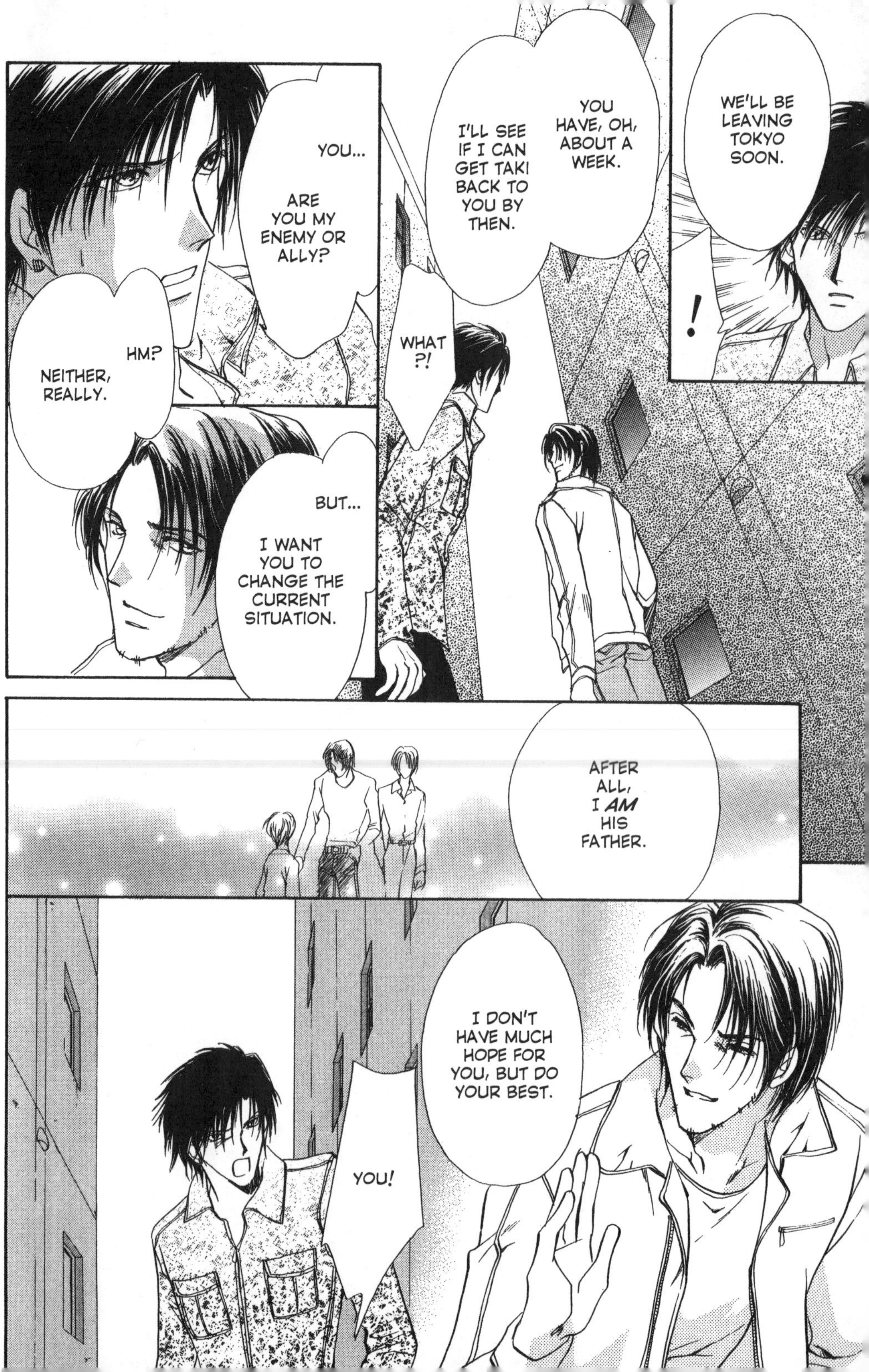
WE'LL BE LEAVING TOKYO SOON.
!
YOU HAVE, OH, ABOUT A WEEK.
I'LL SEE IF I CAN GET TAKI BACK TO YOU BY THEN.
WHAT?!
YOU...
ARE YOU MY ENEMY OR ALLY?
HM?
NEITHER, REALLY.
BUT...
I WANT YOU TO CHANGE THE CURRENT SITUATION.
AFTER ALL, I *AM* HIS FATHER.
I DON'T HAVE MUCH HOPE FOR YOU, BUT DO YOUR BEST.
YOU!

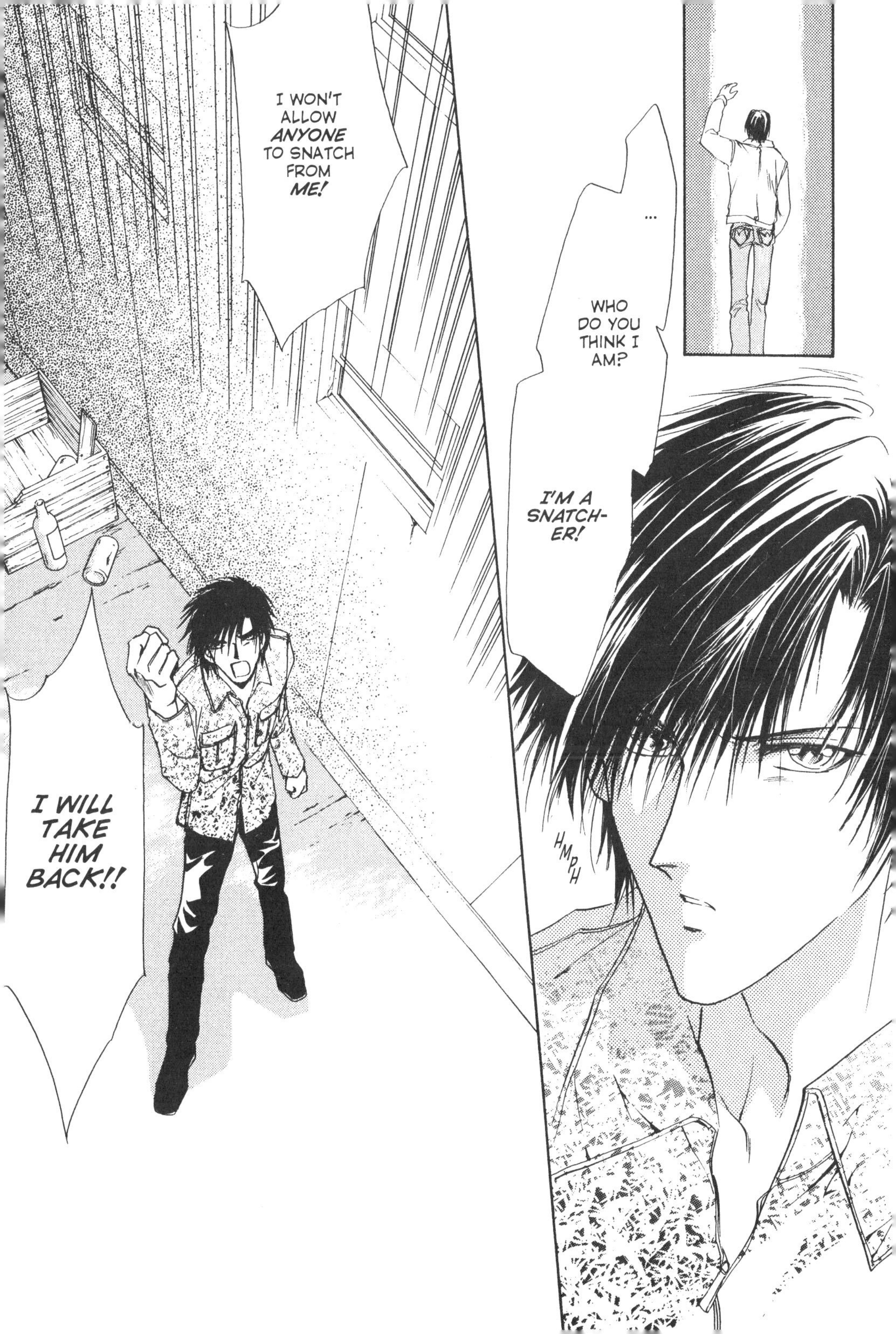
...
WHO DO YOU THINK I AM?
I'M A SNATCH-ER!
HMPH
I WON'T ALLOW ANYONE TO SNATCH FROM ME!
I WILL TAKE HIM BACK!!

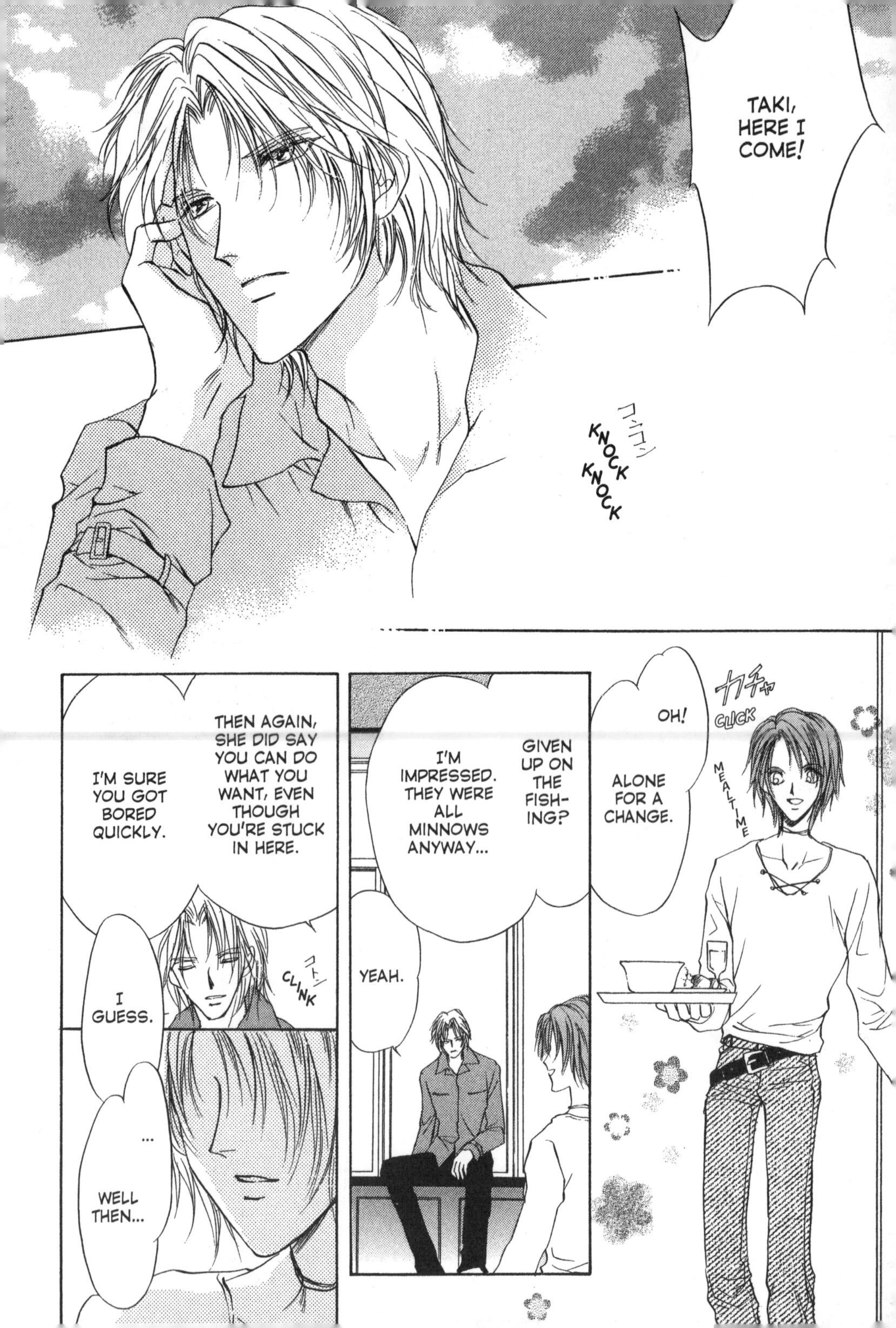
TAKI, HERE I COME!
コンコン
KNOCK KNOCK
カチャ
CLICK
OH!
ALONE FOR A CHANGE.
MEALTIME
GIVEN UP ON THE FISHING?
I'M IMPRESSED. THEY WERE ALL MINNOWS ANYWAY...
YEAH.
THEN AGAIN, SHE DID SAY YOU CAN DO WHAT YOU WANT, EVEN THOUGH YOU'RE STUCK IN HERE.
I'M SURE YOU GOT BORED QUICKLY.
I GUESS.
コトン
CLINK
...
WELL THEN...

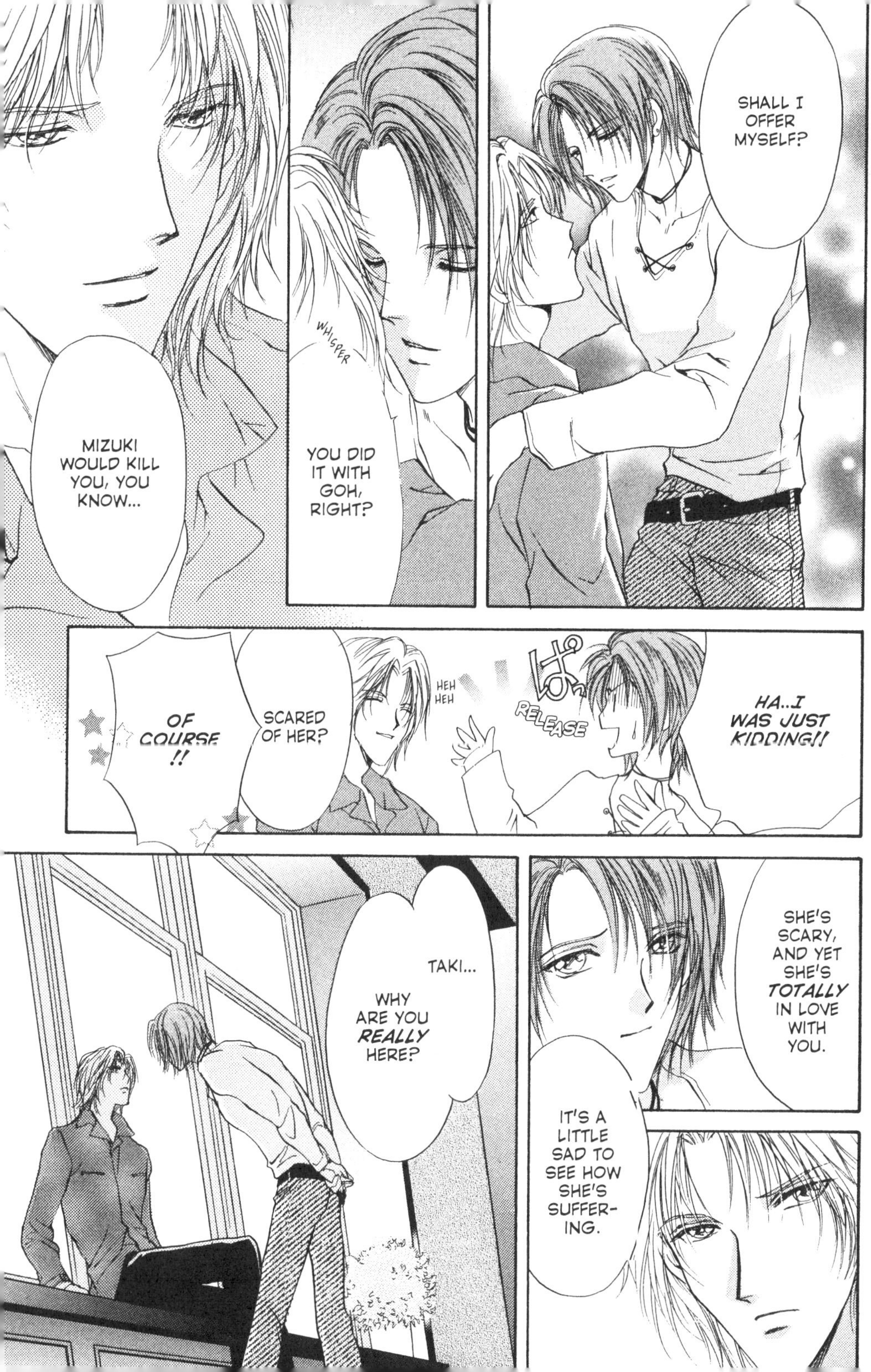
SHALL I OFFER MYSELF?
WHISPER
YOU DID IT WITH GOH, RIGHT?
MIZUKI WOULD KILL YOU, YOU KNOW...
HA..I WAS JUST KIDDING!!
ぱっ
RELEASE
HEH HEH
SCARED OF HER?
OF COURSE !!
SHE'S SCARY, AND YET SHE'S TOTALLY IN LOVE WITH YOU.
IT'S A LITTLE SAD TO SEE HOW SHE'S SUFFERING.
TAKI... WHY ARE YOU REALLY HERE?

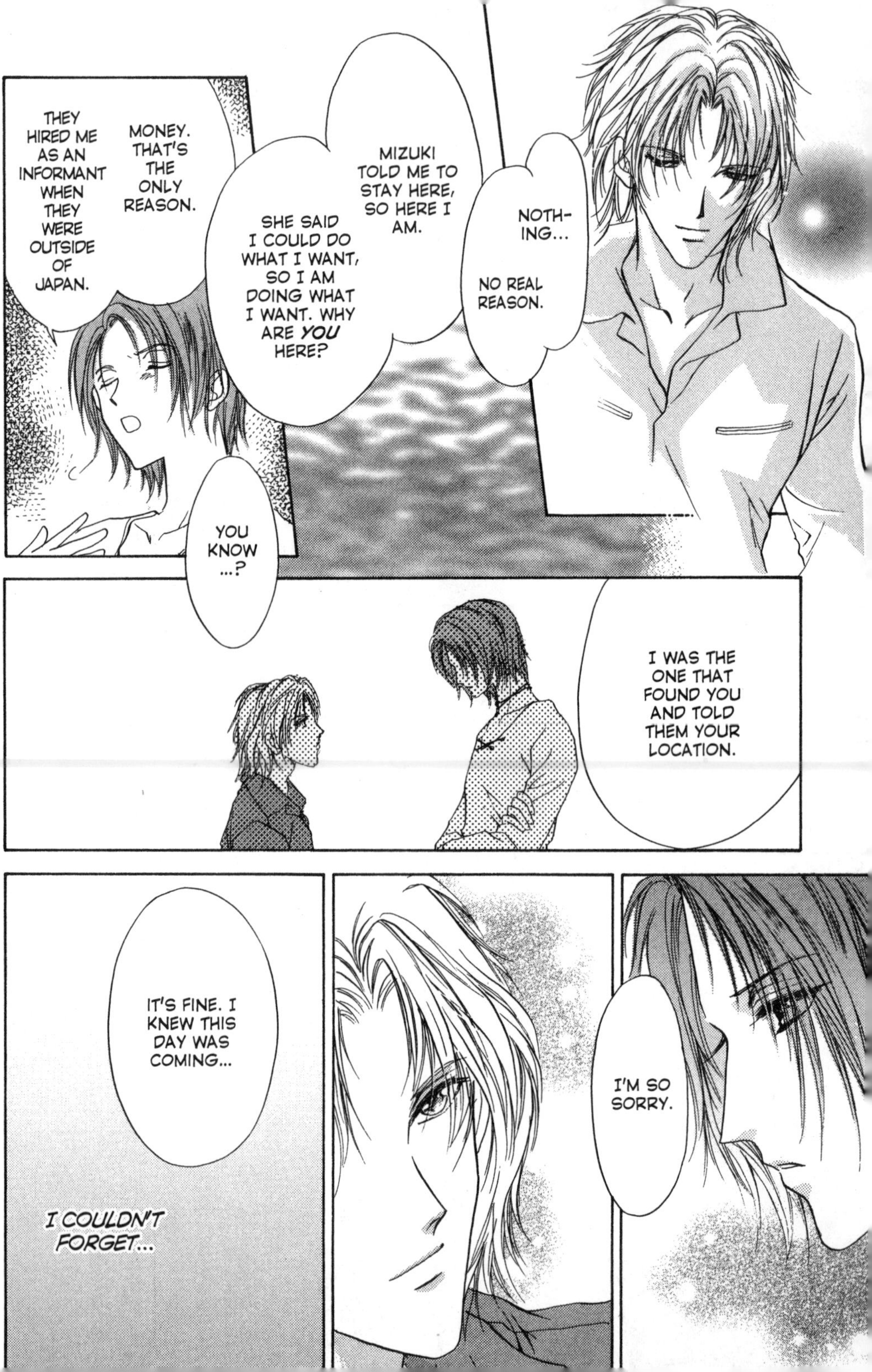

MIZUKI TOLD ME TO STAY HERE, SO HERE I AM.
SHE SAID I COULD DO WHAT I WANT, SO I AM DOING WHAT I WANT. WHY ARE *YOU* HERE?
NOTHING...
NO REAL REASON.
MONEY. THAT'S THE ONLY REASON.
THEY HIRED ME AS AN INFORMANT WHEN THEY WERE OUTSIDE OF JAPAN.
YOU KNOW ...?
I WAS THE ONE THAT FOUND YOU AND TOLD THEM YOUR LOCATION.
I'M SO SORRY.
IT'S FINE. I KNEW THIS DAY WAS COMING...
I COULDN'T FORGET...

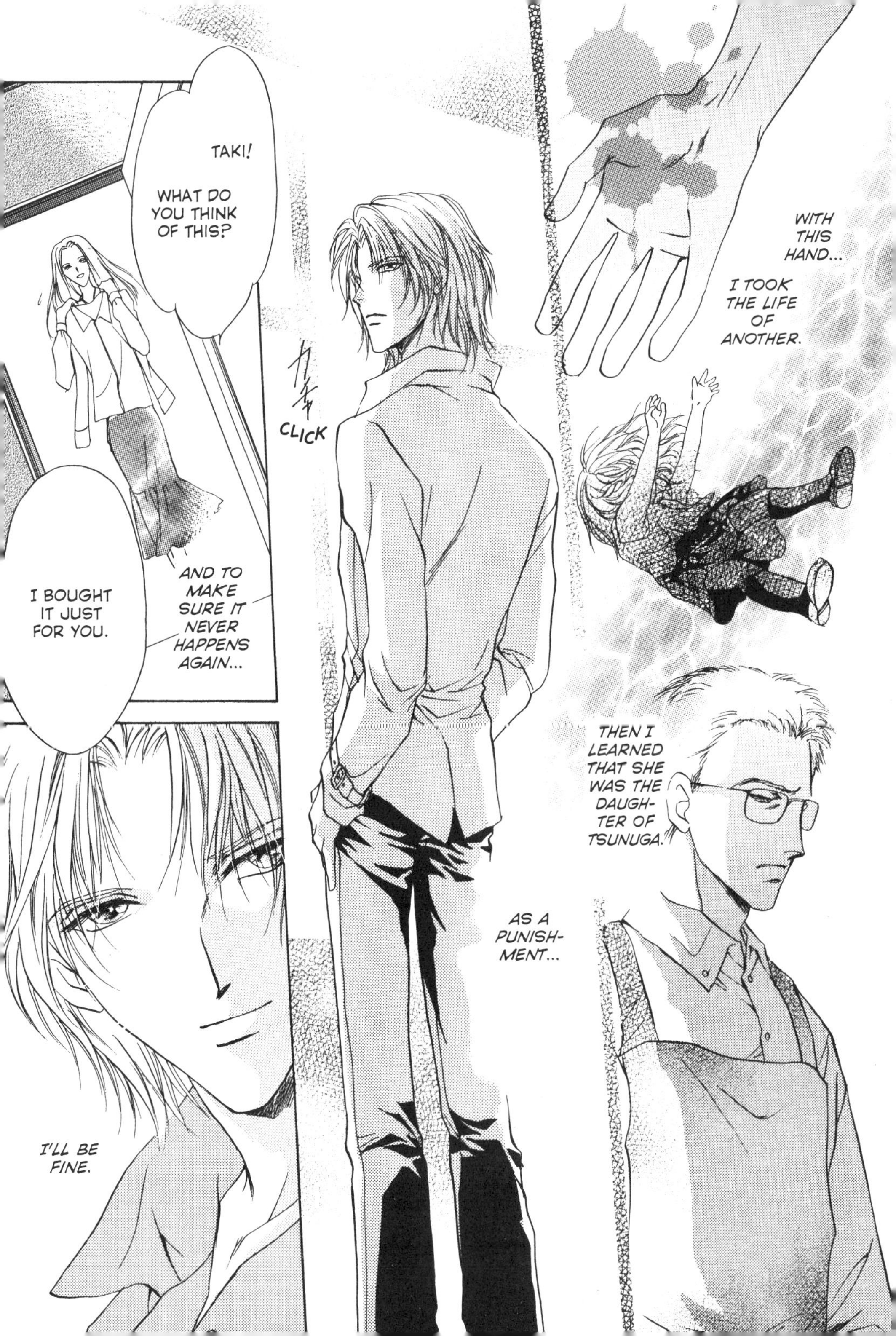
WITH THIS HAND...
I TOOK THE LIFE OF ANOTHER.
THEN I LEARNED THAT SHE WAS THE DAUGHTER OF TSUNUGA.
カチャ
CLICK
AS A PUNISHMENT...
TAKI!
WHAT DO YOU THINK OF THIS?
I BOUGHT IT JUST FOR YOU.
AND TO MAKE SURE IT NEVER HAPPENS AGAIN...
I'LL BE FINE.

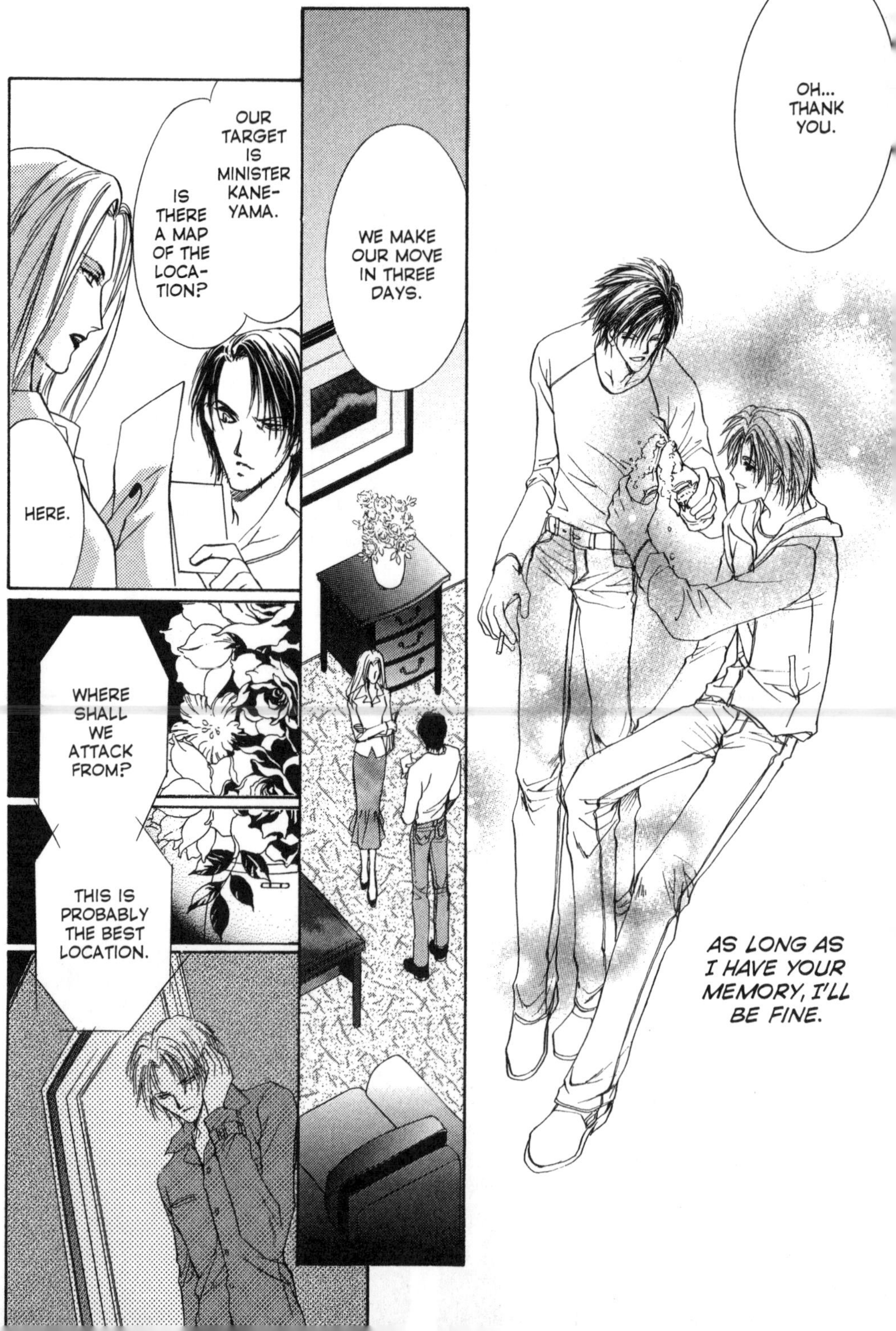
OH... THANK YOU.
AS LONG AS I HAVE YOUR MEMORY, I'LL BE FINE.
WE MAKE OUR MOVE IN THREE DAYS.
OUR TARGET IS MINISTER KANE-YAMA.
IS THERE A MAP OF THE LOCA-TION?
HERE.
WHERE SHALL WE ATTACK FROM?
THIS IS PROBABLY THE BEST LOCATION.

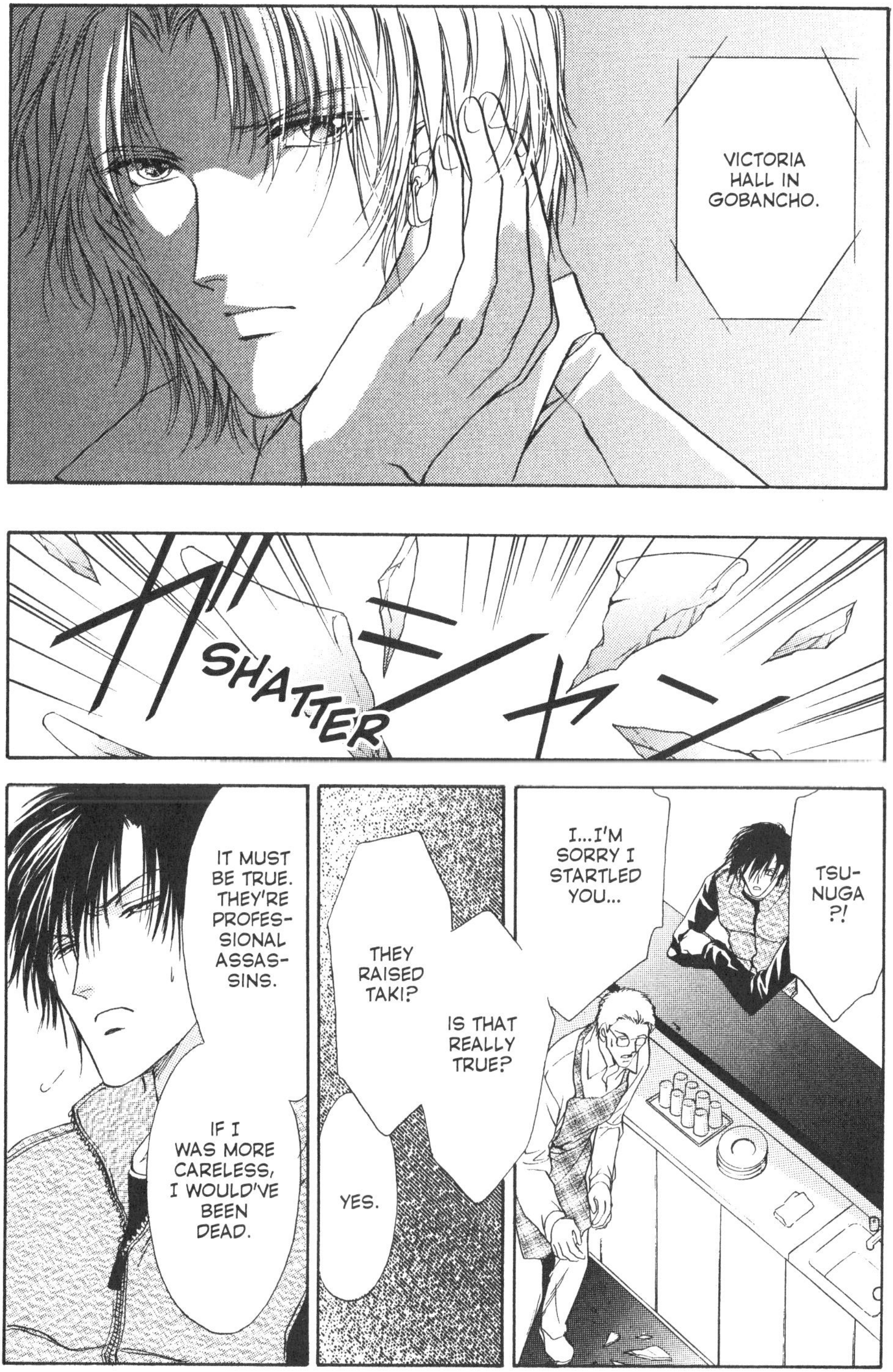
VICTORIA HALL IN GOBANCHO.
SHATTER
TSU-NUGA?!
I...I'M SORRY I STARTLED YOU...
THEY RAISED TAKI?
IS THAT REALLY TRUE?
YES.
IT MUST BE TRUE. THEY'RE PROFES-SIONAL ASSAS-SINS.
IF I WAS MORE CARELESS, I WOULD'VE BEEN DEAD.

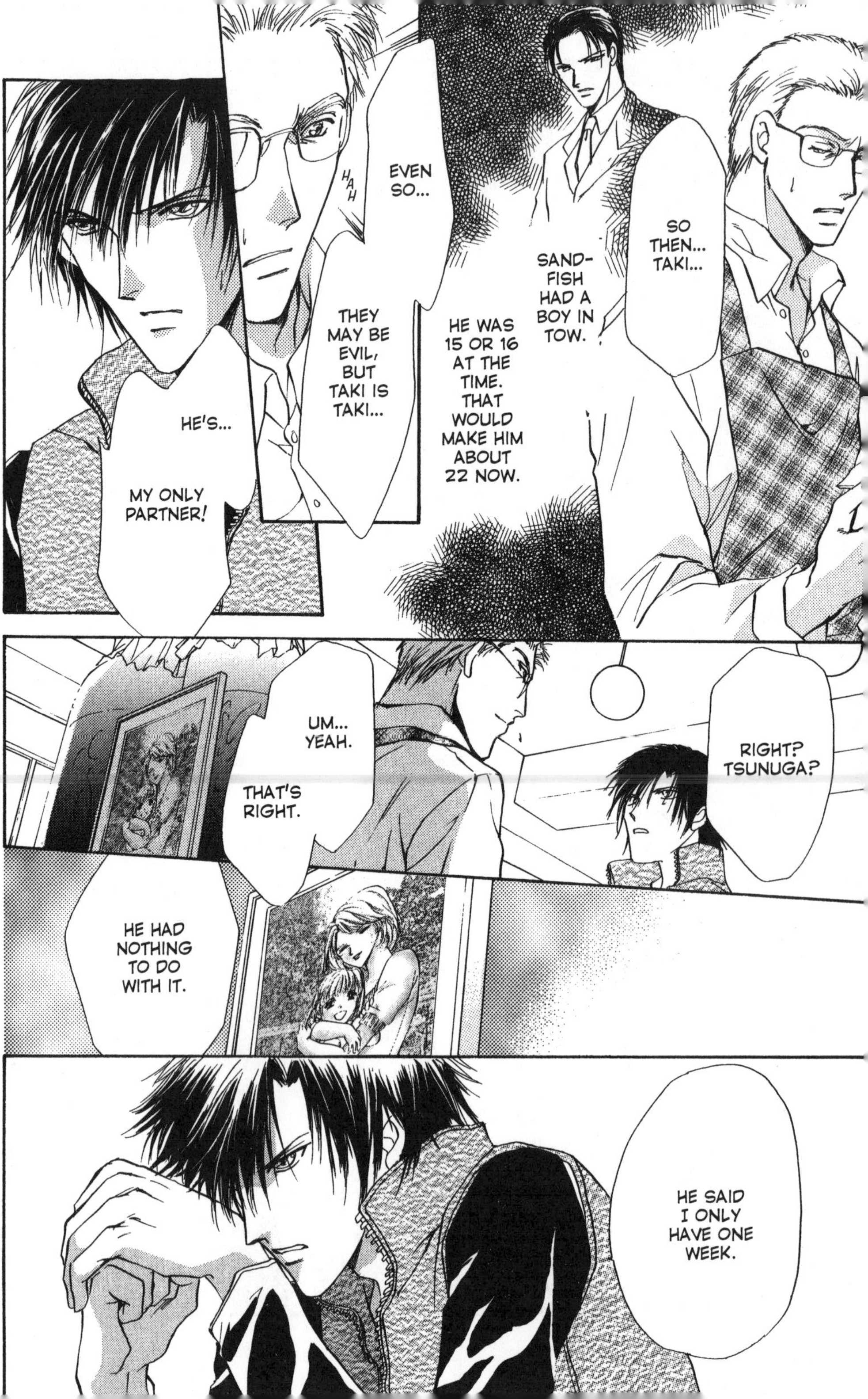
SO THEN... TAKI...
SAND-FISH HAD A BOY IN TOW.
HE WAS 15 OR 16 AT THE TIME. THAT WOULD MAKE HIM ABOUT 22 NOW.
HAH
EVEN SO...
THEY MAY BE EVIL, BUT TAKI IS TAKI...
HE'S...
MY ONLY PARTNER!
RIGHT? TSUNUGA?
UM... YEAH.
THAT'S RIGHT.
HE HAD NOTHING TO DO WITH IT.
HE SAID I ONLY HAVE ONE WEEK.

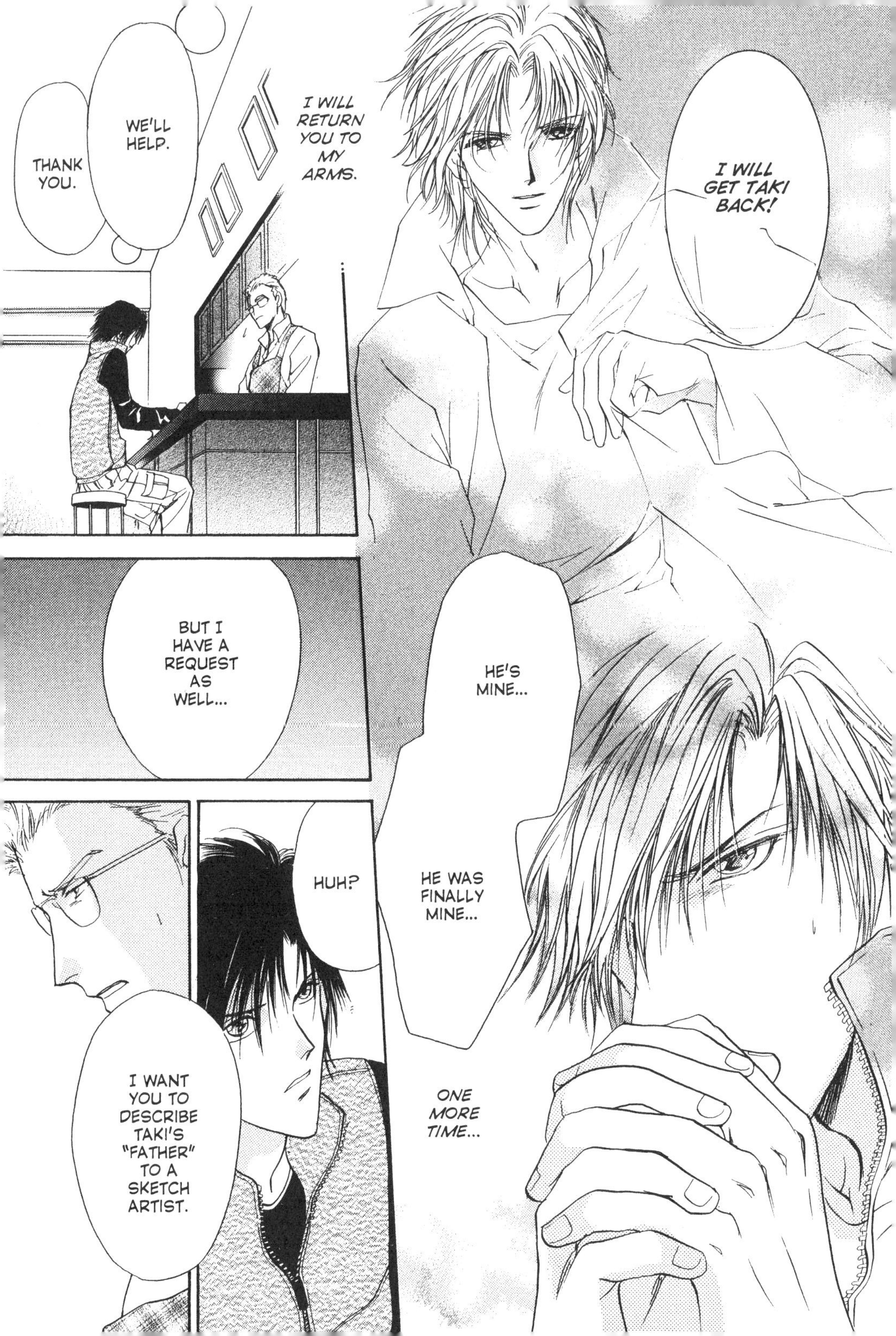
I WILL GET TAKI BACK!
HE'S MINE...
HE WAS FINALLY MINE...
ONE MORE TIME...
I WILL RETURN YOU TO MY ARMS.
WE'LL HELP.
THANK YOU.
BUT I HAVE A REQUEST AS WELL...
HUH?
I WANT YOU TO DESCRIBE TAKI'S "FATHER" TO A SKETCH ARTIST.

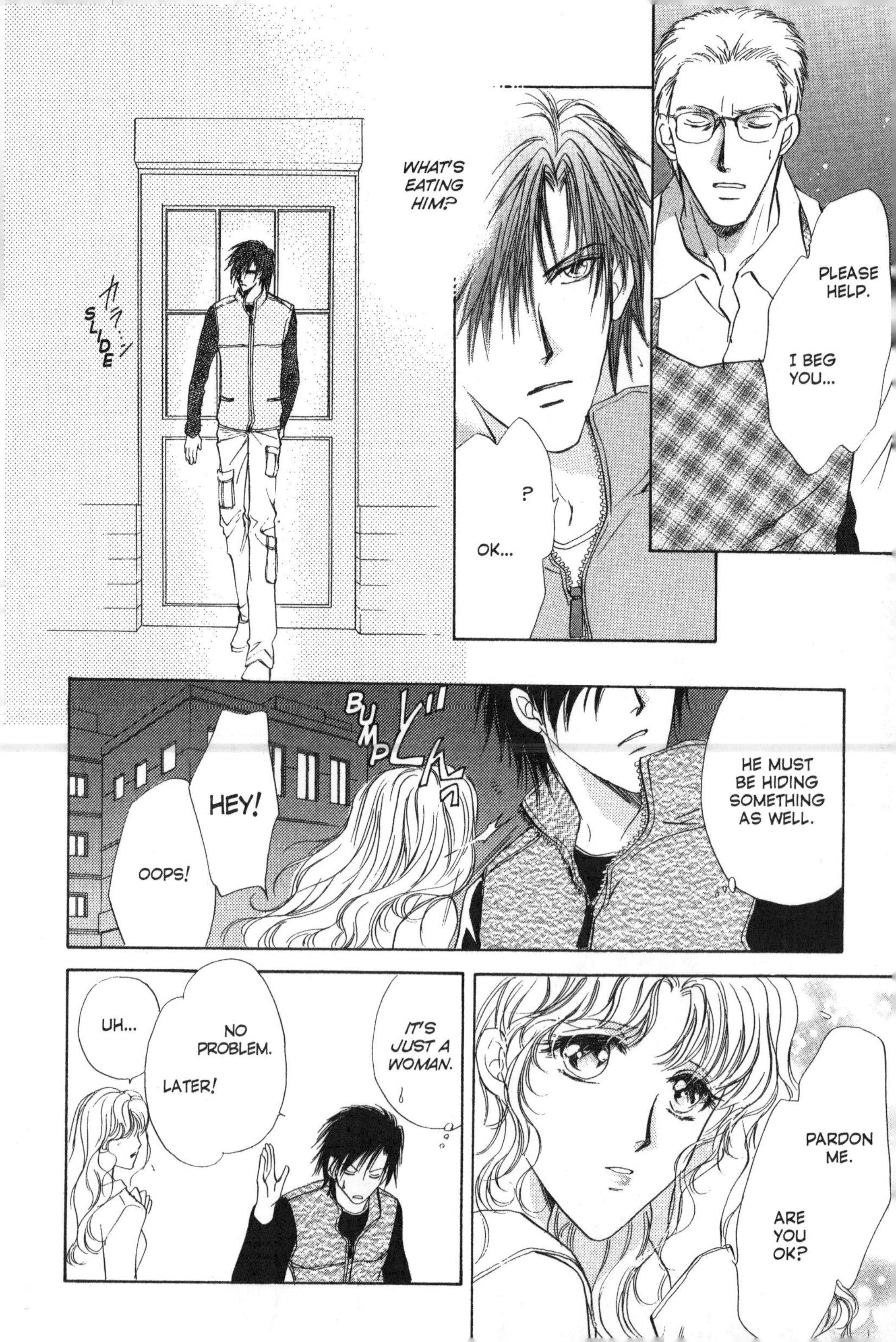
PLEASE HELP.
I BEG YOU...
WHAT'S EATING HIM?
?
OK...
SLIDE
HE MUST BE HIDING SOMETHING AS WELL.
BUMP
HEY!
OOPS!
PARDON ME.
ARE YOU OK?
IT'S JUST A WOMAN.
NO PROBLEM.
LATER!
UH...

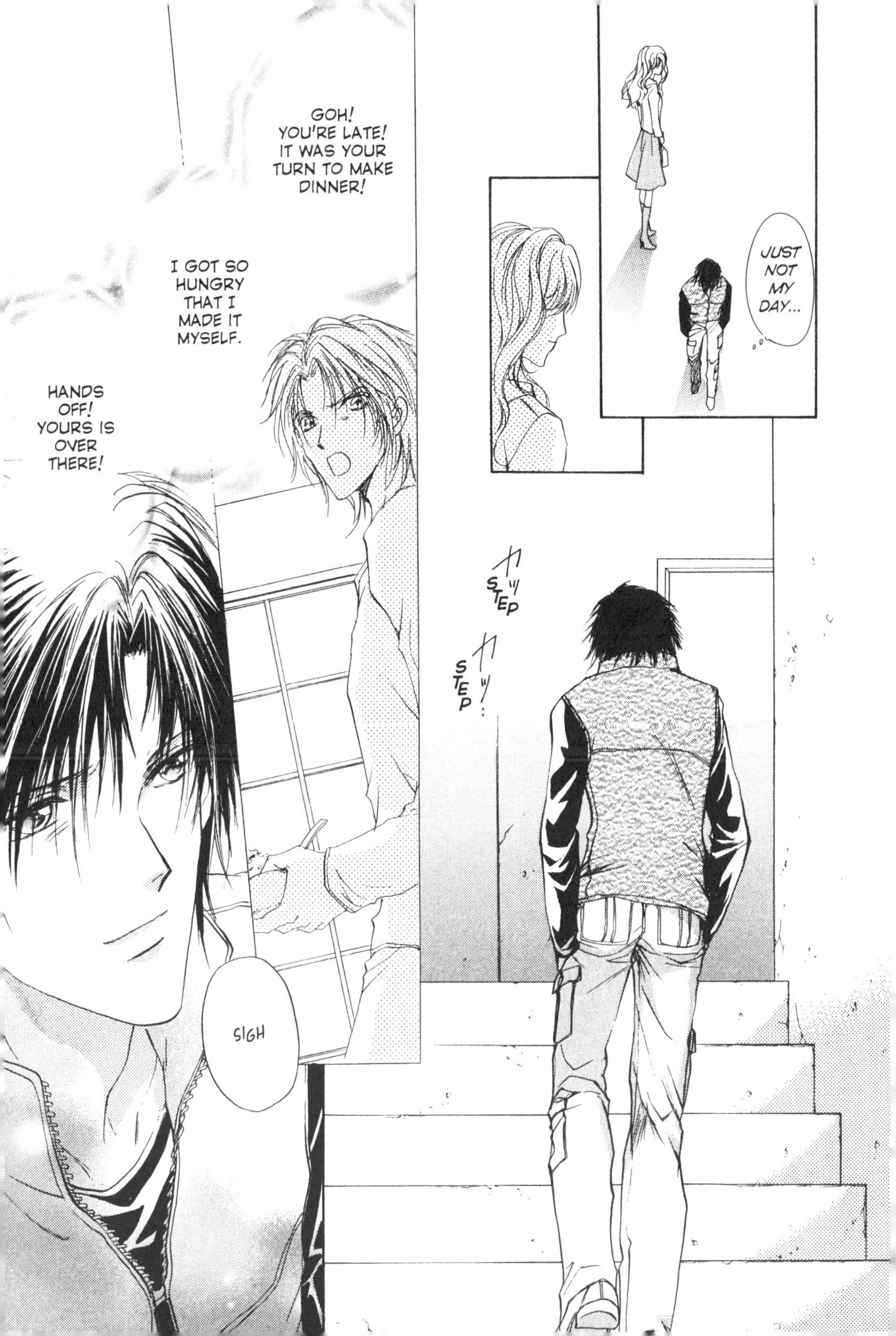
JUST NOT MY DAY...
STEP
STEP
GOH! YOU'RE LATE! IT WAS YOUR TURN TO MAKE DINNER!
I GOT SO HUNGRY THAT I MADE IT MYSELF.
HANDS OFF! YOURS IS OVER THERE!
SIGH

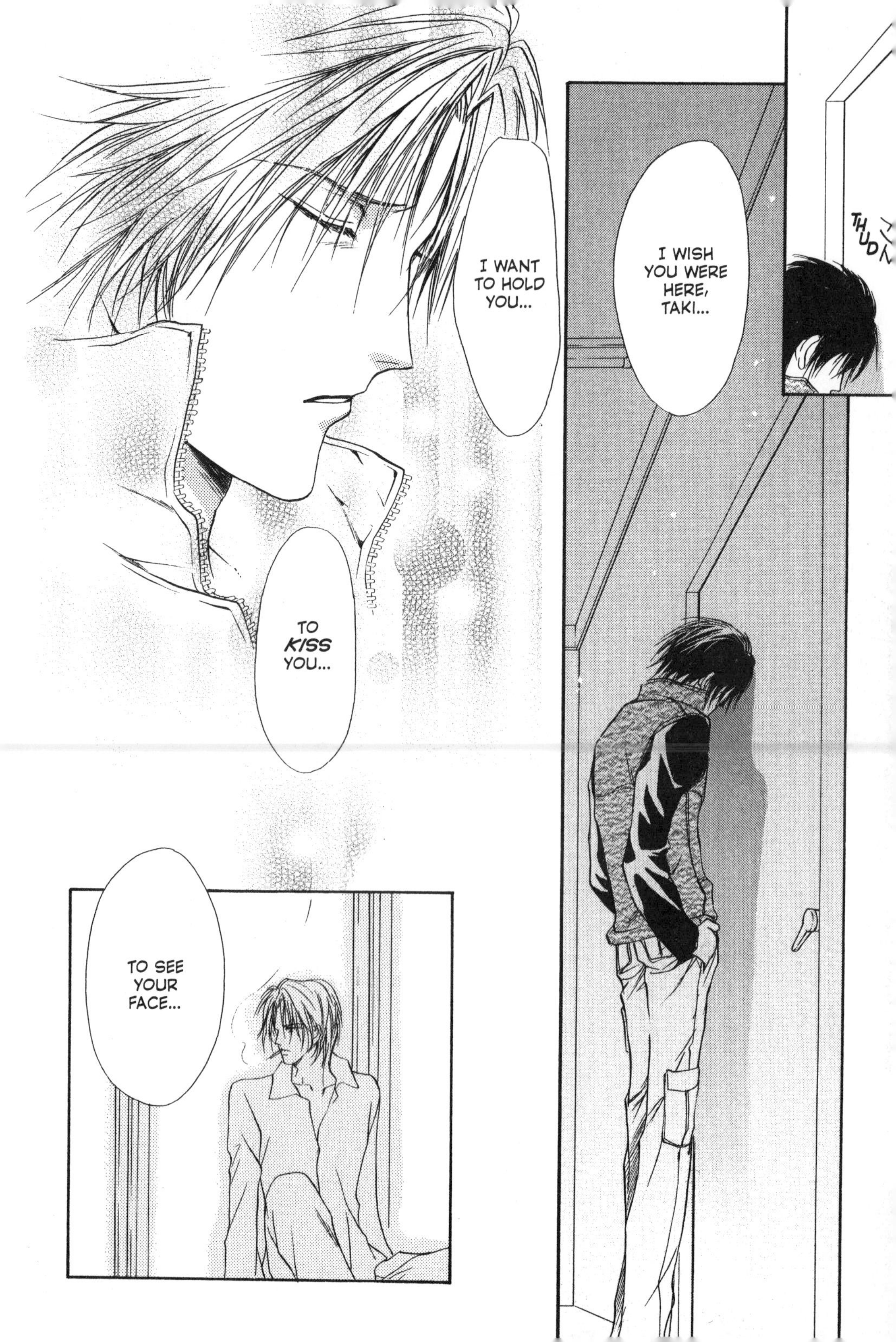
THUD
I WISH YOU WERE HERE, TAKI...
I WANT TO HOLD YOU...
TO *KISS* YOU...
TO SEE YOUR FACE...

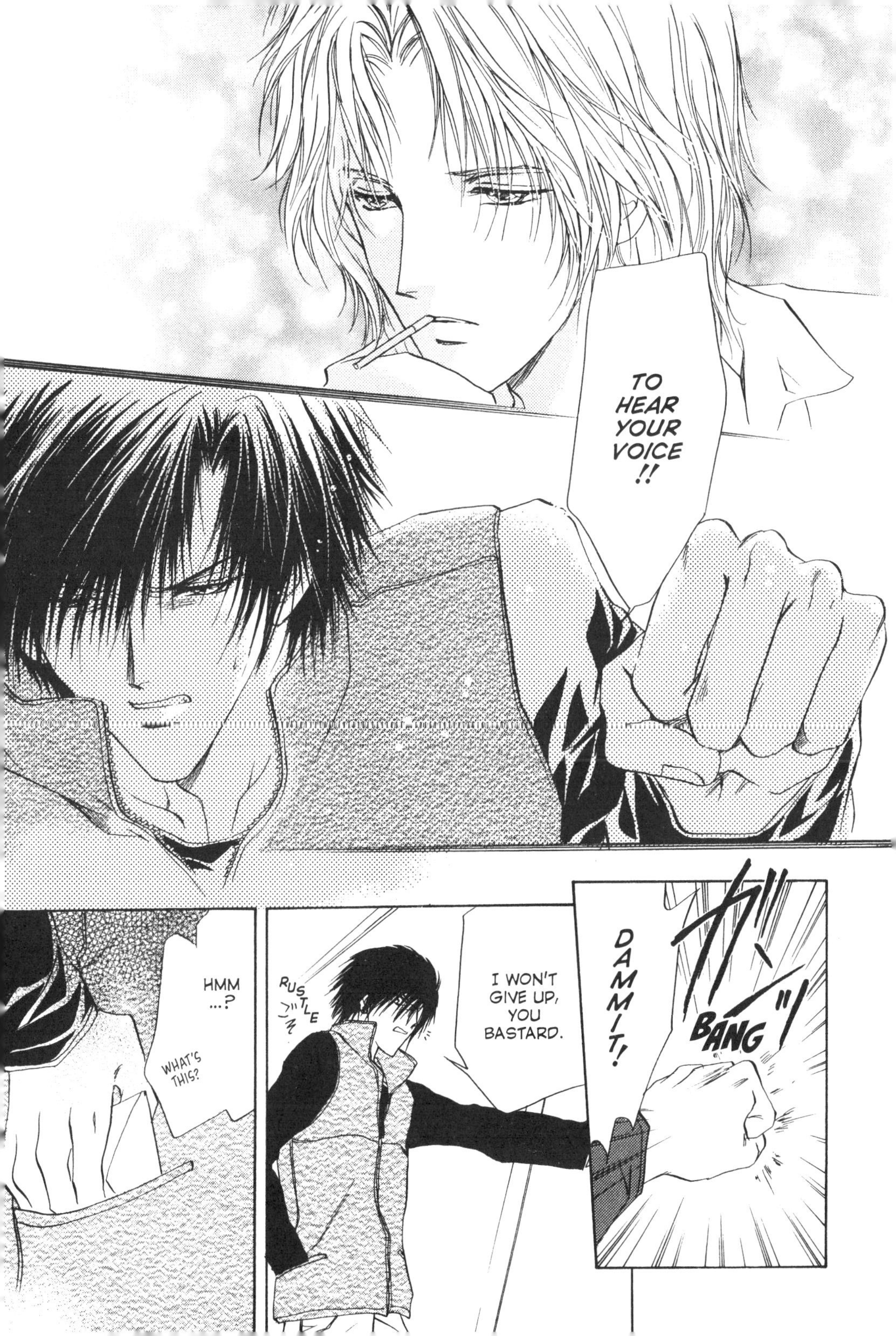
TO HEAR YOUR VOICE !!
DAMMIT!
BANG
I WON'T GIVE UP, YOU BASTARD.
RUSTLE
HMM ...?
WHAT'S THIS?

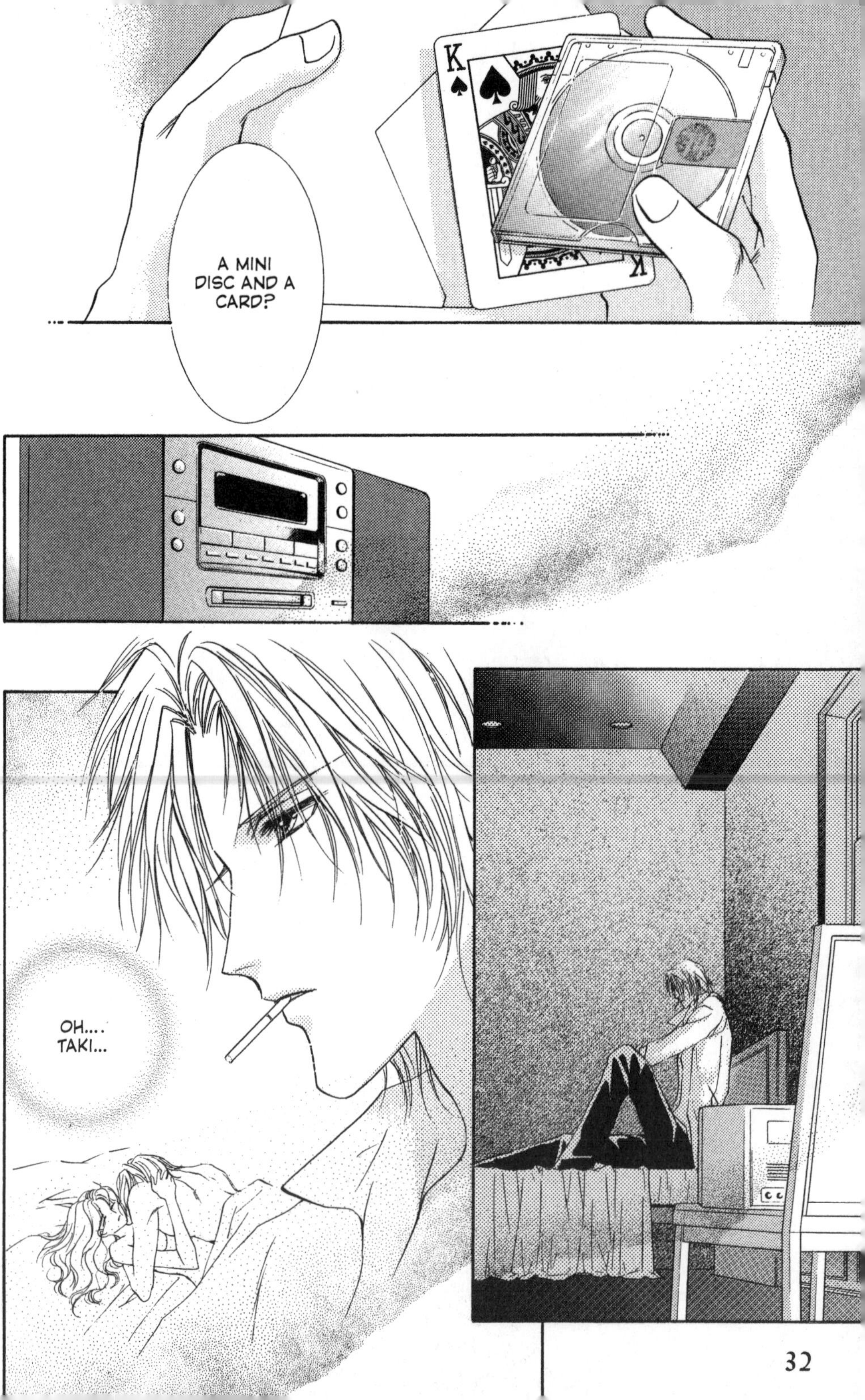
A MINI DISC AND A CARD?
OH.... TAKI...

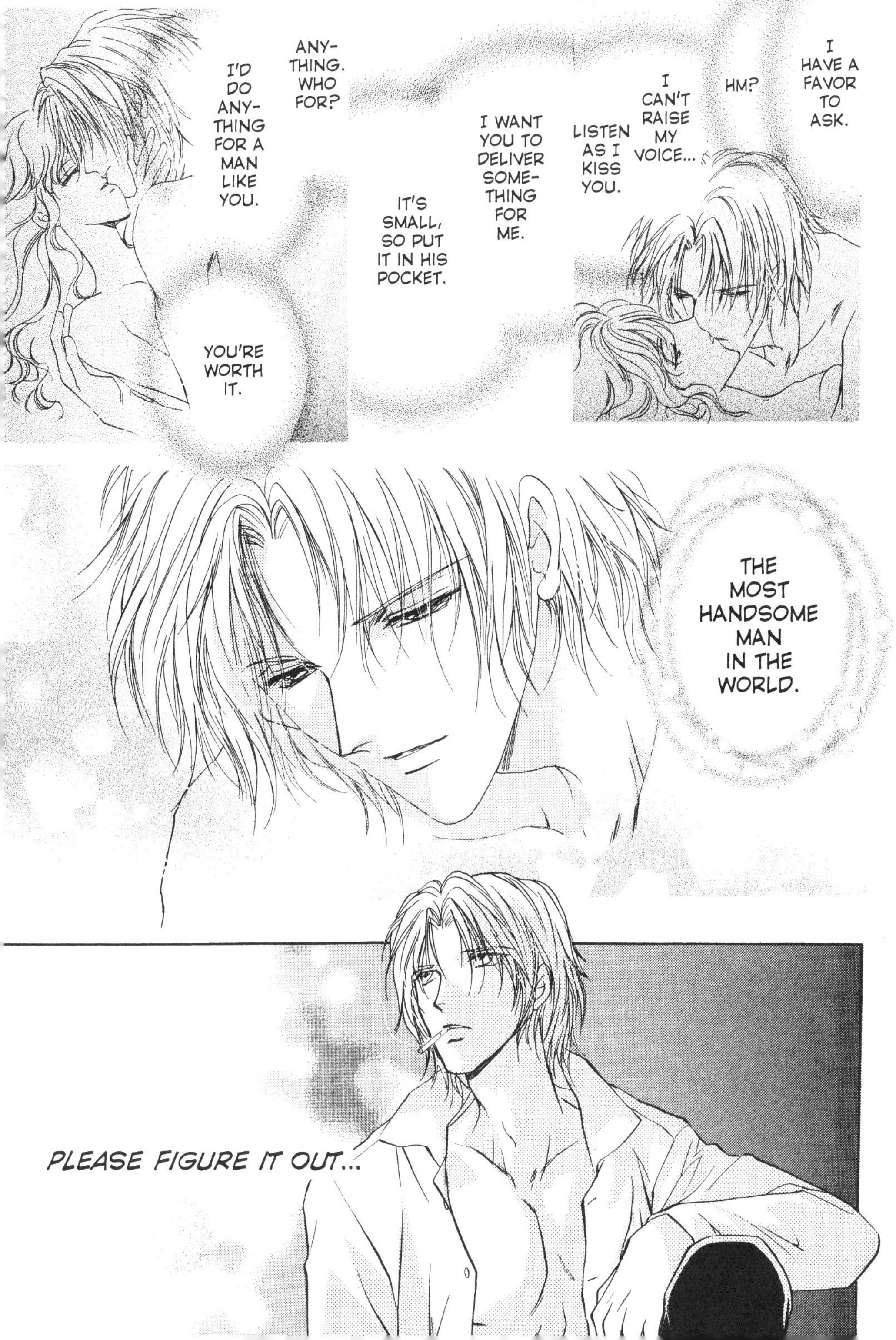
I HAVE A FAVOR TO ASK.
HM?
I CAN'T RAISE MY VOICE...
LISTEN AS I KISS YOU.
I WANT YOU TO DELIVER SOMETHING FOR ME.
IT'S SMALL, SO PUT IT IN HIS POCKET.
ANYTHING. WHO FOR?
I'D DO ANYTHING FOR A MAN LIKE YOU.
YOU'RE WORTH IT.
THE MOST HANDSOME MAN IN THE WORLD.
PLEASE FIGURE IT OUT...

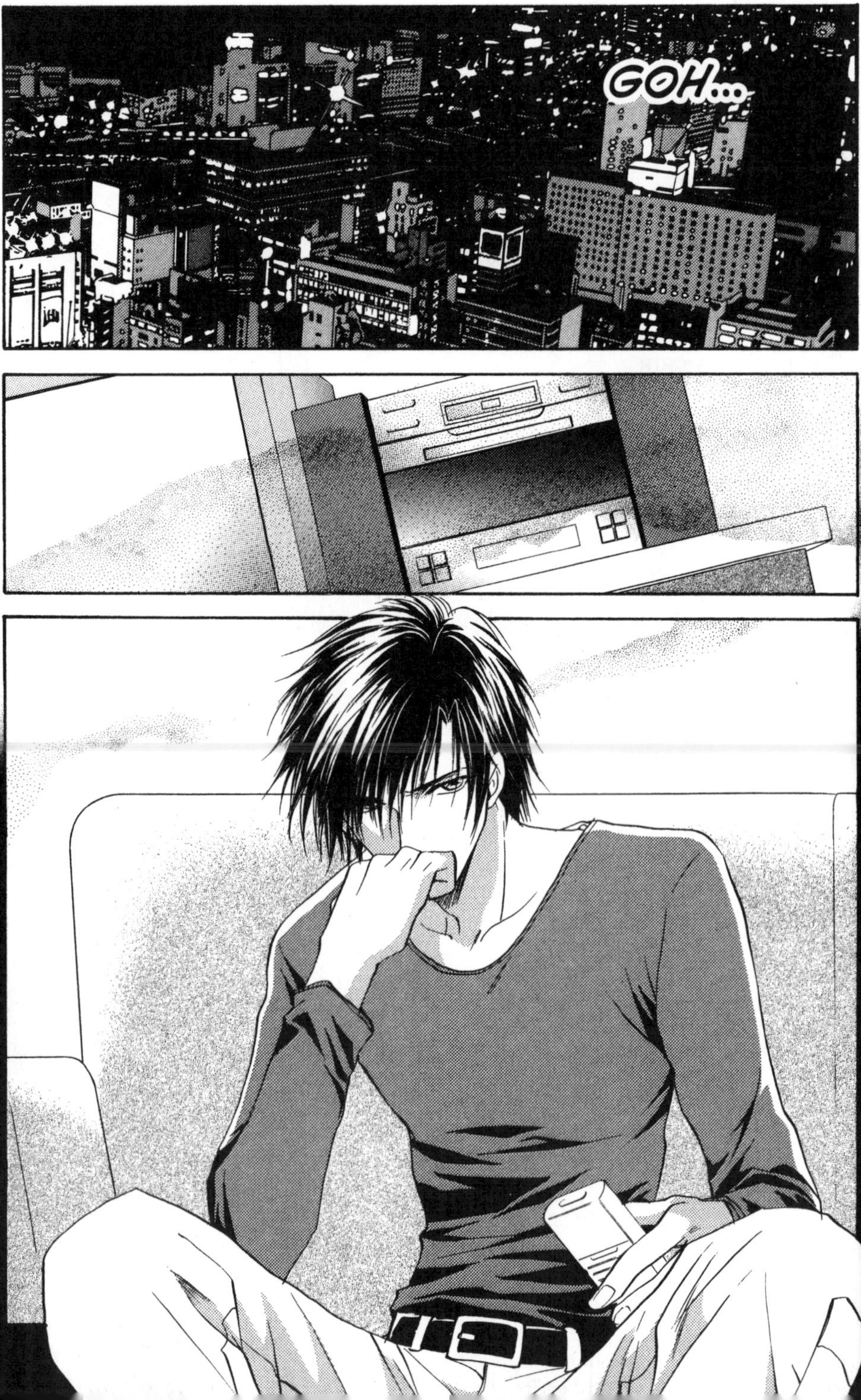
GOH...

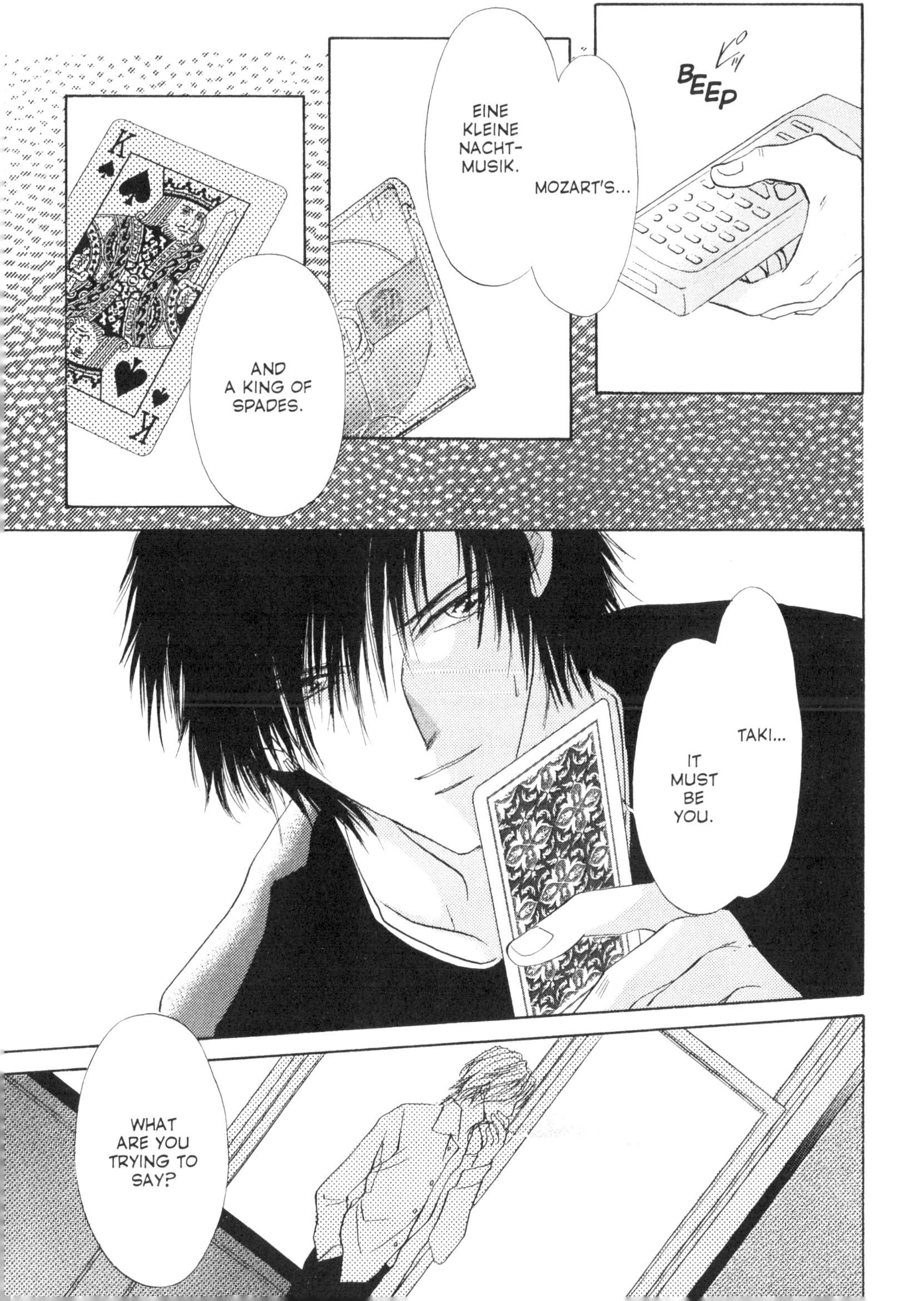
BEEP
ピッ
MOZART'S...
EINE KLEINE NACHT-MUSIK.
AND A KING OF SPADES.
TAKI...
IT MUST BE YOU.
WHAT ARE YOU TRYING TO SAY?

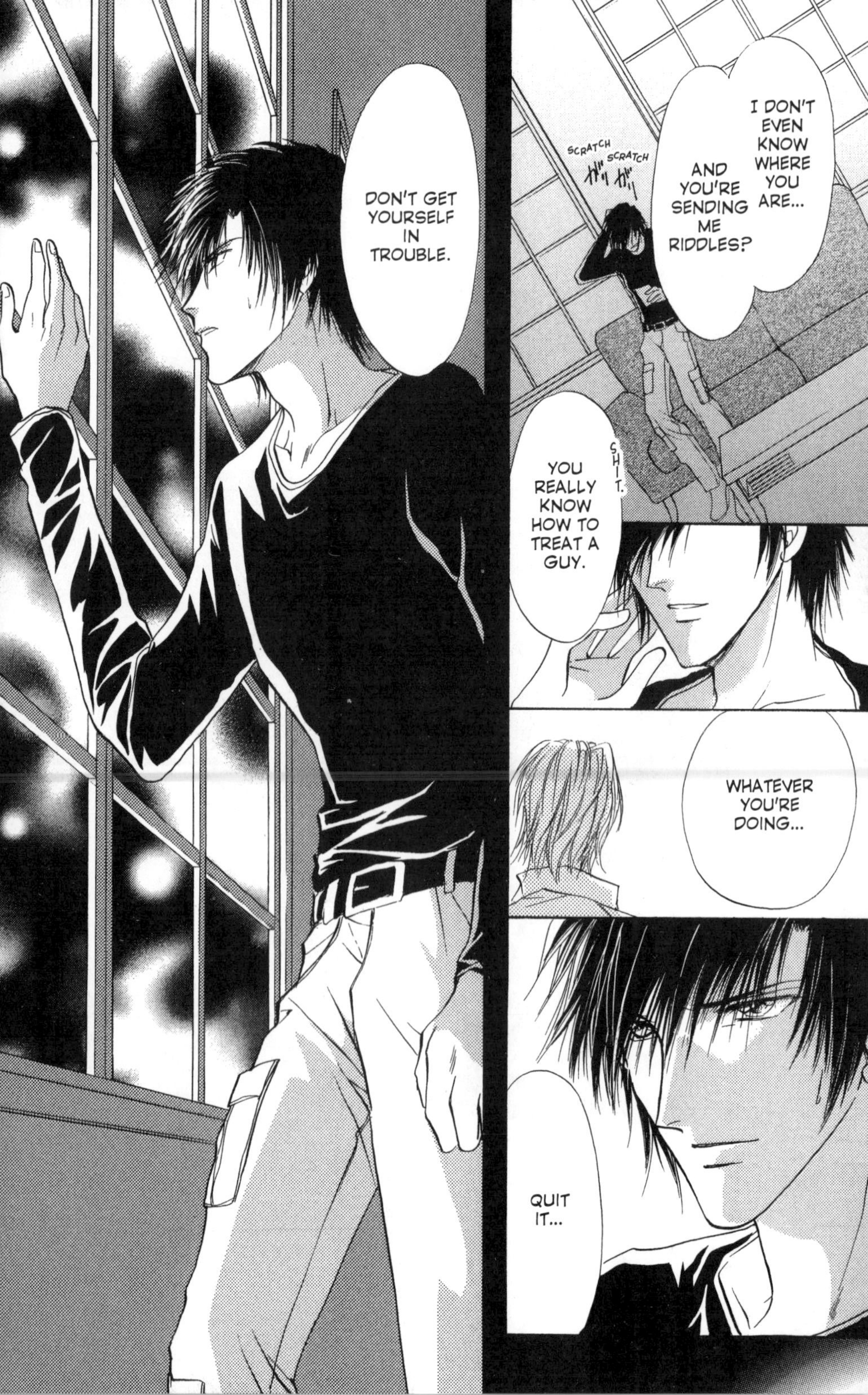
SCRATCH SCRATCH
I DON'T EVEN KNOW WHERE YOU ARE...
AND YOU'RE SENDING ME RIDDLES?
SHIT.
YOU REALLY KNOW HOW TO TREAT A GUY.
WHATEVER YOU'RE DOING...
QUIT IT...
DON'T GET YOURSELF IN TROUBLE.

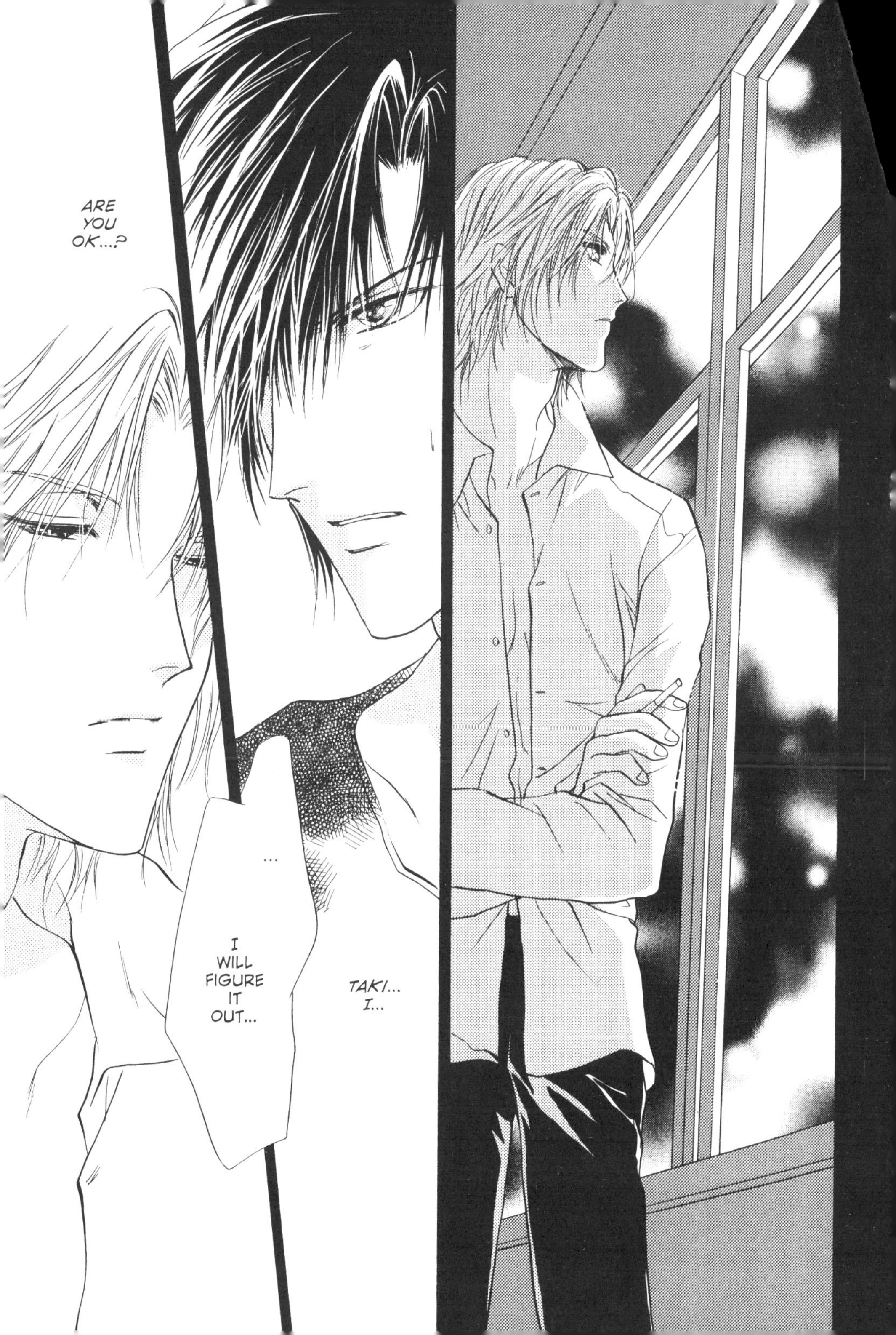
...
TAKI... I...
I WILL FIGURE IT OUT...
ARE YOU OK...?

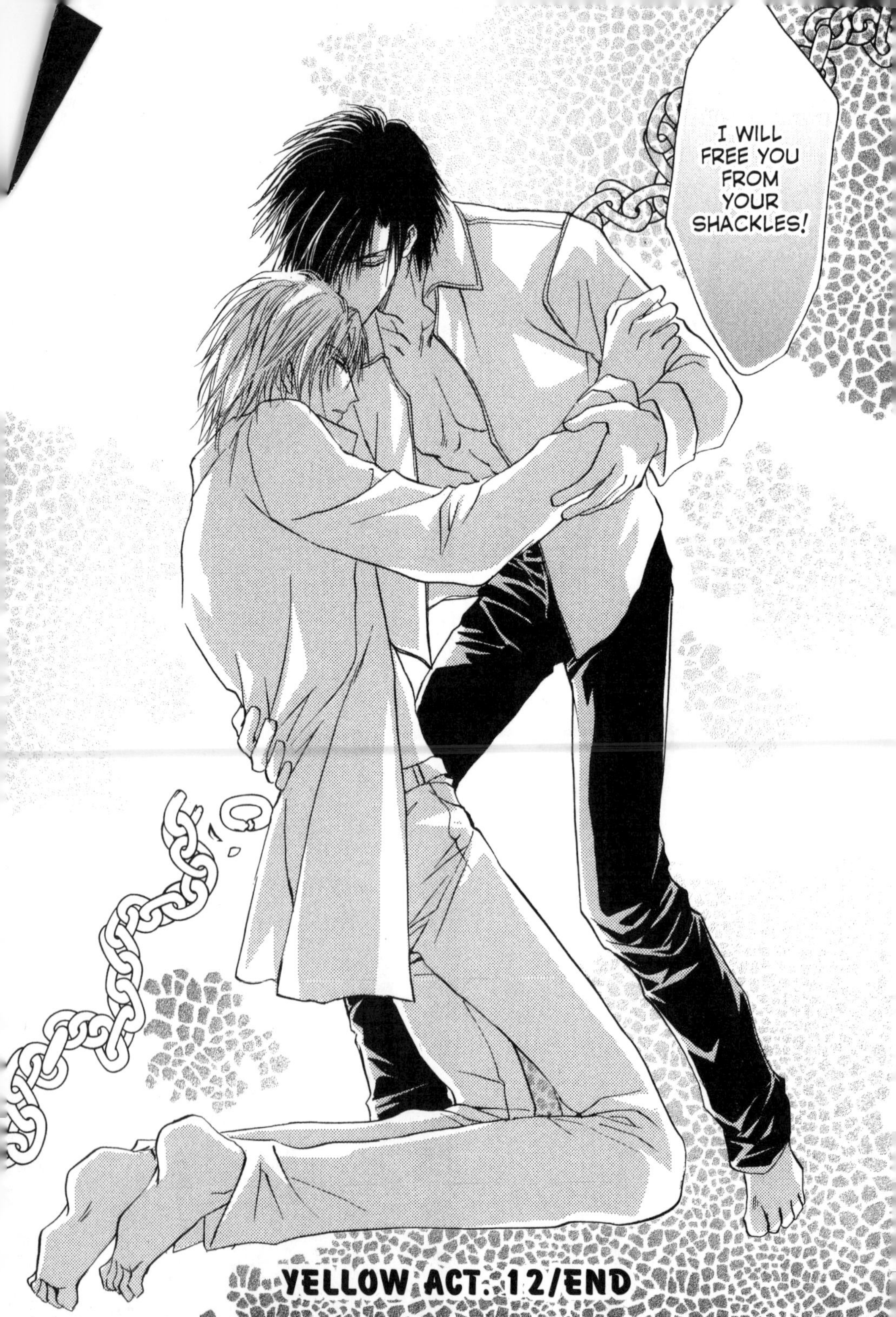
I WILL FREE YOU FROM YOUR SHACKLES!

YELLOW ACT. 12/END

YELLOW

YELLOW

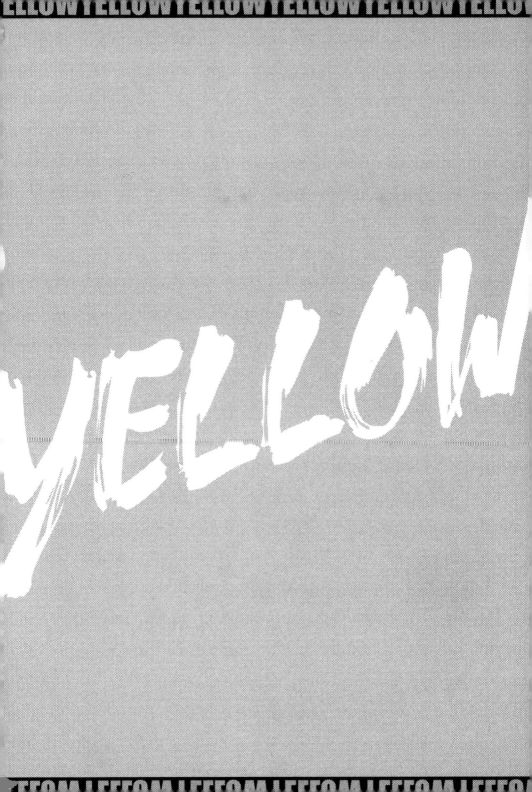

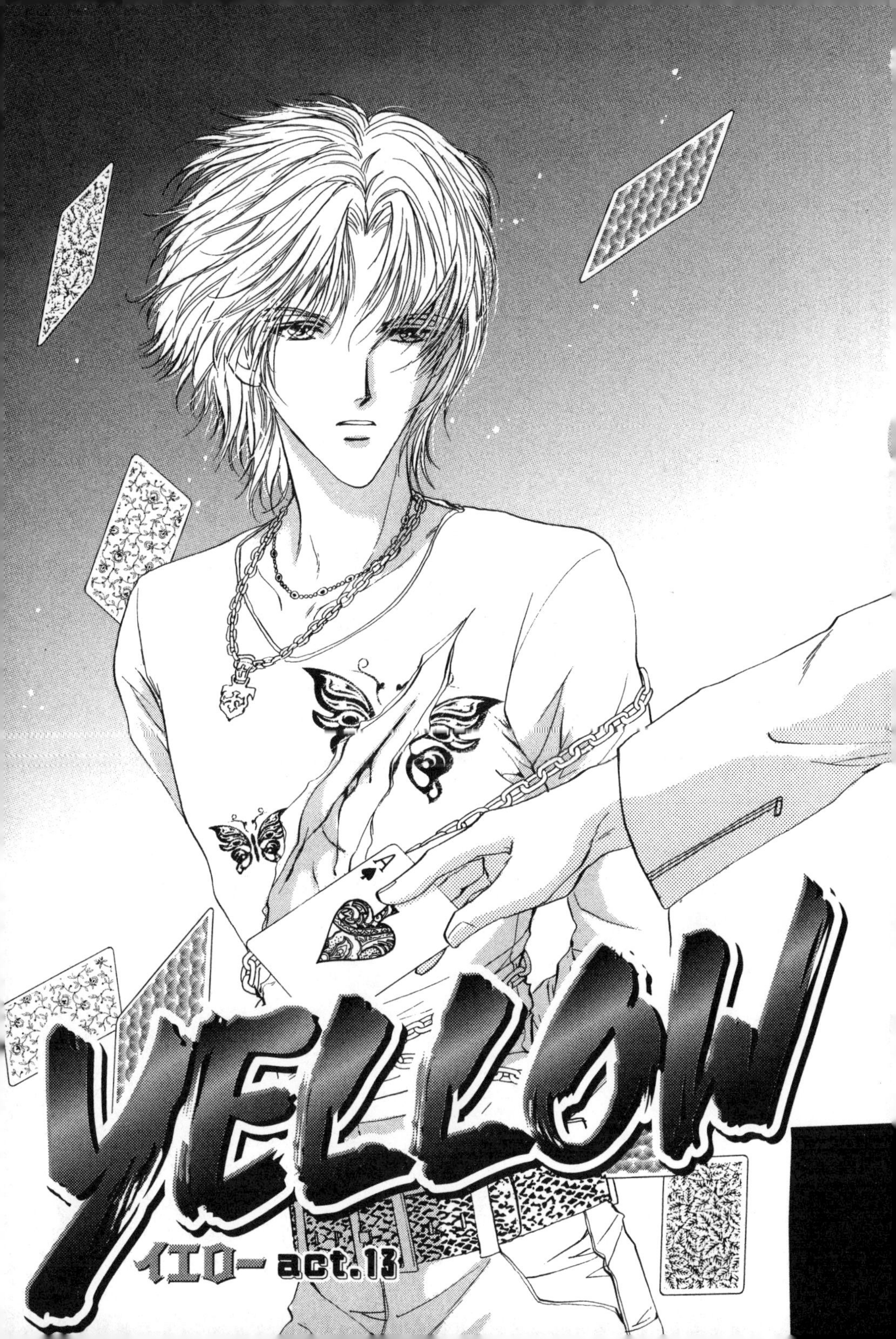
YELLOW
イエロー act.13

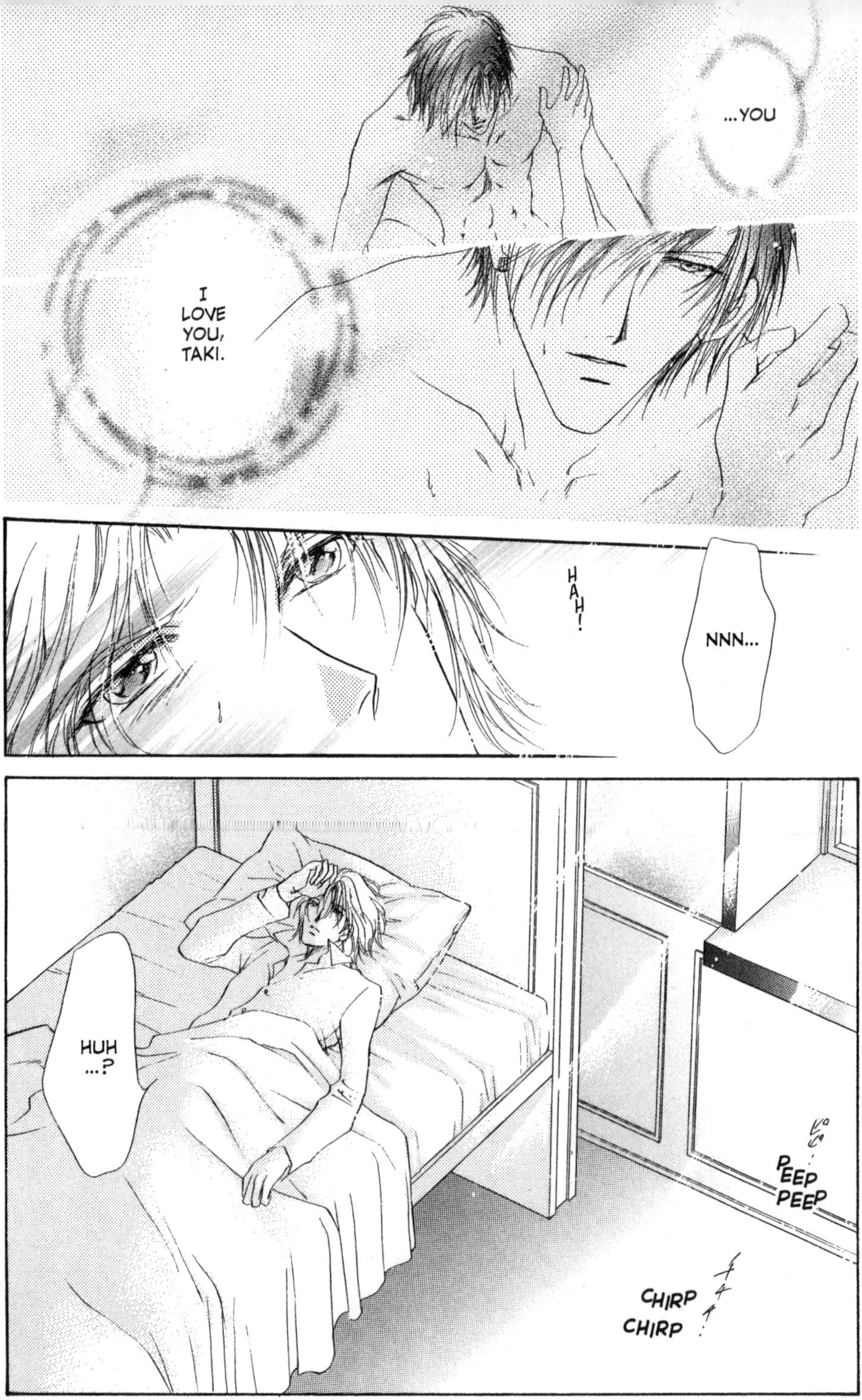
...YOU
I LOVE YOU, TAKI.
NNN...
HAH!
HUH ...?
PEEP PEEP
CHIRP CHIRP

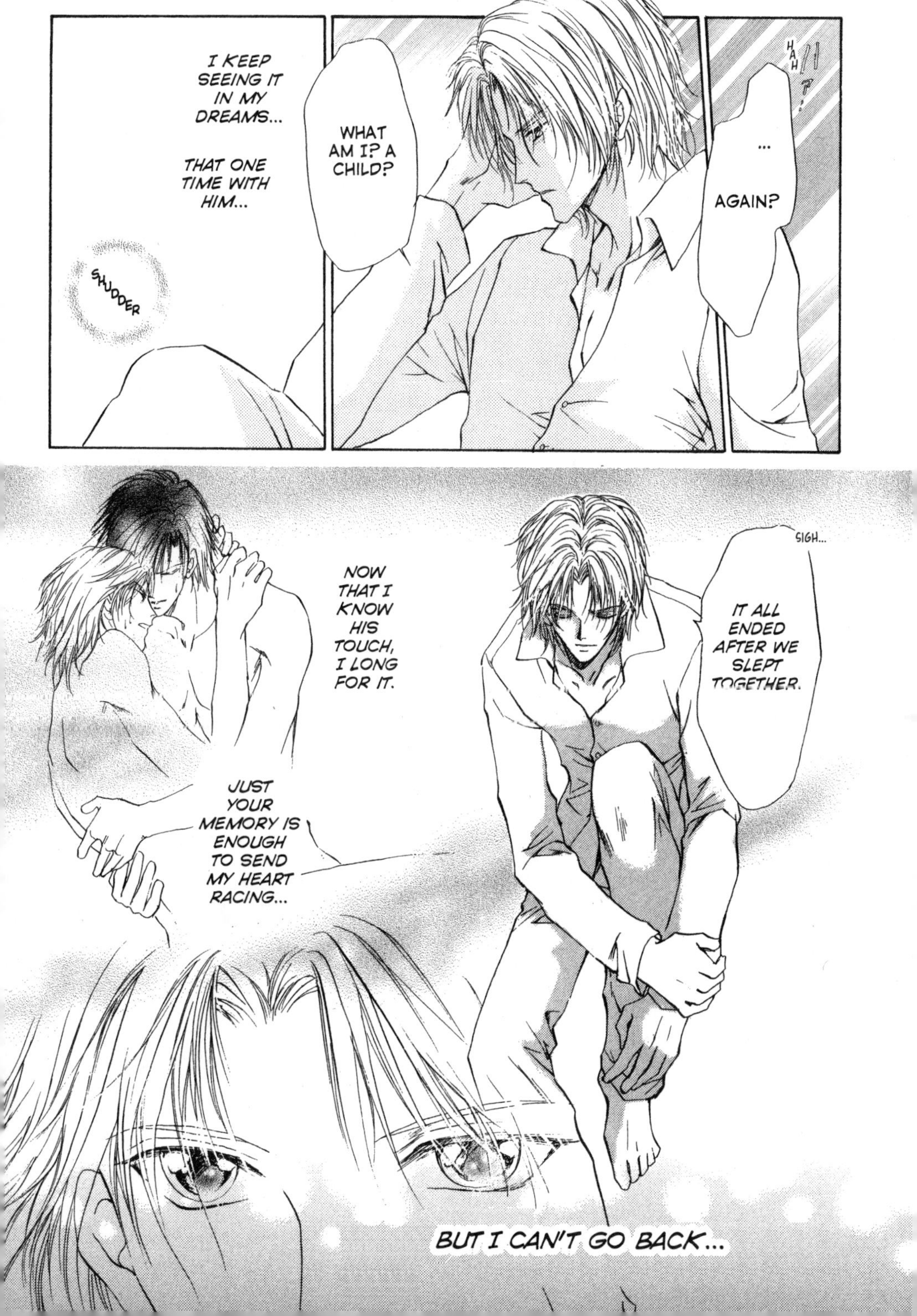
HAH
... AGAIN?
WHAT AM I? A CHILD?
I KEEP SEEING IT IN MY DREAMS...
THAT ONE TIME WITH HIM...
SHUDDER
SIGH...
IT ALL ENDED AFTER WE SLEPT TOGETHER.
NOW THAT I KNOW HIS TOUCH, I LONG FOR IT.
JUST YOUR MEMORY IS ENOUGH TO SEND MY HEART RACING...
BUT I CAN'T GO BACK...

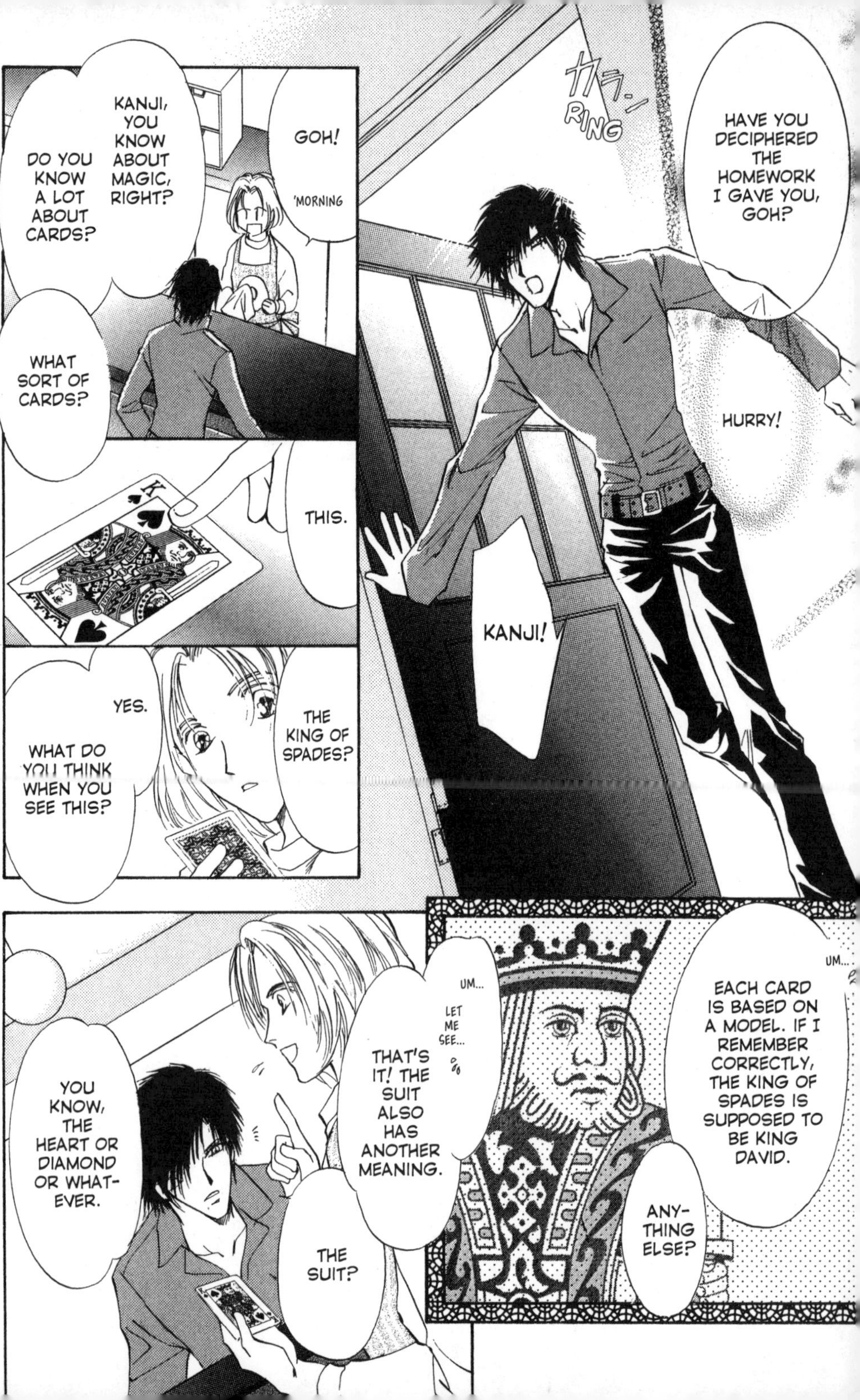
カラーン
RING
HAVE YOU DECIPHERED THE HOMEWORK I GAVE YOU, GOH?
HURRY!
KANJI!
GOH!
'MORNING
KANJI, YOU KNOW ABOUT MAGIC, RIGHT?
DO YOU KNOW A LOT ABOUT CARDS?
WHAT SORT OF CARDS?
THIS.
THE KING OF SPADES?
YES.
WHAT DO YOU THINK WHEN YOU SEE THIS?
UM...
EACH CARD IS BASED ON A MODEL. IF I REMEMBER CORRECTLY, THE KING OF SPADES IS SUPPOSED TO BE KING DAVID.
ANYTHING ELSE?
UM... LET ME SEE...
THAT'S IT! THE SUIT ALSO HAS ANOTHER MEANING.
THE SUIT?
YOU KNOW, THE HEART OR DIAMOND OR WHATEVER.

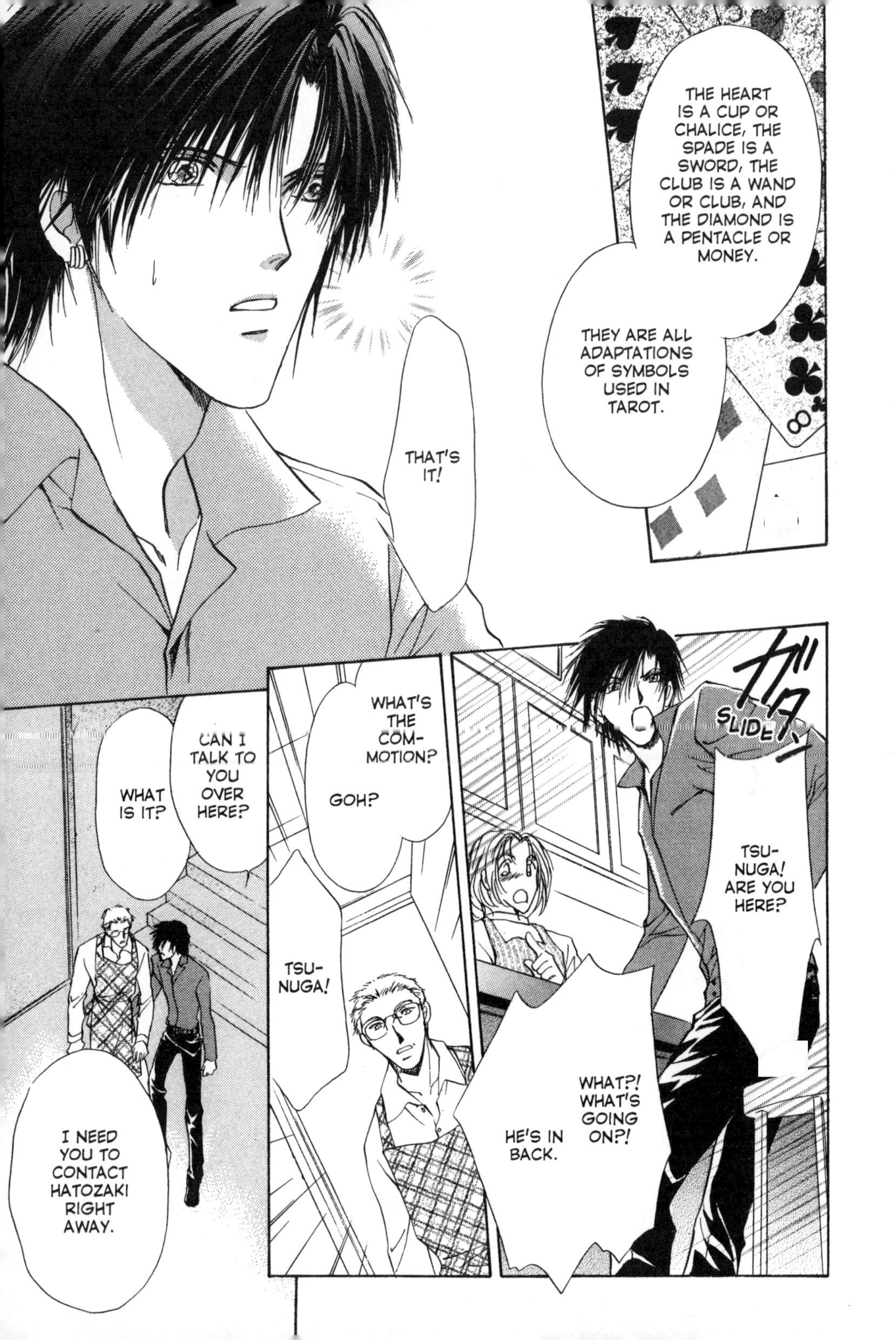

THE HEART IS A CUP OR CHALICE, THE SPADE IS A SWORD, THE CLUB IS A WAND OR CLUB, AND THE DIAMOND IS A PENTACLE OR MONEY.
THEY ARE ALL ADAPTATIONS OF SYMBOLS USED IN TAROT.
THAT'S IT!
ガタ
SLIDE
TSU-NUGA! ARE YOU HERE?
WHAT?! WHAT'S GOING ON?!
WHAT'S THE COM-MOTION?
GOH?
TSU-NUGA!
HE'S IN BACK.
CAN I TALK TO YOU OVER HERE?
WHAT IS IT?
I NEED YOU TO CONTACT HATOZAKI RIGHT AWAY.

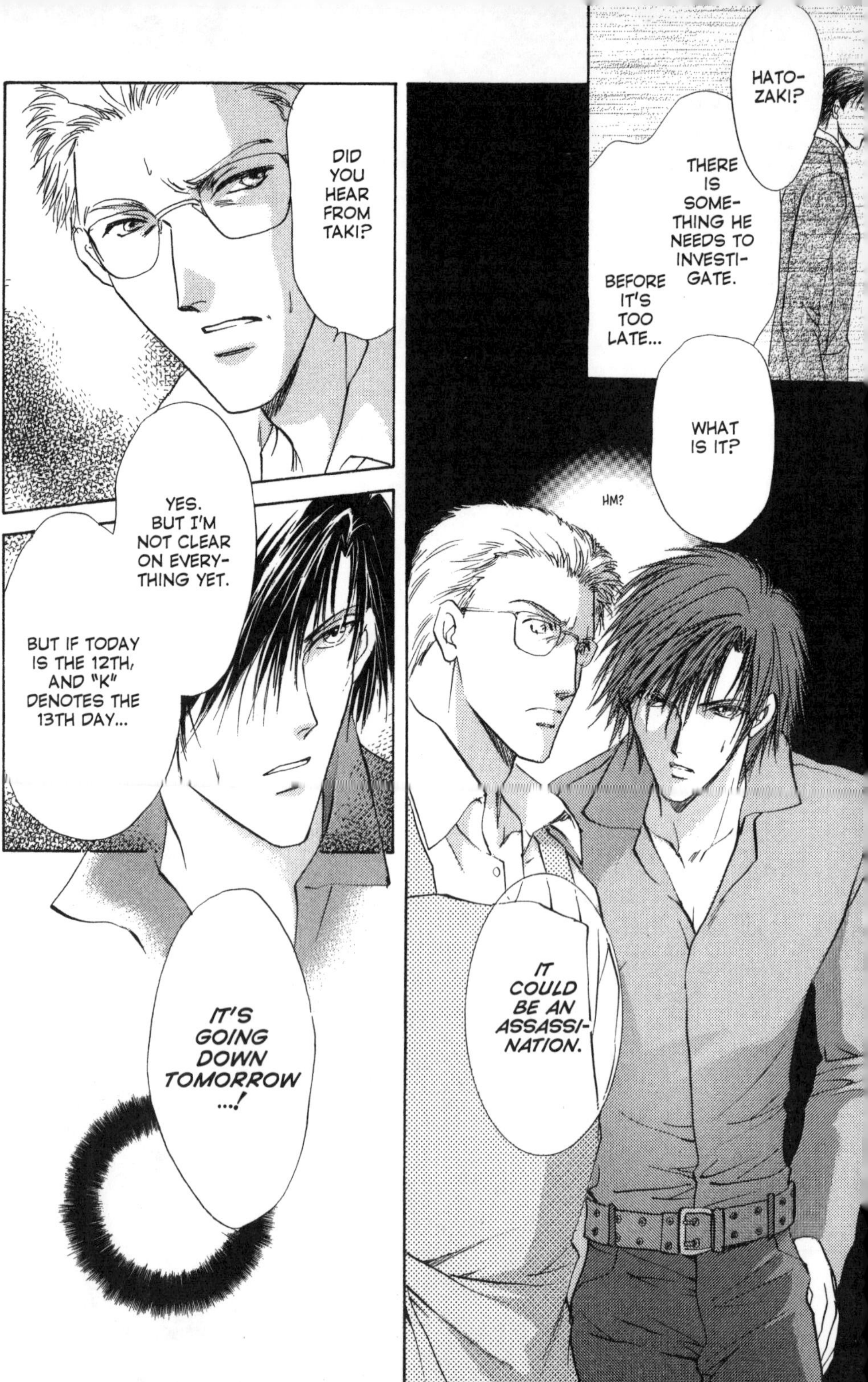
HATO-ZAKI?
THERE IS SOME-THING HE NEEDS TO INVESTI-GATE.
BEFORE IT'S TOO LATE...
WHAT IS IT?
HM?
IT COULD BE AN ASSASSI-NATION.
DID YOU HEAR FROM TAKI?
YES. BUT I'M NOT CLEAR ON EVERY-THING YET.
BUT IF TODAY IS THE 12TH, AND "K" DENOTES THE 13TH DAY...
IT'S GOING DOWN TOMORROW ...!

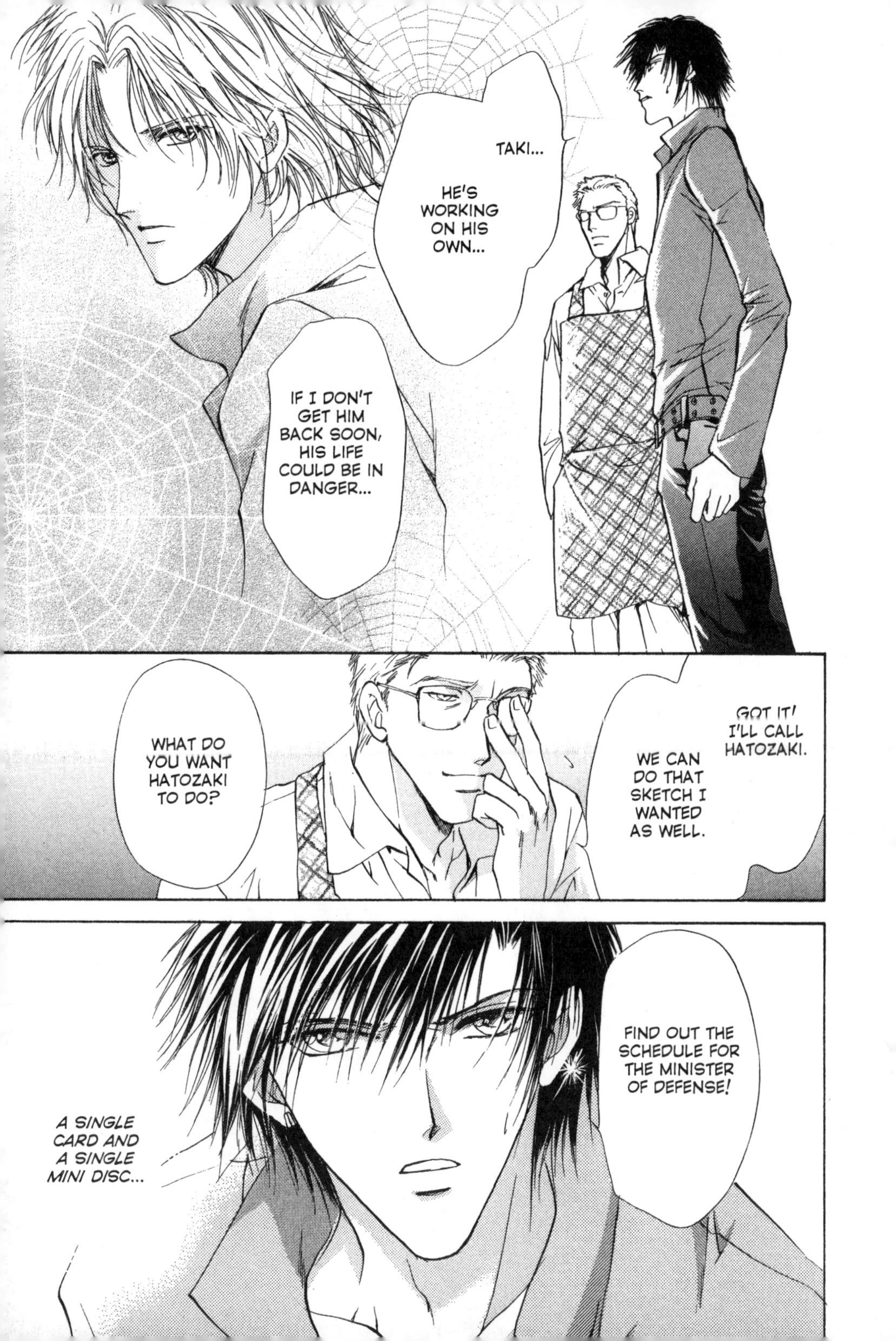
TAKI...
HE'S WORKING ON HIS OWN...
IF I DON'T GET HIM BACK SOON, HIS LIFE COULD BE IN DANGER...
GOT IT! I'LL CALL HATOZAKI.
WE CAN DO THAT SKETCH I WANTED AS WELL.
WHAT DO YOU WANT HATOZAKI TO DO?
FIND OUT THE SCHEDULE FOR THE MINISTER OF DEFENSE!
A SINGLE CARD AND A SINGLE MINI DISC...

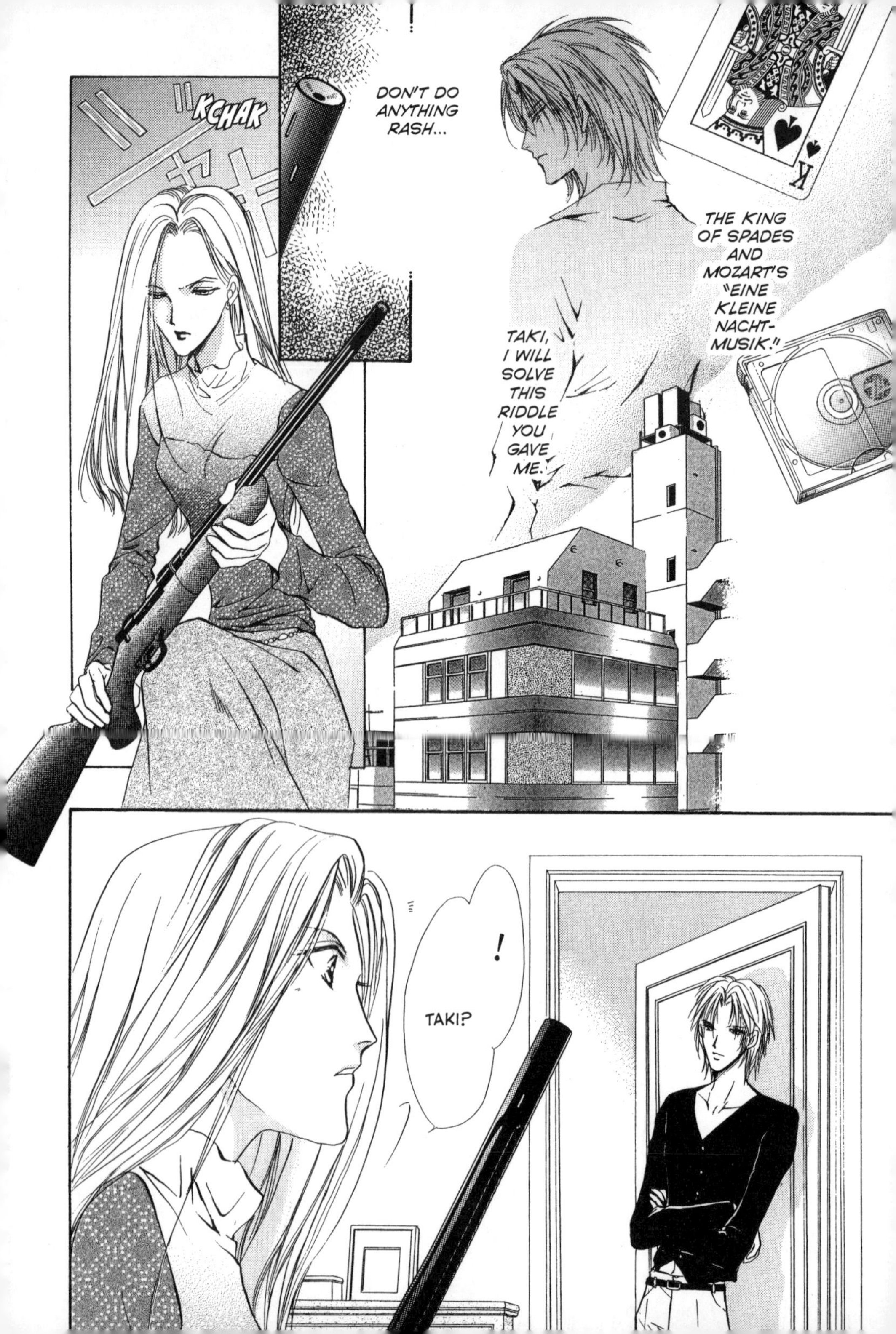
!
DON'T DO ANYTHING RASH...
THE KING OF SPADES AND MOZART'S "EINE KLEINE NACHT-MUSIK."
TAKI, I WILL SOLVE THIS RIDDLE YOU GAVE ME.
KCHAK
!
TAKI?

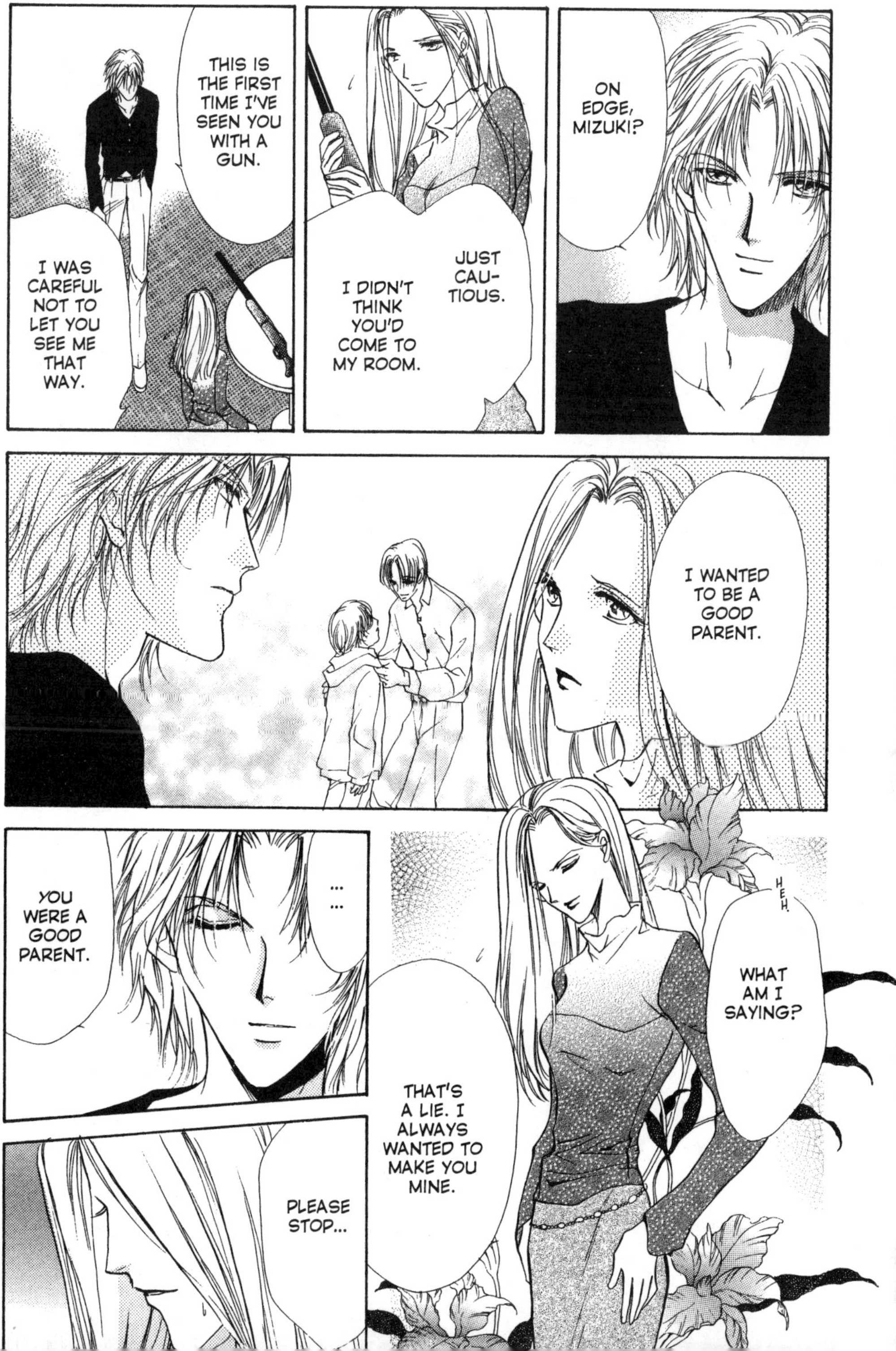
ON EDGE, MIZUKI?
JUST CAUTIOUS.
I DIDN'T THINK YOU'D COME TO MY ROOM.
THIS IS THE FIRST TIME I'VE SEEN YOU WITH A GUN.
I WAS CAREFUL NOT TO LET YOU SEE ME THAT WAY.
I WANTED TO BE A GOOD PARENT.
HEH.
WHAT AM I SAYING?
THAT'S A LIE. I ALWAYS WANTED TO MAKE YOU MINE.
......
YOU WERE A GOOD PARENT.
PLEASE STOP...

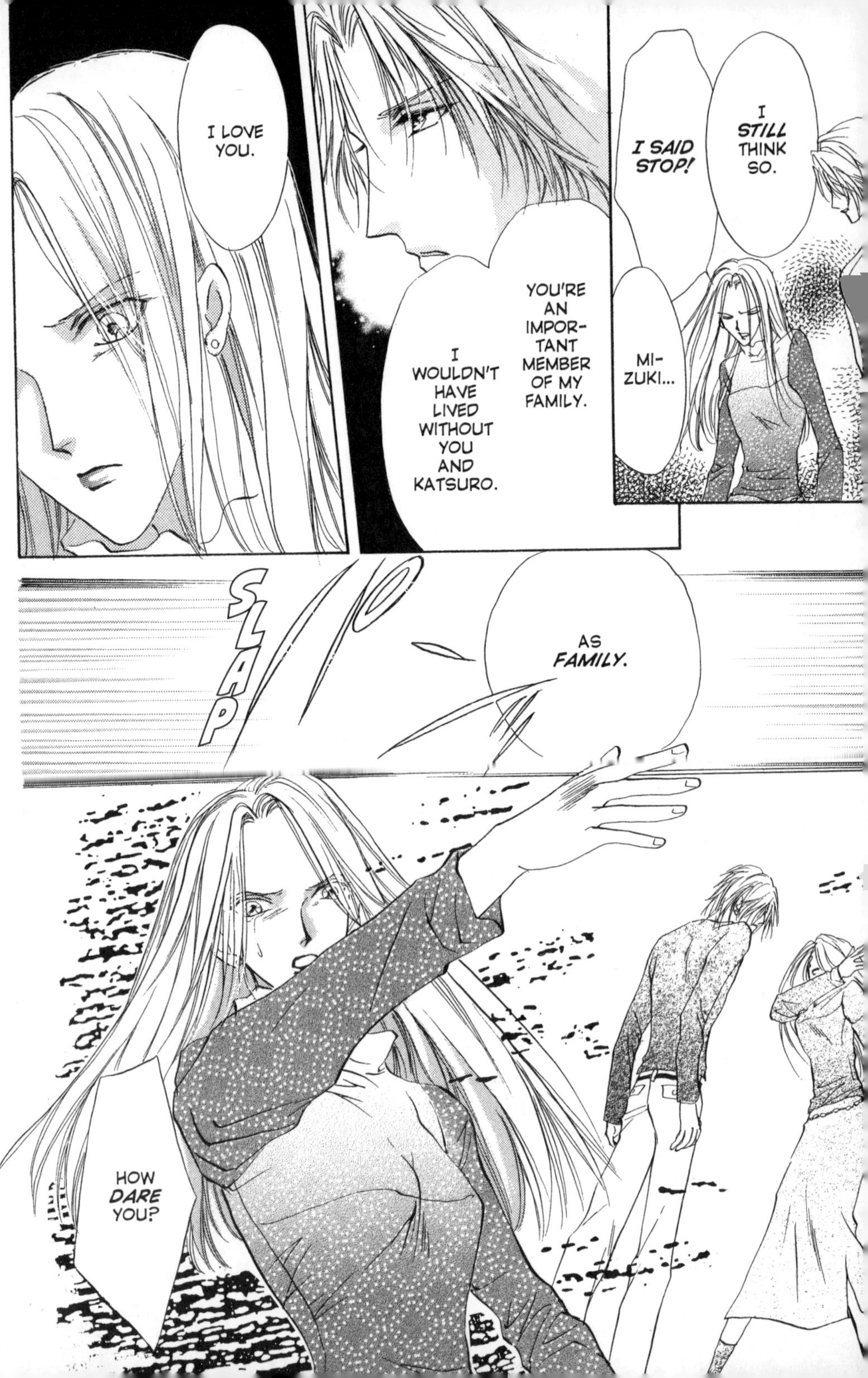
I STILL THINK SO.
I SAID STOP!
MI-ZUKI...
YOU'RE AN IMPOR-TANT MEMBER OF MY FAMILY.
I WOULDN'T HAVE LIVED WITHOUT YOU AND KATSURO.
I LOVE YOU.
AS FAMILY.
SLAP
HOW DARE YOU?

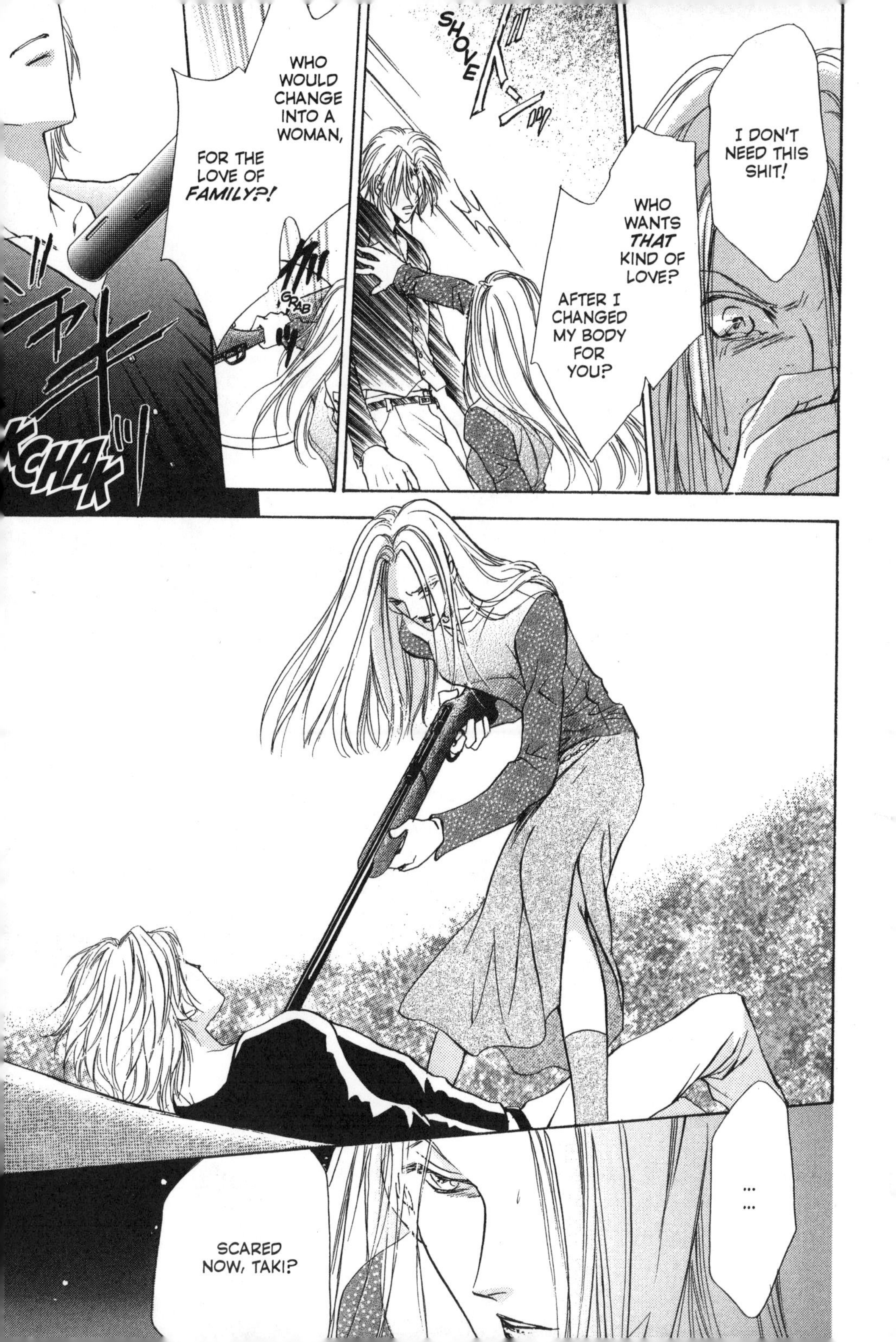
I DON'T NEED THIS SHIT!
SHOVE
WHO WANTS *THAT* KIND OF LOVE?
AFTER I CHANGED MY BODY FOR YOU?
GRAB
WHO WOULD CHANGE INTO A WOMAN,
FOR THE LOVE OF *FAMILY?!*
KCHAK
……
SCARED NOW, TAKI?

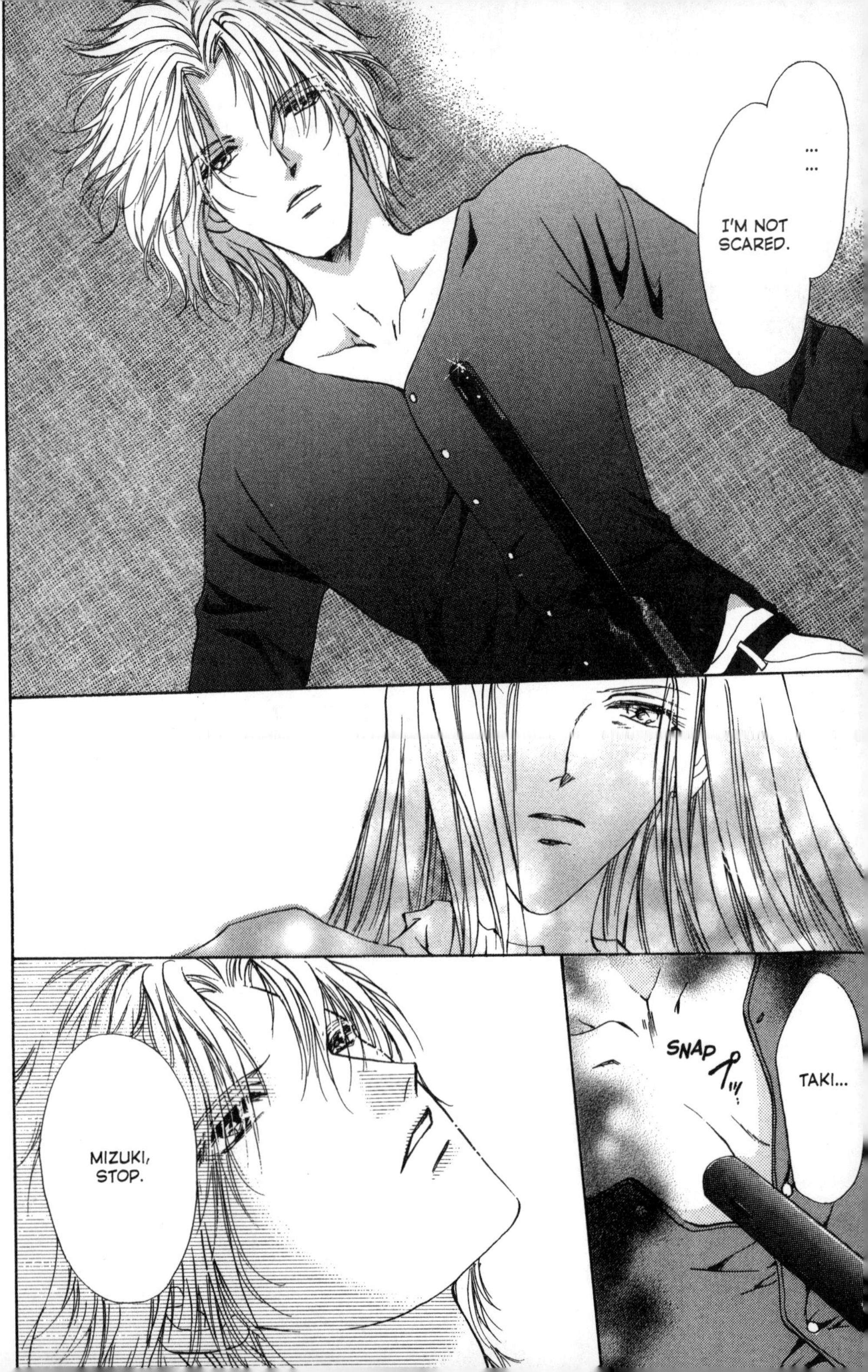
……
I'M NOT SCARED.
TAKI...
SNAP
MIZUKI, STOP.

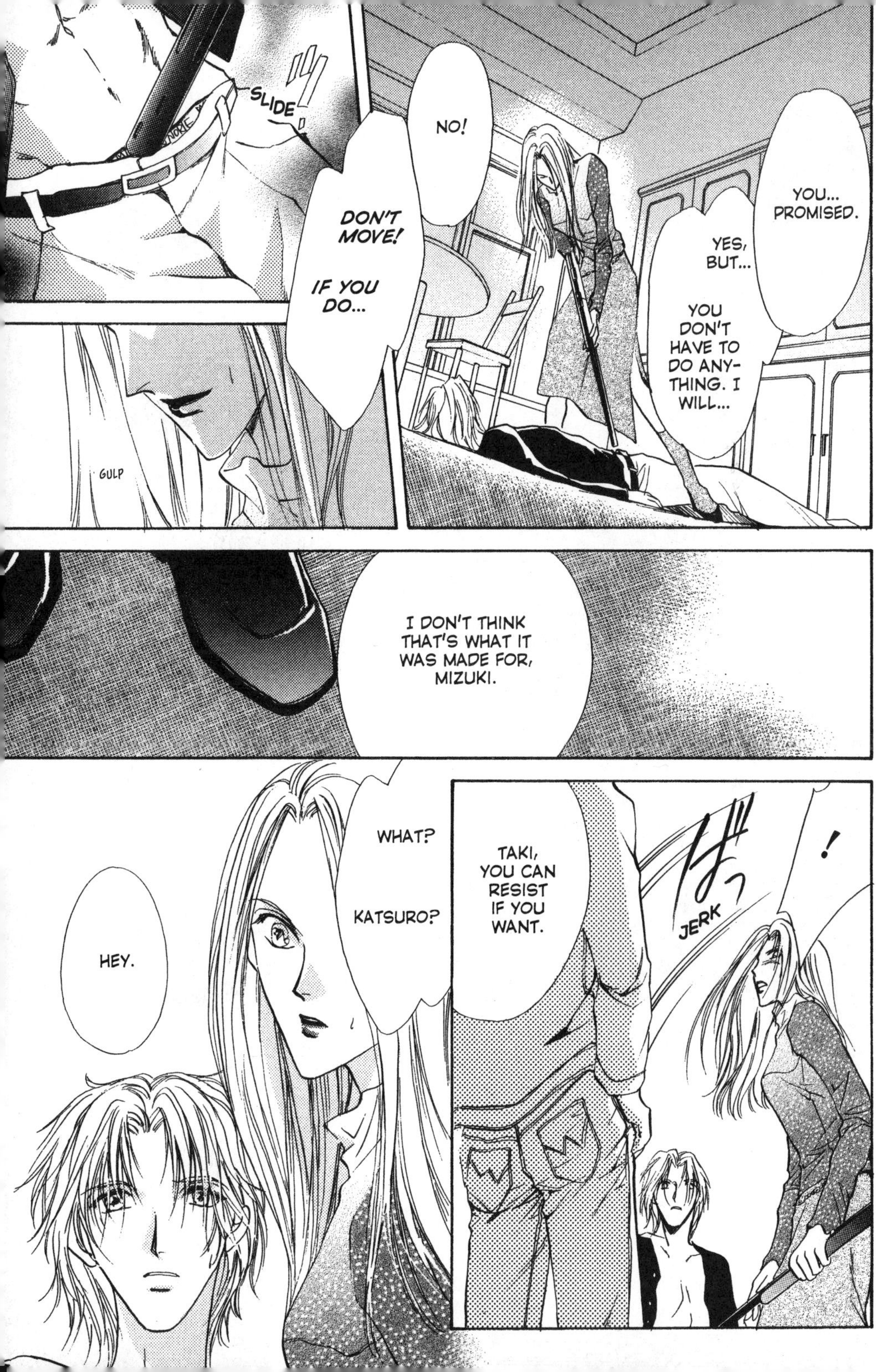
YOU... PROMISED.
YES, BUT...
YOU DON'T HAVE TO DO ANYTHING. I WILL...
NO!
DON'T MOVE!
IF YOU DO...
SLIDE
GULP
I DON'T THINK THAT'S WHAT IT WAS MADE FOR, MIZUKI.
!
JERK
TAKI, YOU CAN RESIST IF YOU WANT.
WHAT?
KATSURO?
HEY.

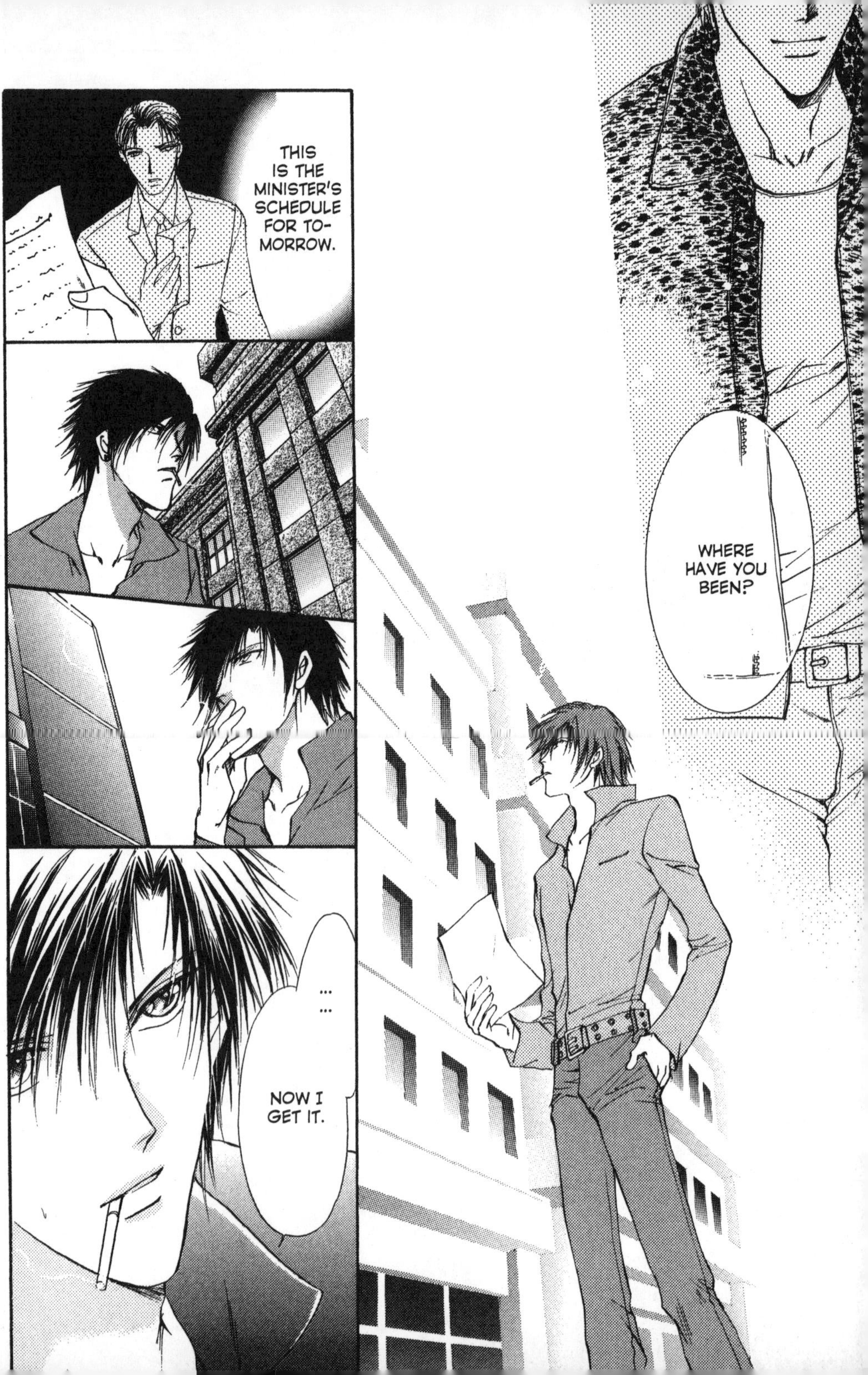
WHERE HAVE YOU BEEN?
THIS IS THE MINISTER'S SCHEDULE FOR TO-MORROW.
... ...
NOW I GET IT.

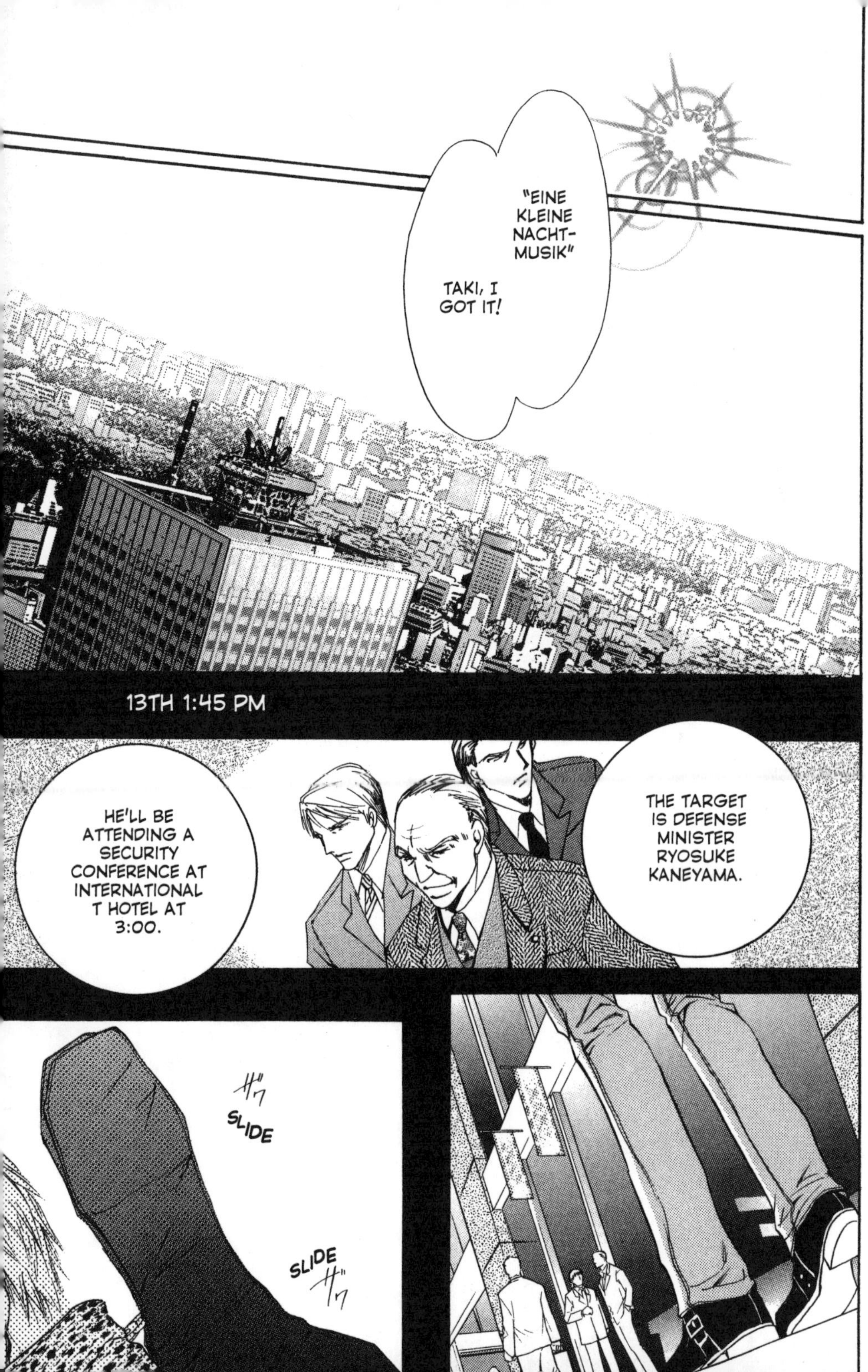
"EINE KLEINE NACHT-MUSIK"
TAKI, I GOT IT!
13TH 1:45 PM
THE TARGET IS DEFENSE MINISTER RYOSUKE KANEYAMA.
HE'LL BE ATTENDING A SECURITY CONFERENCE AT INTERNATIONAL T HOTEL AT 3:00.
SLIDE
SLIDE

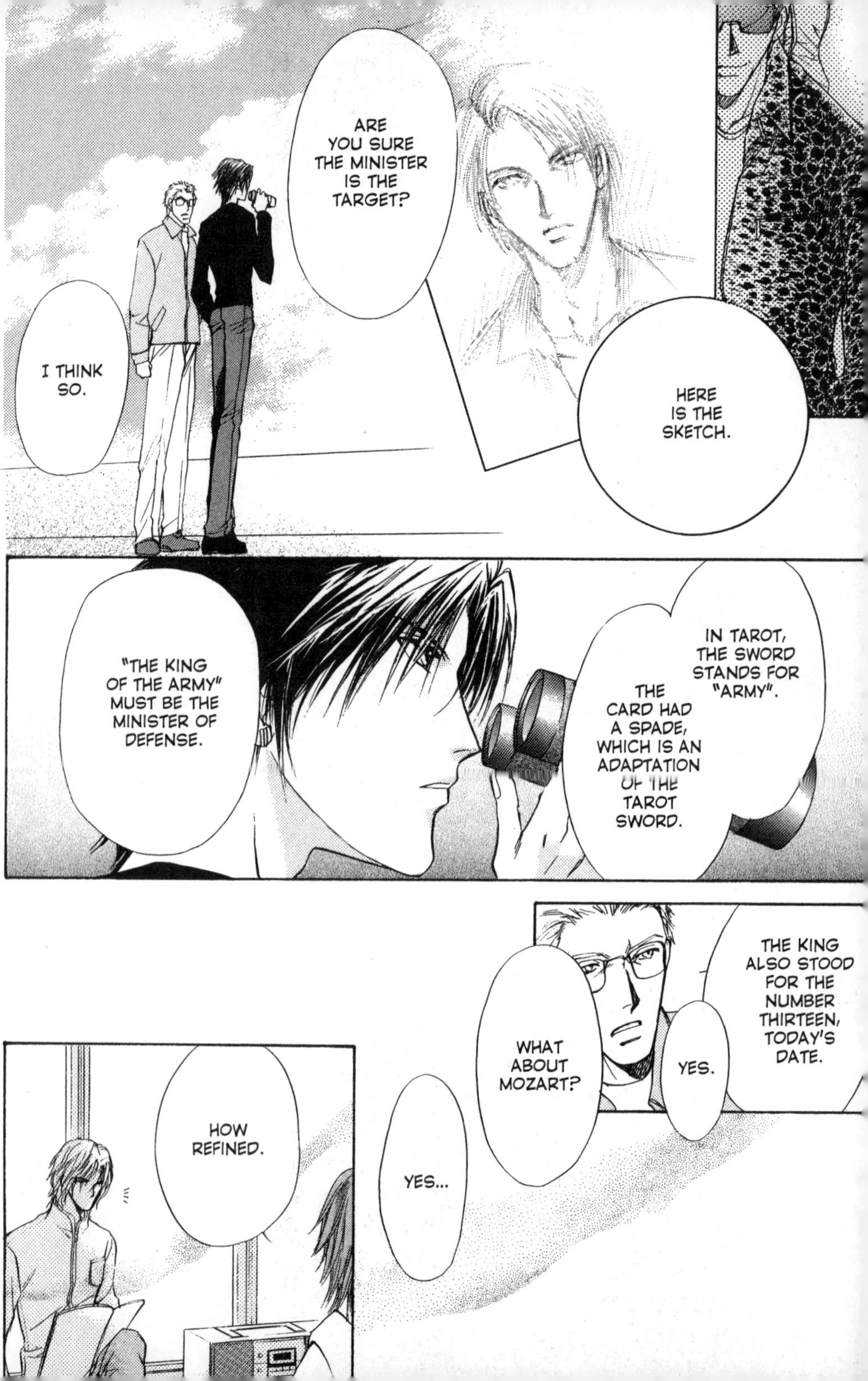
HERE IS THE SKETCH.
ARE YOU SURE THE MINISTER IS THE TARGET?
I THINK SO.
IN TAROT, THE SWORD STANDS FOR "ARMY".
THE CARD HAD A SPADE, WHICH IS AN ADAPTATION OF THE TAROT SWORD.
"THE KING OF THE ARMY" MUST BE THE MINISTER OF DEFENSE.
THE KING ALSO STOOD FOR THE NUMBER THIRTEEN, TODAY'S DATE.
YES.
WHAT ABOUT MOZART?
YES...
HOW REFINED.

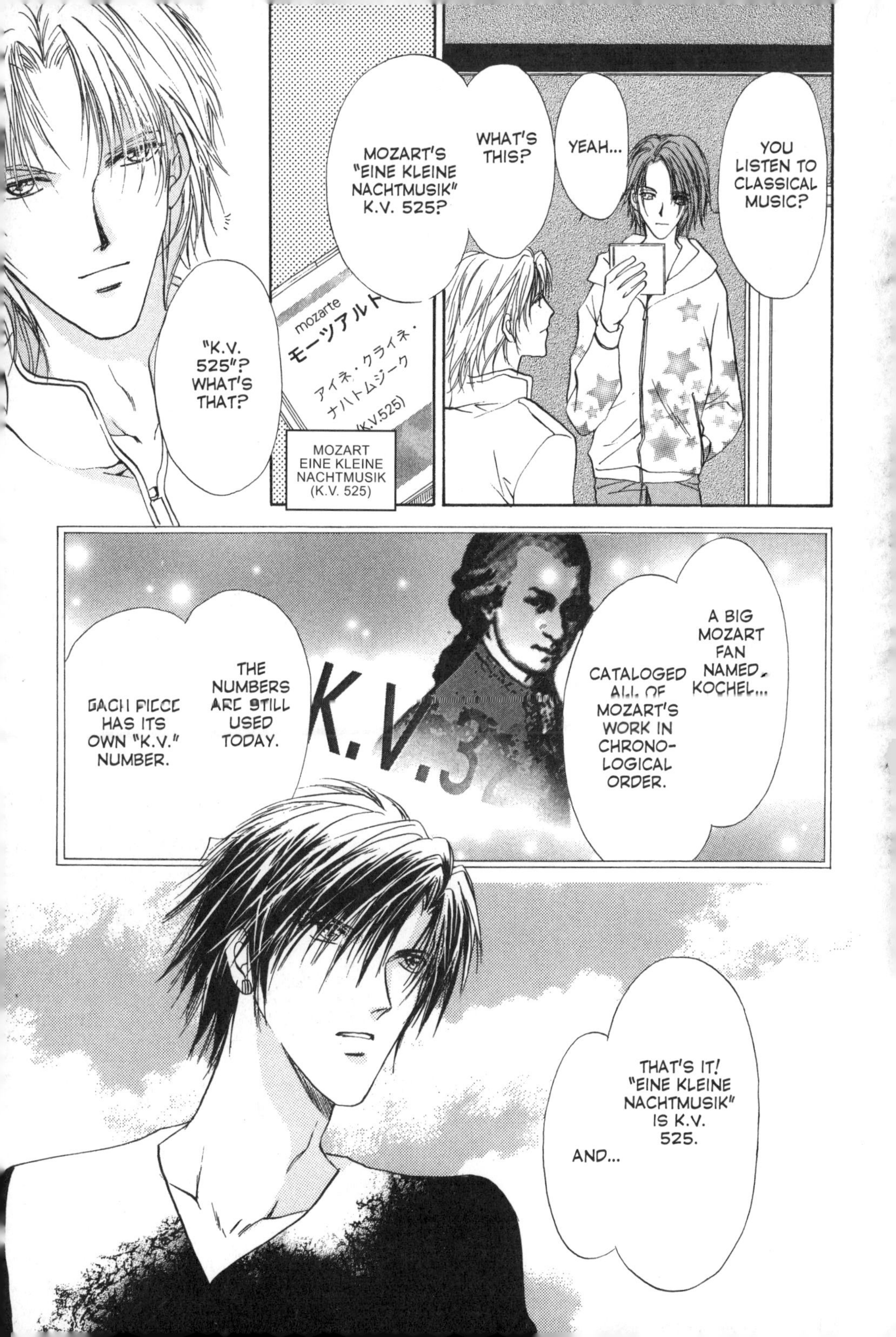
YOU LISTEN TO CLASSICAL MUSIC?
YEAH...
WHAT'S THIS?
MOZART'S "EINE KLEINE NACHTMUSIK" K.V. 525?
mozarte
モーツアルト
アイネ・クライネ・ナハトムジーク
(K.V.525)
MOZART EINE KLEINE NACHTMUSIK (K.V. 525)
"K.V. 525"? WHAT'S THAT?
A BIG MOZART FAN NAMED KOCHEL...
CATALOGED ALL OF MOZART'S WORK IN CHRONO-LOGICAL ORDER.
K.V.3
THE NUMBERS ARE STILL USED TODAY.
EACH PIECE HAS ITS OWN "K.V." NUMBER.
THAT'S IT! "EINE KLEINE NACHTMUSIK" IS K.V. 525.
AND...

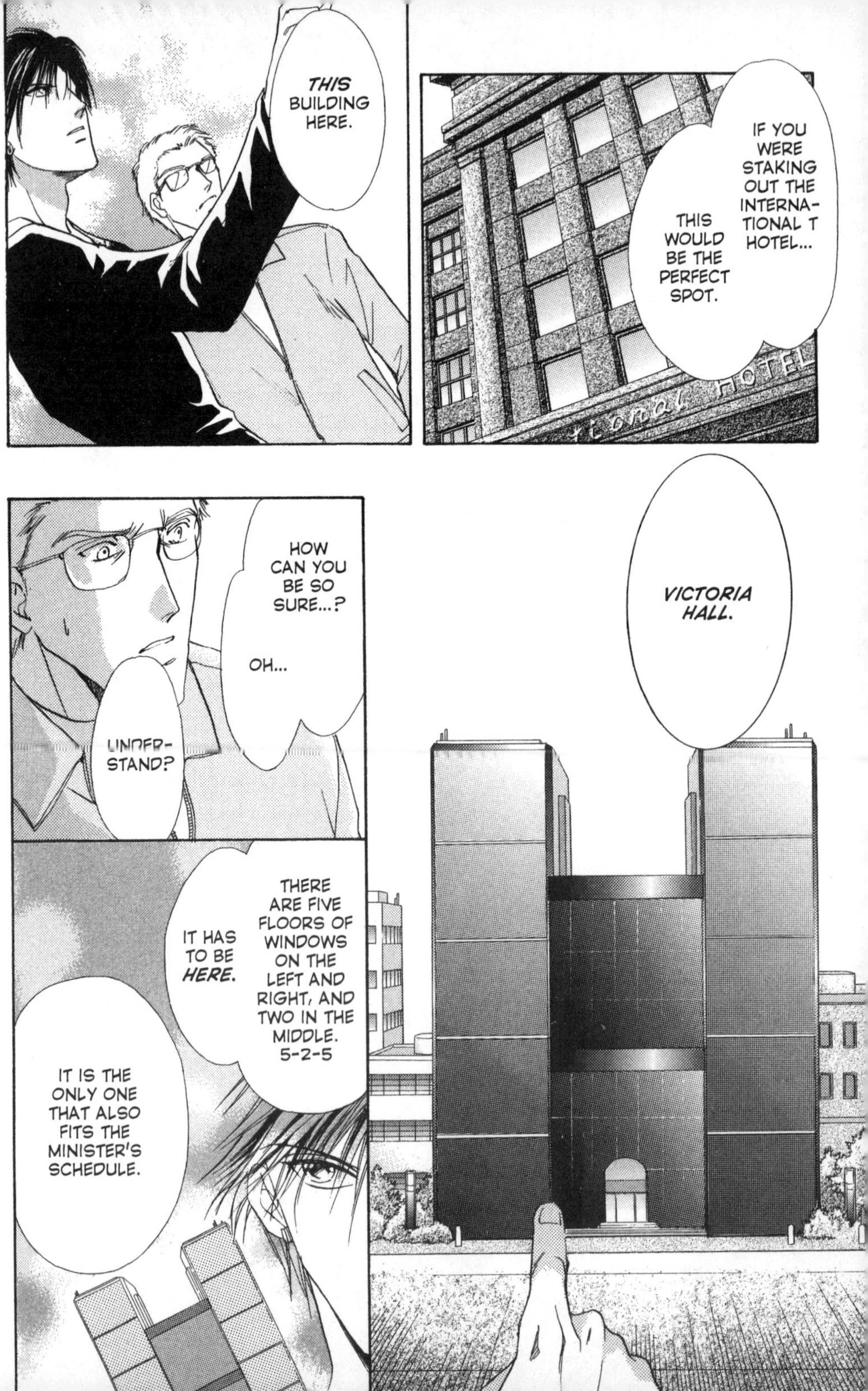
IF YOU WERE STAKING OUT THE INTERNA-TIONAL T HOTEL...
THIS WOULD BE THE PERFECT SPOT.
THIS BUILDING HERE.
VICTORIA HALL.
HOW CAN YOU BE SO SURE...?
OH...
UNDER-STAND?
THERE ARE FIVE FLOORS OF WINDOWS ON THE LEFT AND RIGHT, AND TWO IN THE MIDDLE. 5-2-5
IT HAS TO BE *HERE*.
IT IS THE ONLY ONE THAT ALSO FITS THE MINISTER'S SCHEDULE.

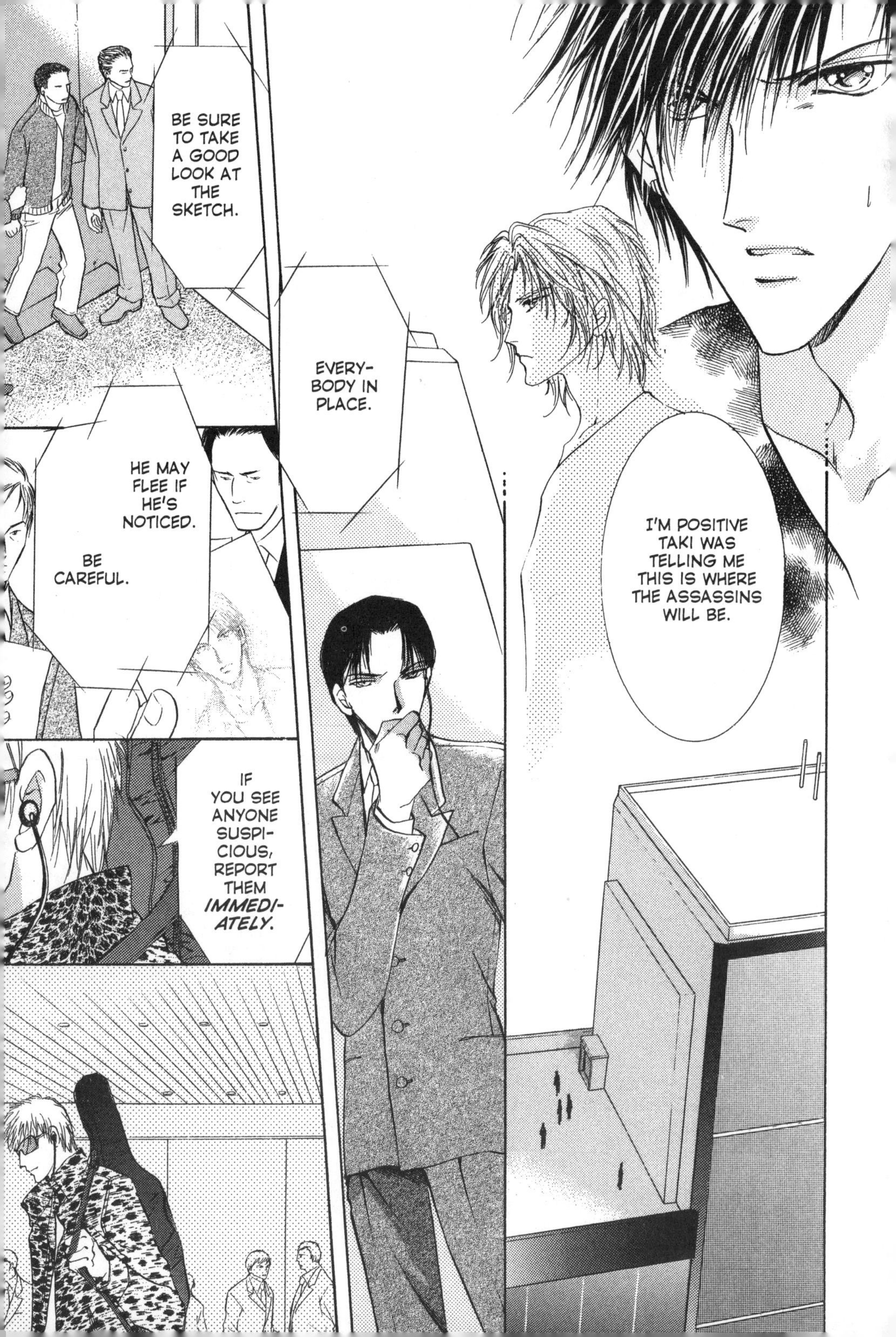
I'M POSITIVE TAKI WAS TELLING ME THIS IS WHERE THE ASSASSINS WILL BE.
EVERY-BODY IN PLACE.
BE SURE TO TAKE A GOOD LOOK AT THE SKETCH.
HE MAY FLEE IF HE'S NOTICED.
BE CAREFUL.
IF YOU SEE ANYONE SUSPICIOUS, REPORT THEM *IMMEDIATELY*.

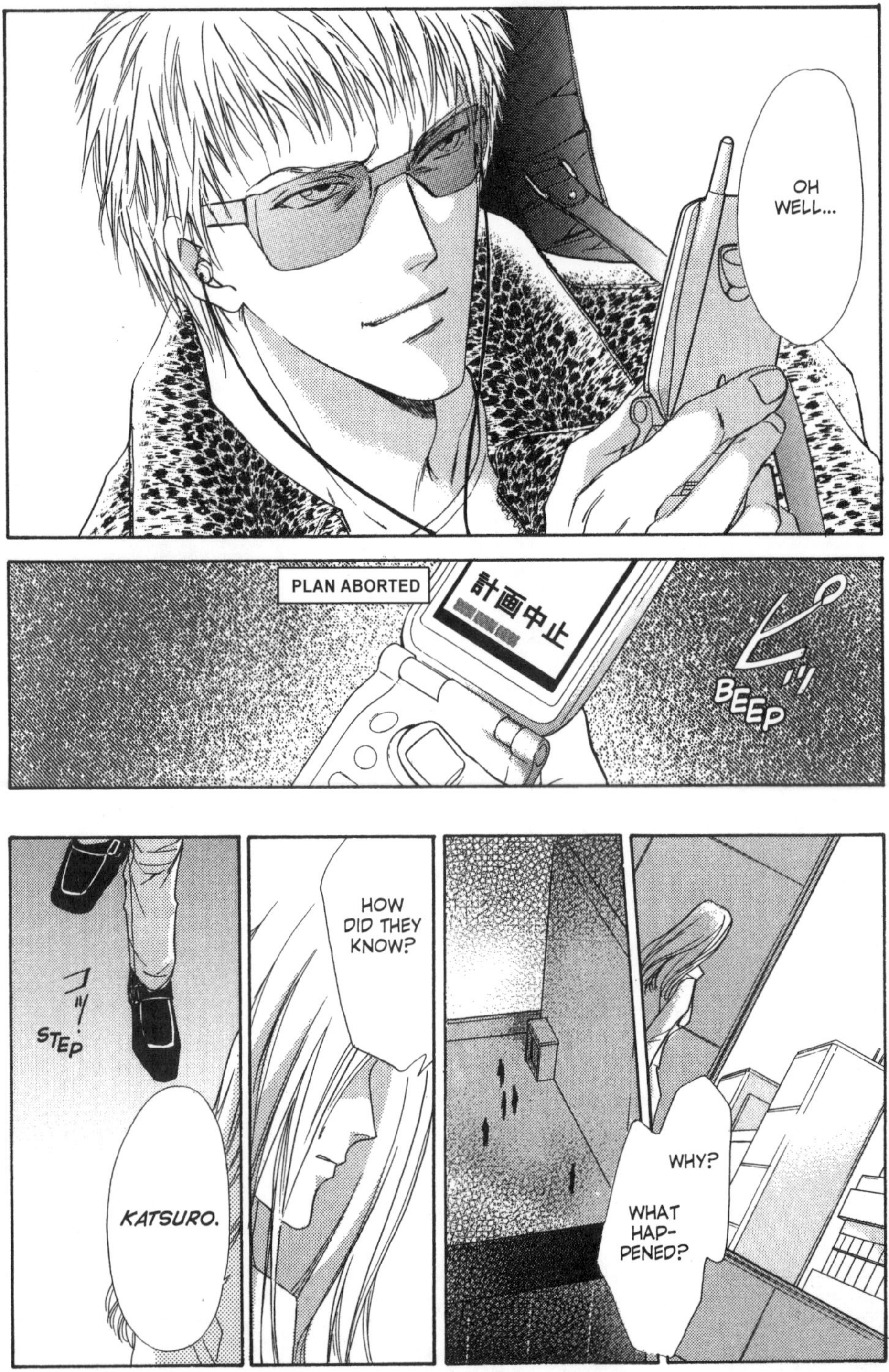
OH WELL...
PLAN ABORTED
計画中止
ピッ
BEEP
WHY?
WHAT HAP-PENED?
HOW DID THEY KNOW?
コツ!
STEP
KATSURO.

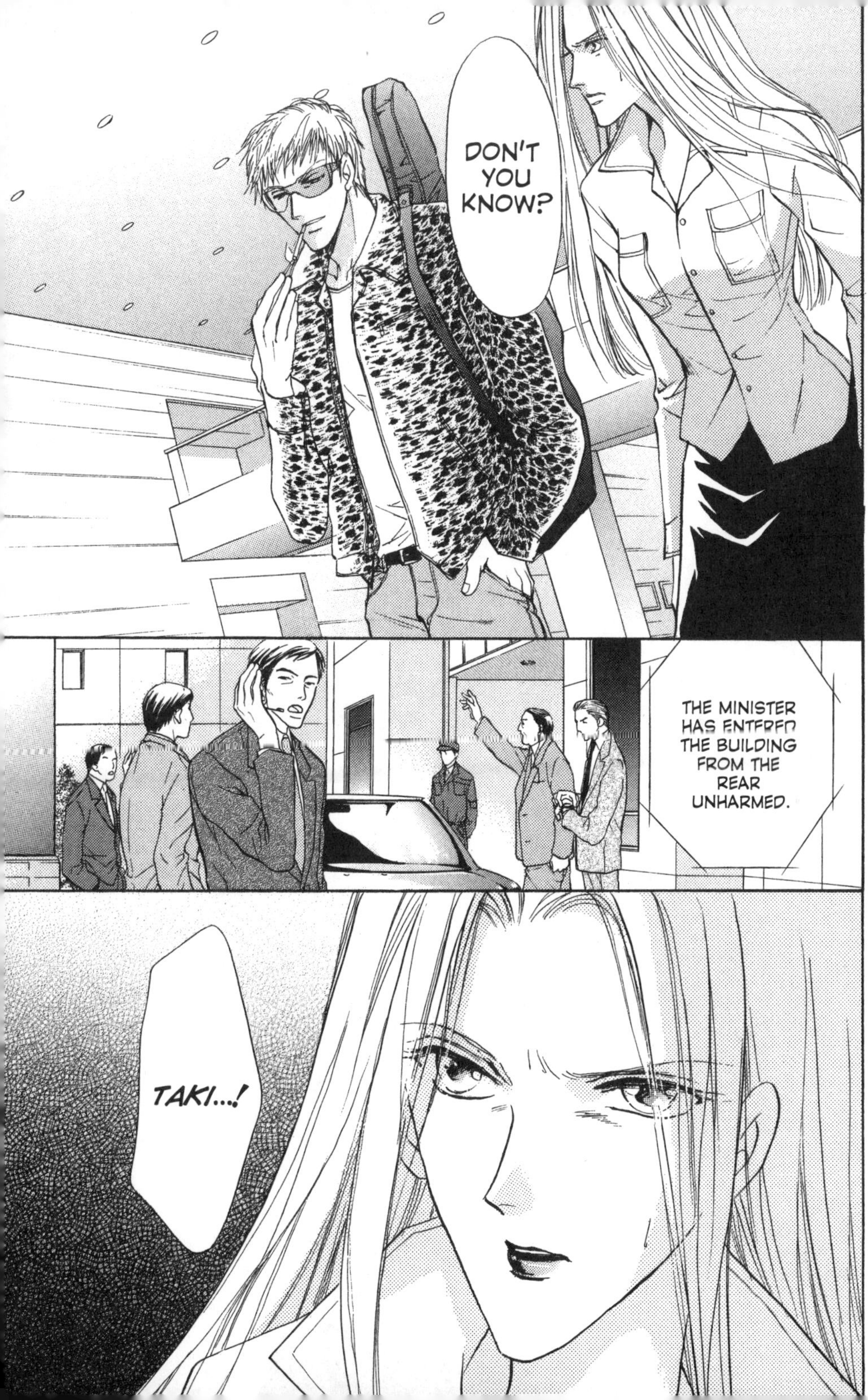
DON'T YOU KNOW?
THE MINISTER HAS ENTERED THE BUILDING FROM THE REAR UNHARMED.
TAKI...!

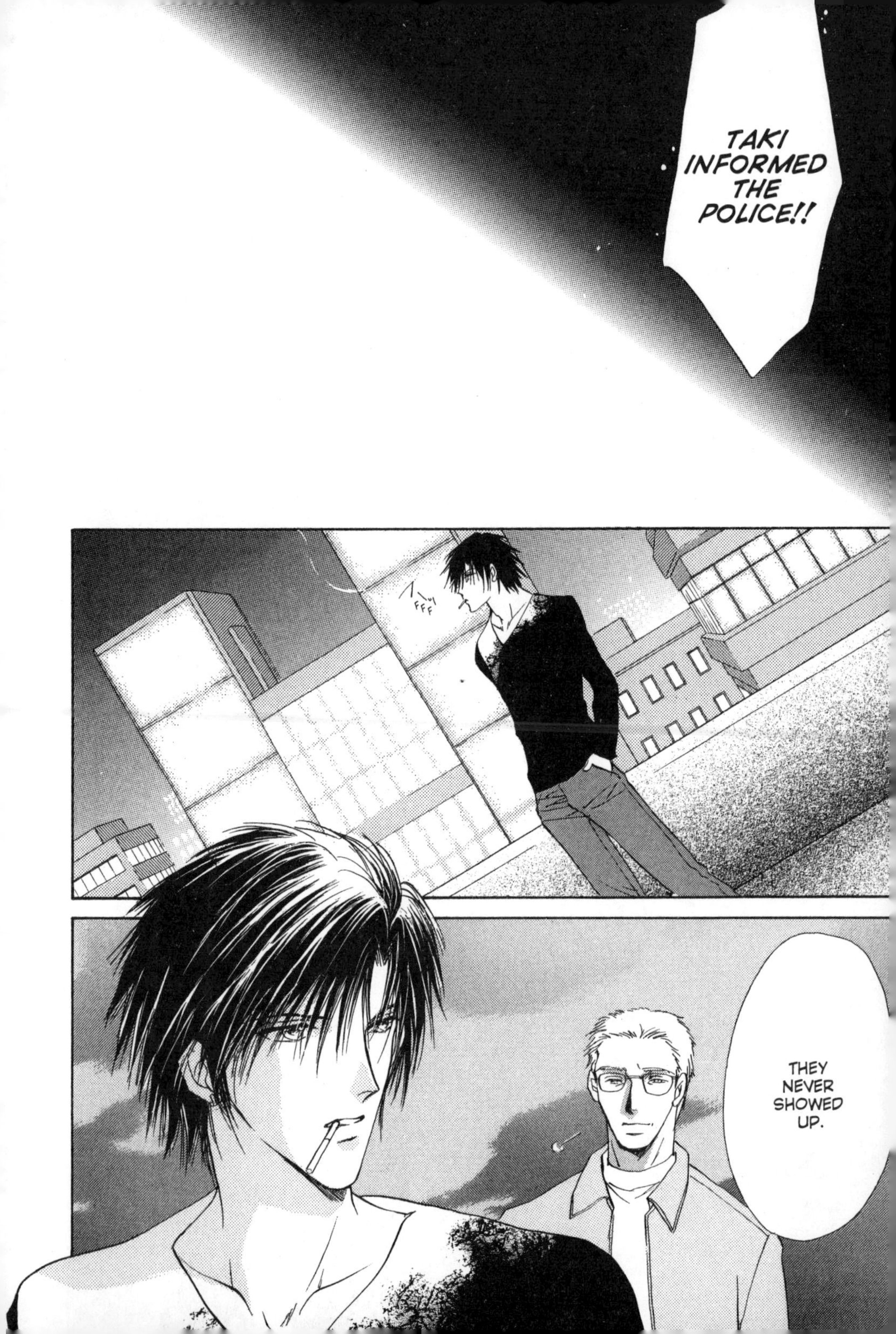
TAKI INFORMED THE POLICE!!
FFF
THEY NEVER SHOWED UP.

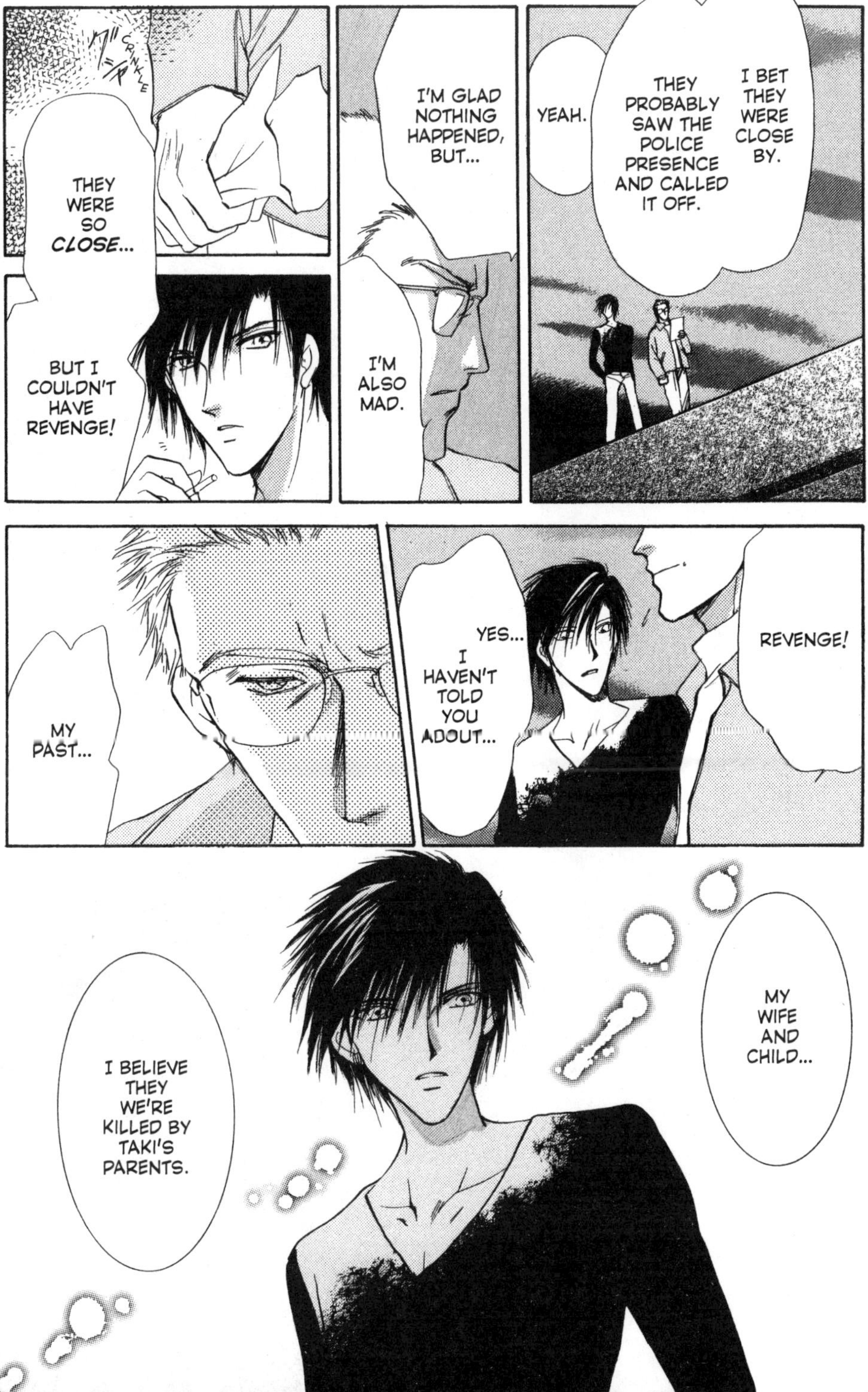
I BET THEY WERE CLOSE BY.
THEY PROBABLY SAW THE POLICE PRESENCE AND CALLED IT OFF.
YEAH.
I'M GLAD NOTHING HAPPENED, BUT...
I'M ALSO MAD.
CRINKLE
THEY WERE SO *CLOSE*...
BUT I COULDN'T HAVE REVENGE!
REVENGE!
YES... I HAVEN'T TOLD YOU ABOUT...
MY PAST...
MY WIFE AND CHILD...
I BELIEVE THEY WE'RE KILLED BY TAKI'S PARENTS.

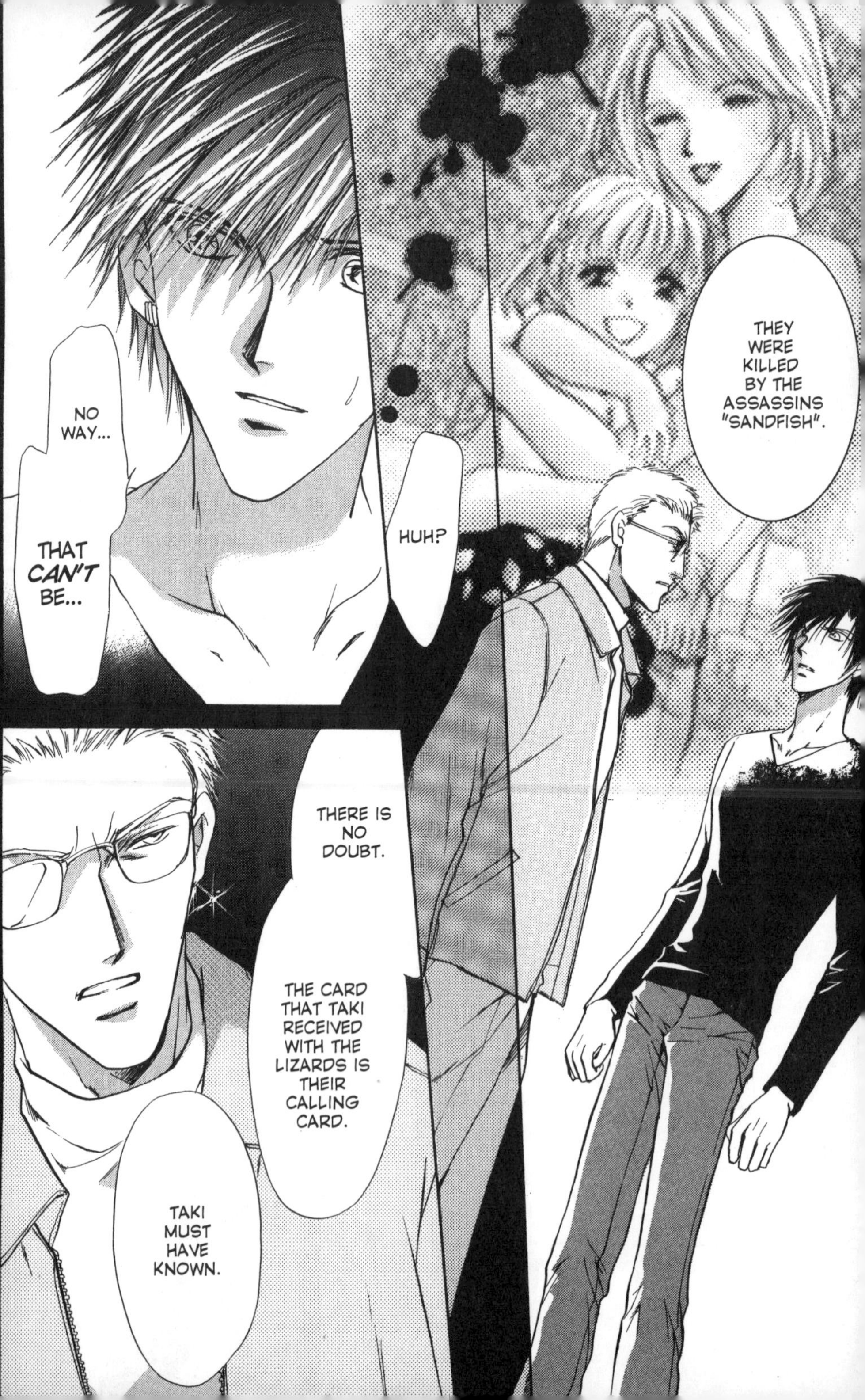
THEY WERE KILLED BY THE ASSASSINS "SANDFISH".
HUH?
NO WAY...
THAT *CAN'T* BE...
THERE IS NO DOUBT.
THE CARD THAT TAKI RECEIVED WITH THE LIZARDS IS THEIR CALLING CARD.
TAKI MUST HAVE KNOWN.

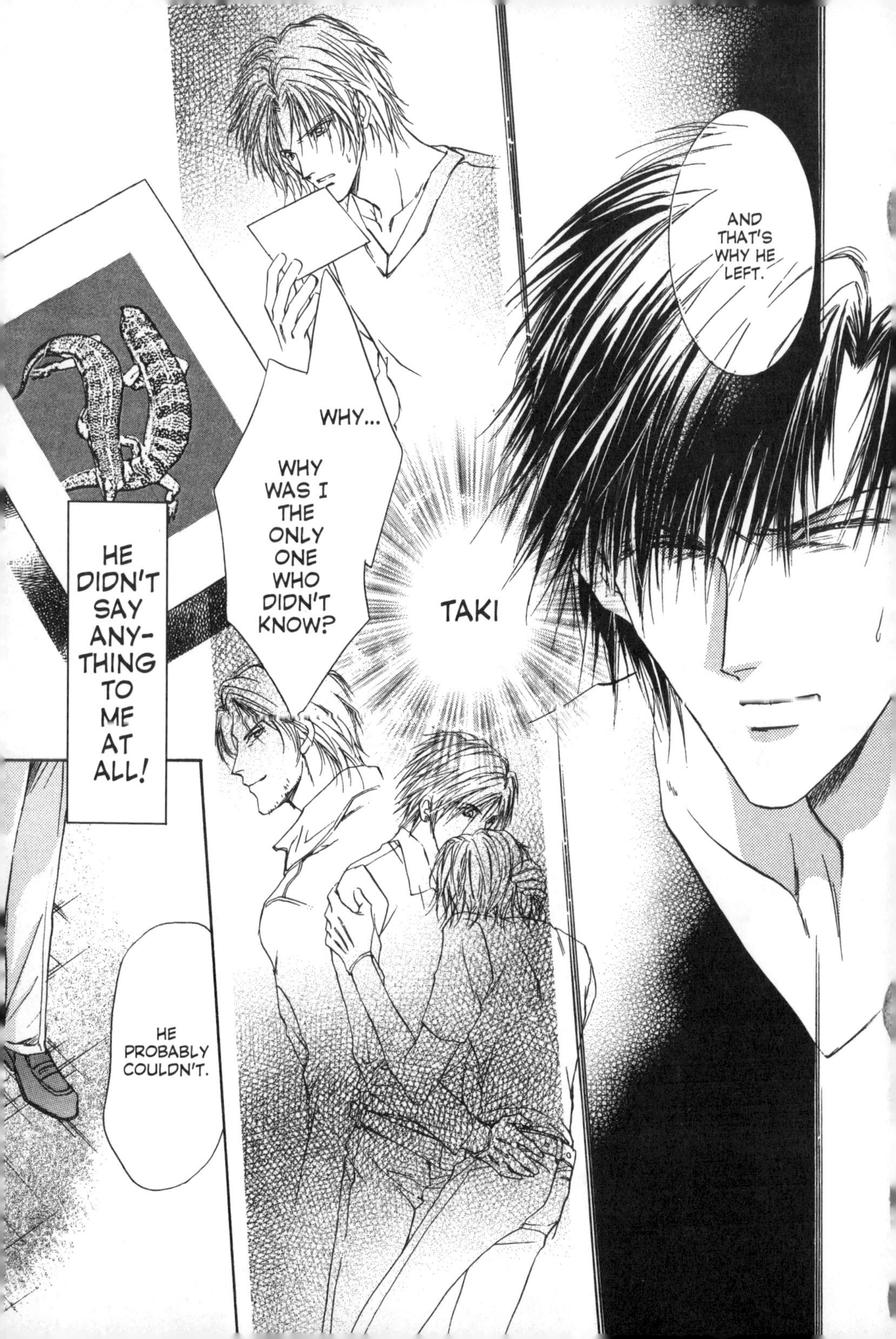
AND THAT'S WHY HE LEFT.
WHY...
WHY WAS I THE ONLY ONE WHO DIDN'T KNOW?
TAKI
HE DIDN'T SAY ANY-THING TO ME AT ALL!
HE PROBABLY COULDN'T.

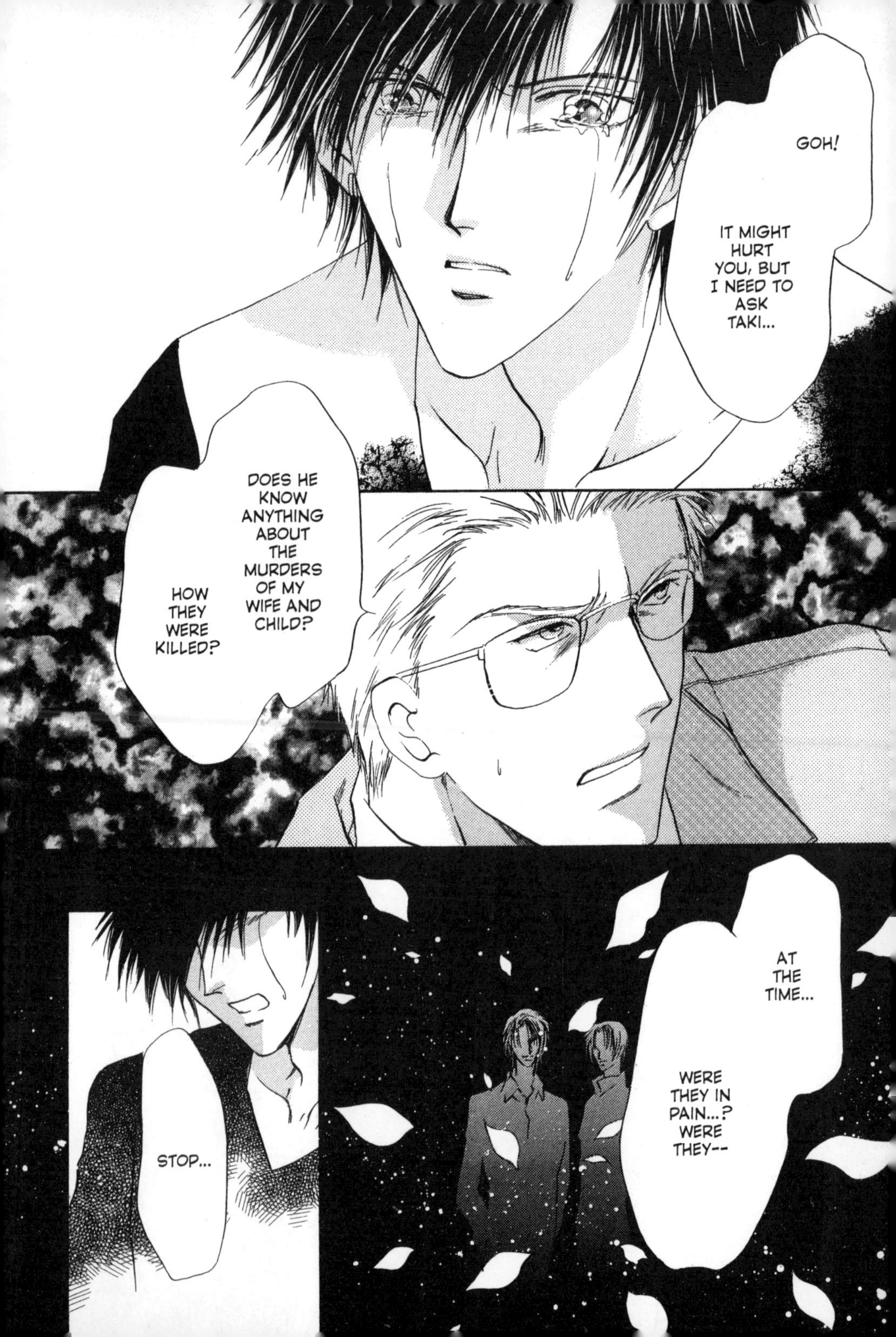
GOH!
IT MIGHT HURT YOU, BUT I NEED TO ASK TAKI...
DOES HE KNOW ANYTHING ABOUT THE MURDERS OF MY WIFE AND CHILD?
HOW THEY WERE KILLED?
AT THE TIME...
WERE THEY IN PAIN...? WERE THEY--
STOP...

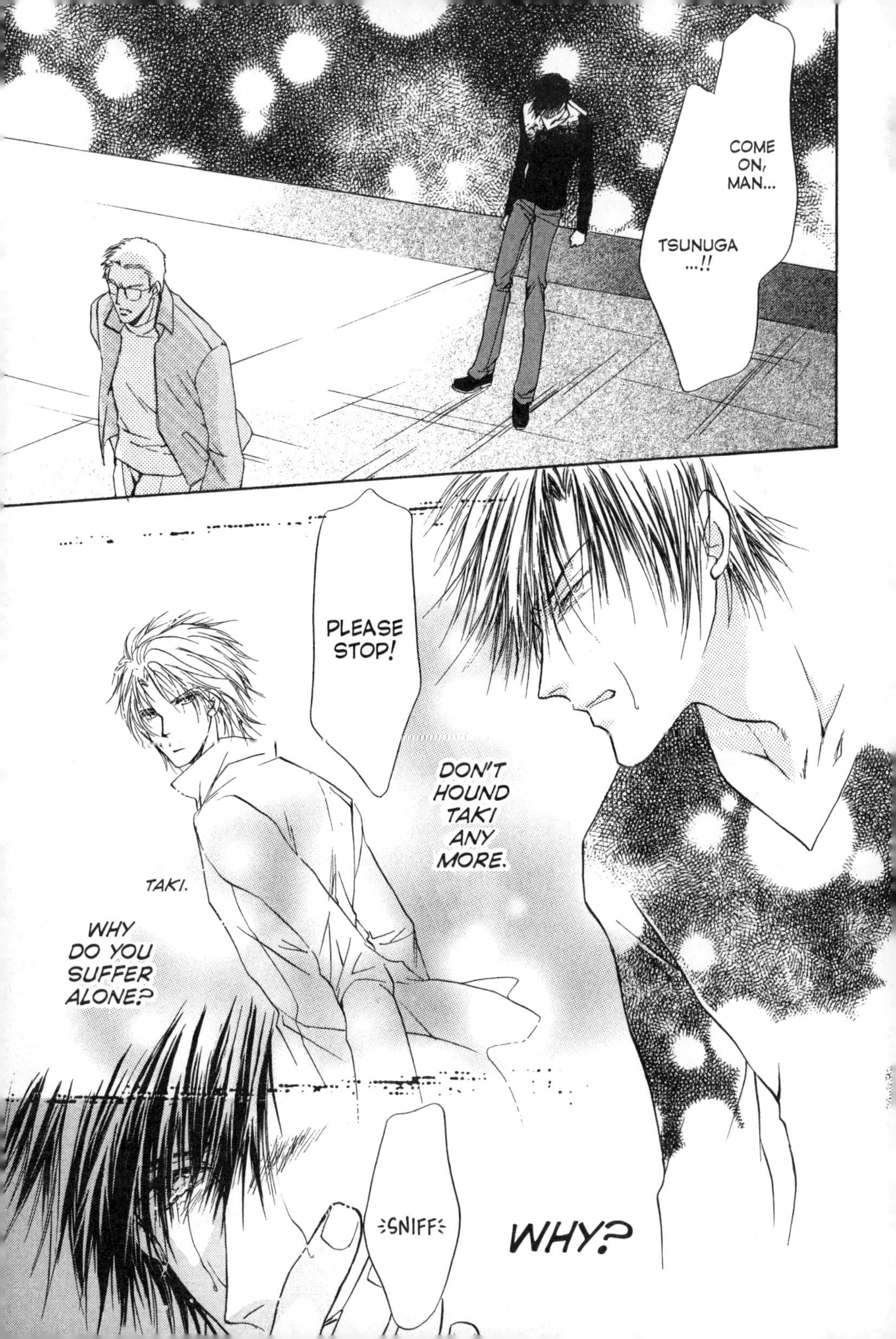
COME ON, MAN...
TSUNUGA ...!!
PLEASE STOP!
DON'T HOUND TAKI ANY MORE.
TAKI.
WHY DO YOU SUFFER ALONE?
WHY?
SNIFF

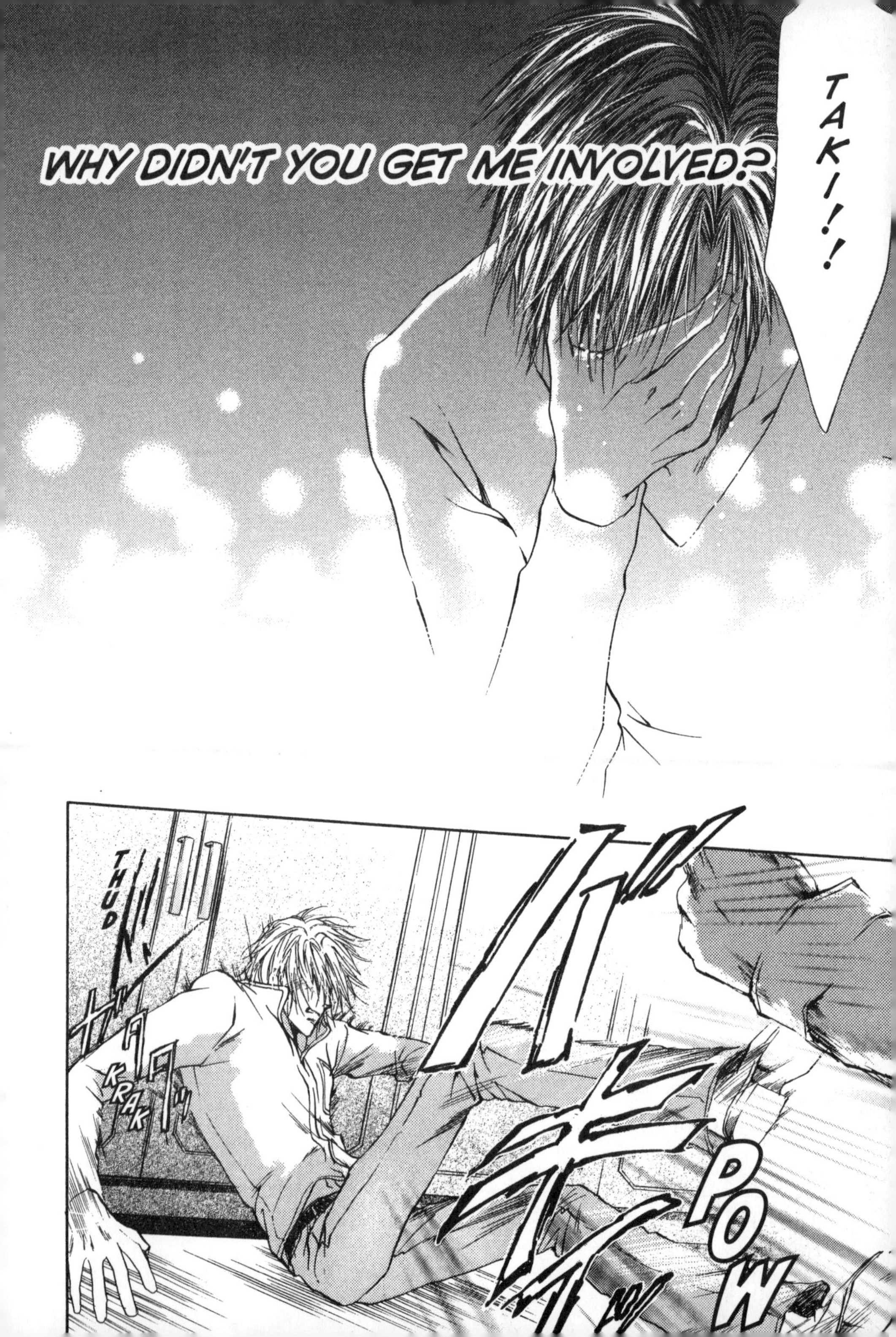
TAKI!!
WHY DIDN'T YOU GET ME INVOLVED?
POW
THUD
KRAK

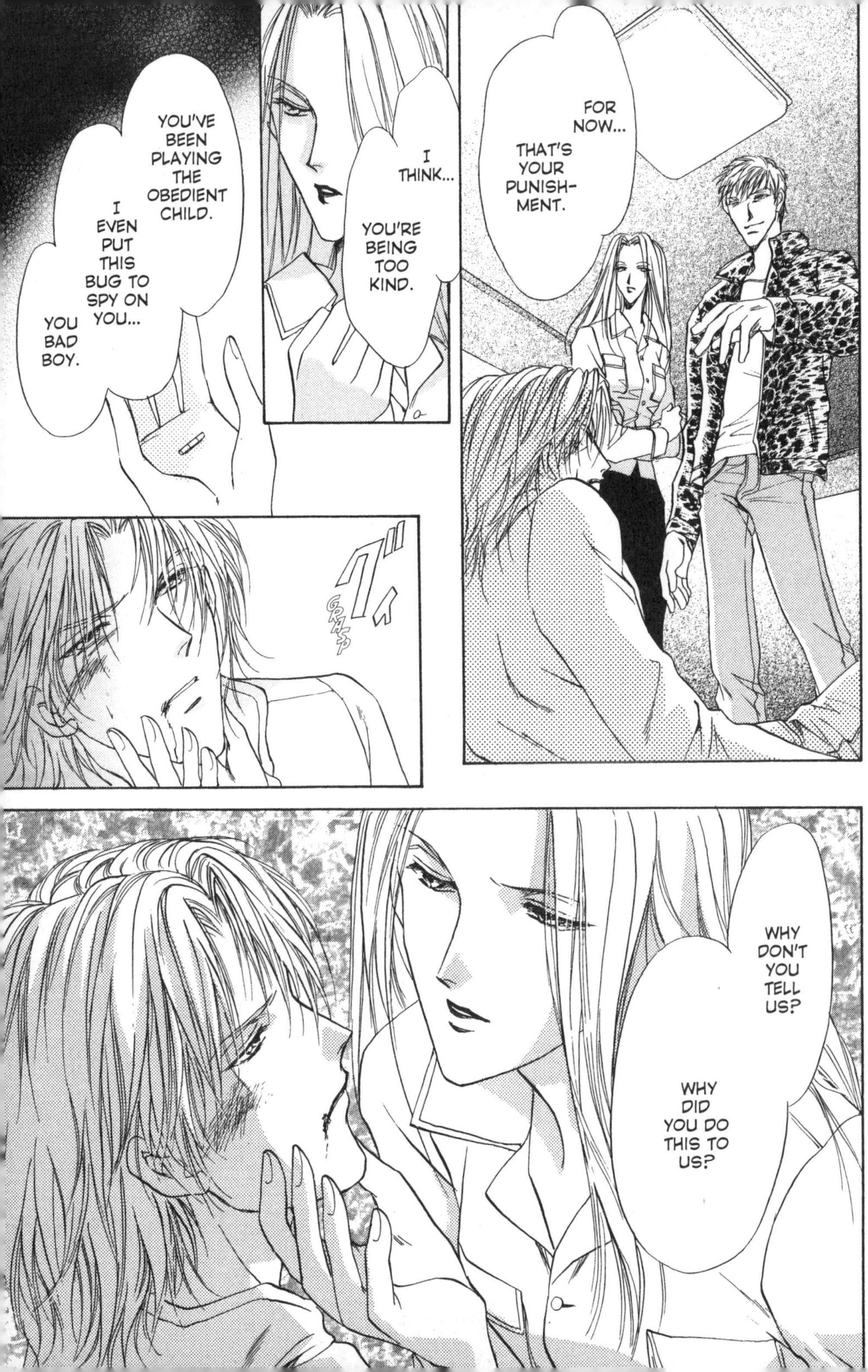

FOR NOW...
THAT'S YOUR PUNISHMENT.
I THINK...
YOU'RE BEING TOO KIND.
YOU'VE BEEN PLAYING THE OBEDIENT CHILD.
I EVEN PUT THIS BUG TO SPY ON YOU...
YOU BAD BOY.
GRASP
WHY DON'T YOU TELL US?
WHY DID YOU DO THIS TO US?

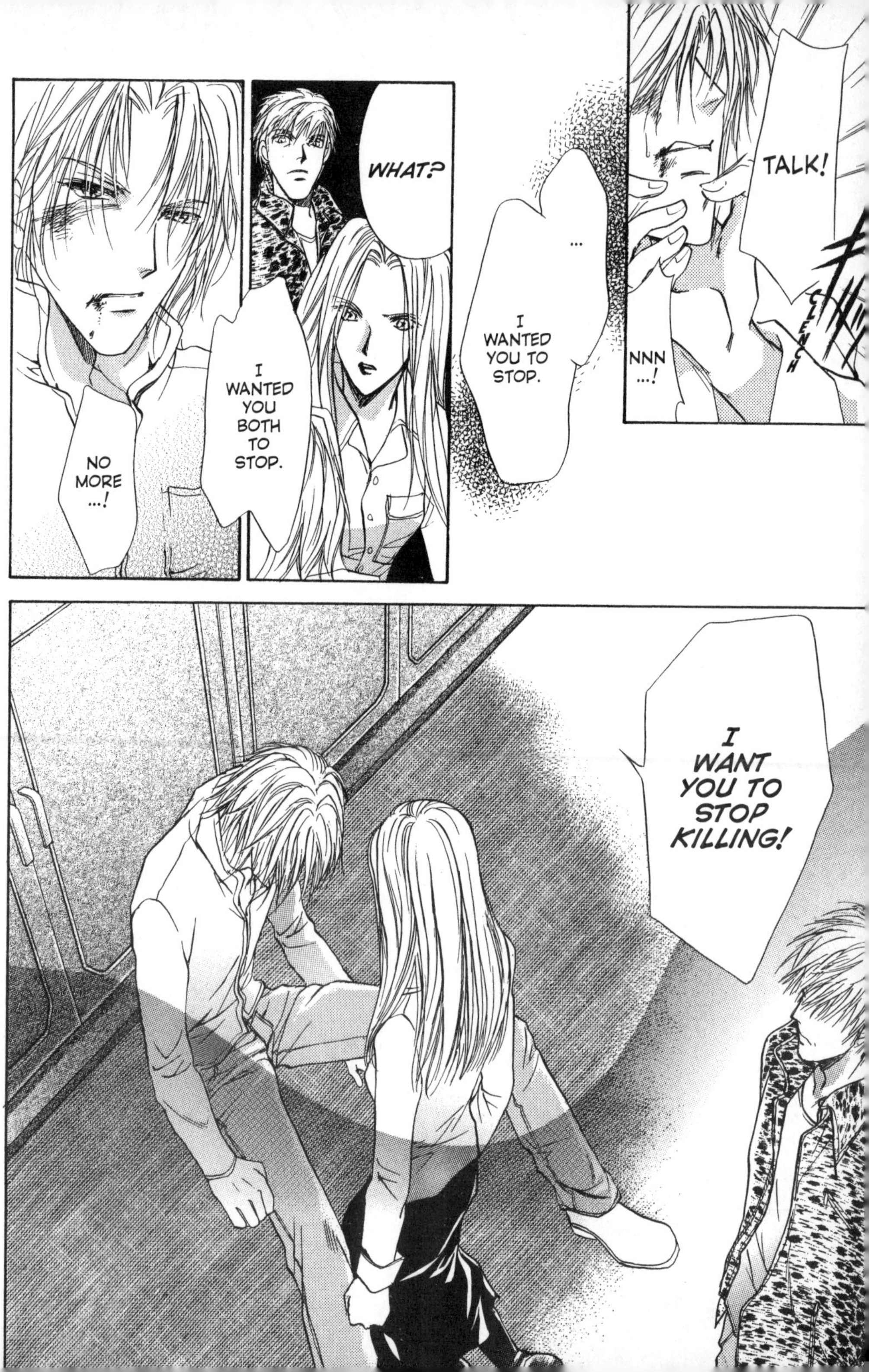

TALK!
CLENCH
NNN ...!
...
I WANTED YOU TO STOP.
WHAT?
I WANTED YOU BOTH TO STOP.
NO MORE ...!
I WANT YOU TO STOP KILLING!

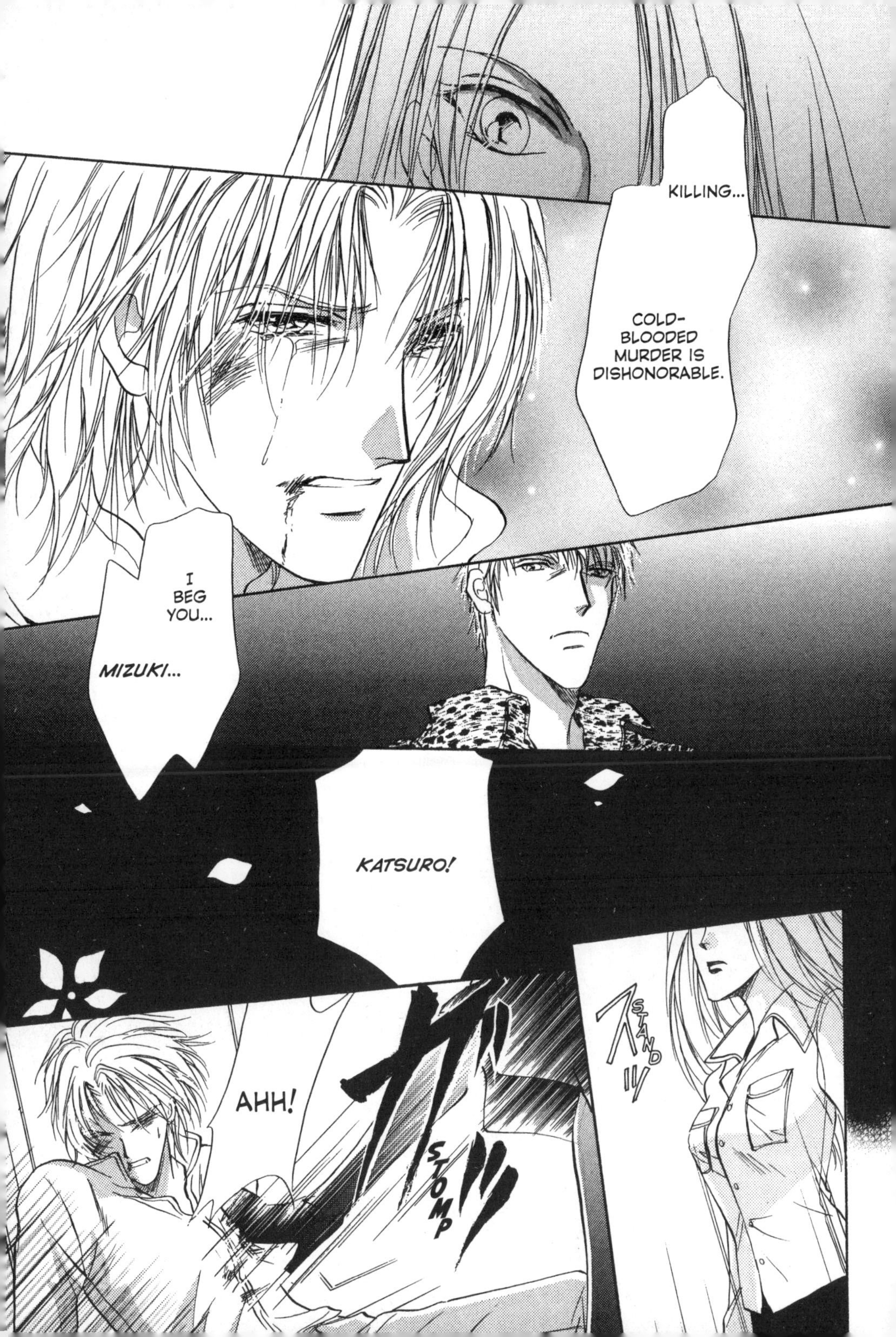
KILLING...
COLD-BLOODED MURDER IS DISHONORABLE.
I BEG YOU...
MIZUKI...
KATSURO!
STAND
STOMP
AHH!

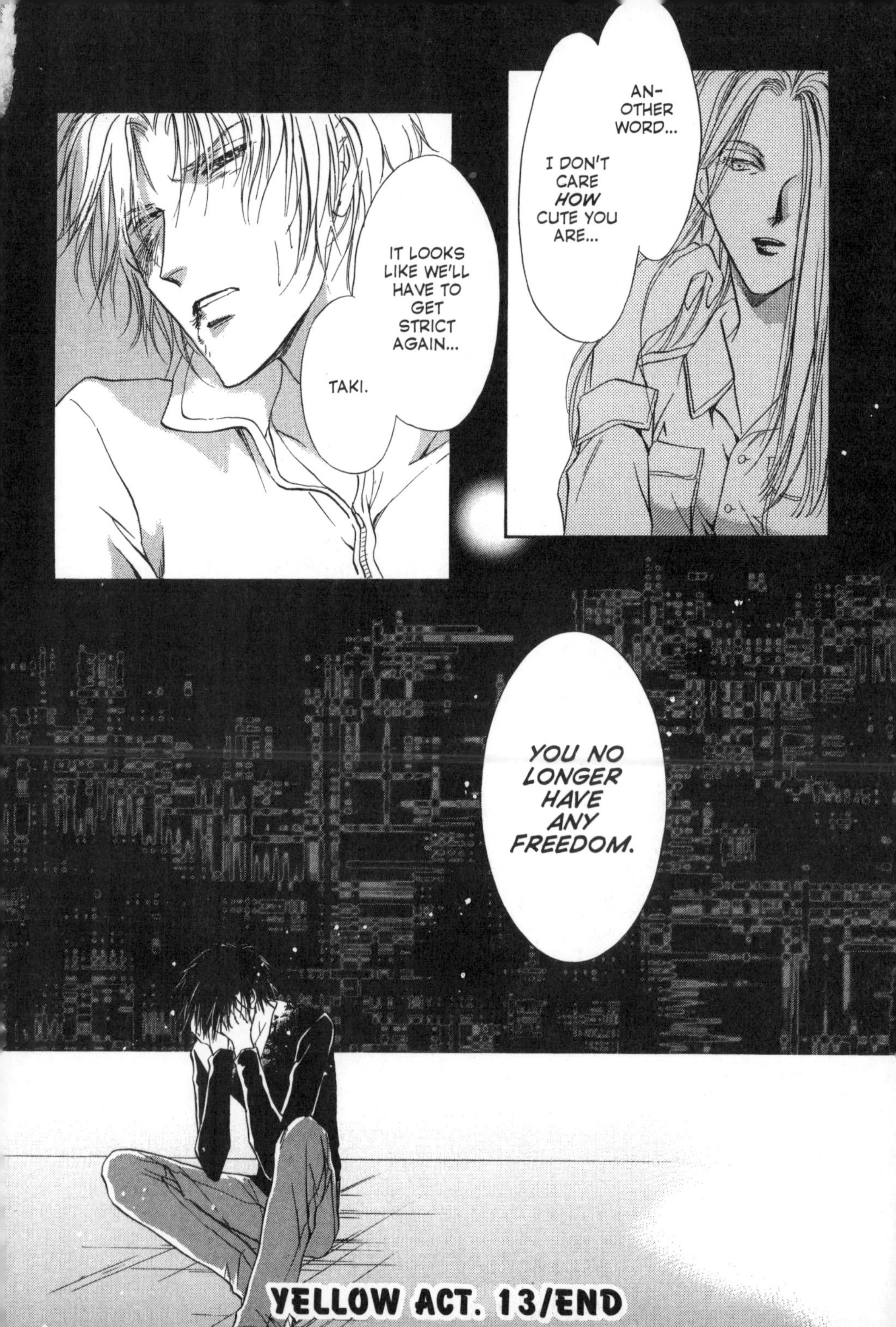
AN-OTHER WORD...
I DON'T CARE *HOW* CUTE YOU ARE...
IT LOOKS LIKE WE'LL HAVE TO GET STRICT AGAIN...
TAKI.
YOU NO LONGER HAVE ANY FREEDOM.
YELLOW ACT. 13/END

YELLOW

YELLOW

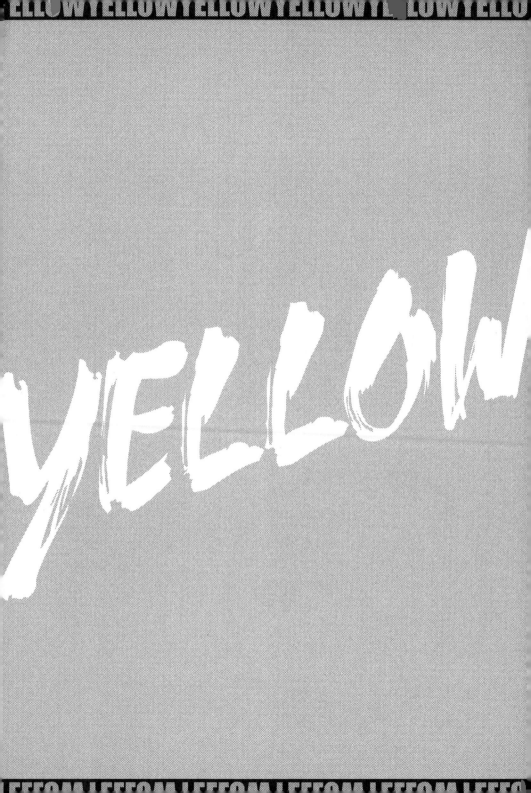

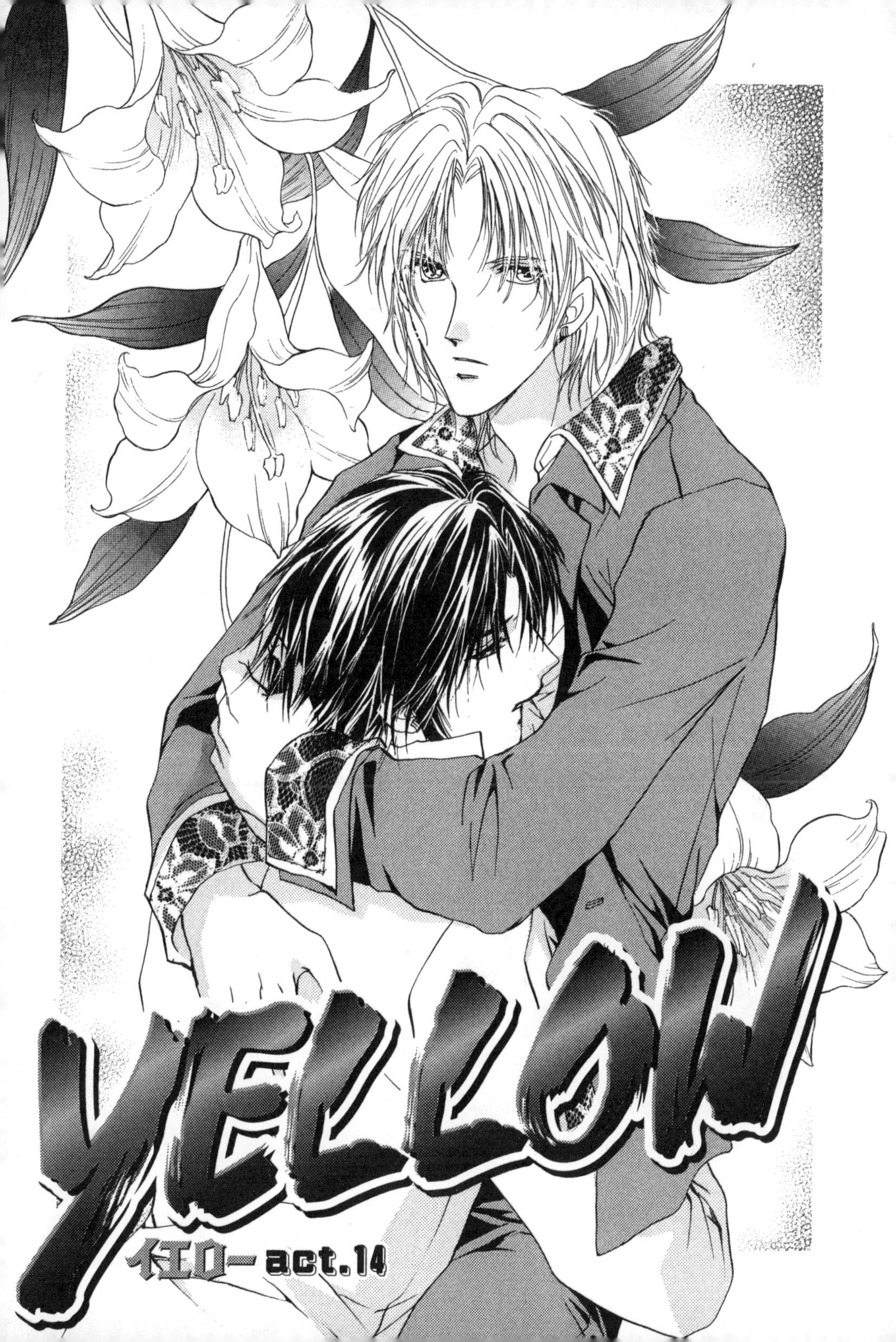
YELLOW
イエロー act.14

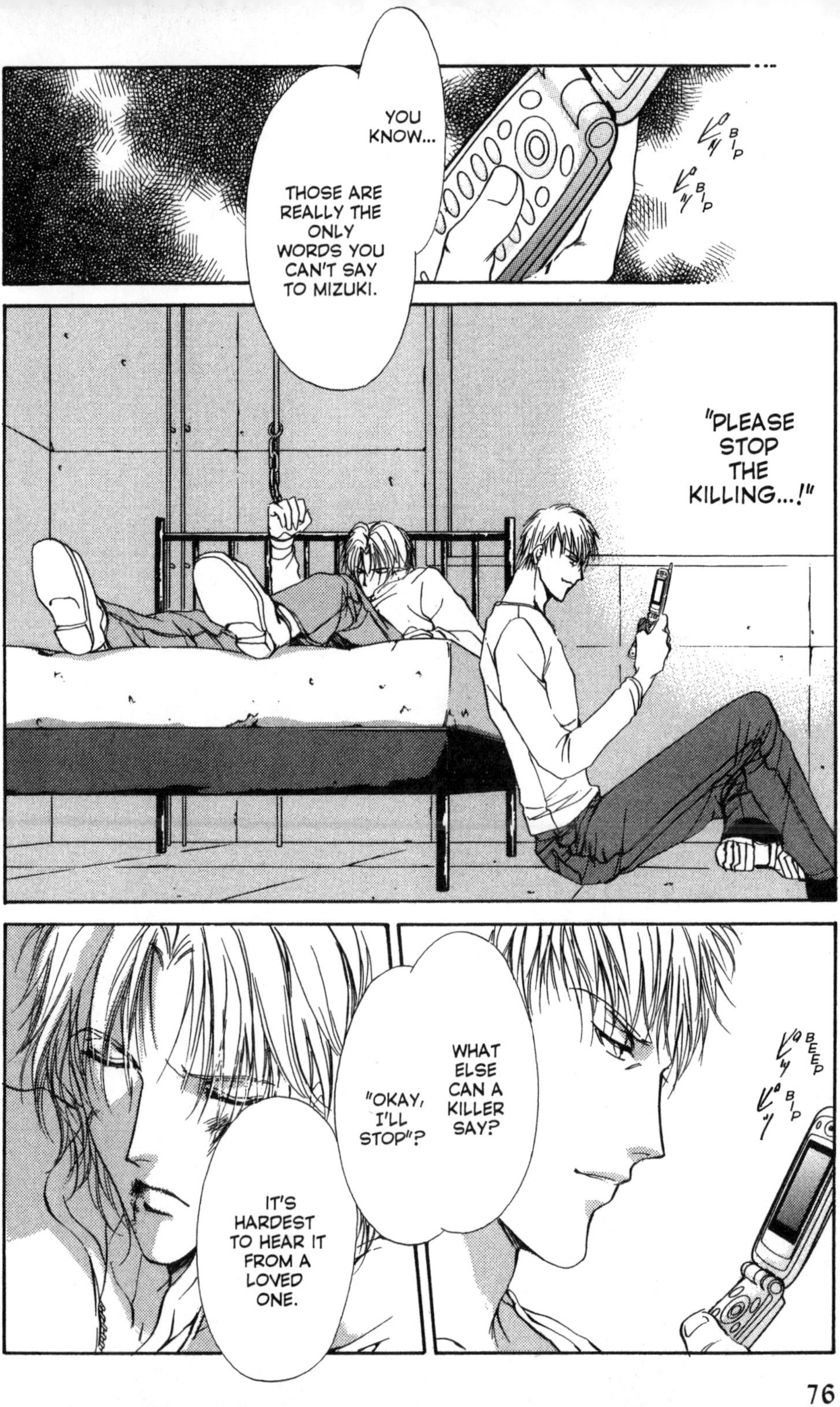
BIP
BIP
YOU KNOW...
THOSE ARE REALLY THE ONLY WORDS YOU CAN'T SAY TO MIZUKI.
"PLEASE STOP THE KILLING...!"
BEEP
BIP
WHAT ELSE CAN A KILLER SAY?
"OKAY, I'LL STOP"?
IT'S HARDEST TO HEAR IT FROM A LOVED ONE.

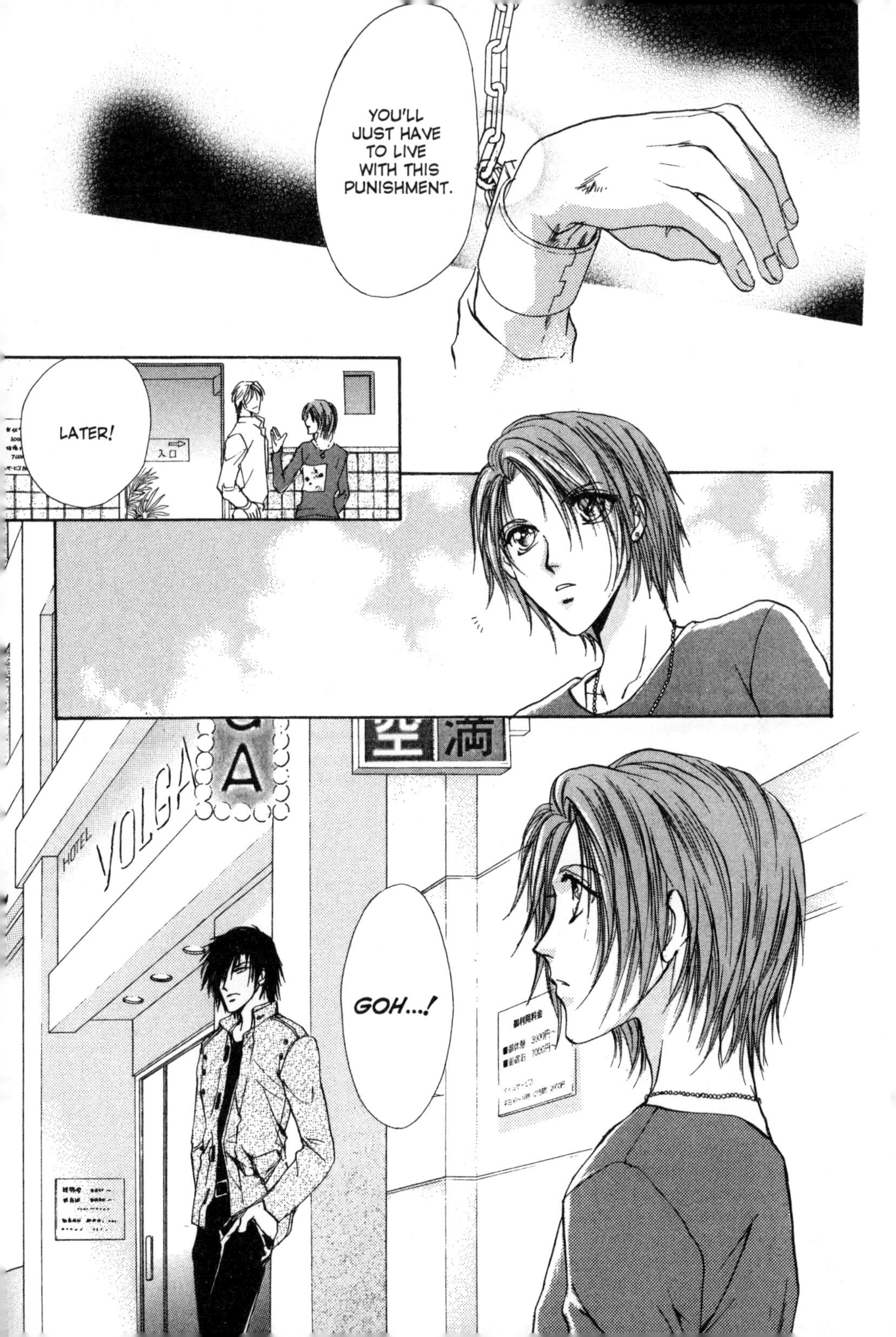
YOU'LL JUST HAVE TO LIVE WITH THIS PUNISHMENT.
入口
LATER!
空
満
HOTEL
VOLGA
GOH...!

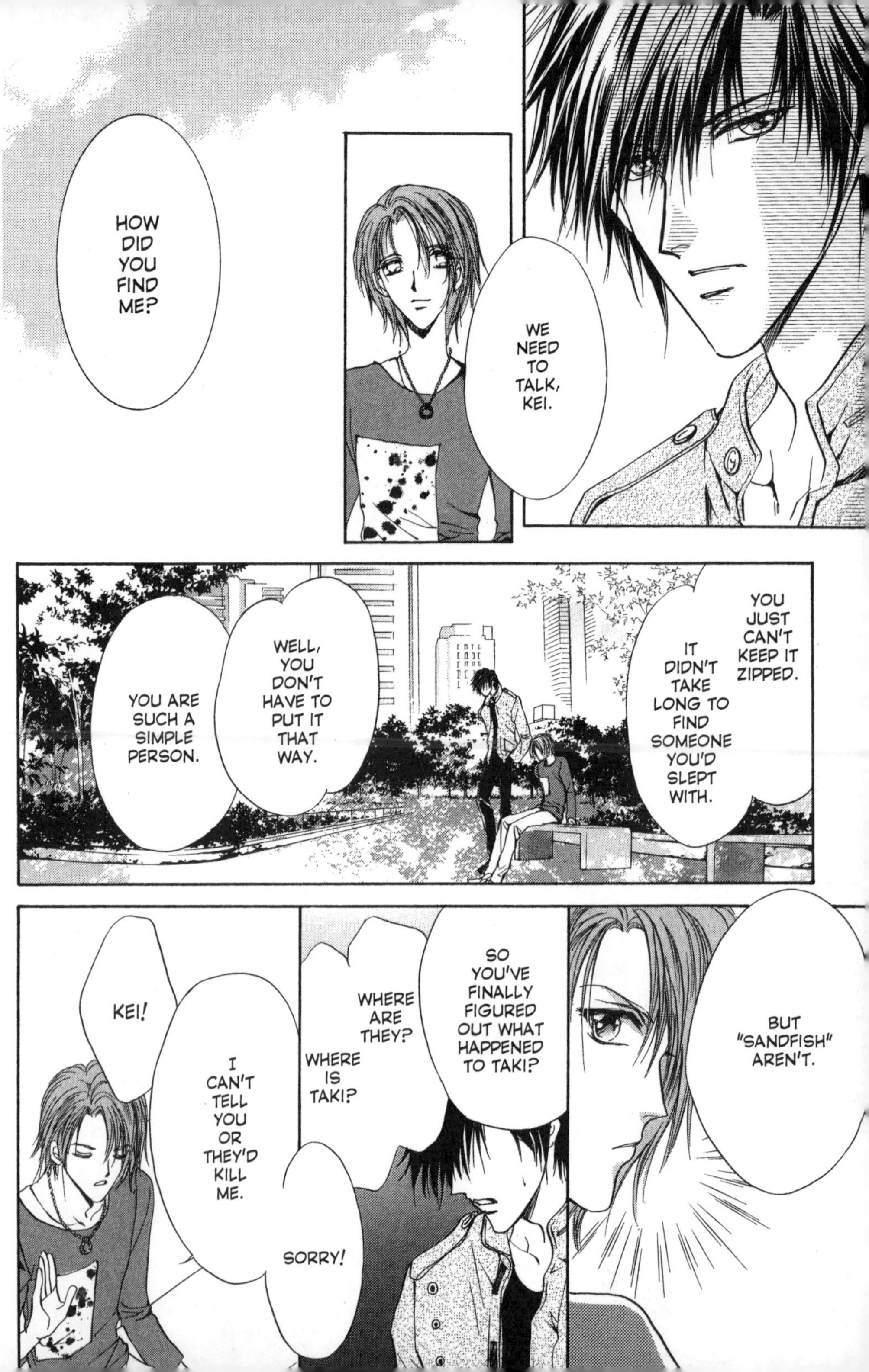
WE NEED TO TALK, KEI.
HOW DID YOU FIND ME?
YOU JUST CAN'T KEEP IT ZIPPED.
IT DIDN'T TAKE LONG TO FIND SOMEONE YOU'D SLEPT WITH.
WELL, YOU DON'T HAVE TO PUT IT THAT WAY.
YOU ARE SUCH A SIMPLE PERSON.
BUT "SANDFISH" AREN'T.
SO YOU'VE FINALLY FIGURED OUT WHAT HAPPENED TO TAKI?
WHERE ARE THEY?
WHERE IS TAKI?
KEI!
I CAN'T TELL YOU OR THEY'D KILL ME.
SORRY!

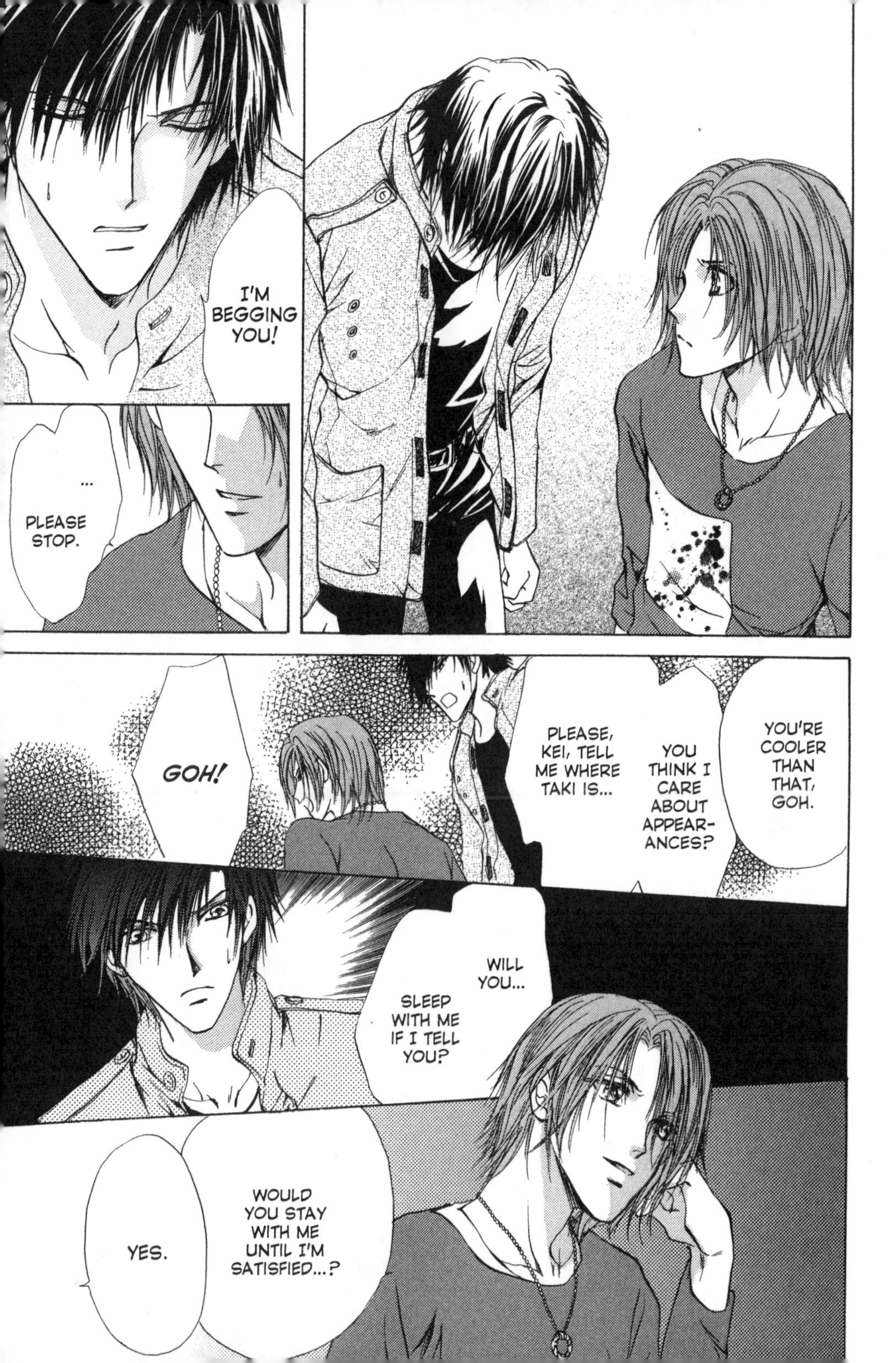
I'M BEGGING YOU!
... PLEASE STOP.
YOU'RE COOLER THAN THAT, GOH.
YOU THINK I CARE ABOUT APPEARANCES?
PLEASE, KEI, TELL ME WHERE TAKI IS...
GOH!
WILL YOU...
SLEEP WITH ME IF I TELL YOU?
WOULD YOU STAY WITH ME UNTIL I'M SATISFIED...?
YES.

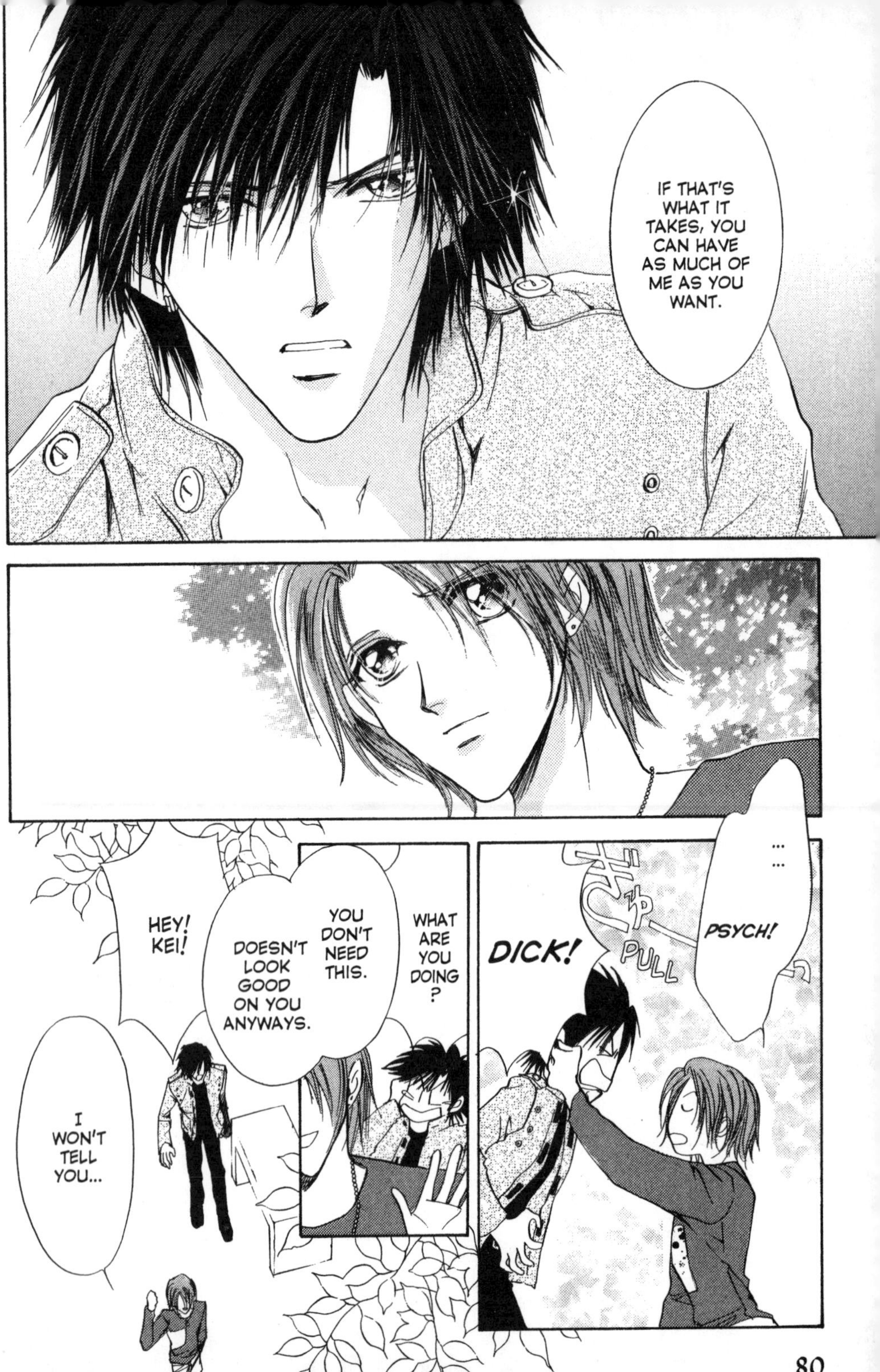
IF THAT'S WHAT IT TAKES, YOU CAN HAVE AS MUCH OF ME AS YOU WANT.
......
PSYCH!
PULL
DICK!
WHAT ARE YOU DOING?
YOU DON'T NEED THIS.
DOESN'T LOOK GOOD ON YOU ANYWAYS.
HEY! KEI!
I WON'T TELL YOU...

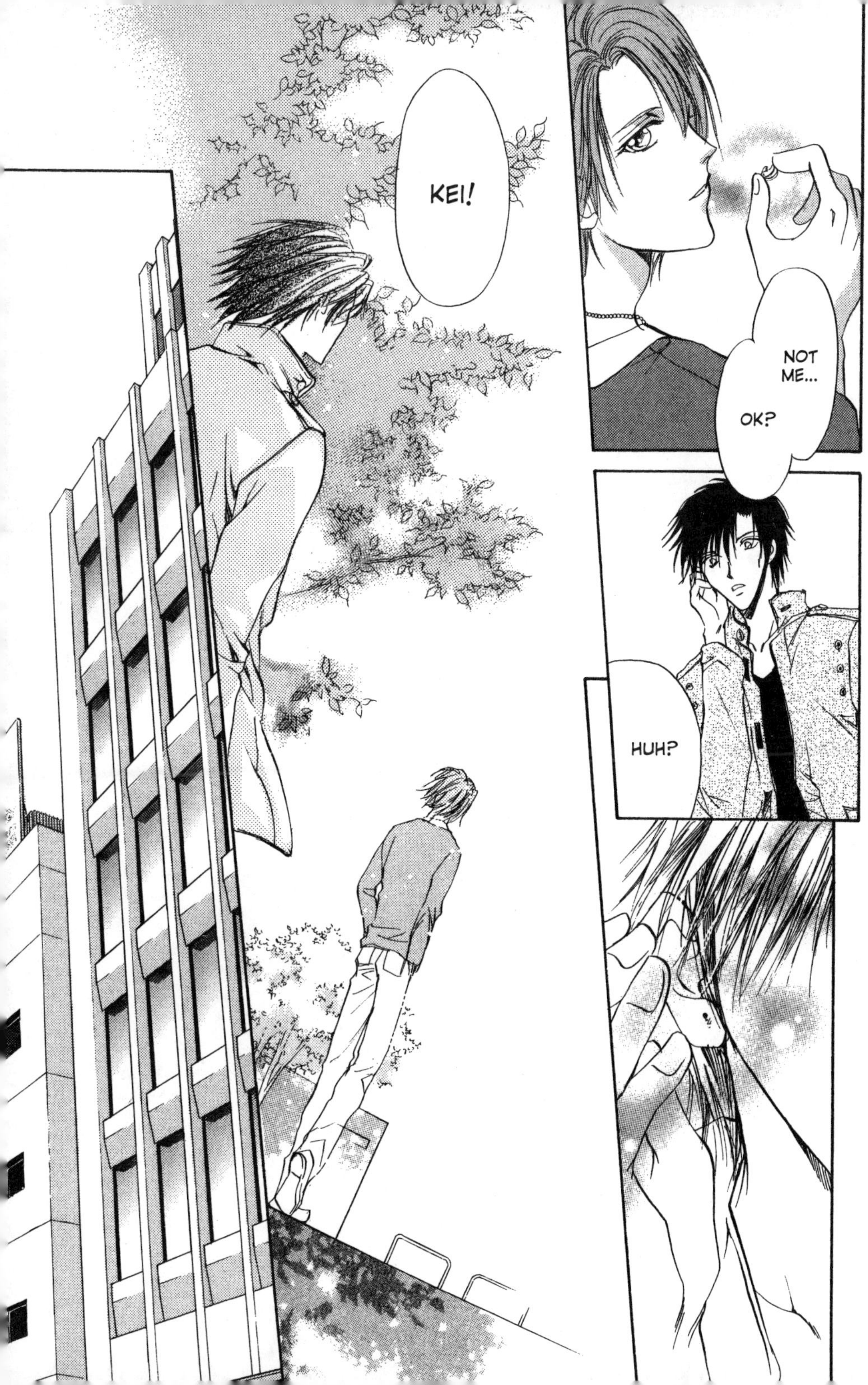
NOT ME...
OK?
HUH?
KEI!

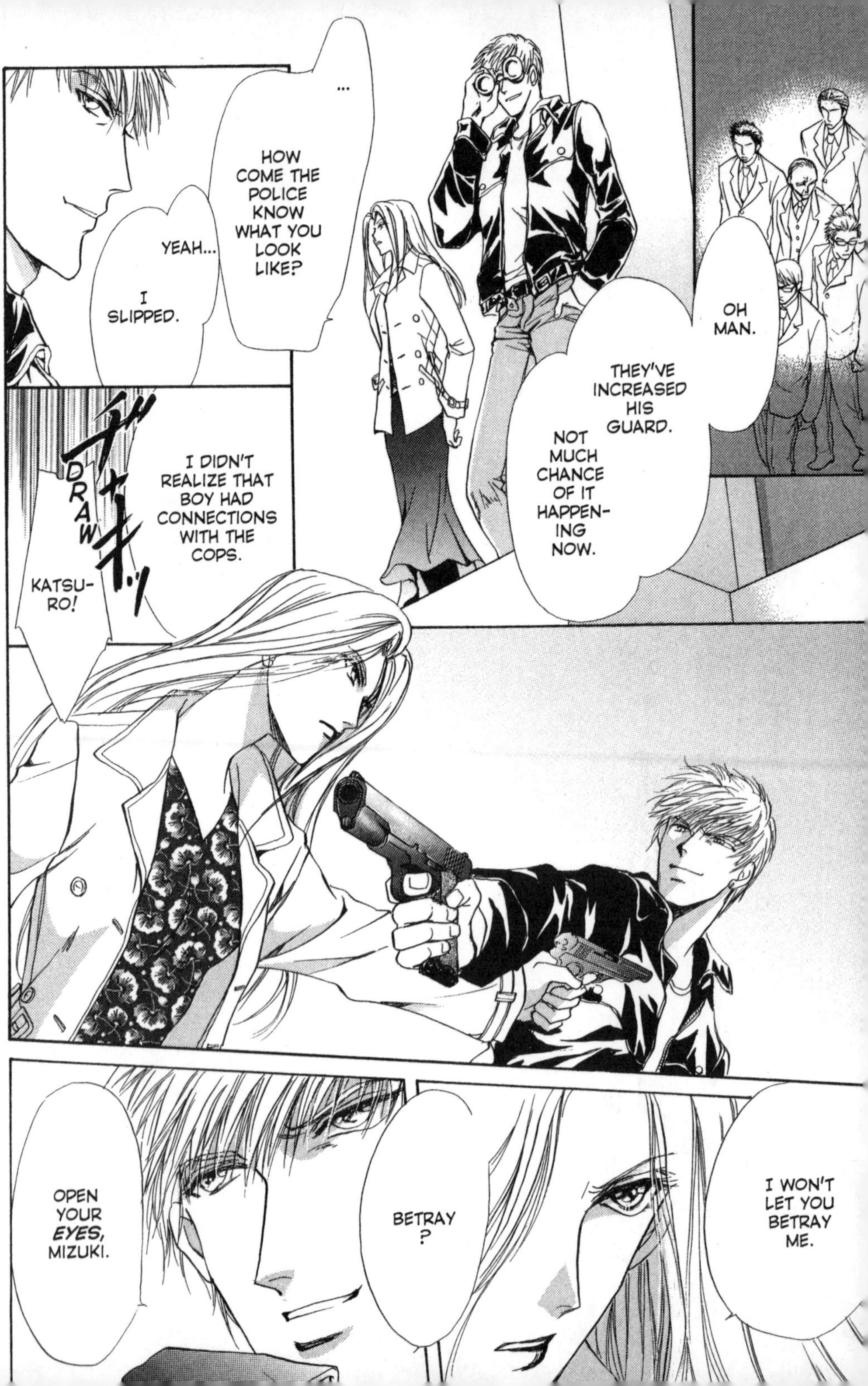
OH MAN.
THEY'VE INCREASED HIS GUARD.
NOT MUCH CHANCE OF IT HAPPENING NOW.
...
HOW COME THE POLICE KNOW WHAT YOU LOOK LIKE?
YEAH...
I SLIPPED.
I DIDN'T REALIZE THAT BOY HAD CONNECTIONS WITH THE COPS.
DRAW
KATSURO!
I WON'T LET YOU BETRAY ME.
BETRAY?
OPEN YOUR *EYES*, MIZUKI.

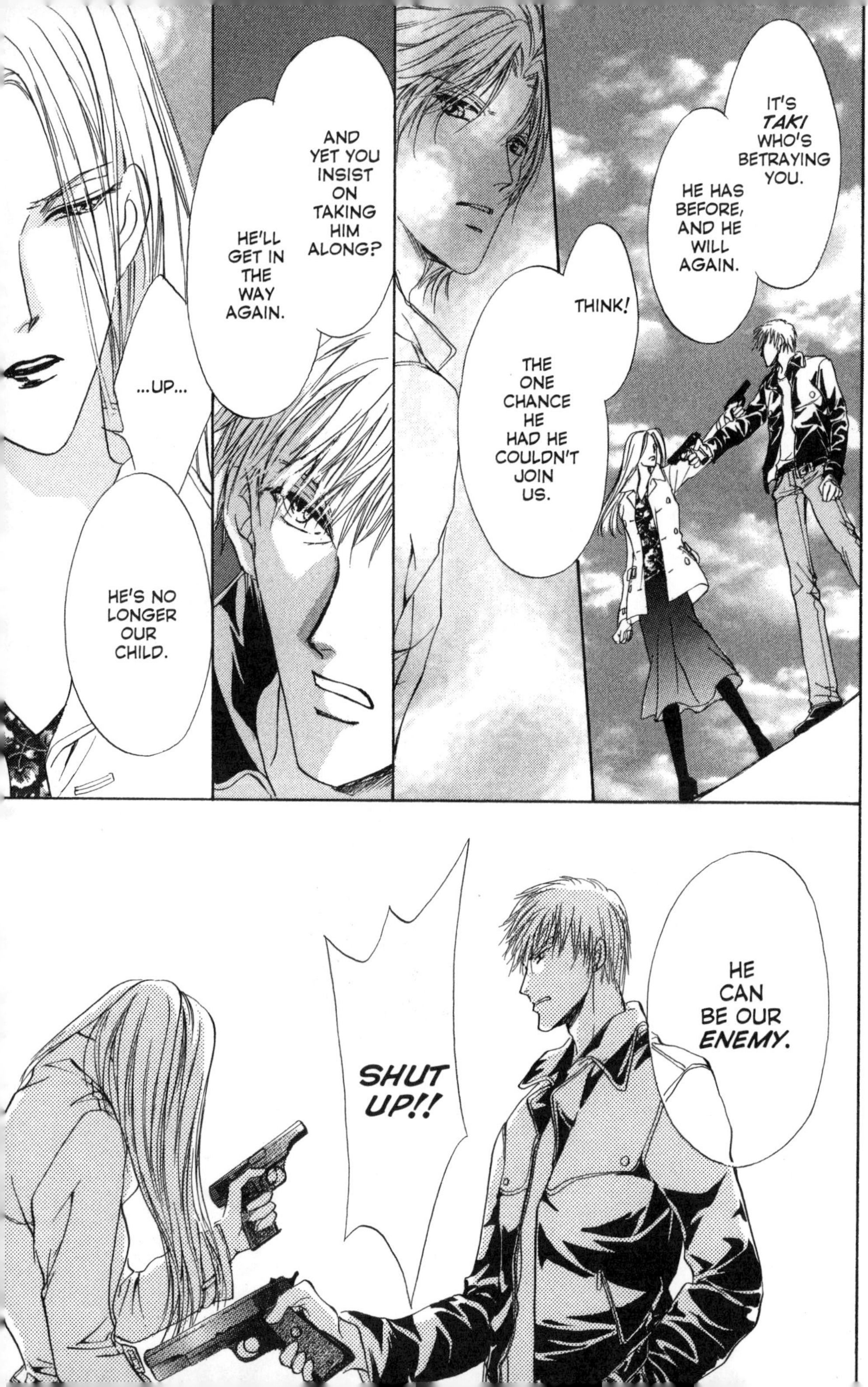
IT'S *TAKI* WHO'S BETRAYING YOU.
HE HAS BEFORE, AND HE WILL AGAIN.
THINK!
THE ONE CHANCE HE HAD HE COULDN'T JOIN US.
AND YET YOU INSIST ON TAKING HIM ALONG?
HE'LL GET IN THE WAY AGAIN.
...UP...
HE'S NO LONGER OUR CHILD.
HE CAN BE OUR *ENEMY*.
SHUT UP!!

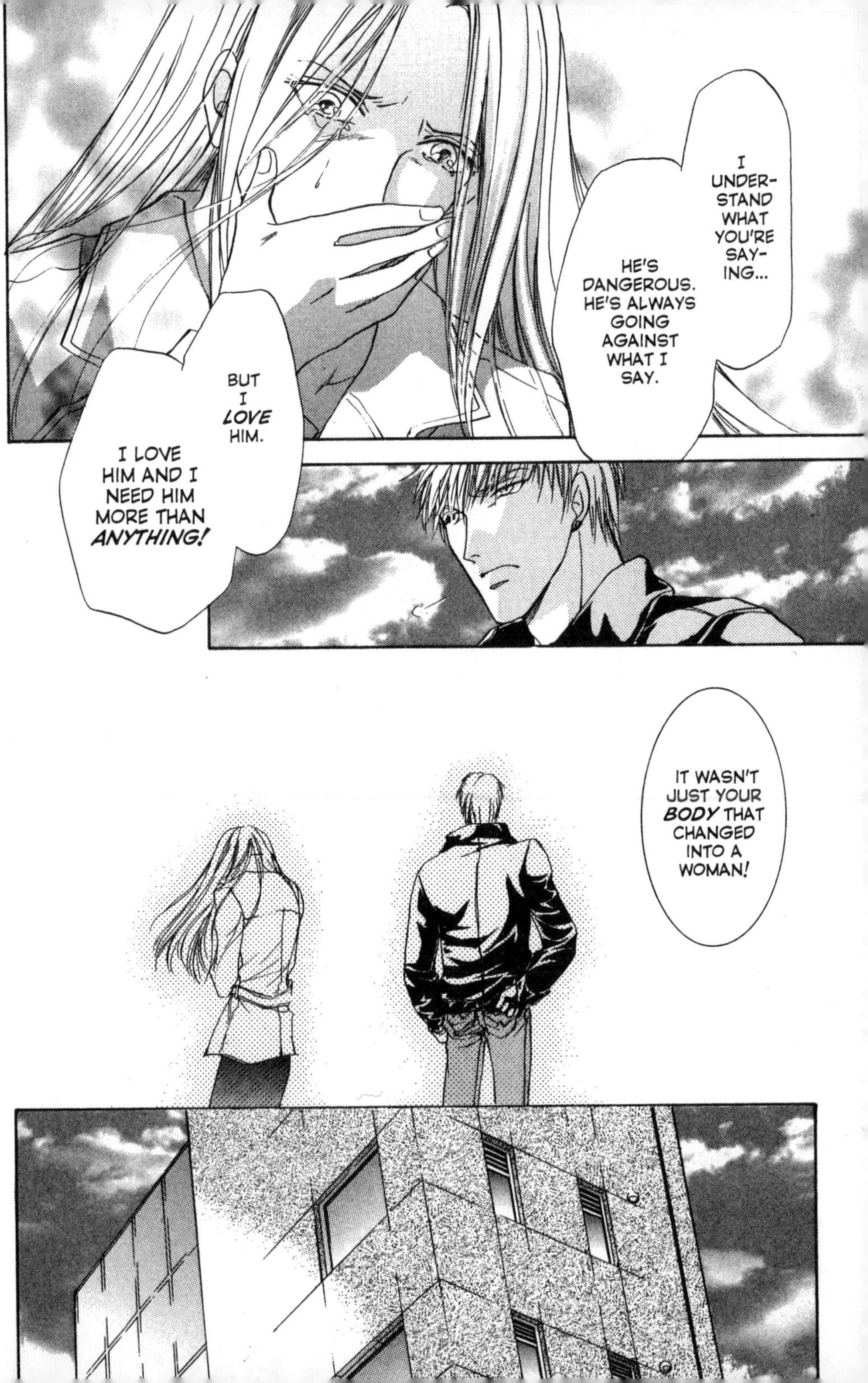
I UNDERSTAND WHAT YOU'RE SAYING...
HE'S DANGEROUS. HE'S ALWAYS GOING AGAINST WHAT I SAY.
BUT I *LOVE* HIM.
I LOVE HIM AND I NEED HIM MORE THAN *ANYTHING!*
IT WASN'T JUST YOUR *BODY* THAT CHANGED INTO A WOMAN!

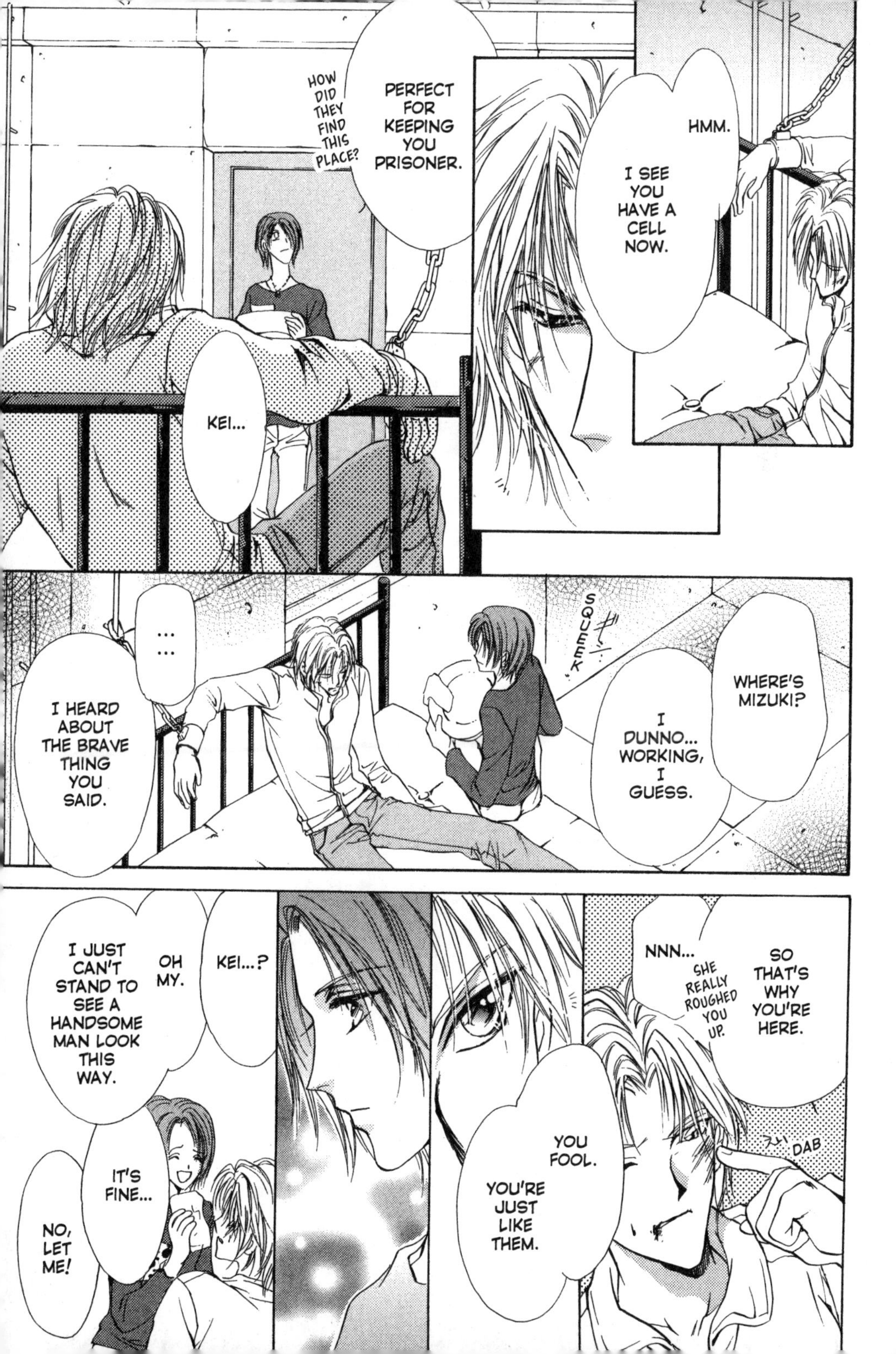
HMM.
I SEE YOU HAVE A CELL NOW.
PERFECT FOR KEEPING YOU PRISONER.
HOW DID THEY FIND THIS PLACE?
KEI...
WHERE'S MIZUKI?
SQUEEK
I DUNNO... WORKING, I GUESS.
......
I HEARD ABOUT THE BRAVE THING YOU SAID.
SO THAT'S WHY YOU'RE HERE.
NNN...
SHE REALLY ROUGHED YOU UP.
DAB
YOU FOOL.
YOU'RE JUST LIKE THEM.
KEI...?
OH MY.
I JUST CAN'T STAND TO SEE A HANDSOME MAN LOOK THIS WAY.
IT'S FINE...
NO, LET ME!

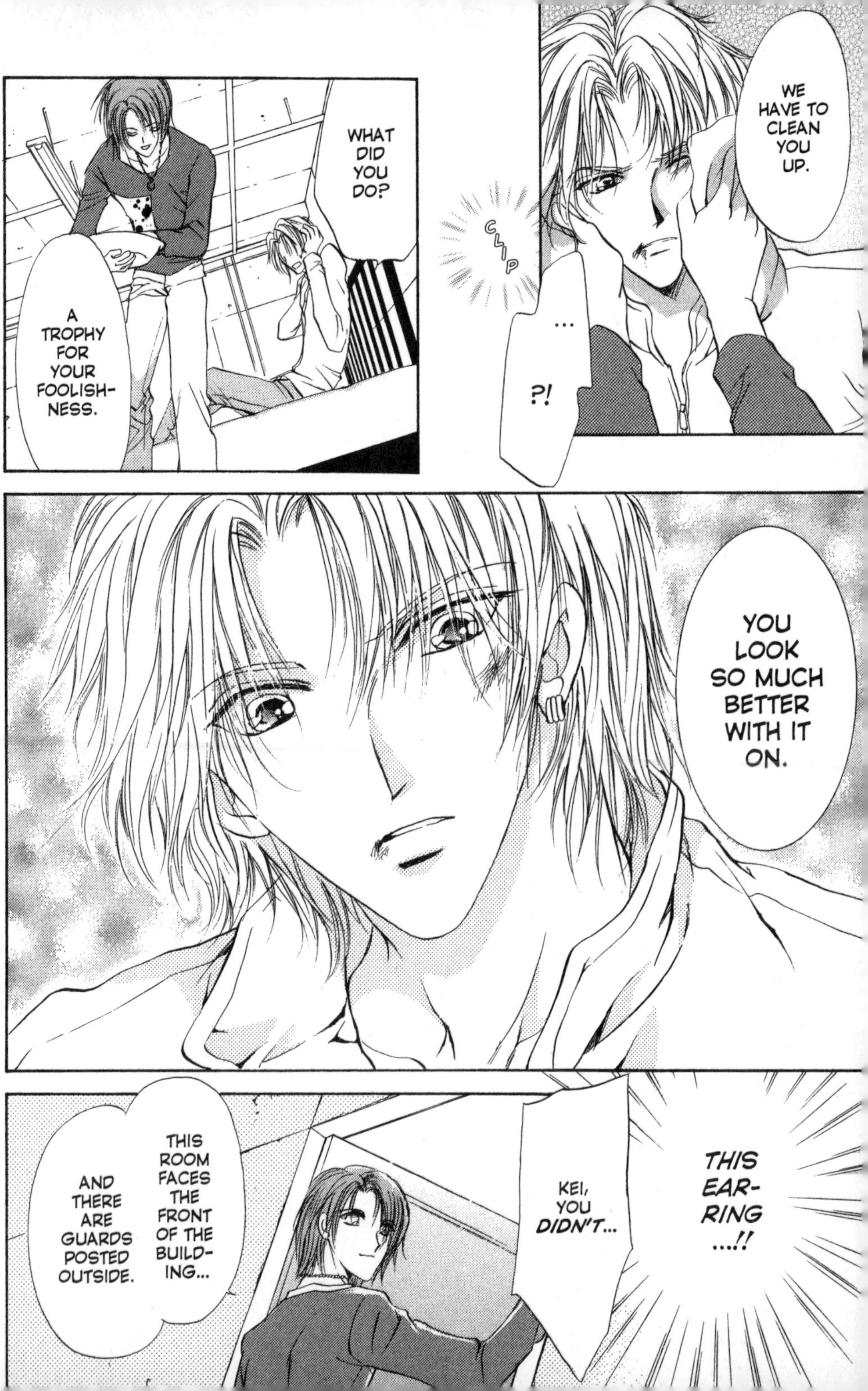

WE HAVE TO CLEAN YOU UP.
CLIP
...
?!
WHAT DID YOU DO?
A TROPHY FOR YOUR FOOLISHNESS.
YOU LOOK SO MUCH BETTER WITH IT ON.
THIS EARRING...!!
KEI, YOU DIDN'T...
THIS ROOM FACES THE FRONT OF THE BUILDING...
AND THERE ARE GUARDS POSTED OUTSIDE.

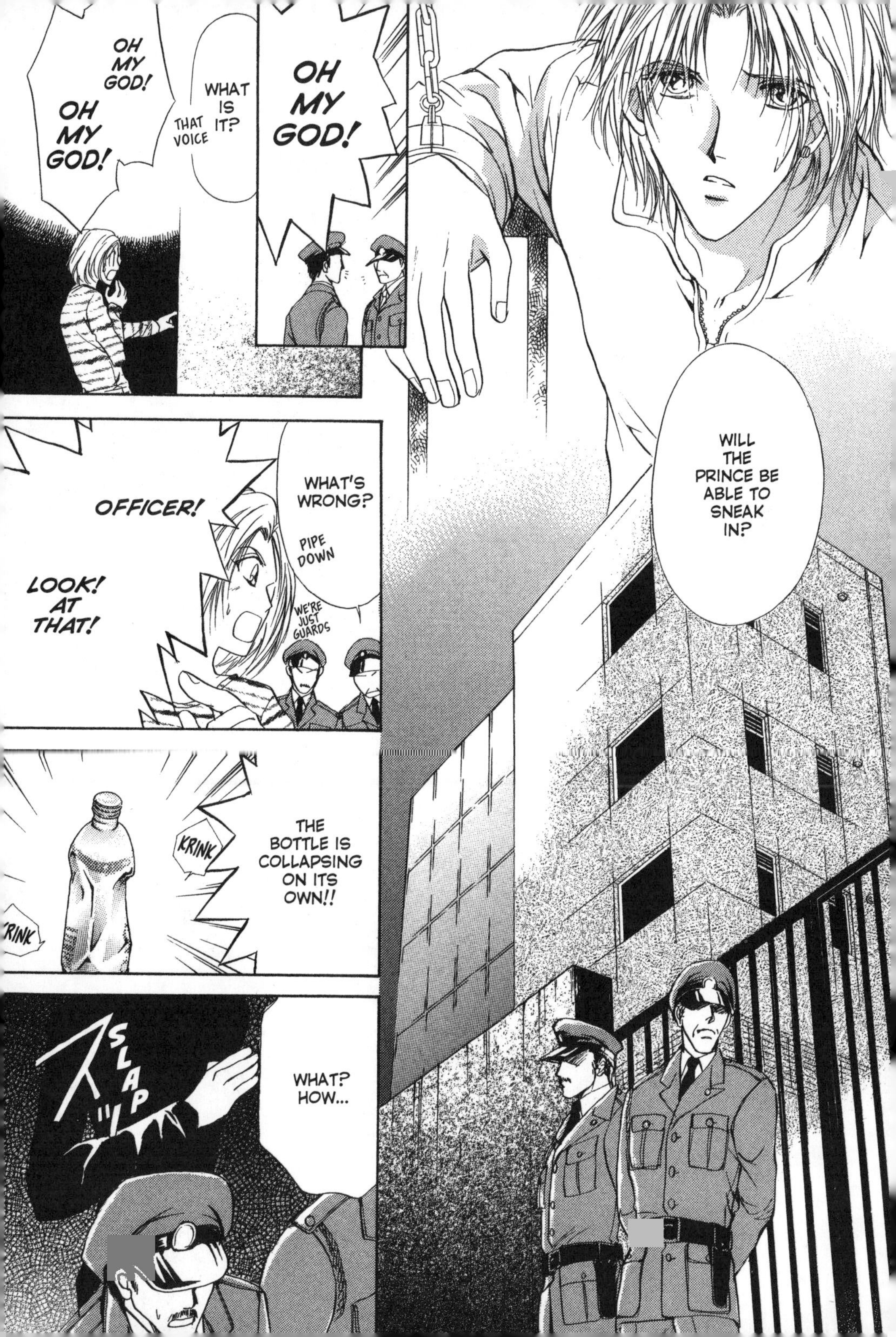
WILL THE PRINCE BE ABLE TO SNEAK IN?
OH MY GOD!
WHAT IS IT?
THAT VOICE
OH MY GOD!
OH MY GOD!
WHAT'S WRONG?
PIPE DOWN
WE'RE JUST GUARDS
OFFICER!
LOOK! AT THAT!
THE BOTTLE IS COLLAPSING ON ITS OWN!!
KRINK
RINK
WHAT? HOW...
SLAP

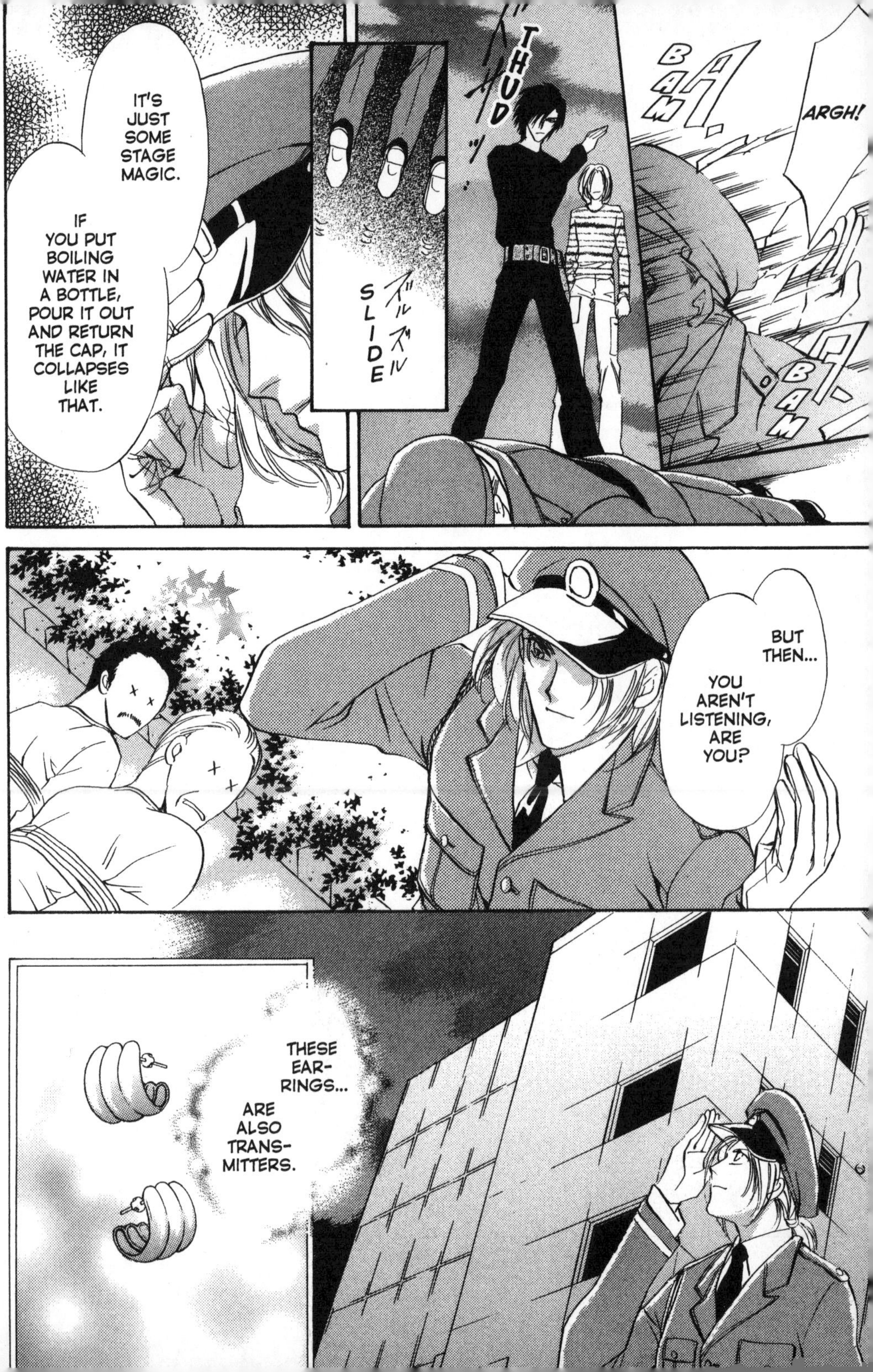
ARGH!
BAM BAM
BAM BAM
THUD
SLIDE
IT'S JUST SOME STAGE MAGIC.
IF YOU PUT BOILING WATER IN A BOTTLE, POUR IT OUT AND RETURN THE CAP, IT COLLAPSES LIKE THAT.
BUT THEN...
YOU AREN'T LISTENING, ARE YOU?
THESE EAR-RINGS...
ARE ALSO TRANS-MITTERS.

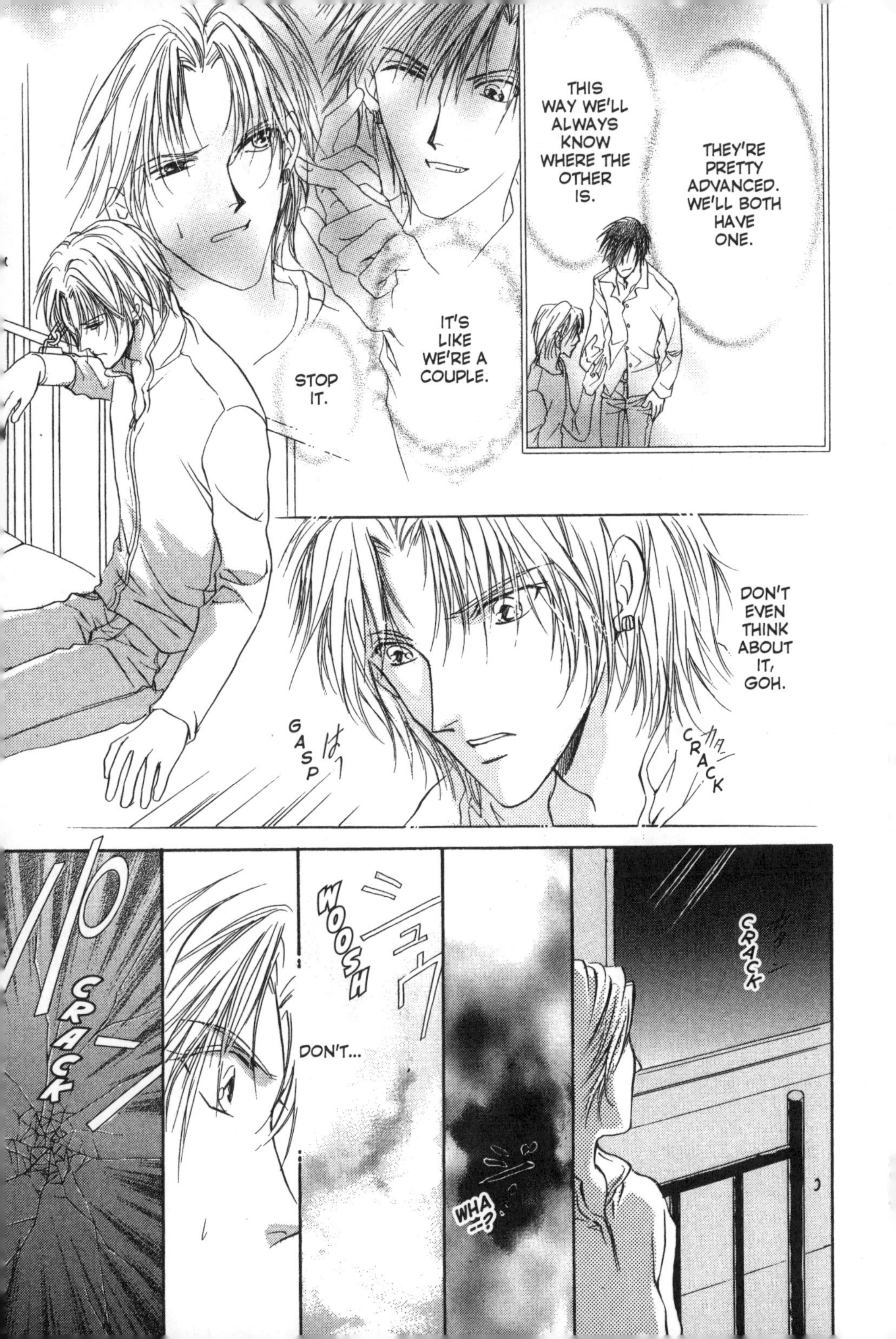
THEY'RE PRETTY ADVANCED. WE'LL BOTH HAVE ONE.
THIS WAY WE'LL ALWAYS KNOW WHERE THE OTHER IS.
IT'S LIKE WE'RE A COUPLE.
STOP IT.
DON'T EVEN THINK ABOUT IT, GOH.
CRACK
GASP
CRACK
WHA--!?
DON'T...
WOOSH
CRACK

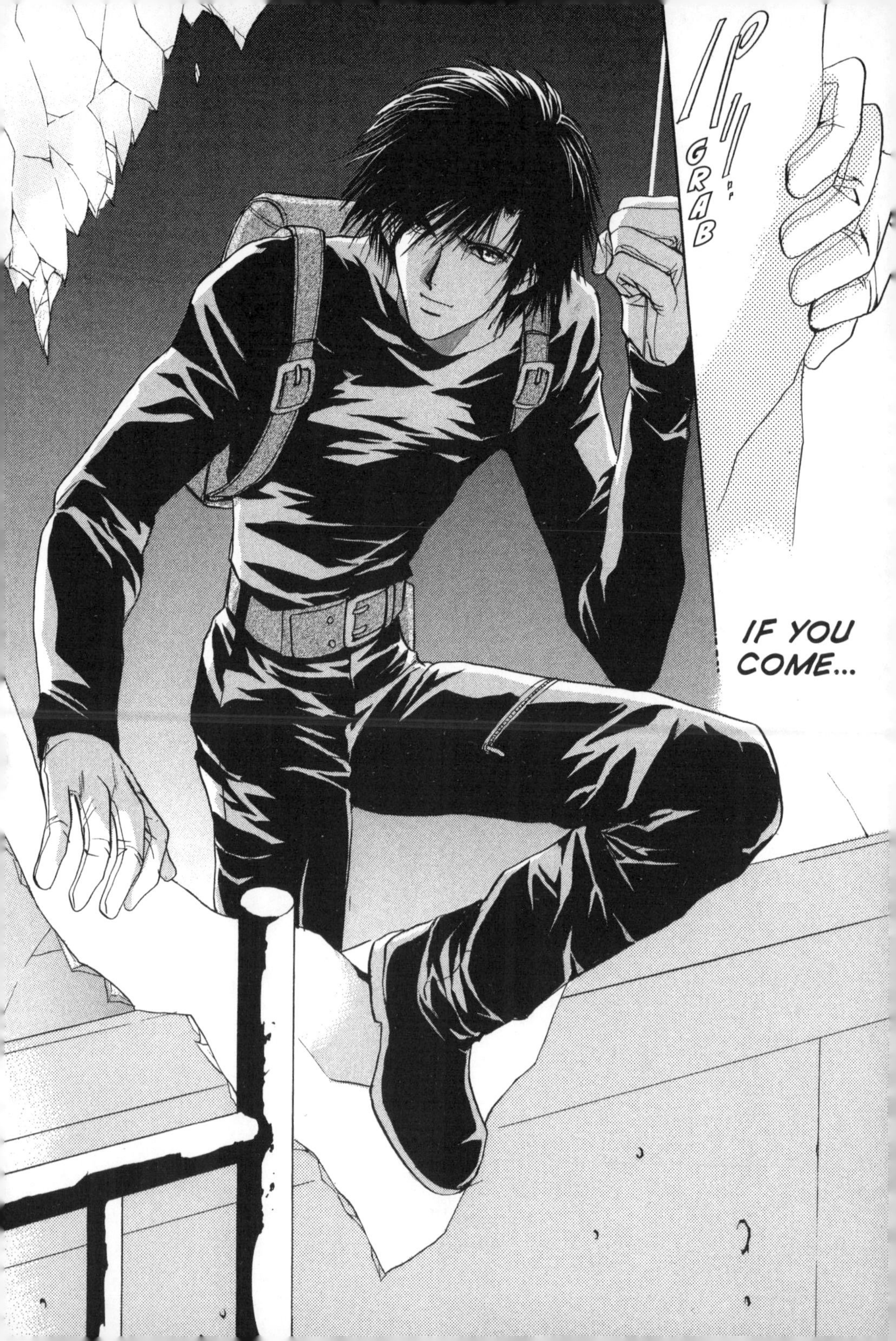
GRAB
IF YOU COME...

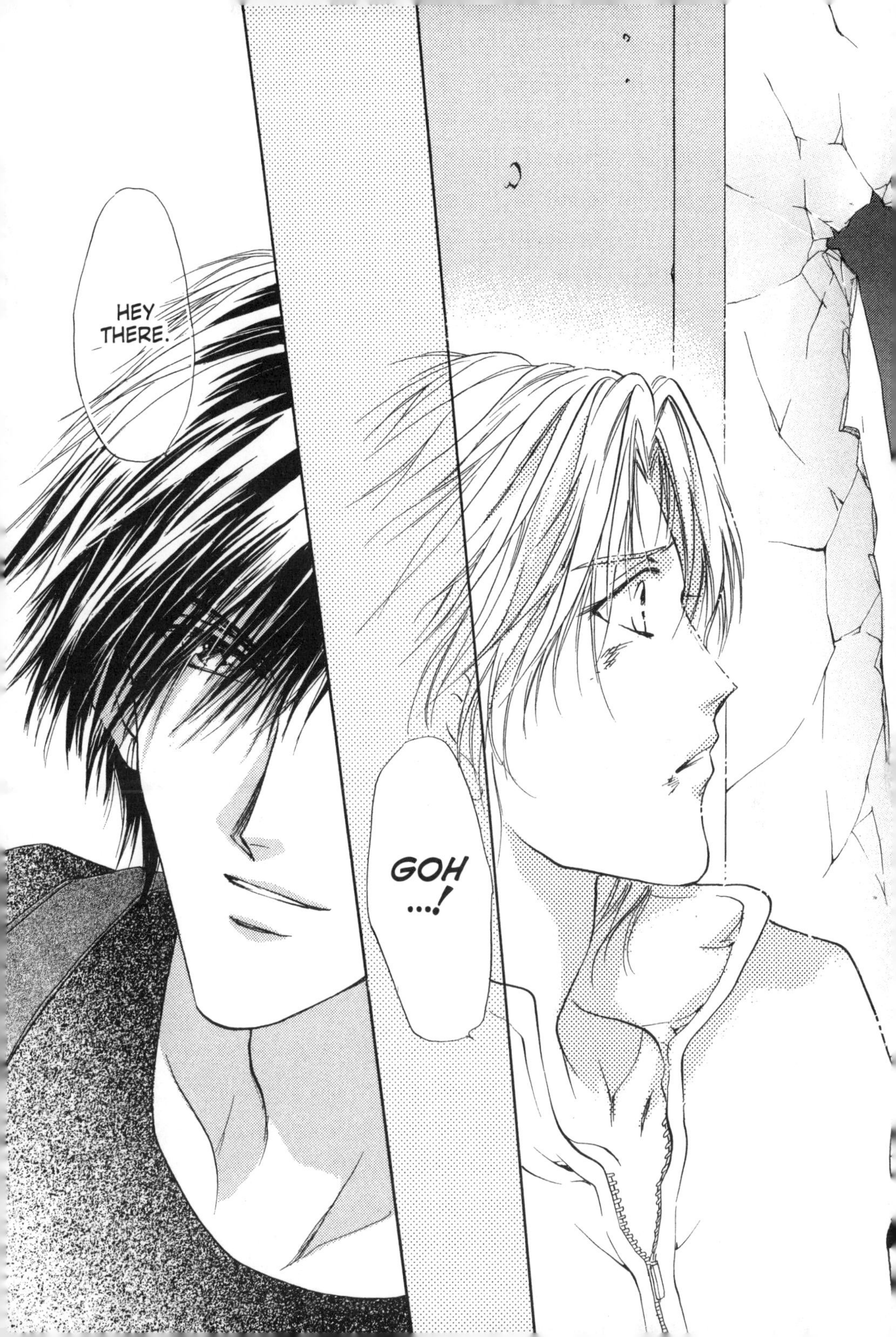
GOH ...!
HEY THERE.

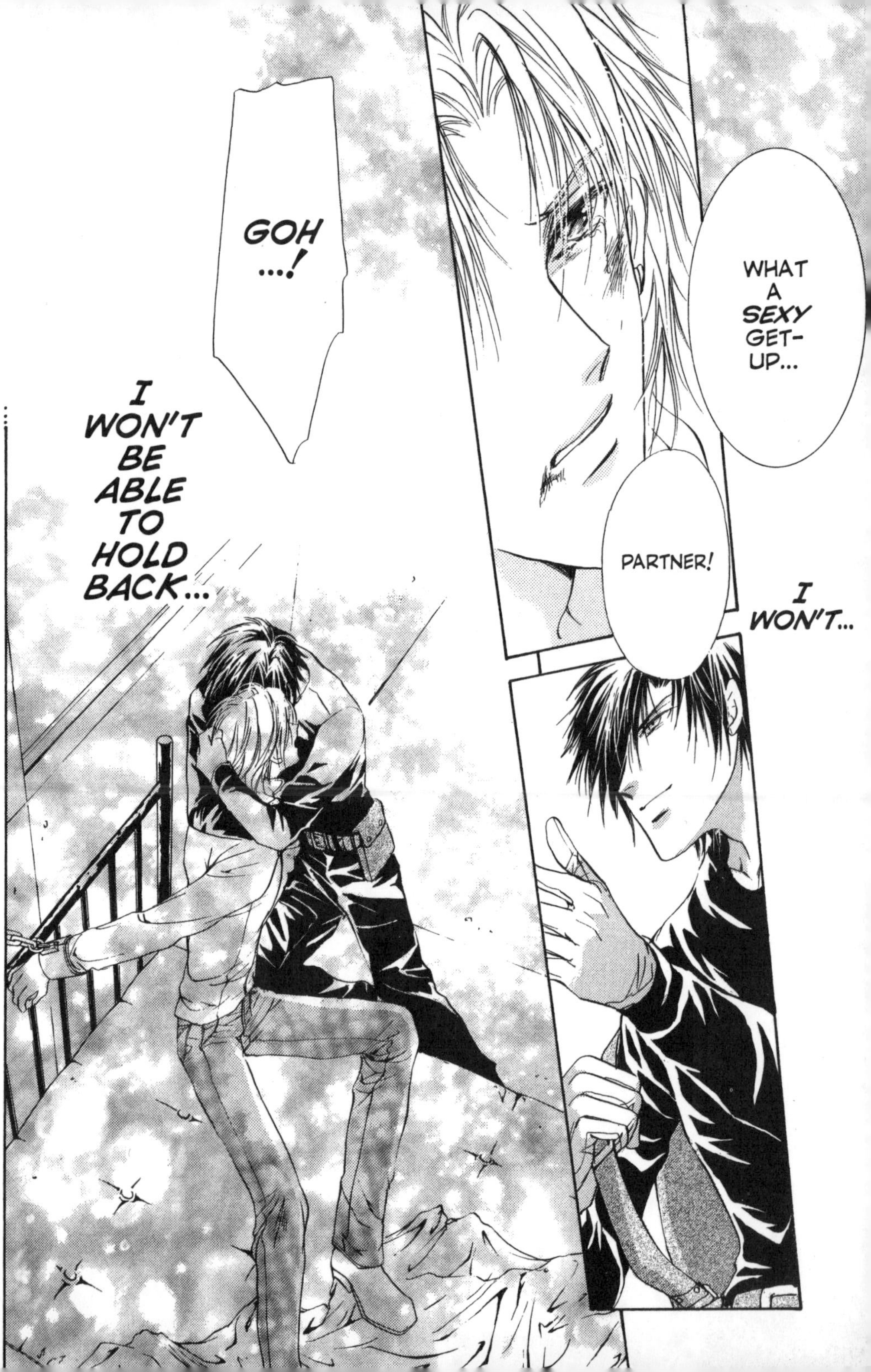
WHAT A SEXY GET-UP...
PARTNER!
I WON'T...
GOH ...!
I WON'T BE ABLE TO HOLD BACK...

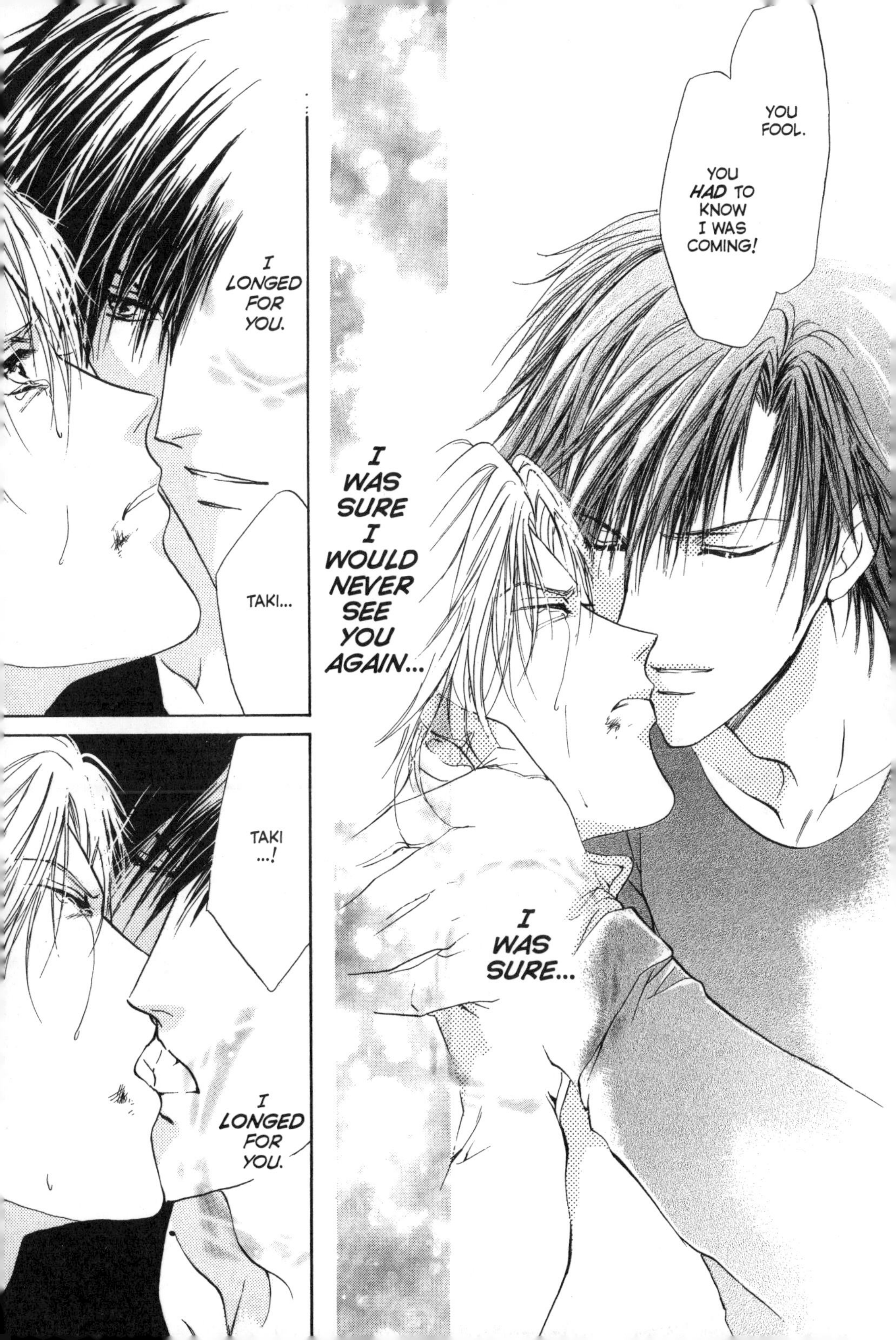
YOU FOOL.
YOU HAD TO KNOW I WAS COMING!
I WAS SURE I WOULD NEVER SEE YOU AGAIN...
I WAS SURE...
I LONGED FOR YOU.
TAKI...
TAKI ...!
I LONGED FOR YOU.

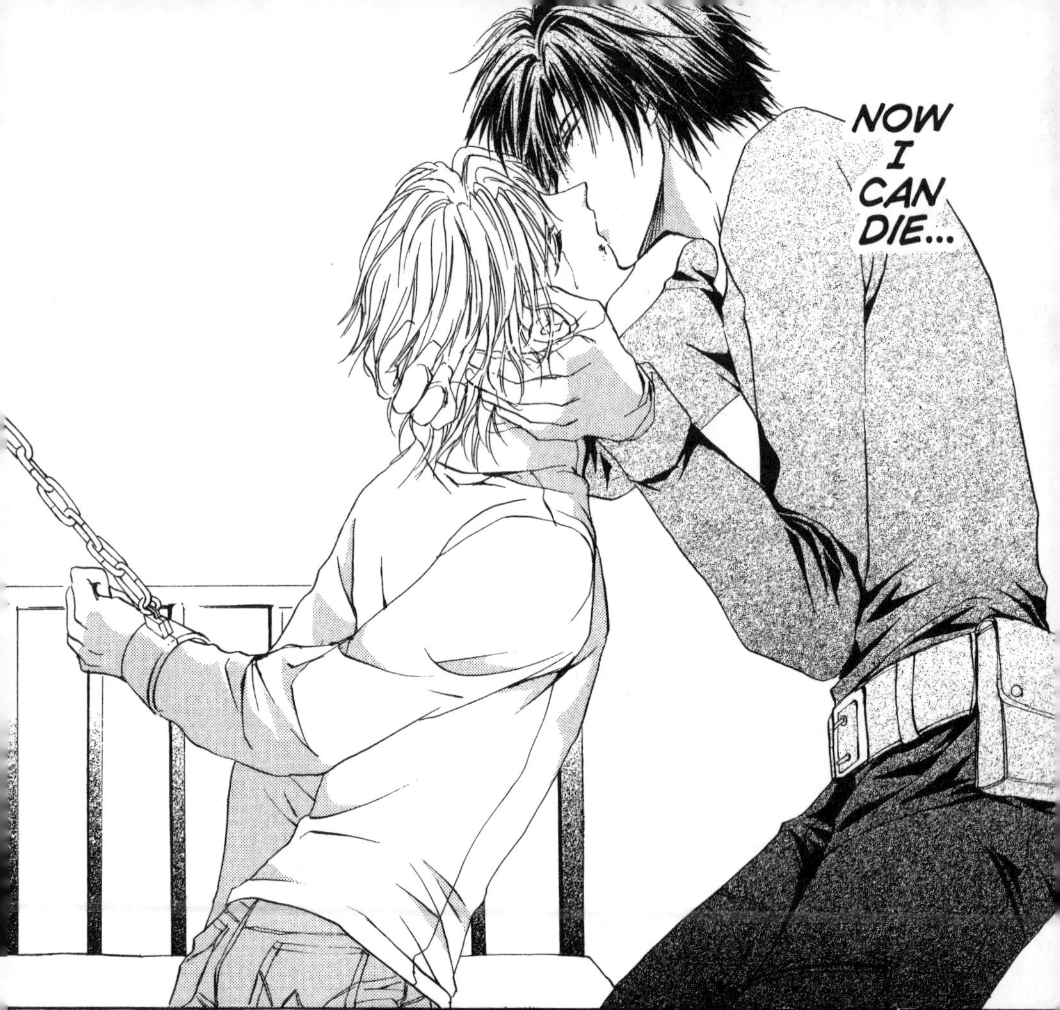
NOW I CAN DIE...
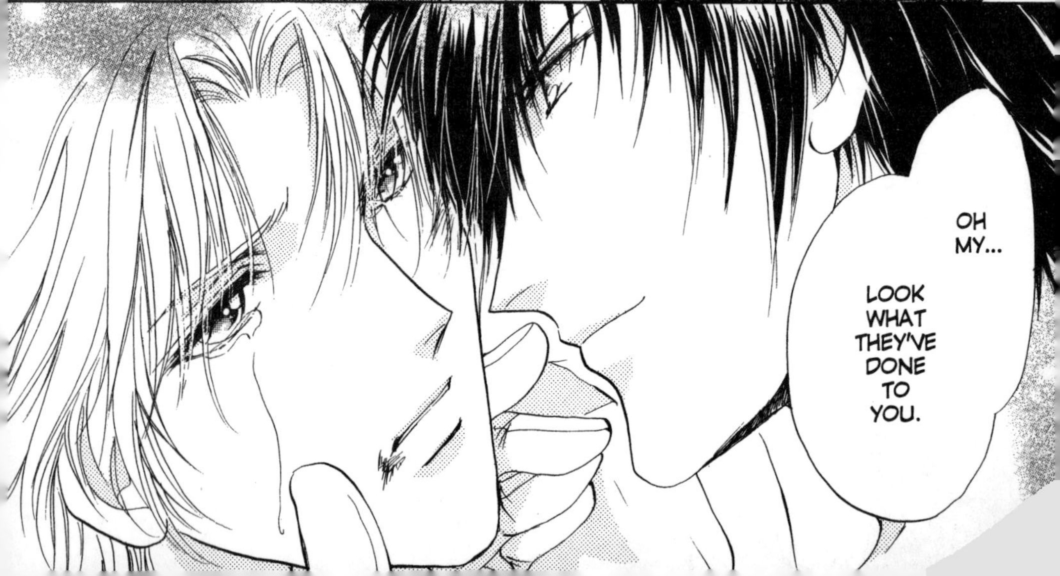
OH MY...
LOOK WHAT THEY'VE DONE TO YOU.

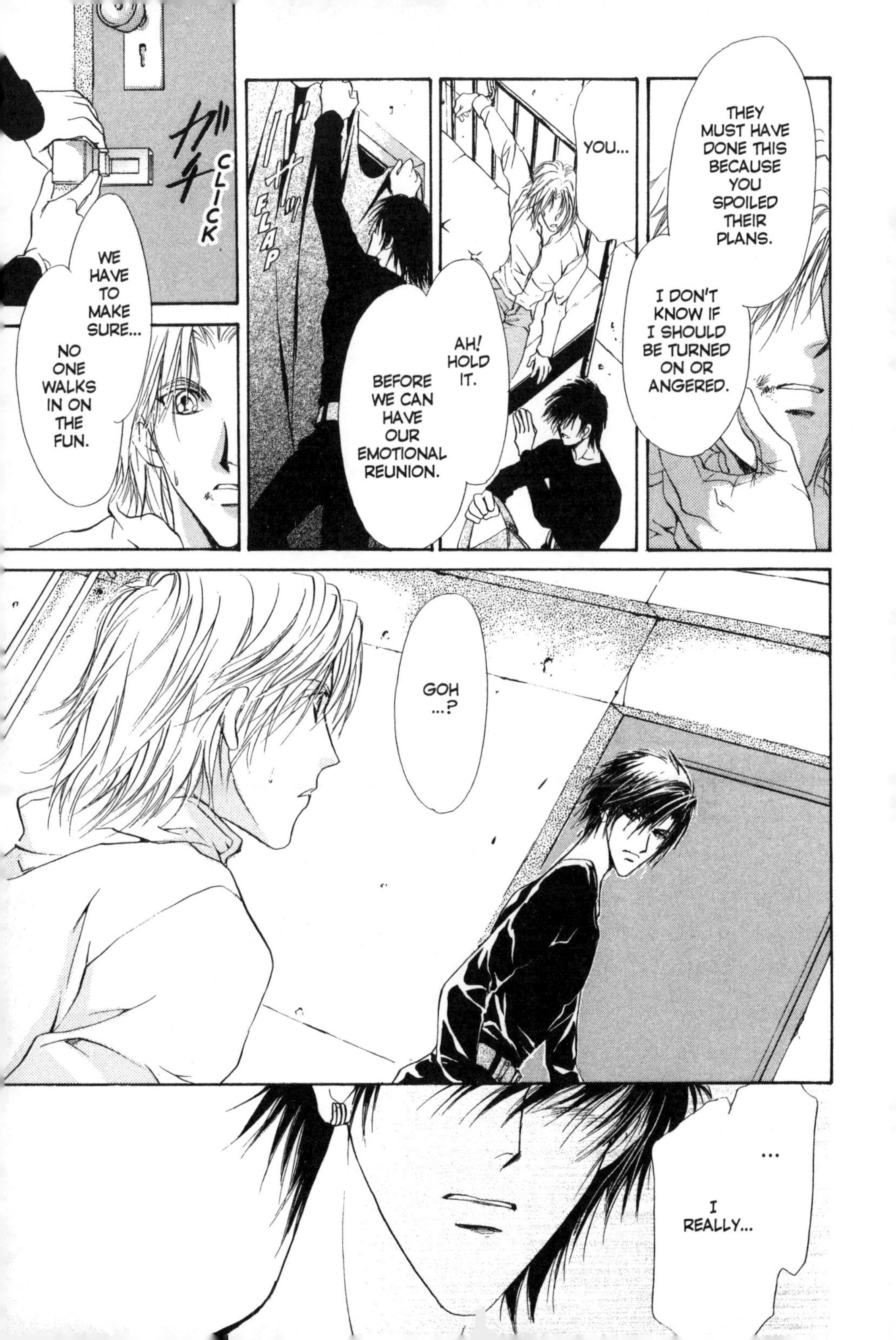
THEY MUST HAVE DONE THIS BECAUSE YOU SPOILED THEIR PLANS.
I DON'T KNOW IF I SHOULD BE TURNED ON OR ANGERED.
YOU...
AH! HOLD IT.
BEFORE WE CAN HAVE OUR EMOTIONAL REUNION.
FLAP
CLICK
WE HAVE TO MAKE SURE...
NO ONE WALKS IN ON THE FUN.
GOH ...?
...
I REALLY...

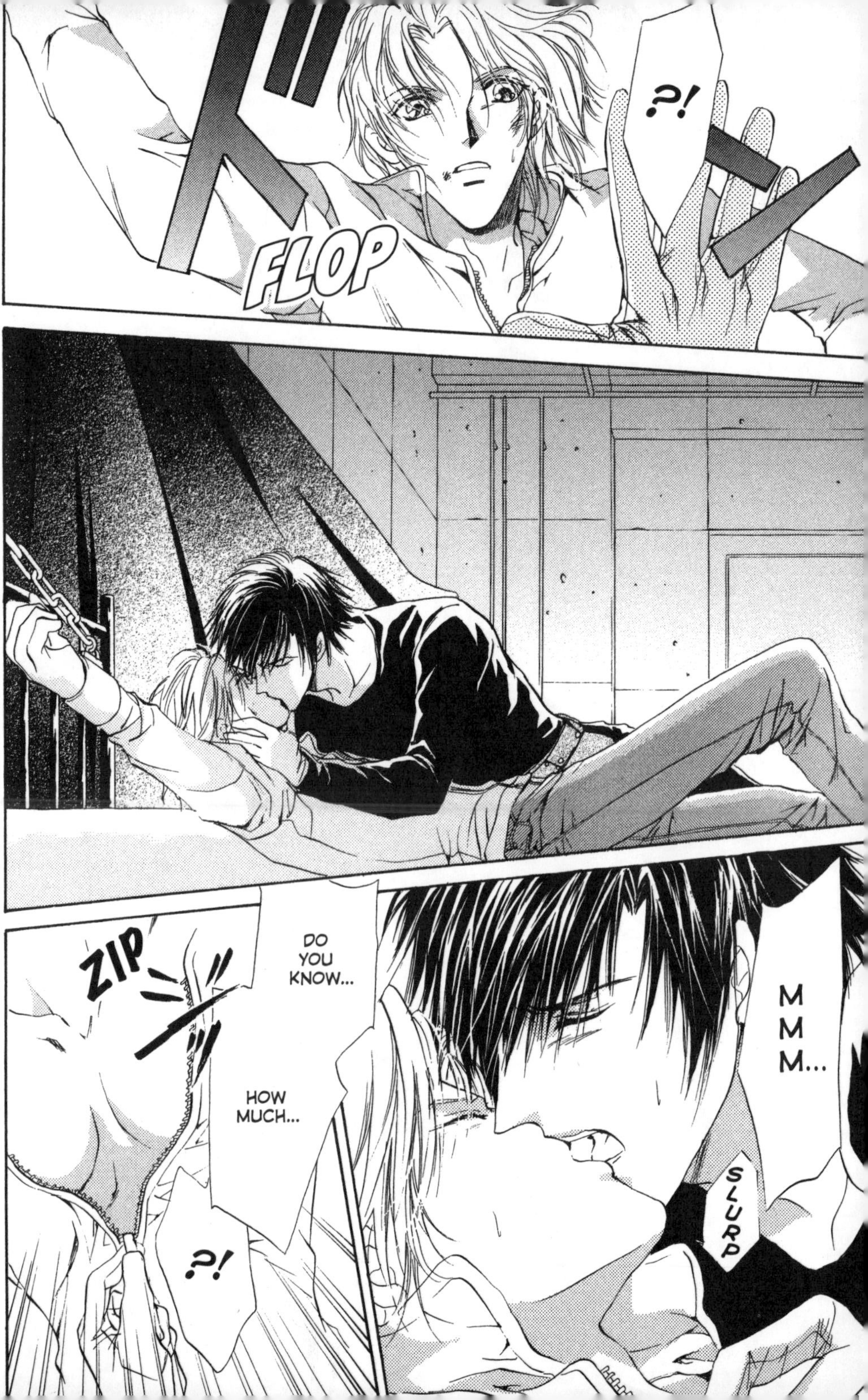
?!
FLOP
MMM...
SLURP
DO YOU KNOW...
HOW MUCH...
ZIP
?!

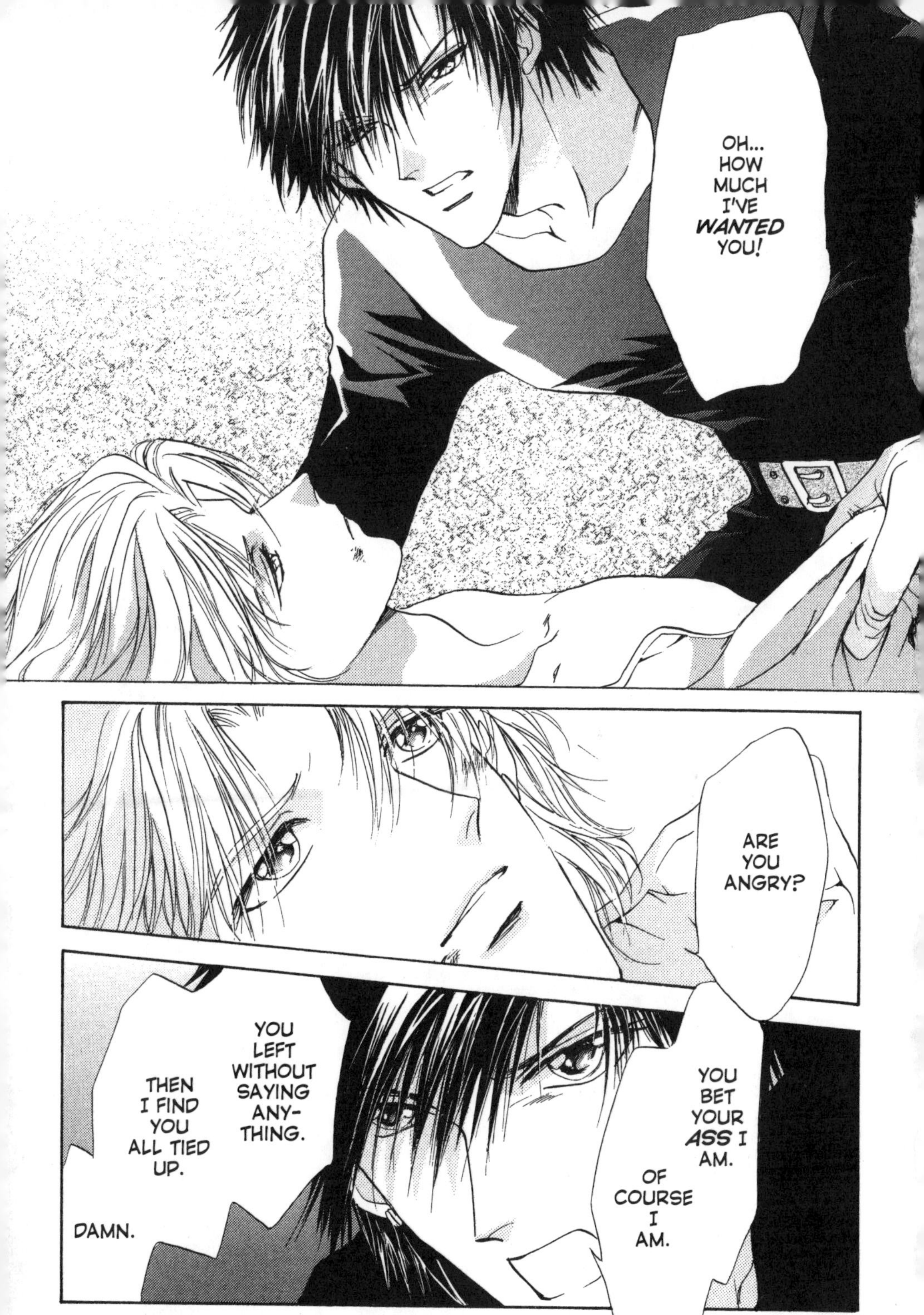
OH... HOW MUCH I'VE *WANTED* YOU!
ARE YOU ANGRY?
YOU BET YOUR *ASS* I AM.
OF COURSE I AM.
YOU LEFT WITHOUT SAYING ANY-THING.
THEN I FIND YOU ALL TIED UP.
DAMN.

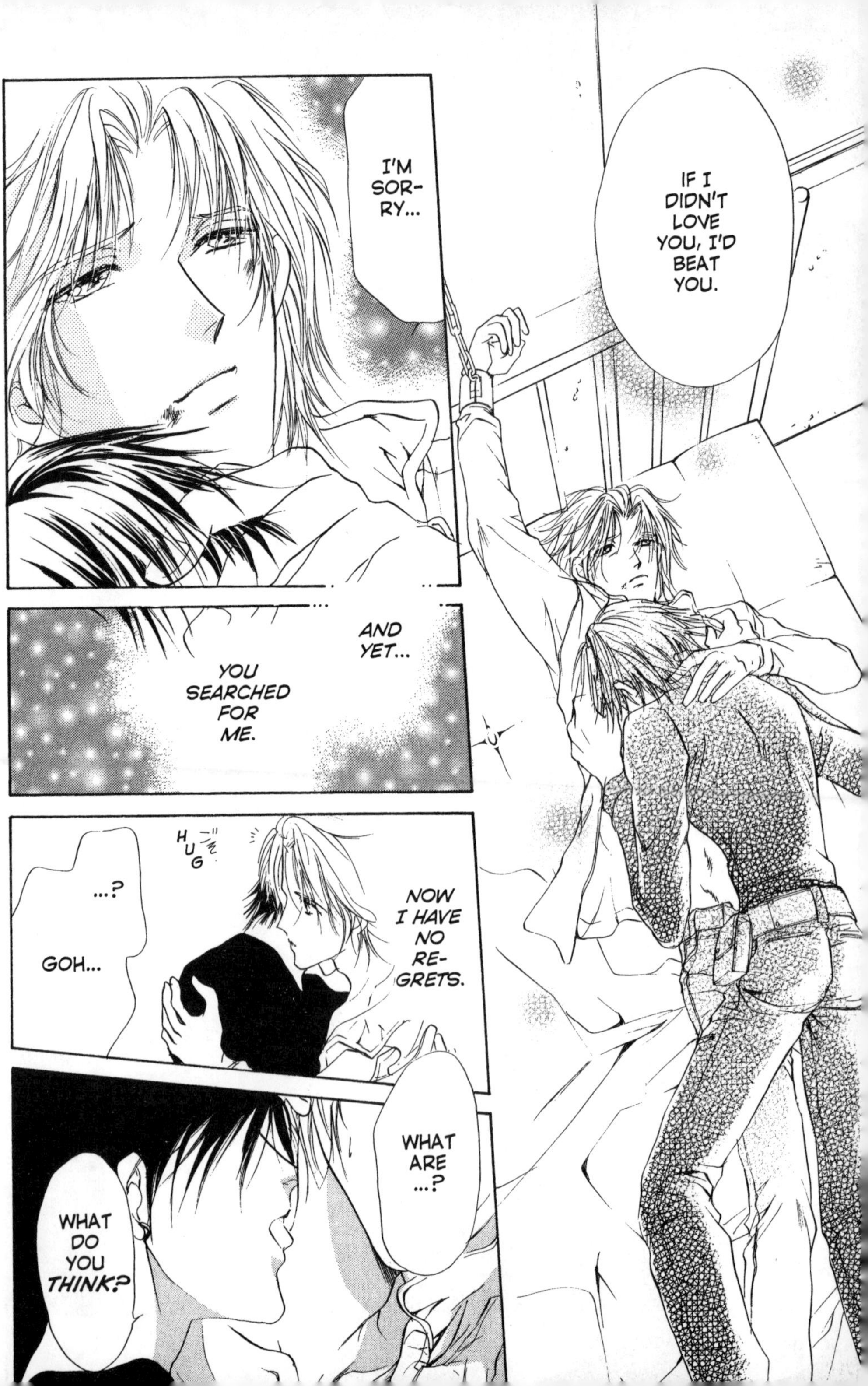
IF I DIDN'T LOVE YOU, I'D BEAT YOU.
I'M SOR-RY...
AND YET...
YOU SEARCHED FOR ME.
HUG
NOW I HAVE NO RE-GRETS.
...?
GOH...
WHAT ARE ...?
WHAT DO YOU *THINK?*

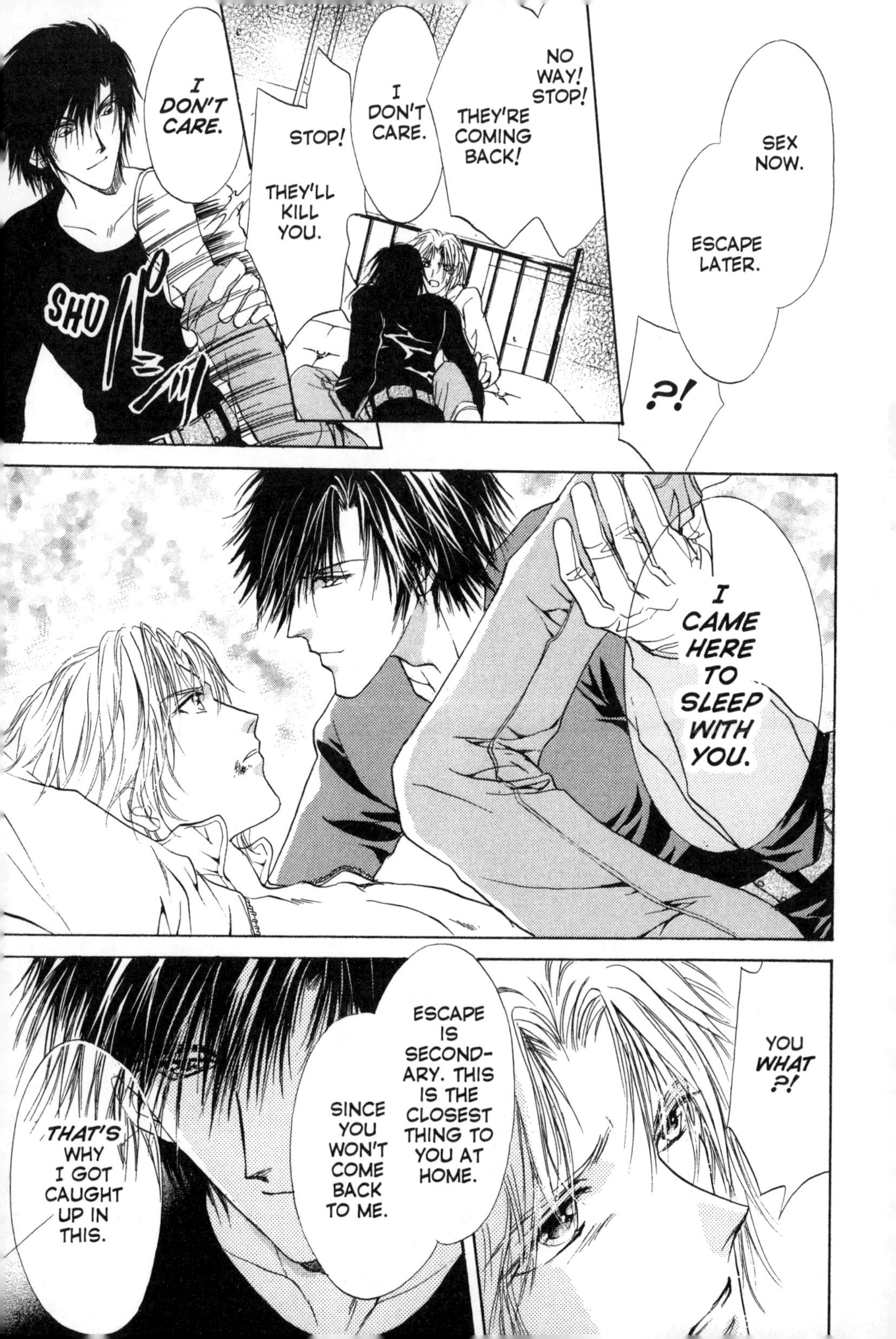
SEX NOW.
ESCAPE LATER.
?!
NO WAY! STOP!
THEY'RE COMING BACK!
I DON'T CARE.
STOP!
THEY'LL KILL YOU.
I DON'T CARE.
SHU
I CAME HERE TO SLEEP WITH YOU.
YOU WHAT?!
ESCAPE IS SECONDARY. THIS IS THE CLOSEST THING TO YOU AT HOME.
SINCE YOU WON'T COME BACK TO ME.
THAT'S WHY I GOT CAUGHT UP IN THIS.

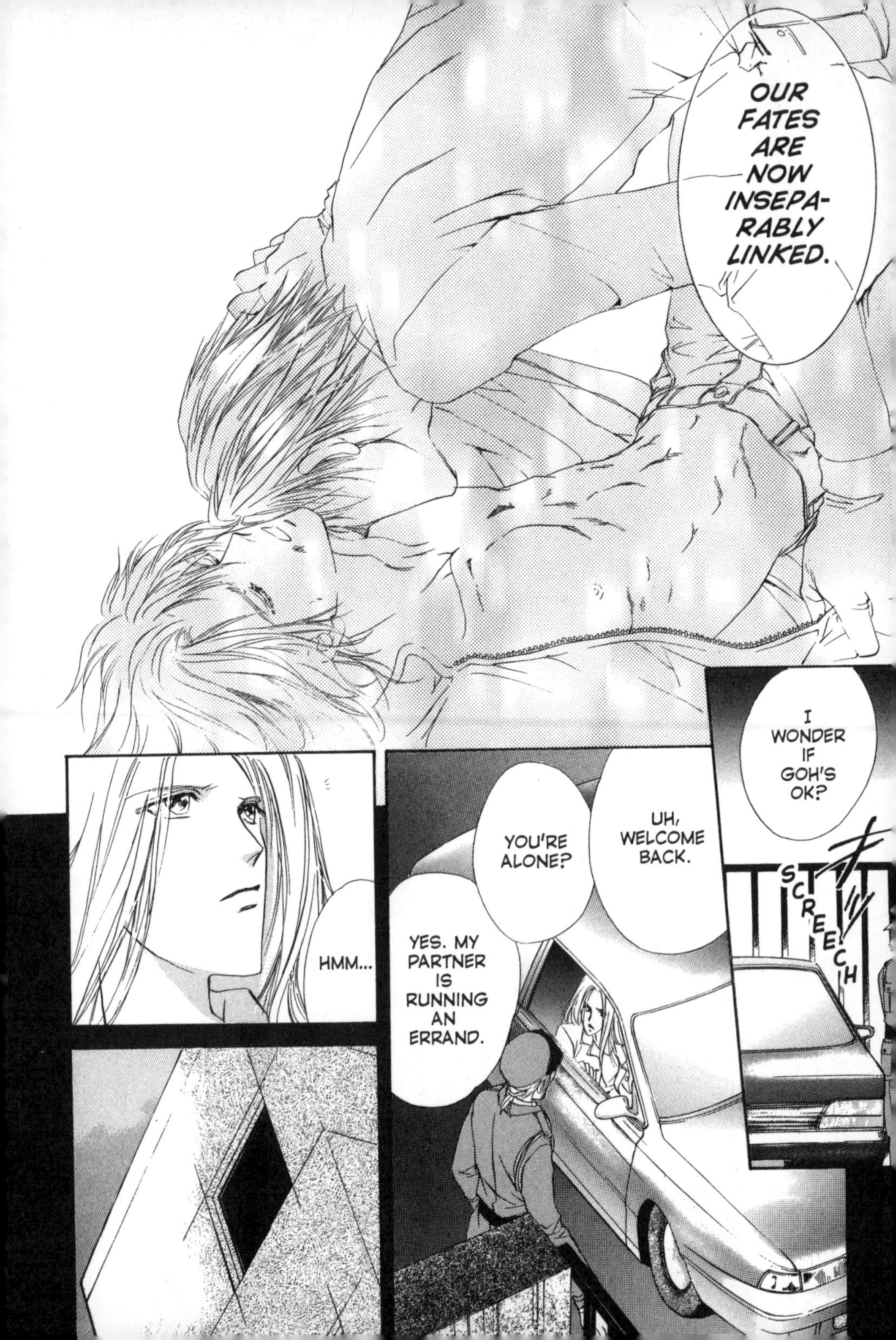
OUR FATES ARE NOW INSEPARABLY LINKED.
I WONDER IF GOH'S OK?
SCREECH
UH, WELCOME BACK.
YOU'RE ALONE?
YES. MY PARTNER IS RUNNING AN ERRAND.
HMM...

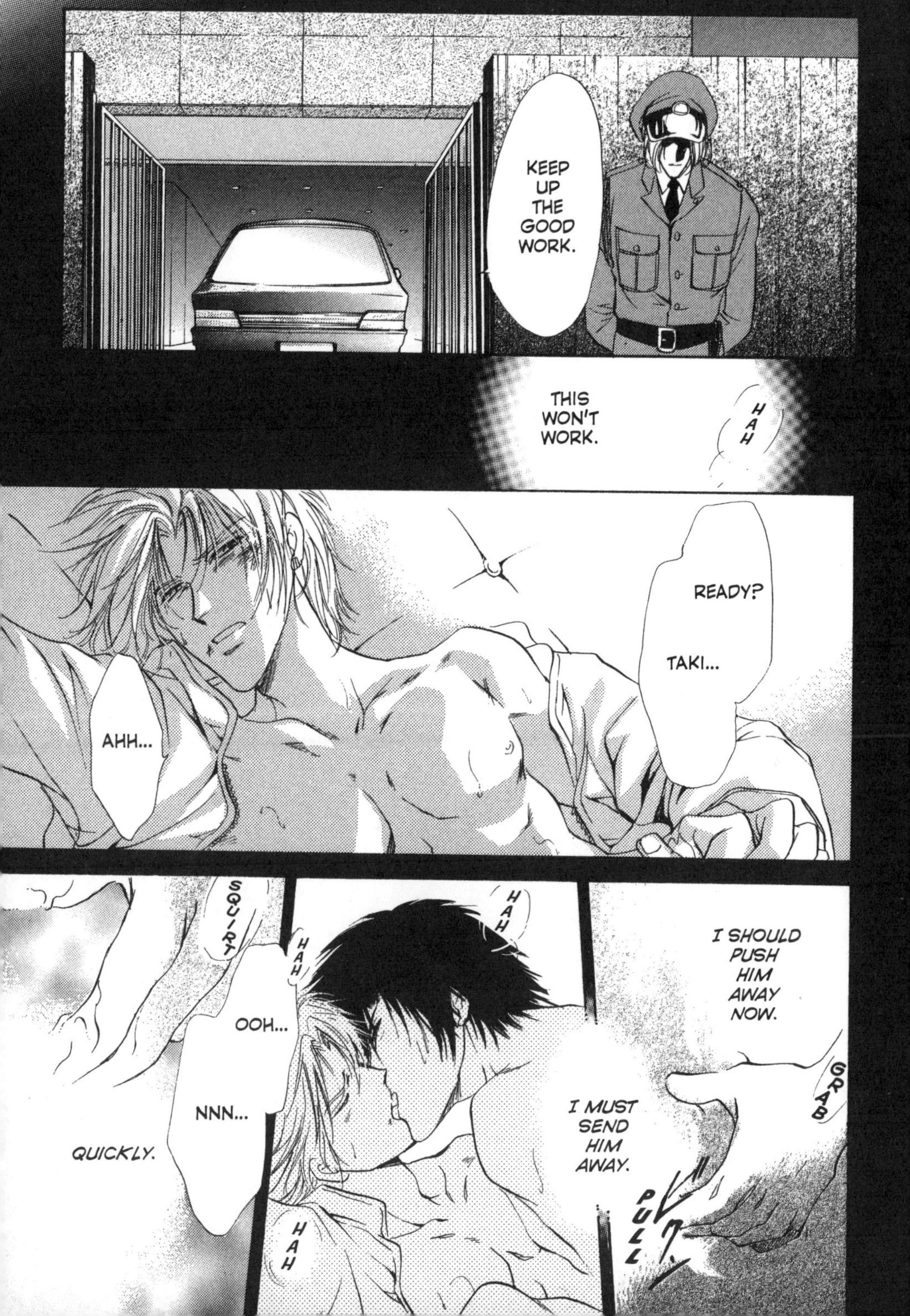
KEEP UP THE GOOD WORK.
HAH
THIS WON'T WORK.
READY?
TAKI...
AHH...
I SHOULD PUSH HIM AWAY NOW.
GRAB
I MUST SEND HIM AWAY.
PULL
HAH
HAH
OOH...
NNN...
HAH
SQUIRT
QUICKLY.

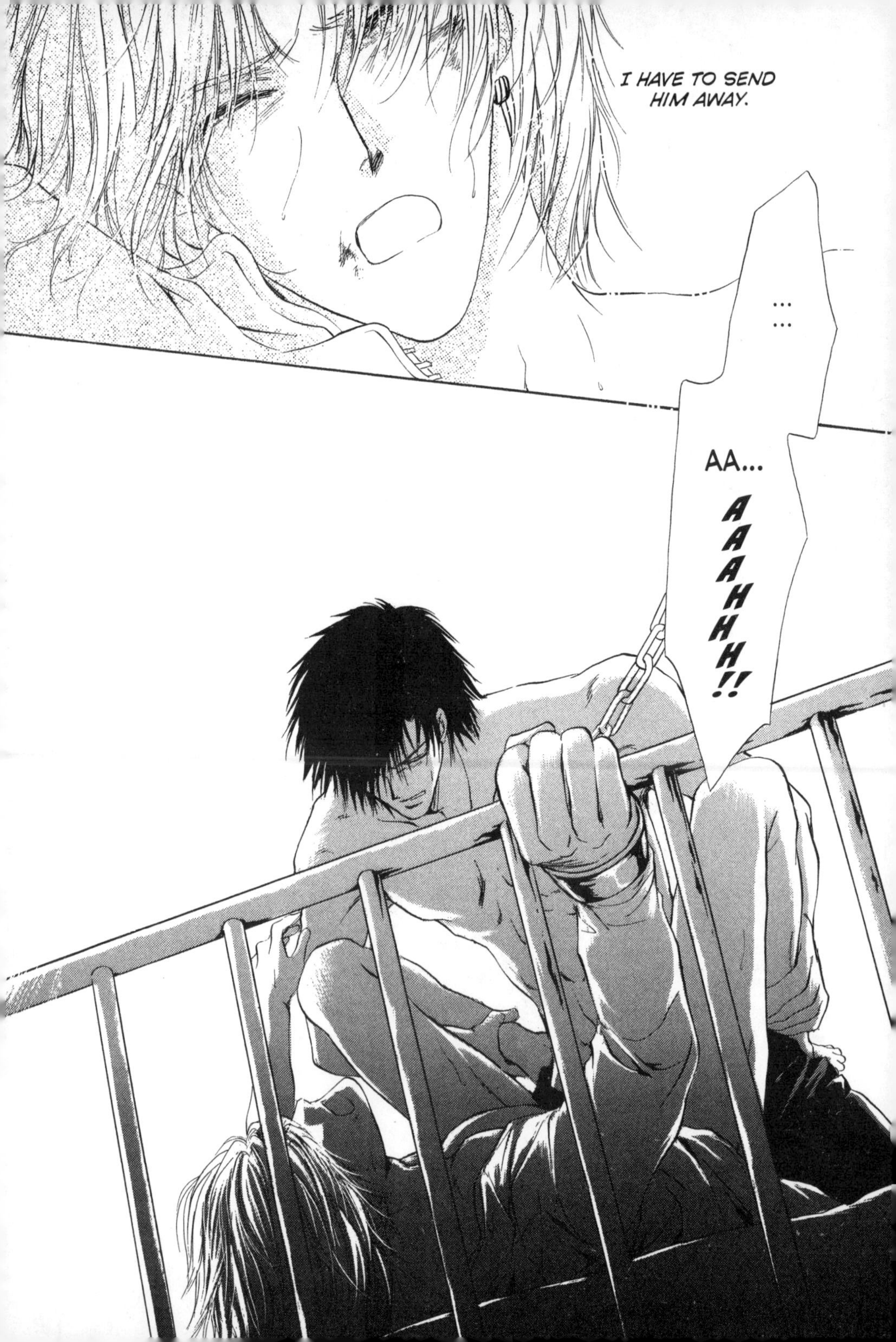
I HAVE TO SEND HIM AWAY.
......
AA... AAAAHHH!!

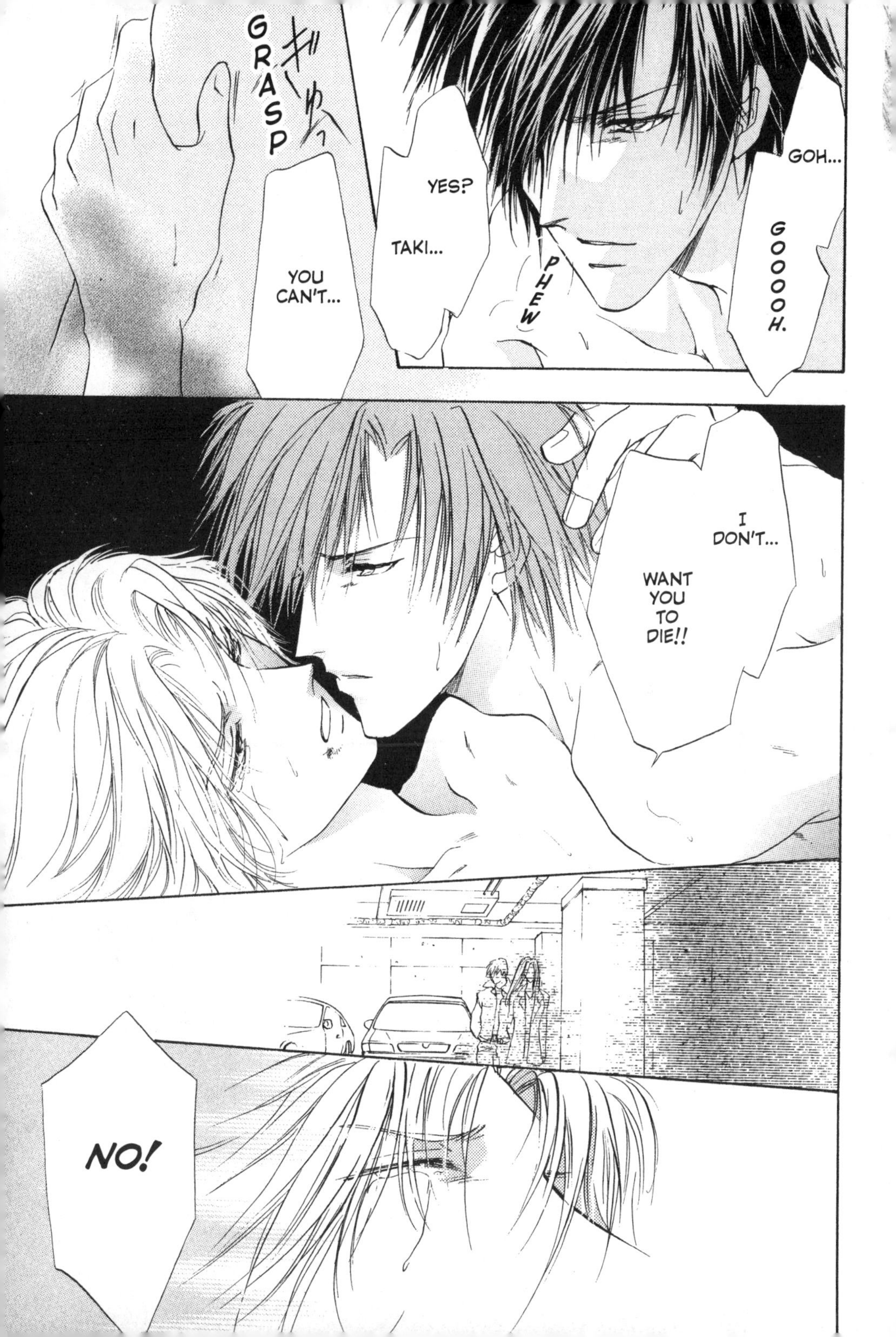
GOH...
GOOOOOH.
PHEW
YES?
TAKI...
YOU CAN'T...
GRASP
I DON'T...
WANT YOU TO DIE!!
NO!

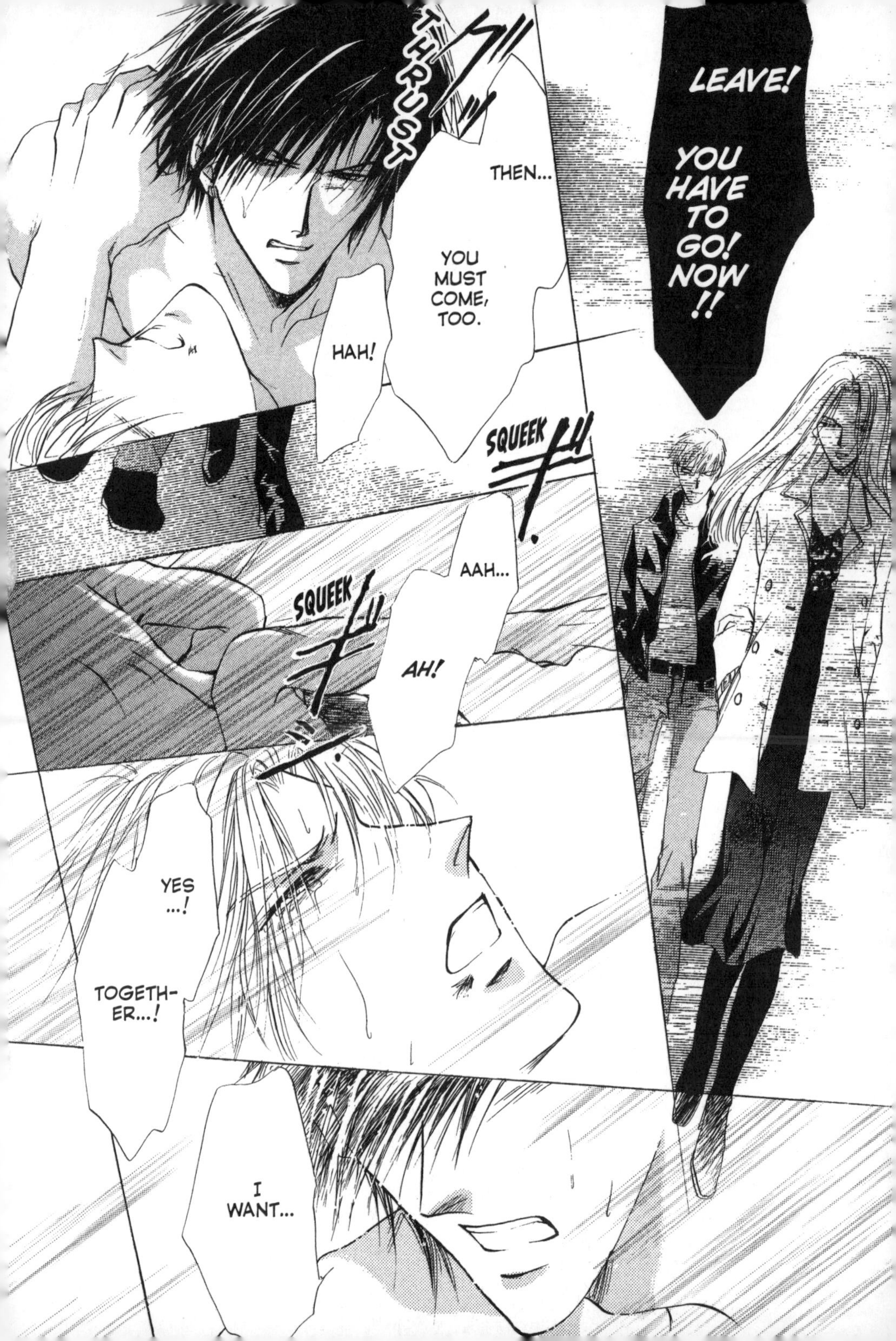
LEAVE!
YOU HAVE TO GO! NOW!!
THEN...
YOU MUST COME, TOO.
THRUST
HAH!
SQUEEK
AAH...
SQUEEK
AH!
YES ...!
TOGETHER...!
I WANT...

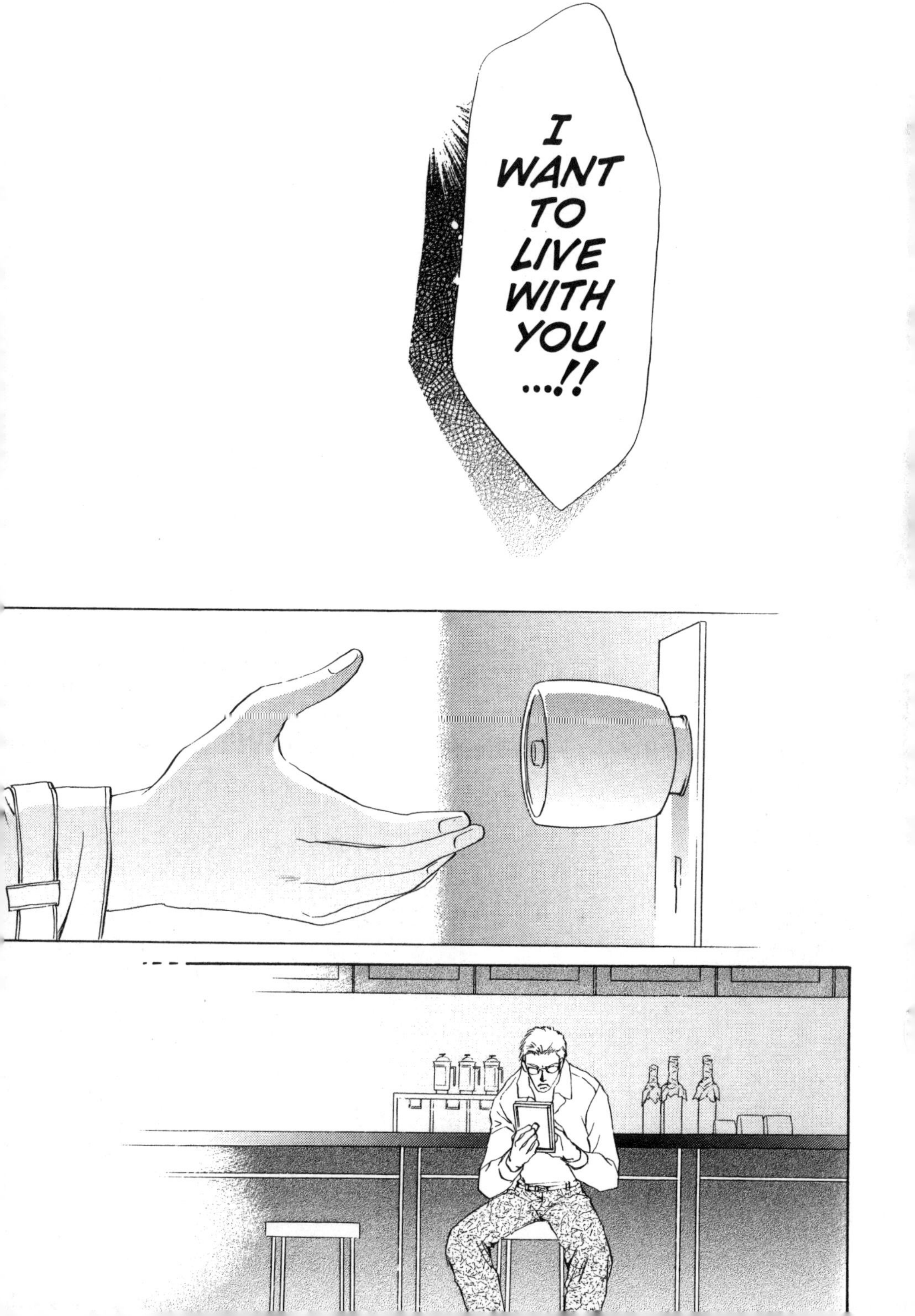
I WANT TO LIVE WITH YOU ...!!

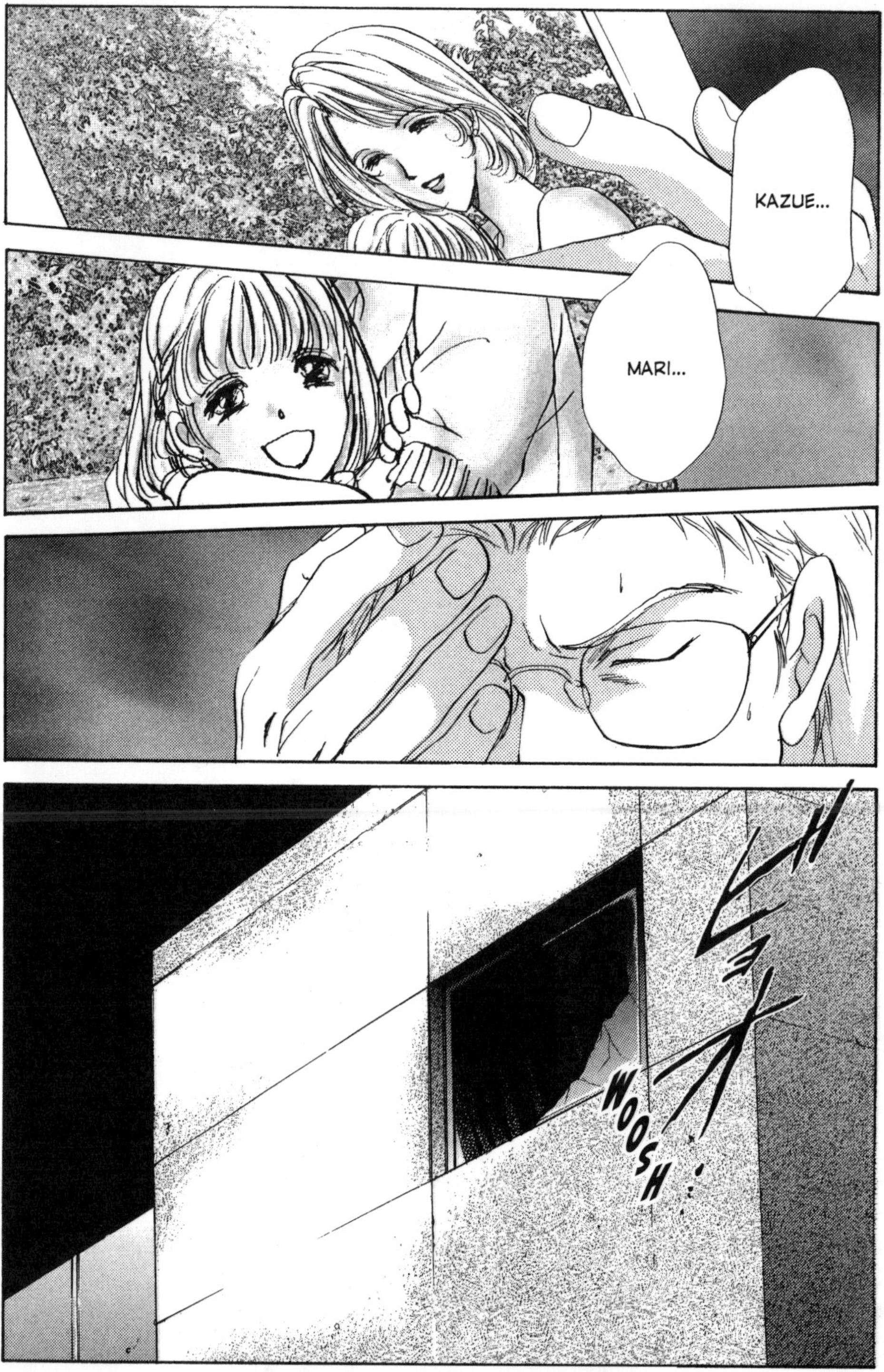
KAZUE...
MARI...
WOOSH...

YELLOW ACT. 14/END

YELLOW

YELLOW

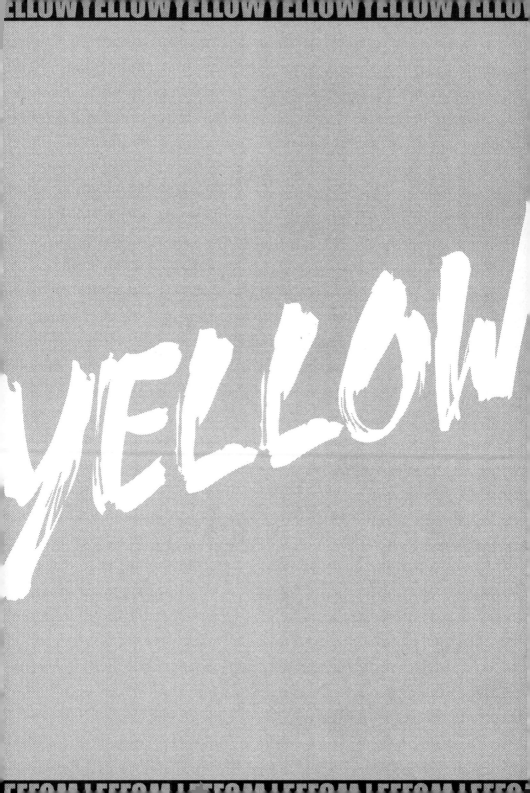

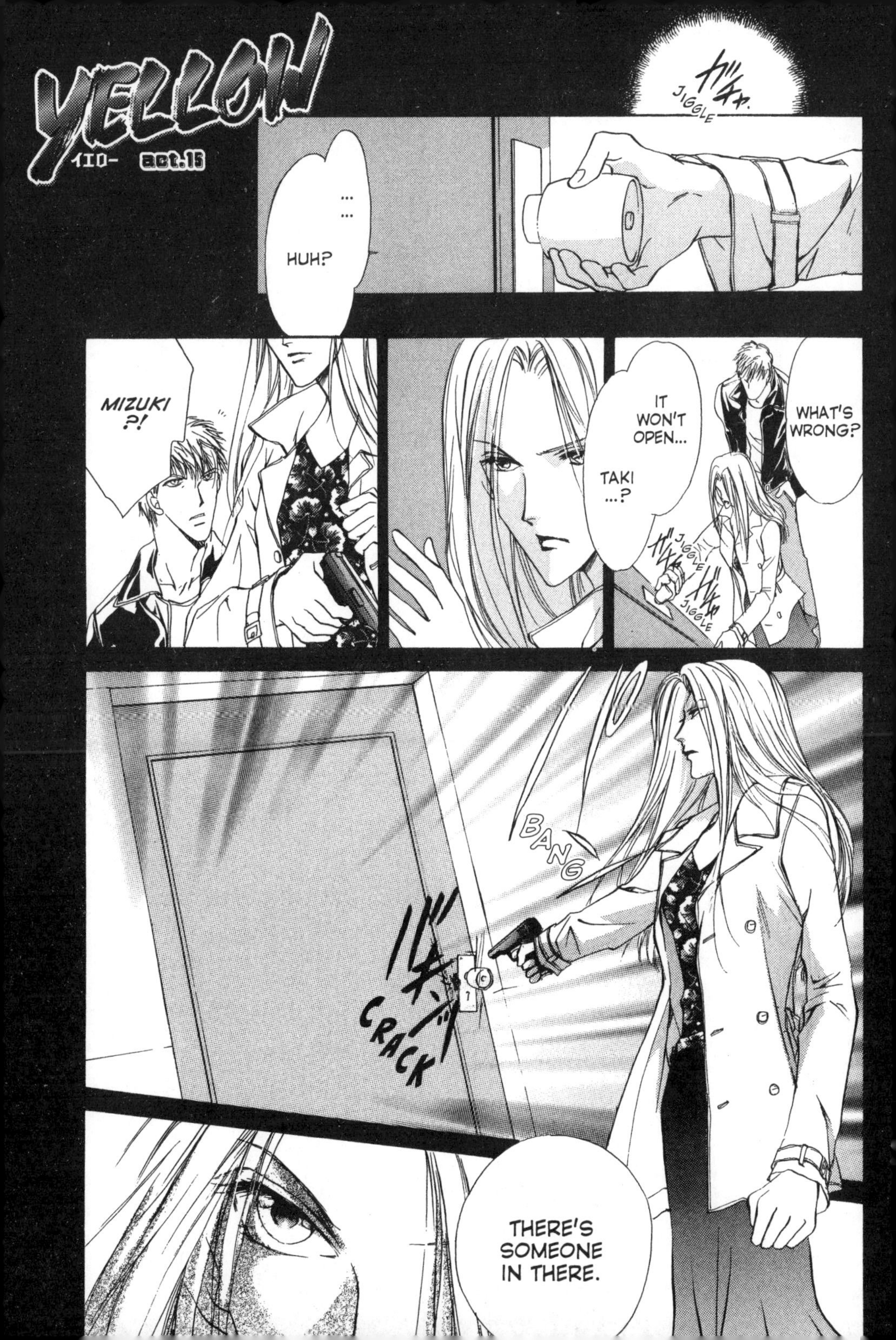
YELLOW
イエロー act.15
JIGGLE
...
...
HUH?
WHAT'S WRONG?
IT WON'T OPEN...
TAKI ...?
JIGGLE
JIGGLE
MIZUKI ?!
BANG
CRACK
THERE'S SOMEONE IN THERE.

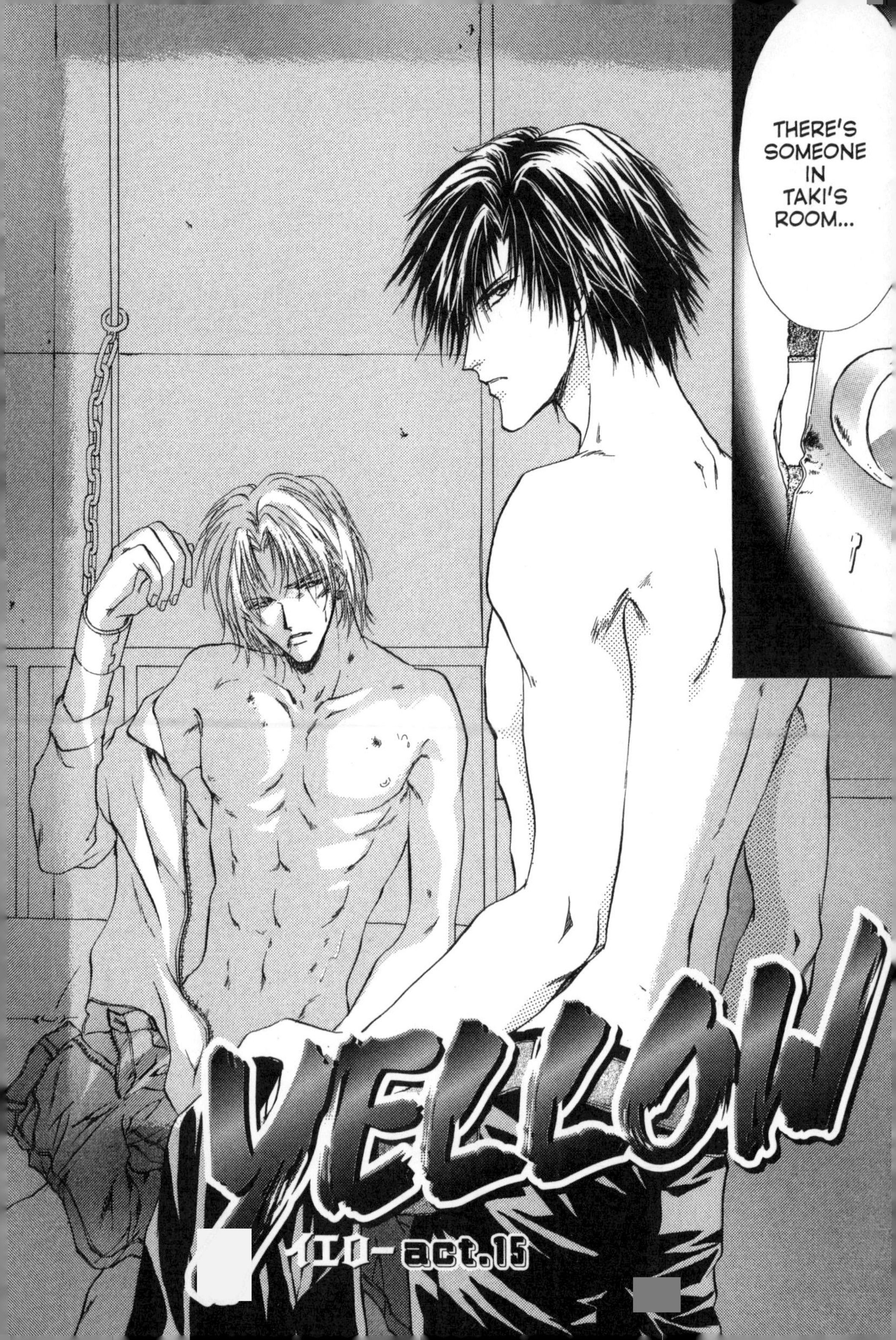
THERE'S SOMEONE IN TAKI'S ROOM...
YELLOW
イエロー act.15

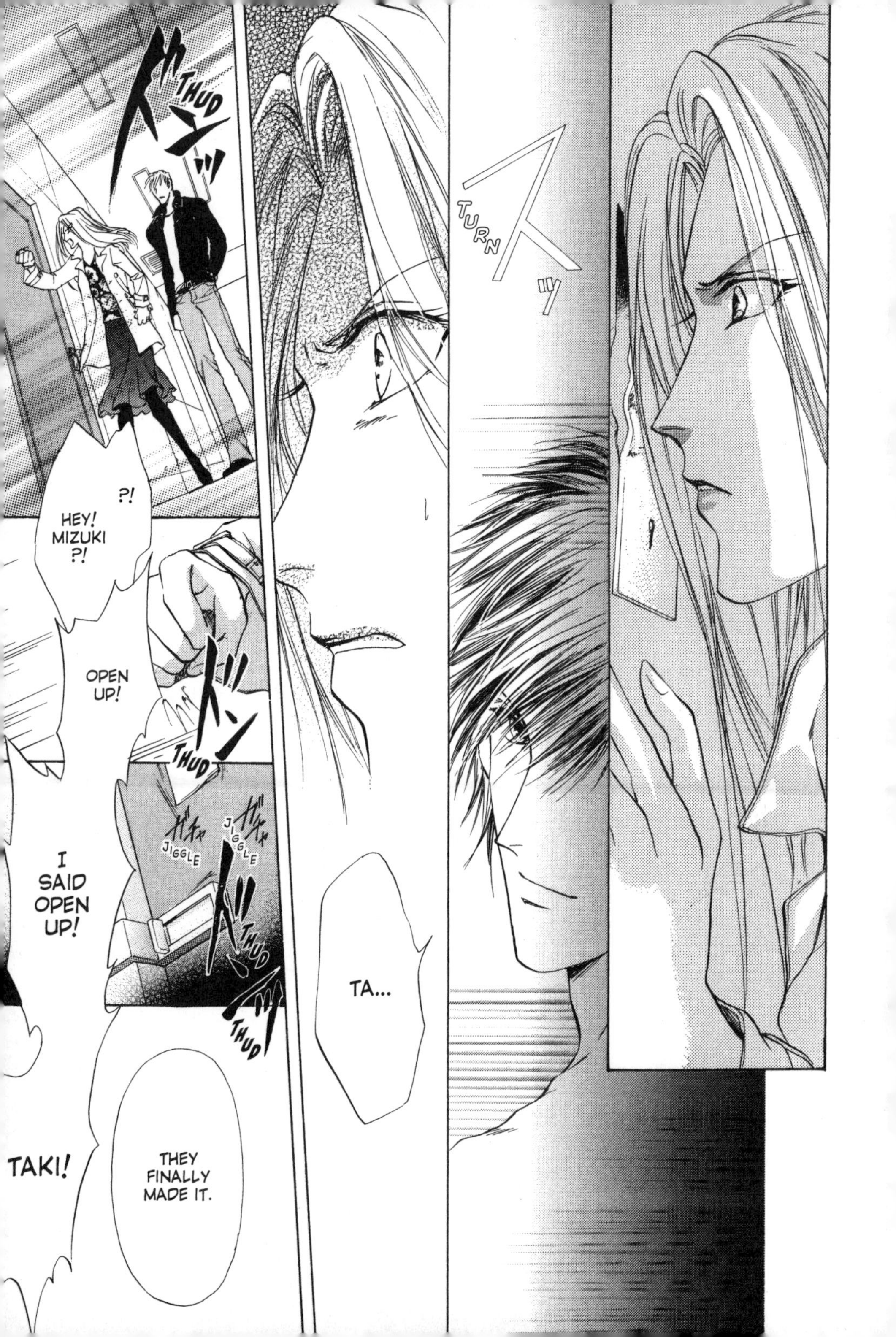
TURN
TA...
THEY FINALLY MADE IT.
THUD
?!
HEY! MIZUKI?!
OPEN UP!
THUD
I SAID OPEN UP!
JIGGLE
JIGGLE
THUD
THUD
TAKI!

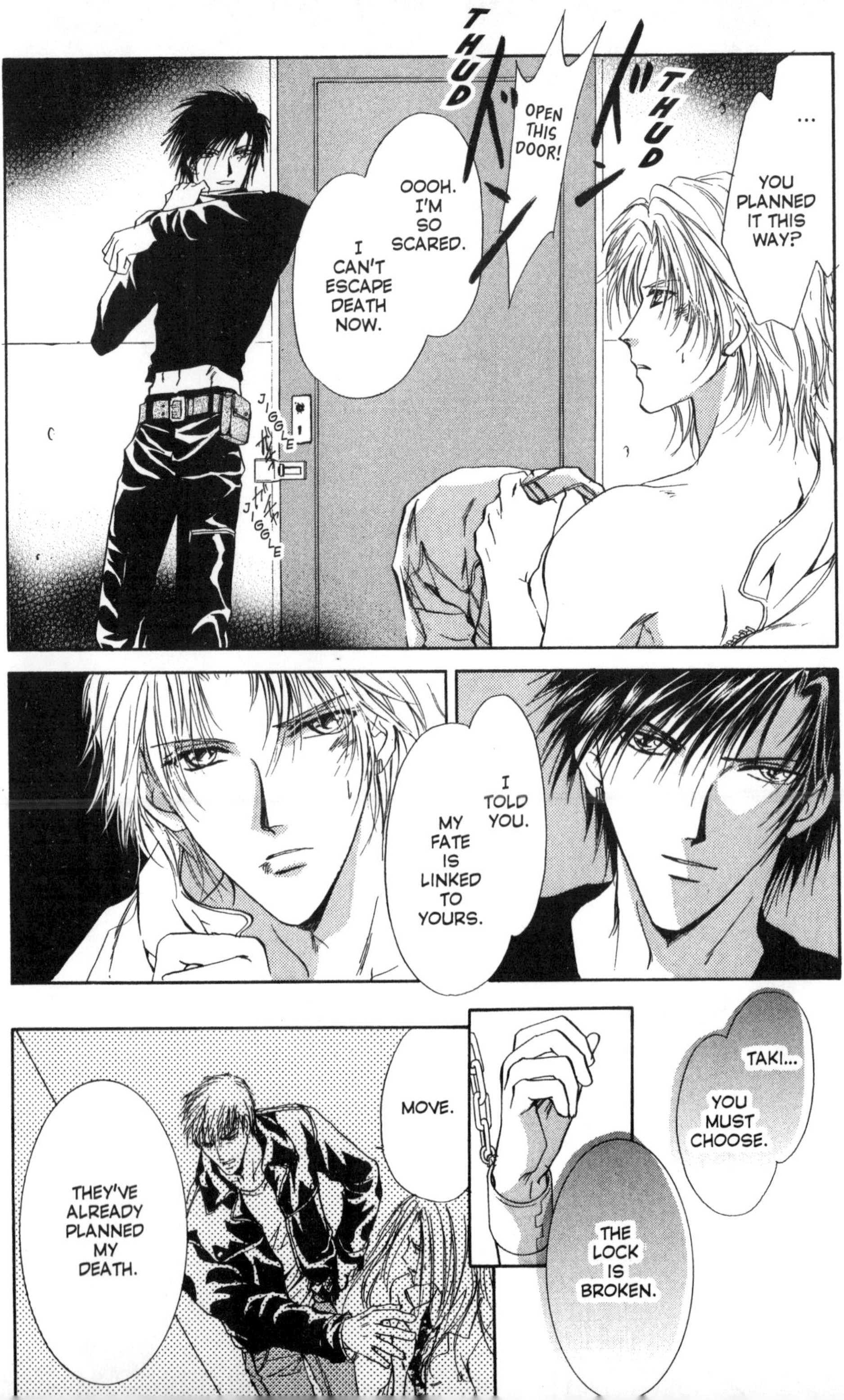
...
YOU PLANNED IT THIS WAY?
THUD
OPEN THIS DOOR!
THUD
OOOH. I'M SO SCARED.
I CAN'T ESCAPE DEATH NOW.
JIGGLE
JIGGLE
I TOLD YOU.
MY FATE IS LINKED TO YOURS.
TAKI...
YOU MUST CHOOSE.
THE LOCK IS BROKEN.
MOVE.
THEY'VE ALREADY PLANNED MY DEATH.

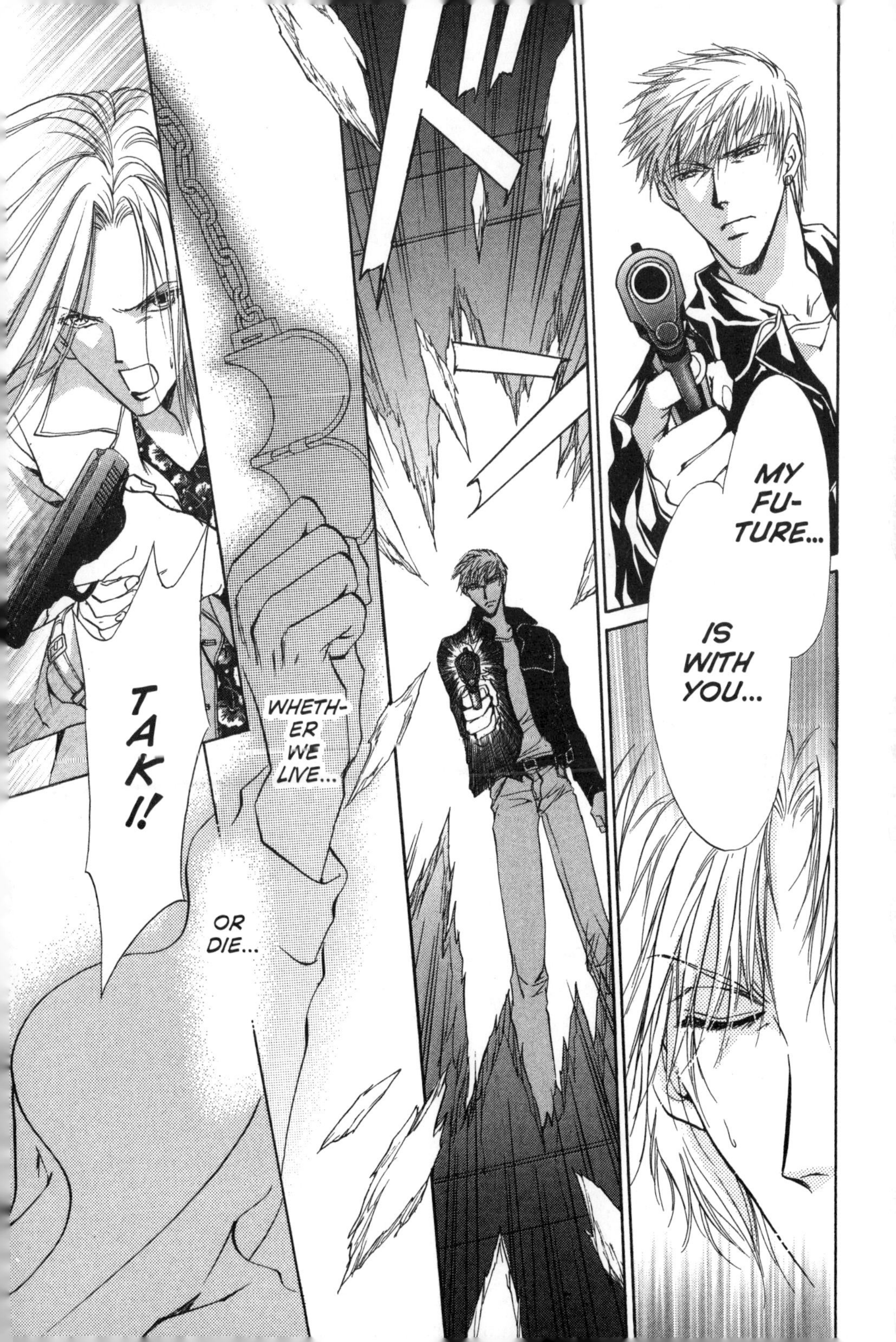
MY FU- TURE...
IS WITH YOU...
WHETH- ER WE LIVE...
OR DIE...
TAKI!

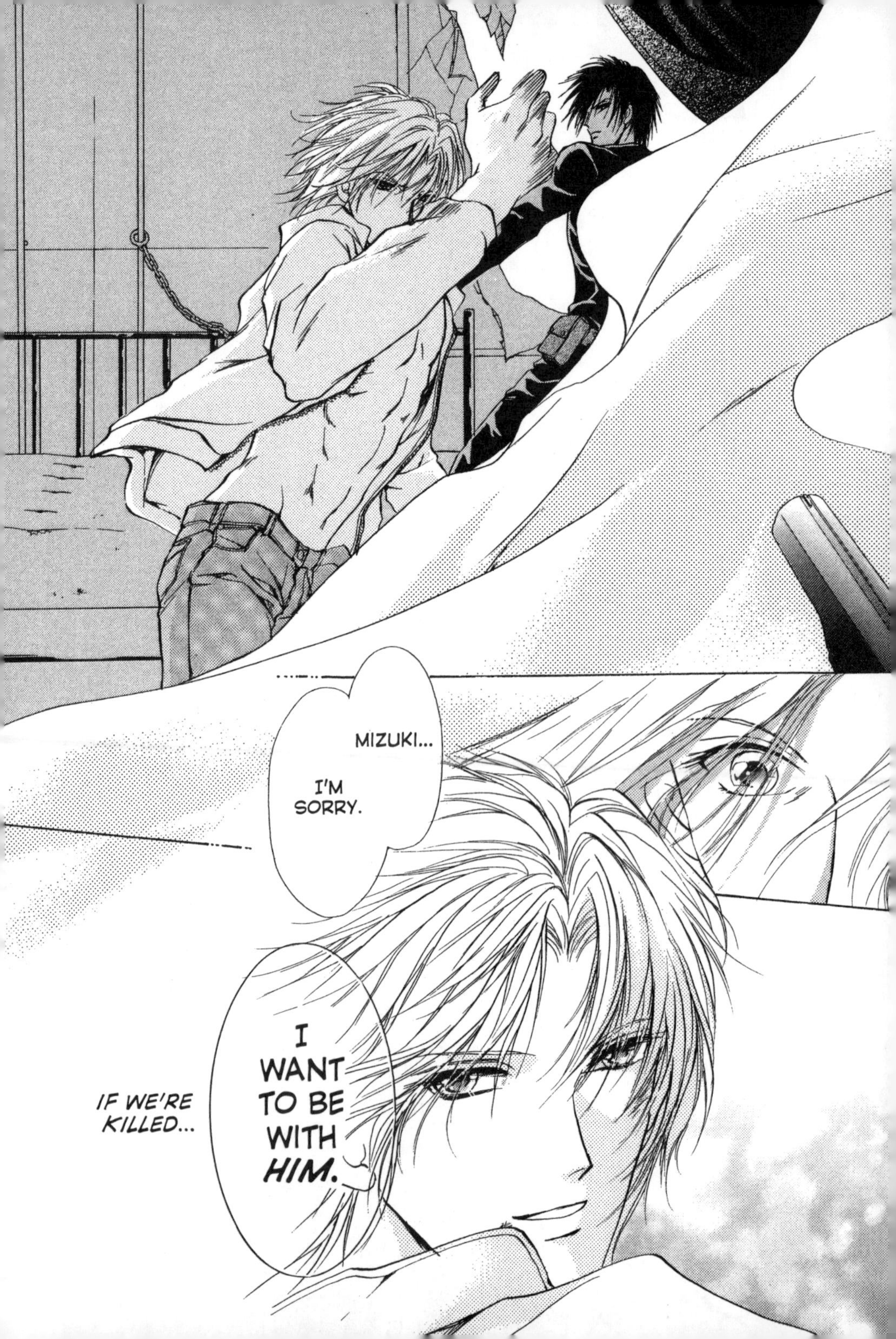
MIZUKI...
I'M SORRY.
I WANT TO BE WITH HIM.
IF WE'RE KILLED...

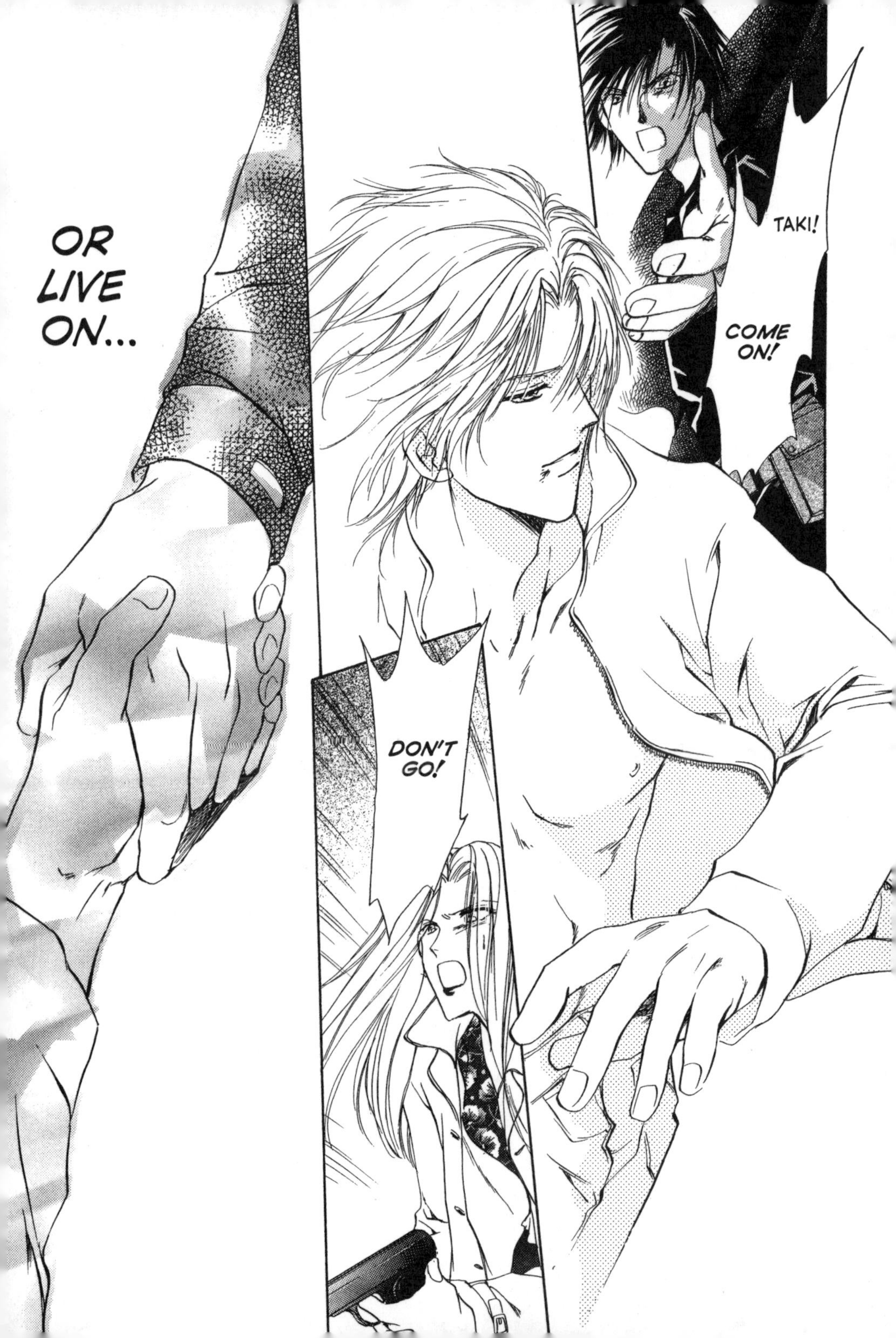
TAKI!
COME ON!
DON'T GO!
OR LIVE ON...

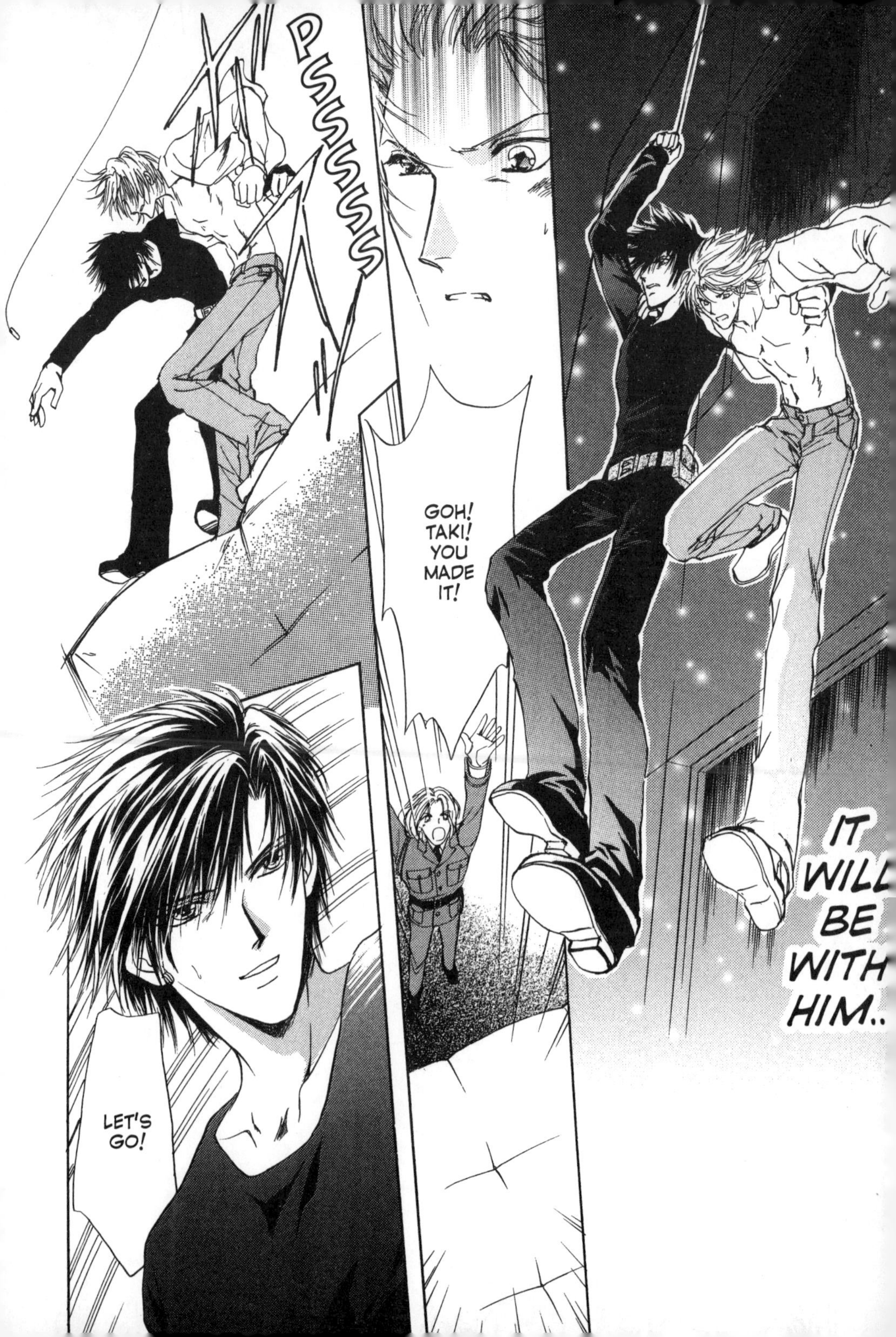
IT WILL BE WITH HIM..
GOH! TAKI! YOU MADE IT!
PSSSSSSS
LET'S GO!

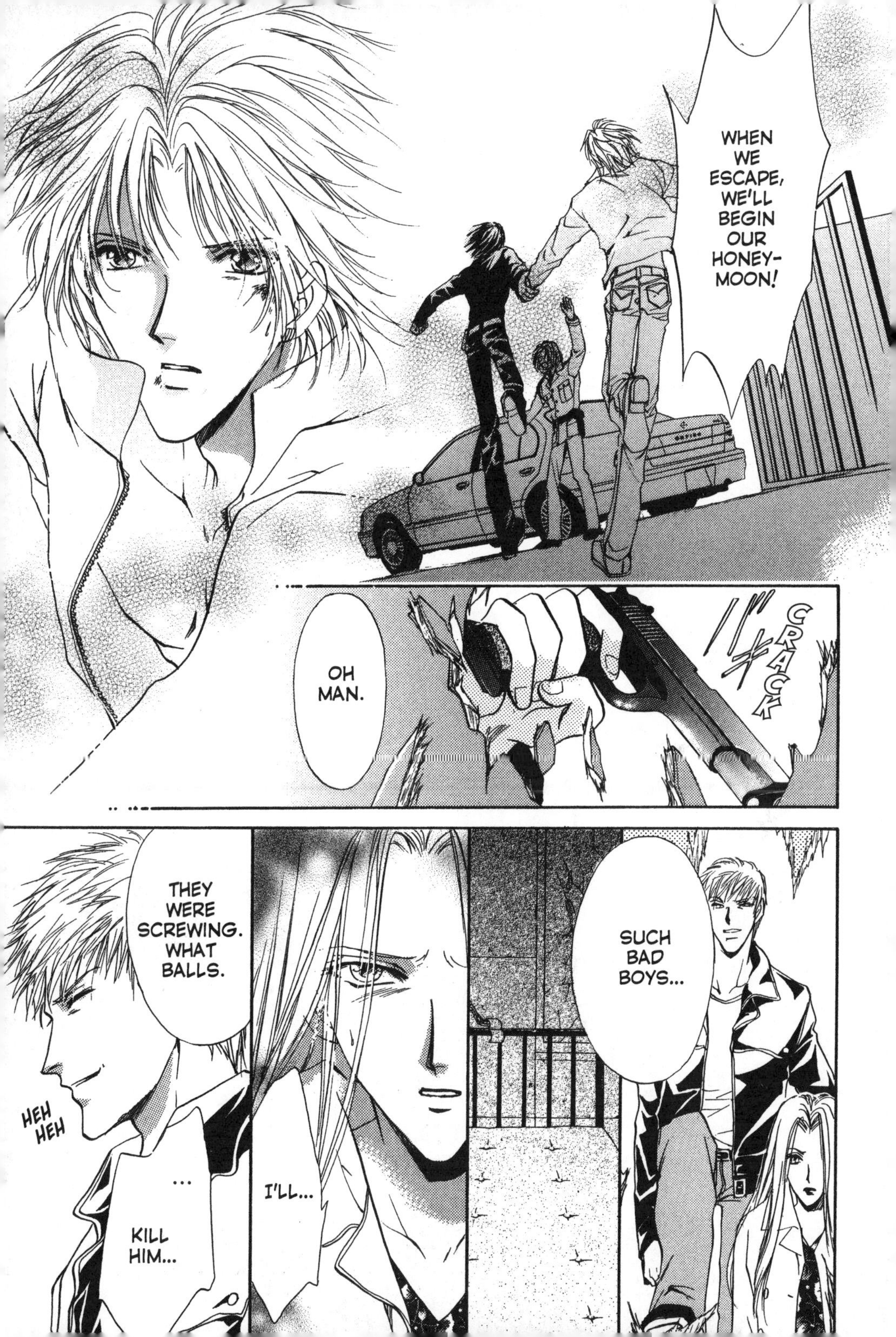
WHEN WE ESCAPE, WE'LL BEGIN OUR HONEY-MOON!
CRACK
OH MAN.
SUCH BAD BOYS...
THEY WERE SCREWING. WHAT BALLS.
HEH HEH
I'LL...
...
KILL HIM...

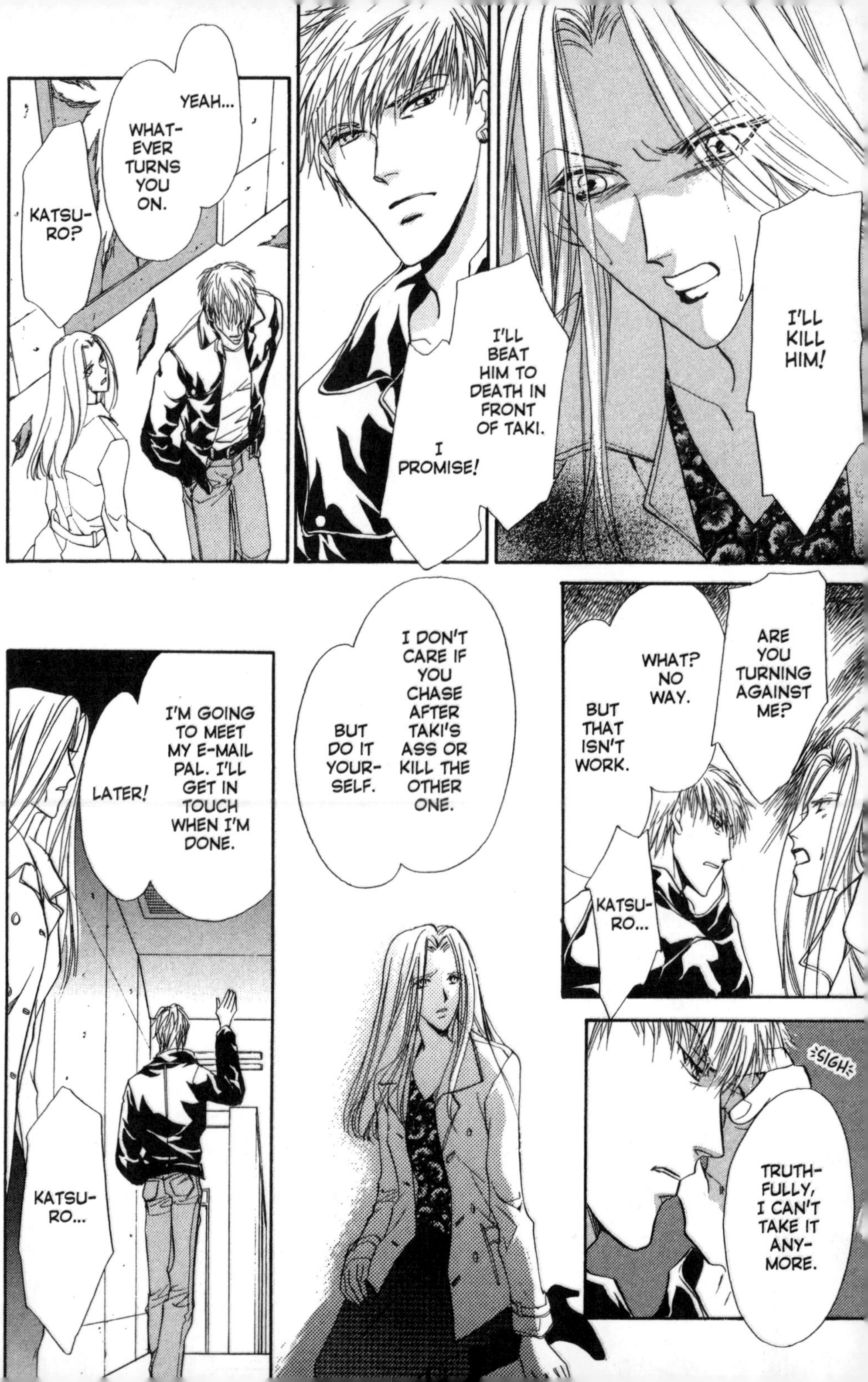
I'LL KILL HIM!
I'LL BEAT HIM TO DEATH IN FRONT OF TAKI.
I PROMISE!
YEAH... WHATEVER TURNS YOU ON.
KATSURO?
ARE YOU TURNING AGAINST ME?
WHAT? NO WAY.
BUT THAT ISN'T WORK.
KATSURO...
SIGH
TRUTHFULLY, I CAN'T TAKE IT ANYMORE.
I DON'T CARE IF YOU CHASE AFTER TAKI'S ASS OR KILL THE OTHER ONE.
BUT DO IT YOURSELF.
I'M GOING TO MEET MY E-MAIL PAL. I'LL GET IN TOUCH WHEN I'M DONE.
LATER!
KATSURO...

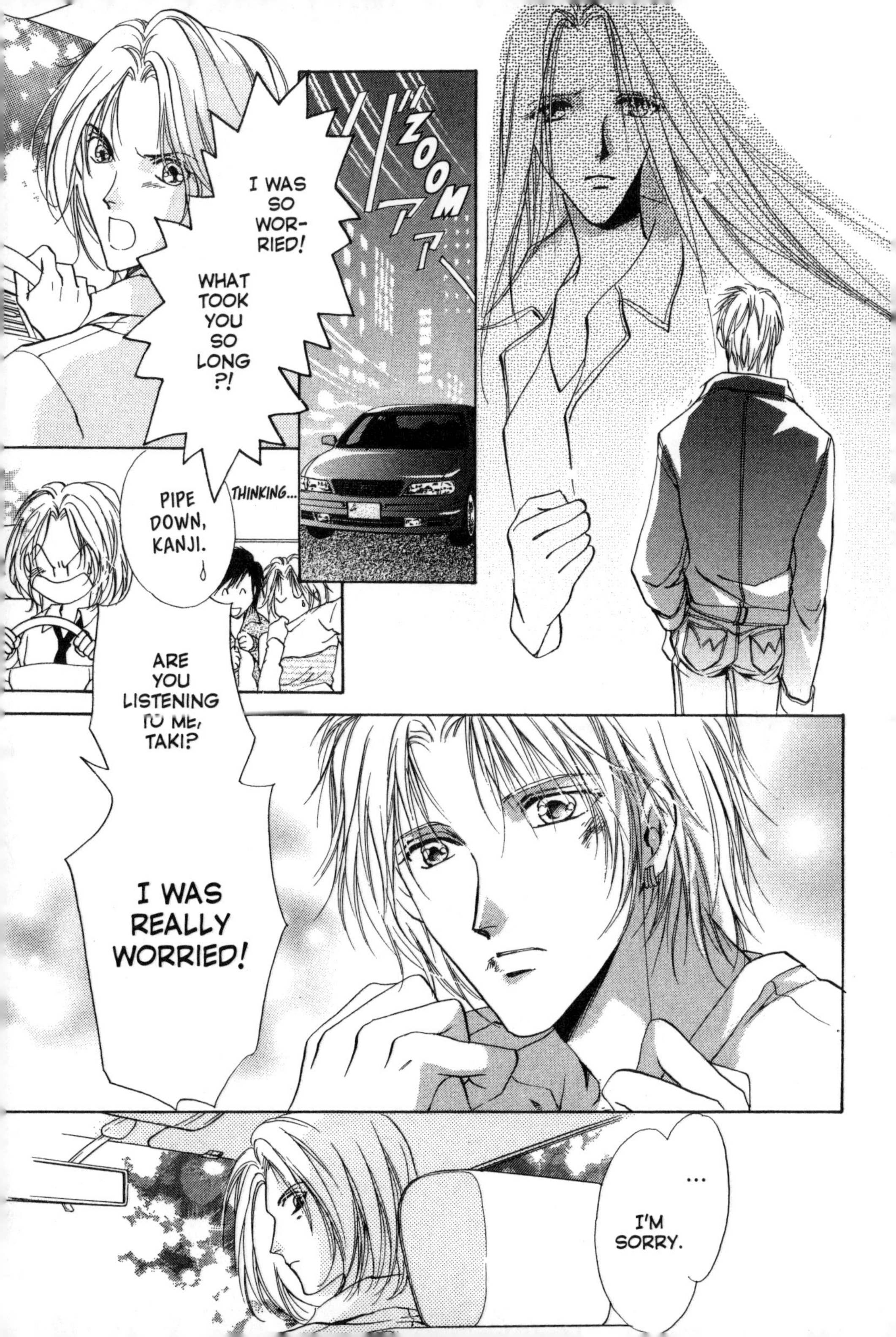
ZOOM
I WAS SO WORRIED!
WHAT TOOK YOU SO LONG?!
THINKING...
PIPE DOWN, KANJI.
ARE YOU LISTENING TO ME, TAKI?
I WAS REALLY WORRIED!
...
I'M SORRY.

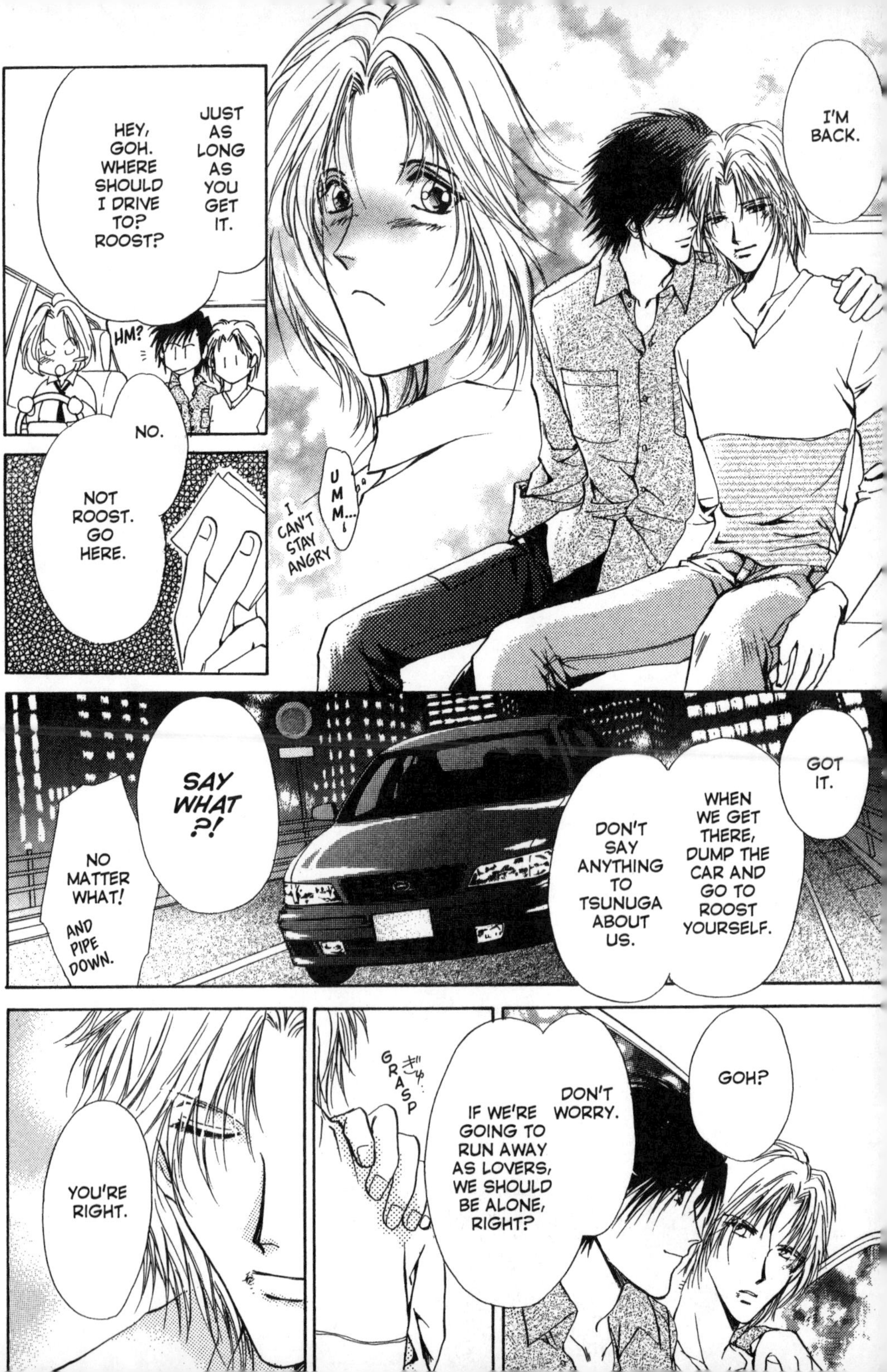
I'M BACK.
UMM...
I CAN'T STAY ANGRY
JUST AS LONG AS YOU GET IT.
HEY, GOH. WHERE SHOULD I DRIVE TO? ROOST?
HM?
NO.
NOT ROOST. GO HERE.
GOT IT.
WHEN WE GET THERE, DUMP THE CAR AND GO TO ROOST YOURSELF.
DON'T SAY ANYTHING TO TSUNUGA ABOUT US.
SAY WHAT?!
NO MATTER WHAT!
AND PIPE DOWN.
GOH?
DON'T WORRY.
IF WE'RE GOING TO RUN AWAY AS LOVERS, WE SHOULD BE ALONE, RIGHT?
ぎゅ
GRASP
YOU'RE RIGHT.

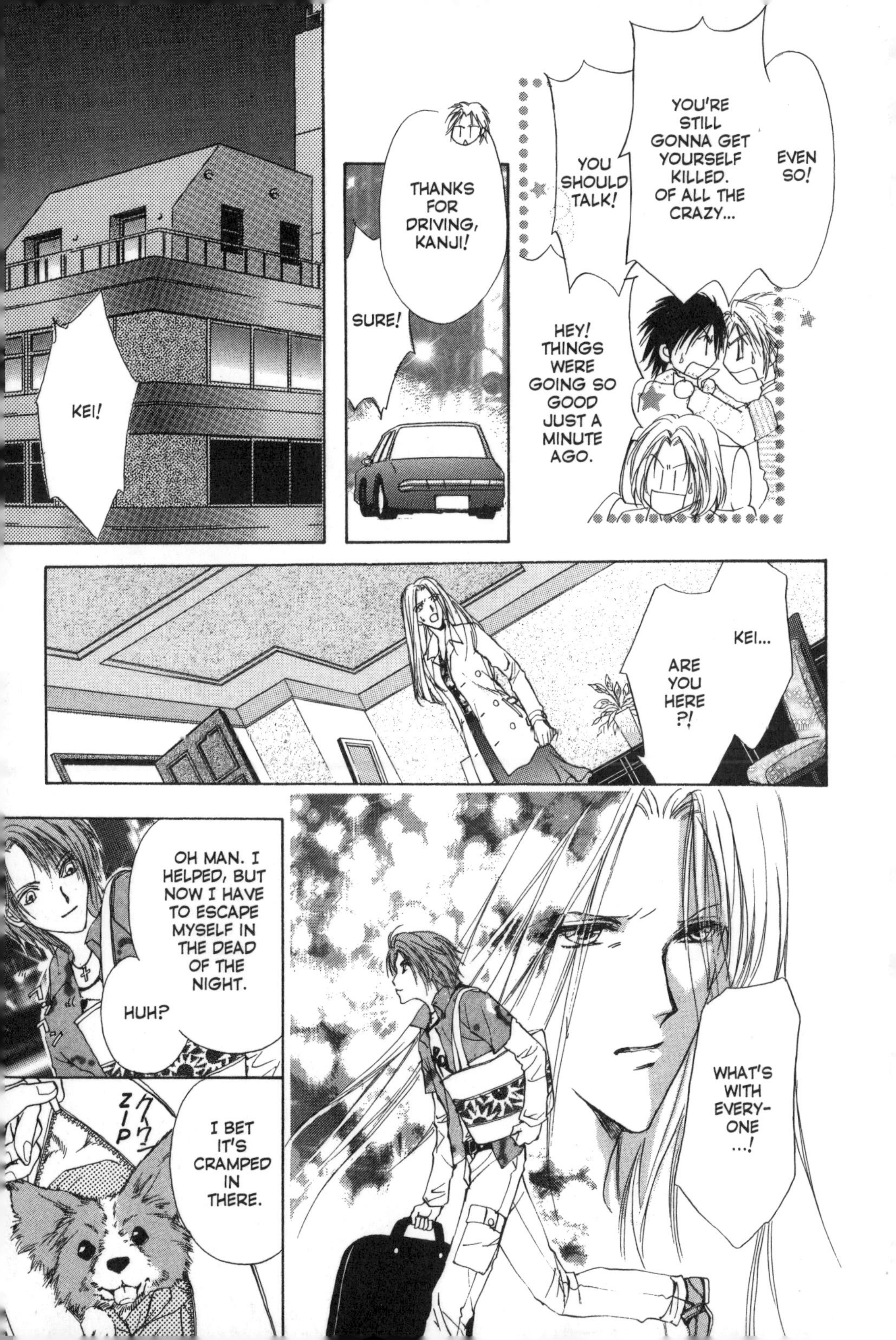
EVEN SO!
YOU'RE STILL GONNA GET YOURSELF KILLED. OF ALL THE CRAZY...
YOU SHOULD TALK!
HEY! THINGS WERE GOING SO GOOD JUST A MINUTE AGO.
THANKS FOR DRIVING, KANJI!
SURE!
KEI!
KEI...
ARE YOU HERE?!
WHAT'S WITH EVERY-ONE ...!
OH MAN. I HELPED, BUT NOW I HAVE TO ESCAPE MYSELF IN THE DEAD OF THE NIGHT.
HUH?
ZIP
I BET IT'S CRAMPED IN THERE.

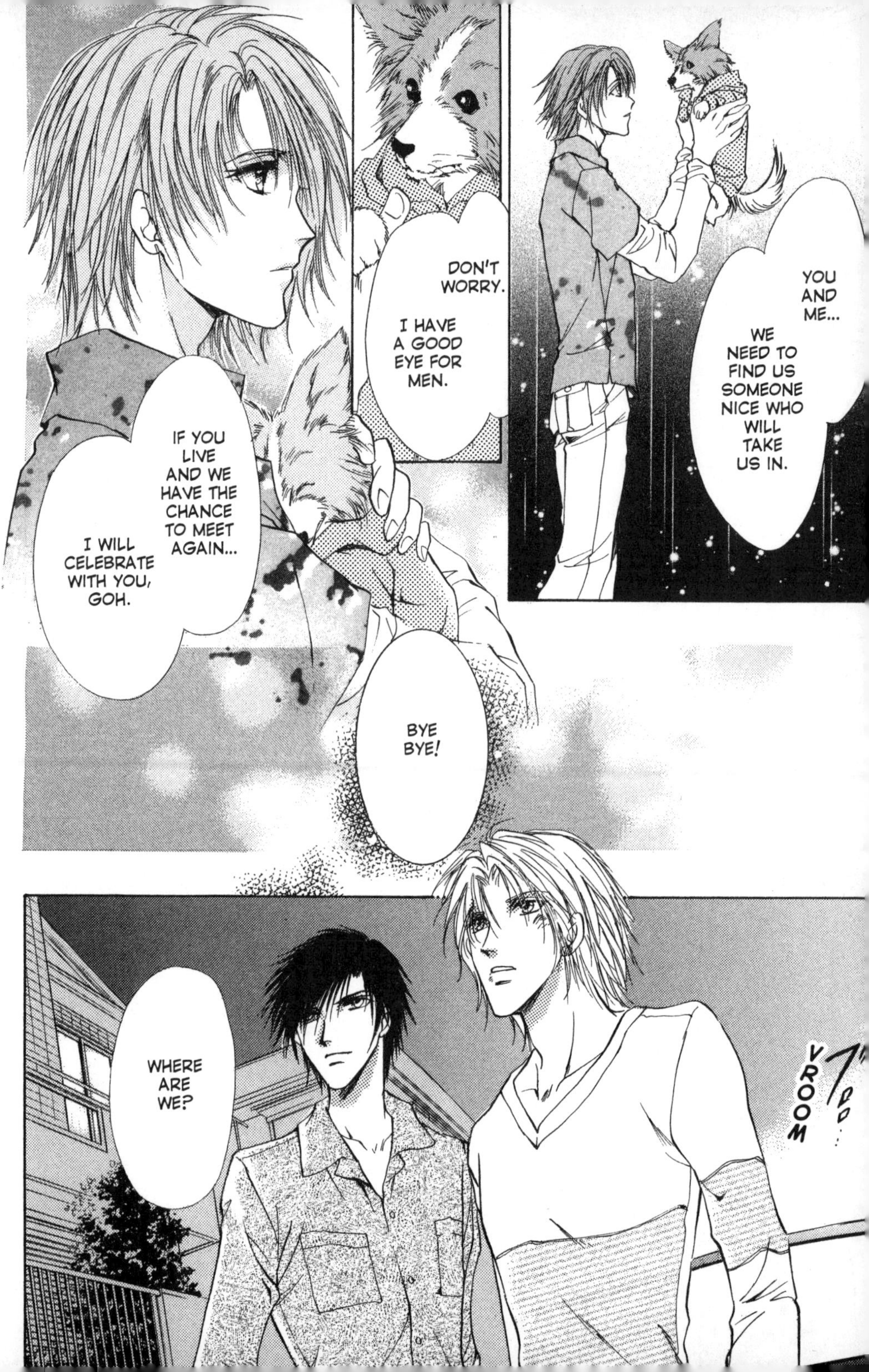
YOU AND ME... WE NEED TO FIND US SOMEONE NICE WHO WILL TAKE US IN.
DON'T WORRY.
I HAVE A GOOD EYE FOR MEN.
IF YOU LIVE AND WE HAVE THE CHANCE TO MEET AGAIN...
I WILL CELEBRATE WITH YOU, GOH.
BYE BYE!
VROOM
WHERE ARE WE?

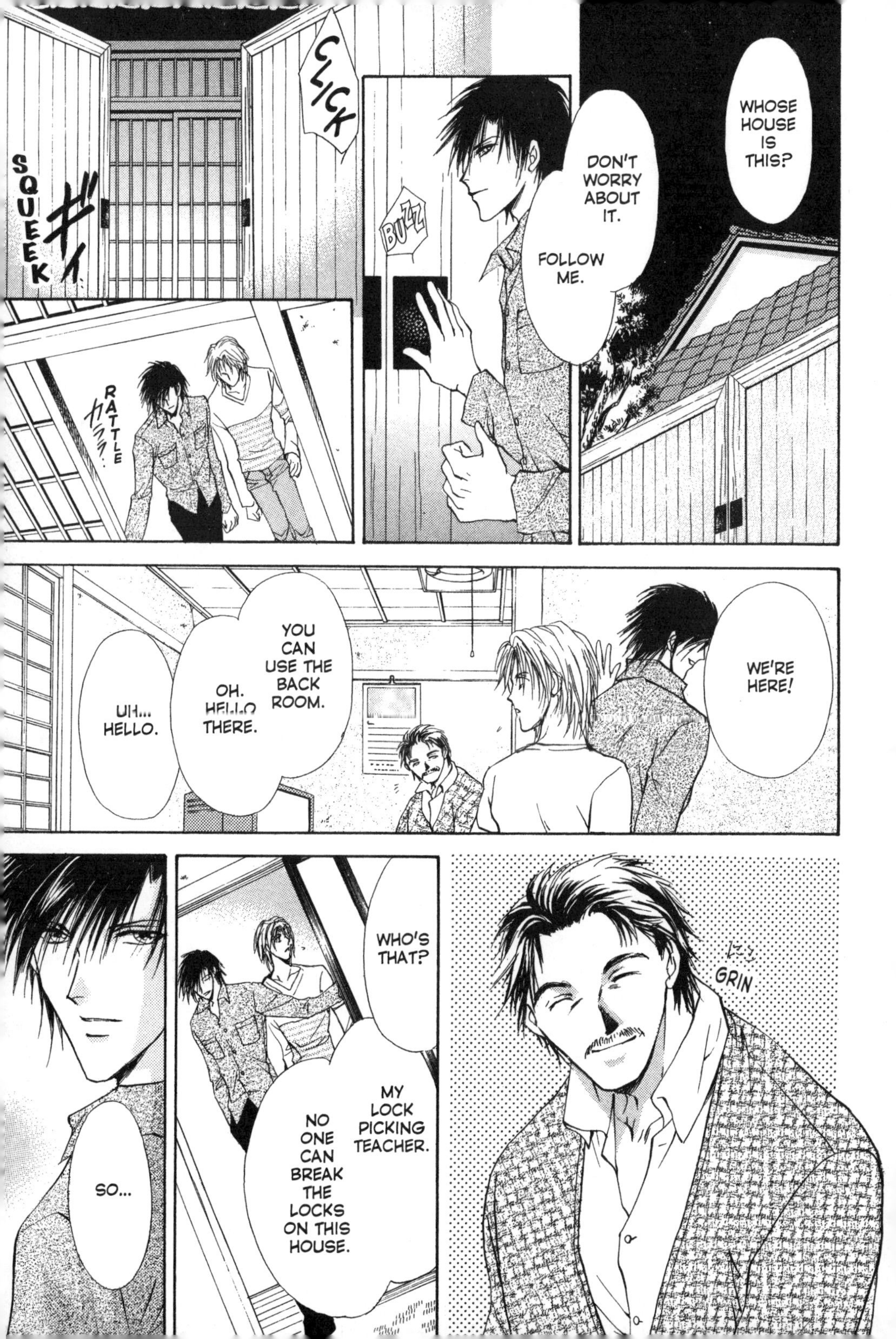
WHOSE HOUSE IS THIS?
BUZZ
DON'T WORRY ABOUT IT.
FOLLOW ME.
CLICK
SQUEEK
RATTLE
WE'RE HERE!
YOU CAN USE THE BACK ROOM.
OH. HELLO THERE.
UH... HELLO.
GRIN
WHO'S THAT?
MY LOCK PICKING TEACHER.
NO ONE CAN BREAK THE LOCKS ON THIS HOUSE.
SO...

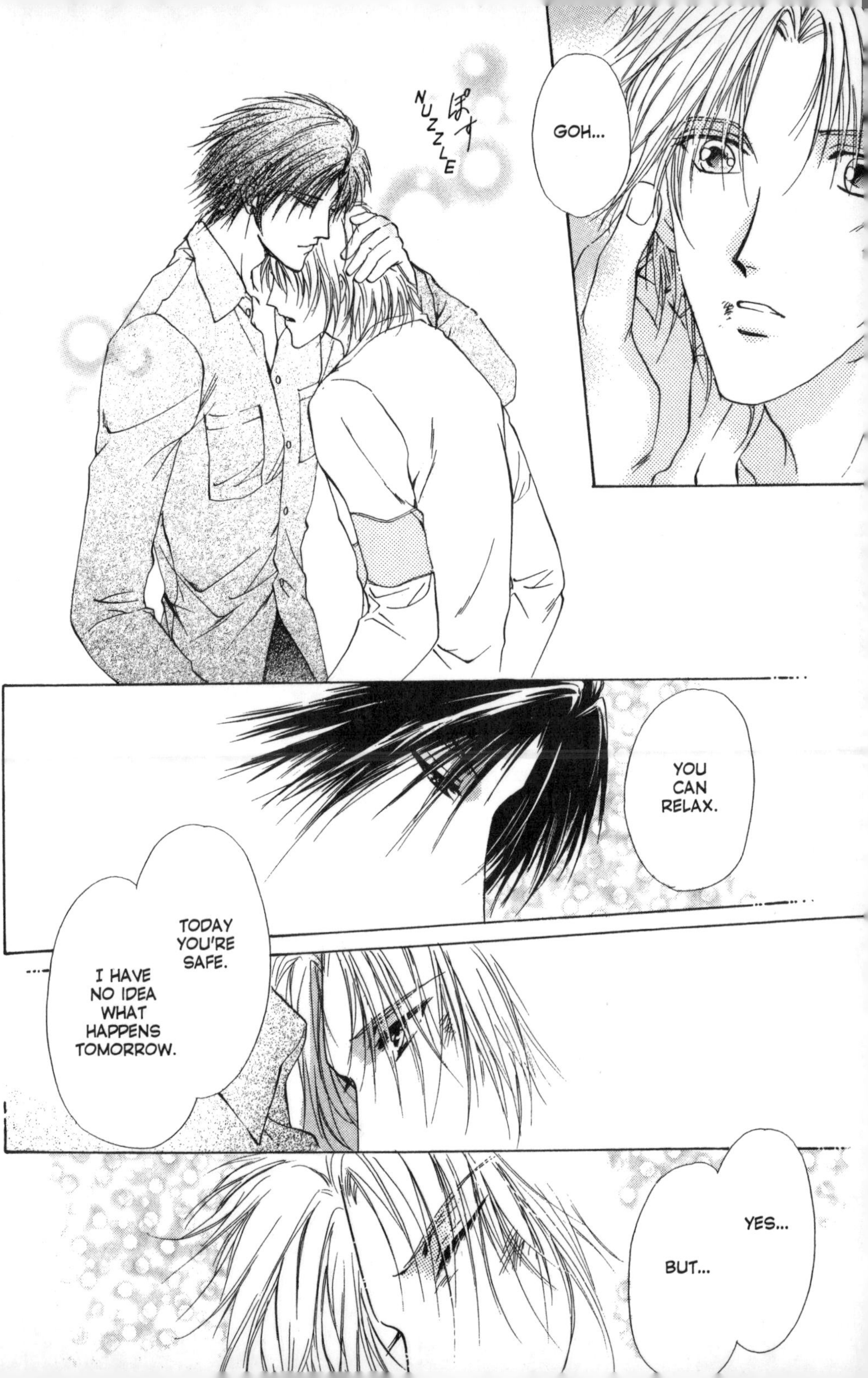
GOH...
ぽす
NUZZLE
YOU CAN RELAX.
TODAY YOU'RE SAFE.
I HAVE NO IDEA WHAT HAPPENS TOMORROW.
YES...
BUT...

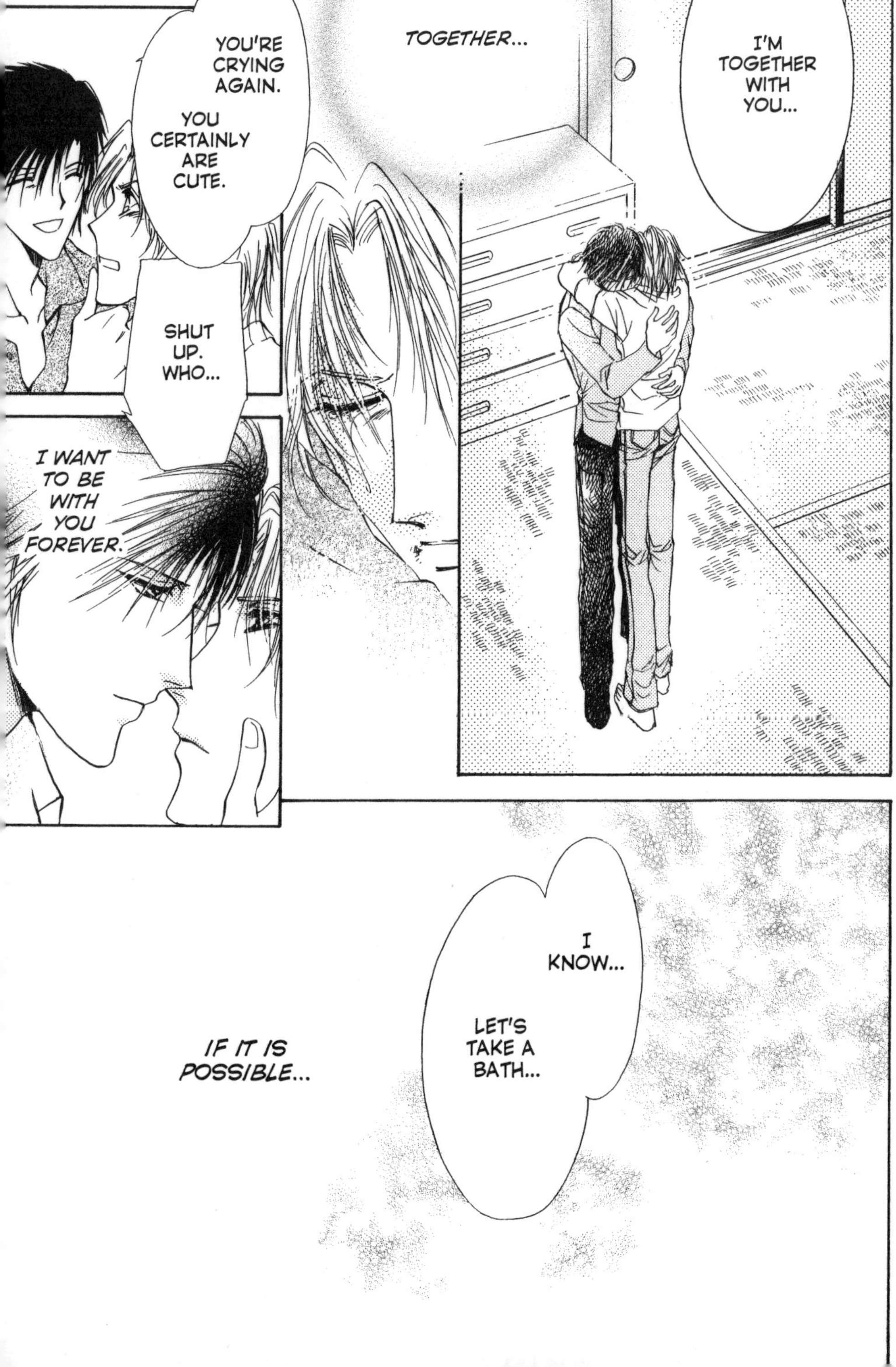
I'M TOGETHER WITH YOU...
TOGETHER...
YOU'RE CRYING AGAIN.
YOU CERTAINLY ARE CUTE.
SHUT UP. WHO...
I WANT TO BE WITH YOU FOREVER.
I KNOW...
LET'S TAKE A BATH...
IF IT IS POSSIBLE...

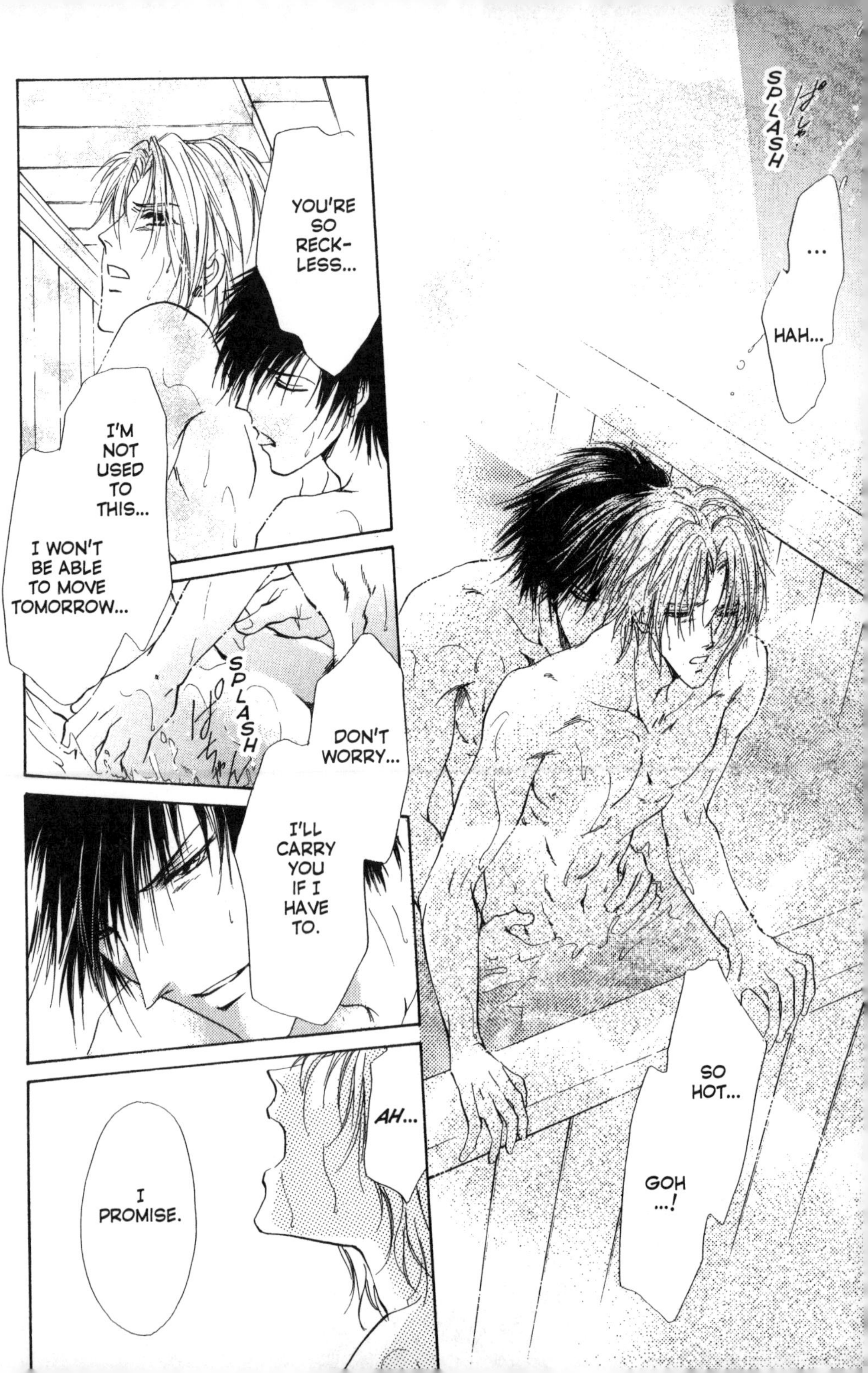
SPLASH
...
HAH...
SO HOT...
GOH ...!
YOU'RE SO RECKLESS...
I'M NOT USED TO THIS...
I WON'T BE ABLE TO MOVE TOMORROW...
SPLASH
DON'T WORRY...
I'LL CARRY YOU IF I HAVE TO.
AH...
I PROMISE.

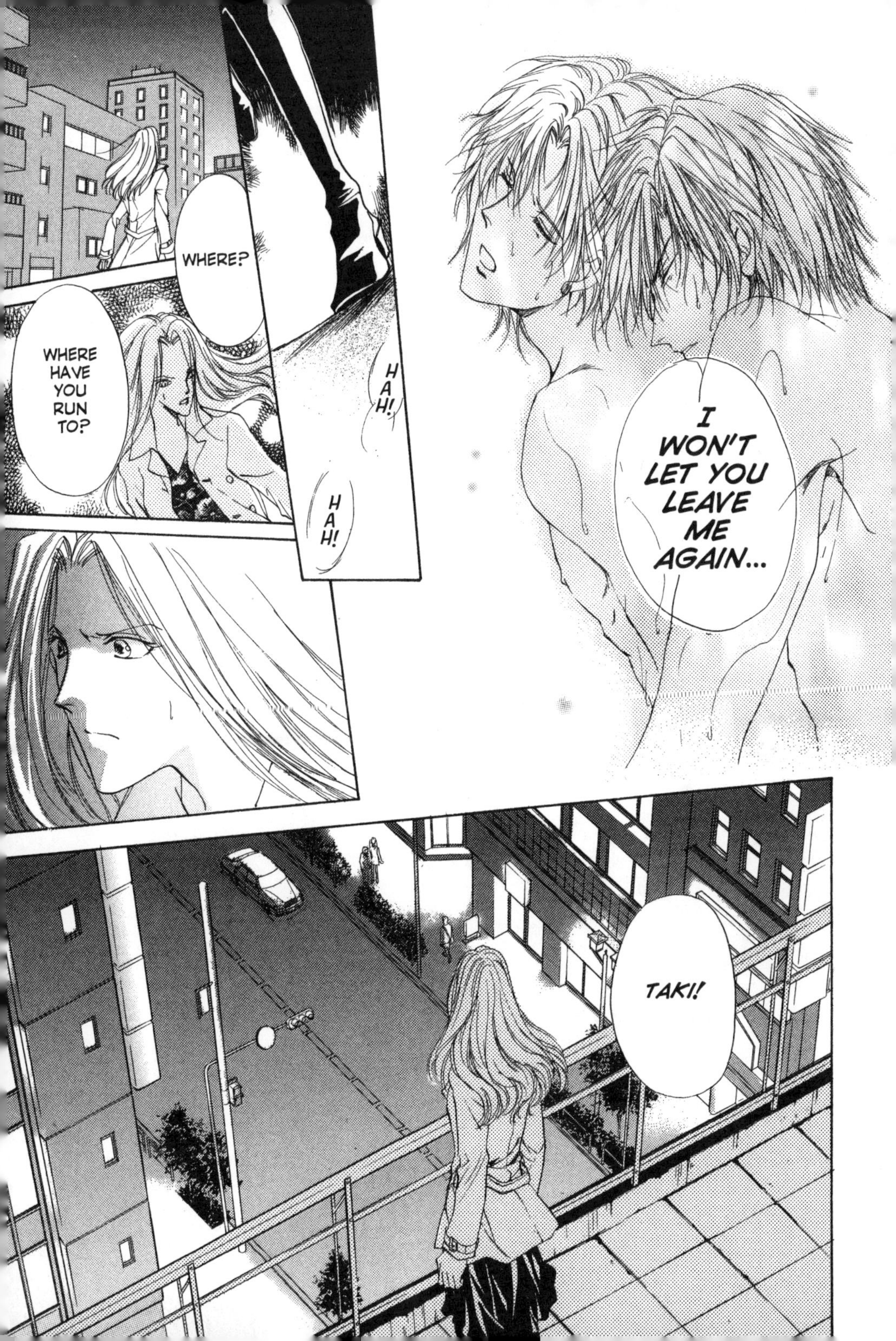
I WON'T LET YOU LEAVE ME AGAIN...
HAH!
HAH!
WHERE?
WHERE HAVE YOU RUN TO?
TAKI!

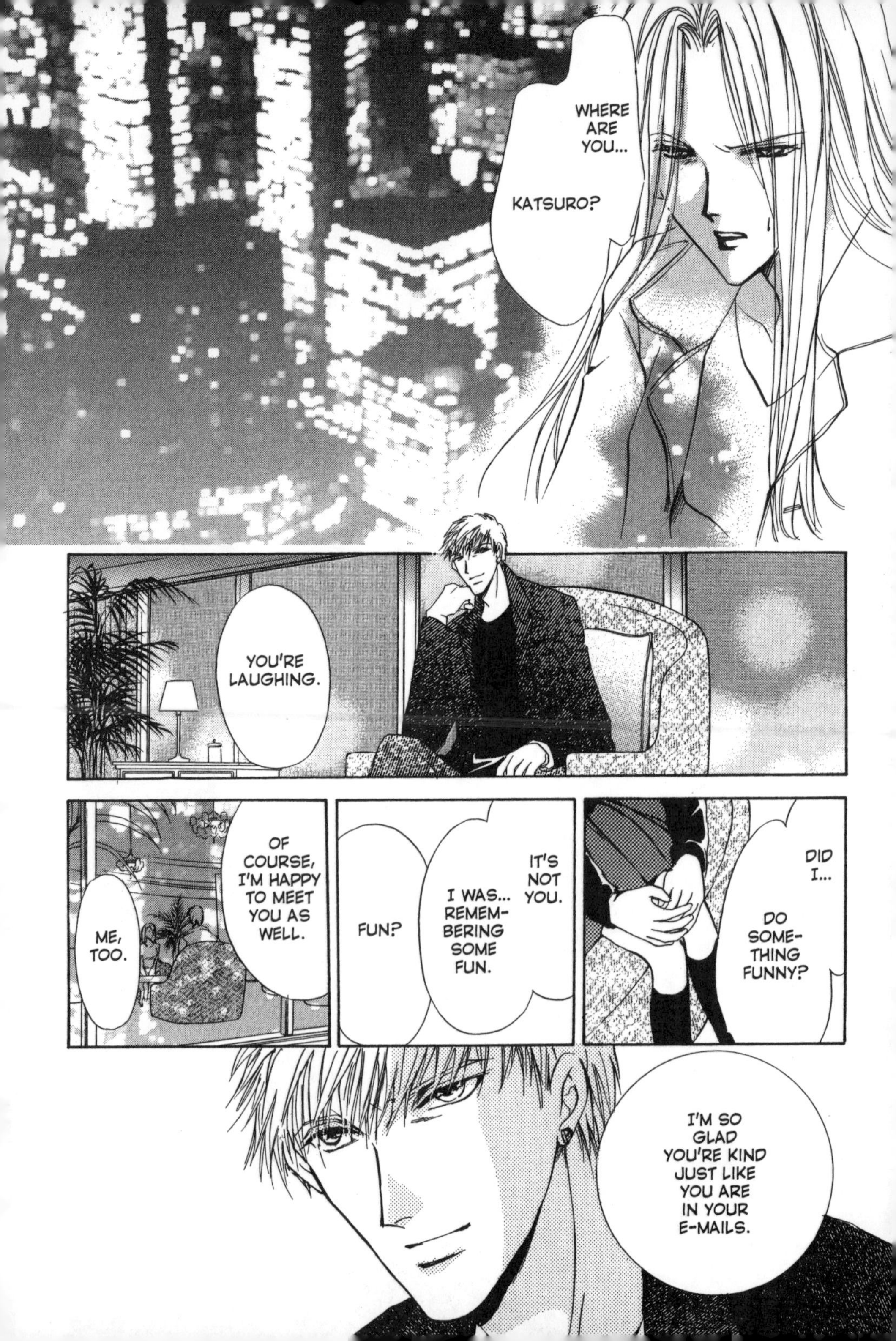
WHERE ARE YOU...
KATSURO?
YOU'RE LAUGHING.
DID I...
DO SOMETHING FUNNY?
IT'S NOT YOU.
I WAS... REMEMBERING SOME FUN.
FUN?
OF COURSE, I'M HAPPY TO MEET YOU AS WELL.
ME, TOO.
I'M SO GLAD YOU'RE KIND JUST LIKE YOU ARE IN YOUR E-MAILS.

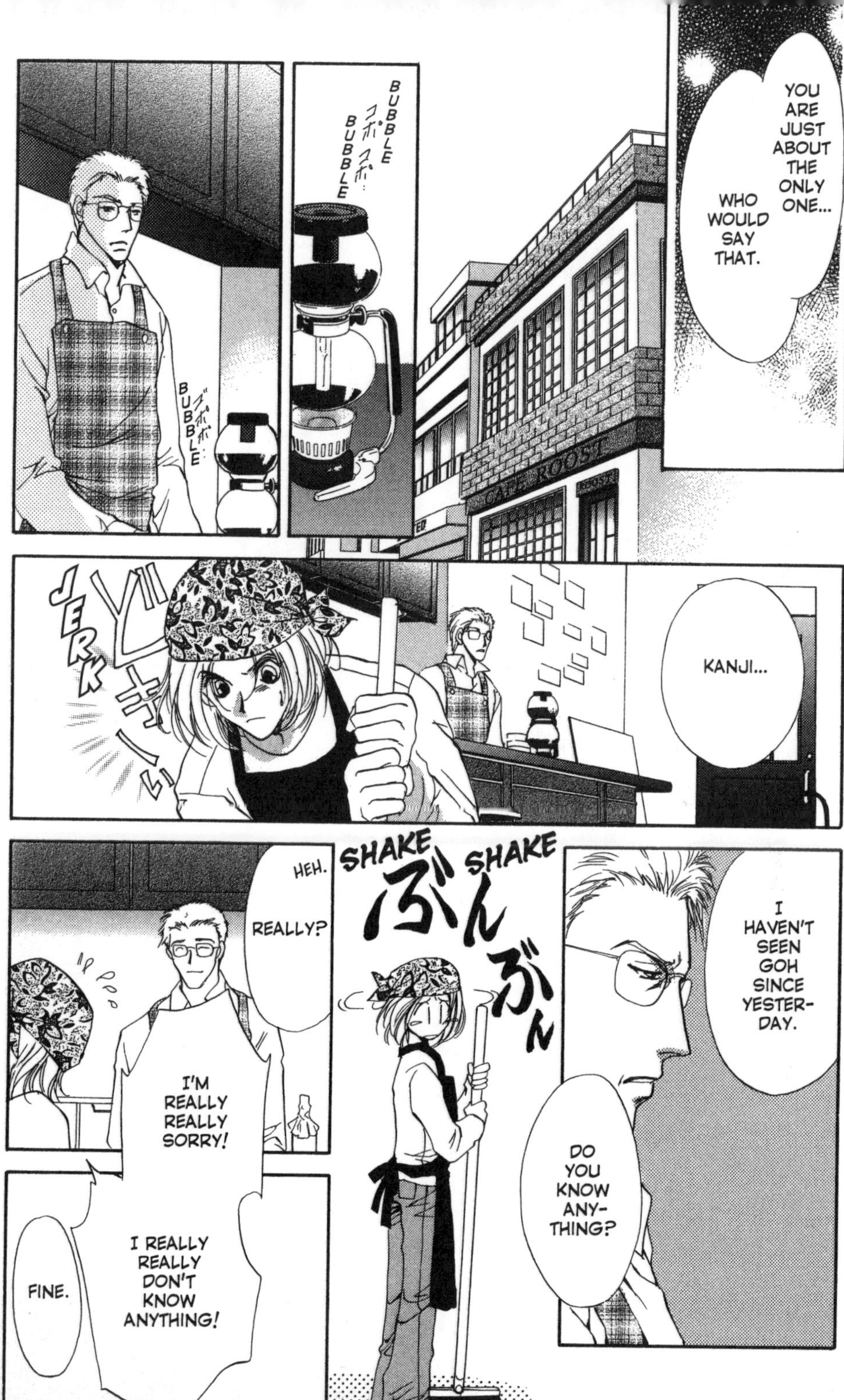
YOU ARE JUST ABOUT THE ONLY ONE...
WHO WOULD SAY THAT.
CAFE ROOST
BUBBLE コポ コポ BUBBLE
BUBBLE BUBBLE
KANJI...
JERK
I HAVEN'T SEEN GOH SINCE YESTER-DAY.
DO YOU KNOW ANY-THING?
SHAKE SHAKE
ぶんぶん
HEH.
REALLY?
I'M REALLY REALLY SORRY!
I REALLY REALLY DON'T KNOW ANYTHING!
FINE.

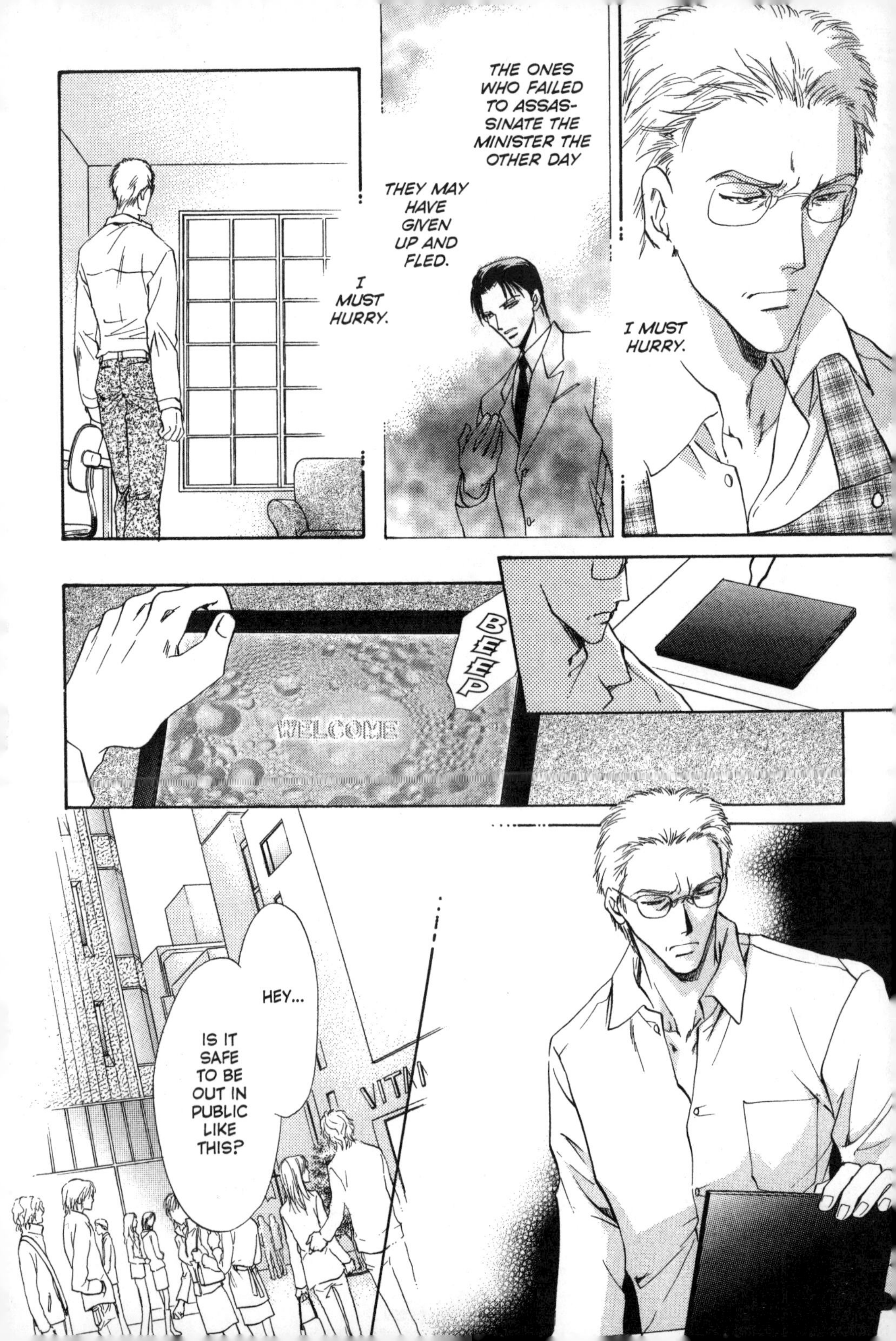
I MUST HURRY.
THE ONES WHO FAILED TO ASSAS-SINATE THE MINISTER THE OTHER DAY
THEY MAY HAVE GIVEN UP AND FLED.
I MUST HURRY.
BEEP
WELCOME
HEY...
IS IT SAFE TO BE OUT IN PUBLIC LIKE THIS?

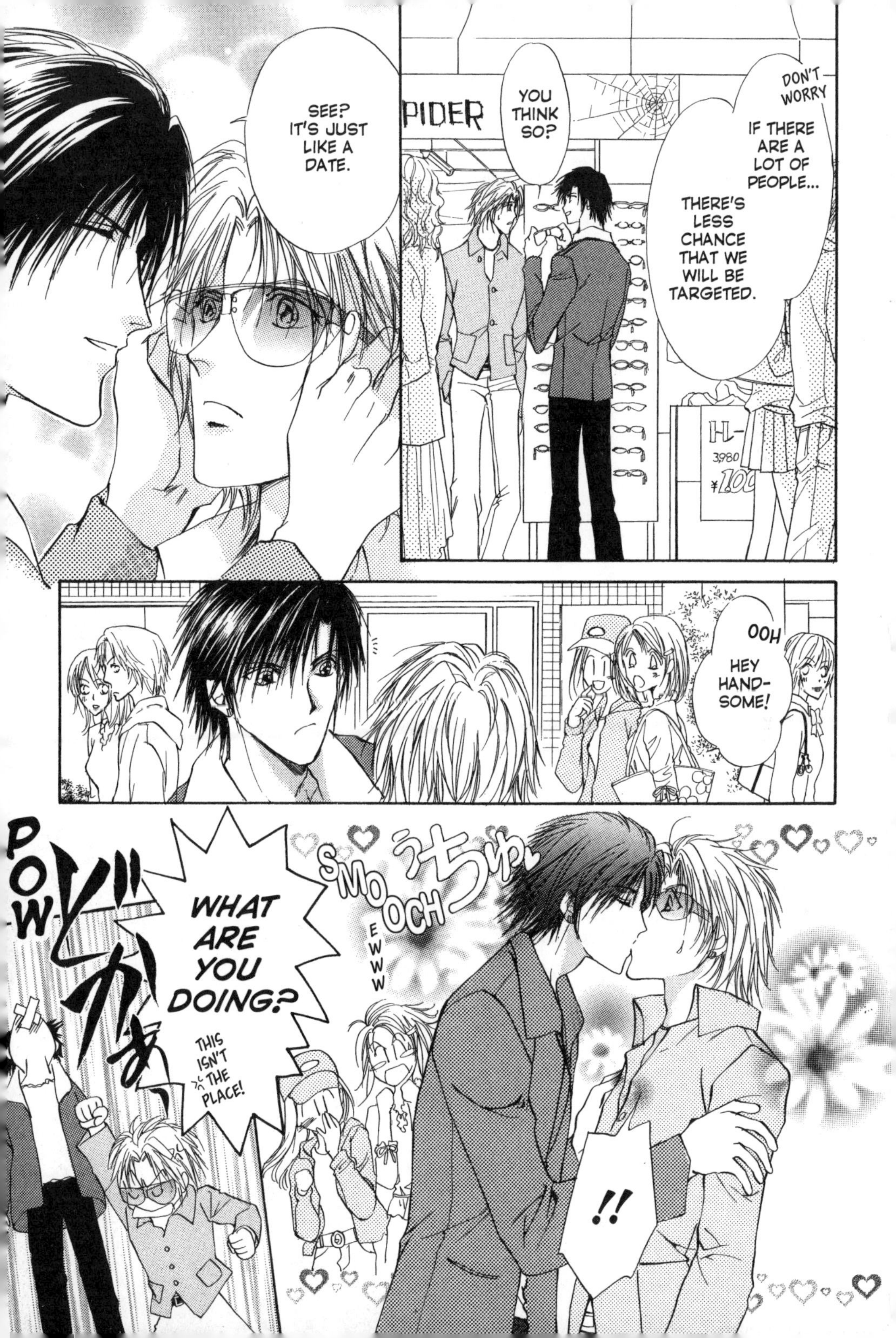
DON'T WORRY
IF THERE ARE A LOT OF PEOPLE...
THERE'S LESS CHANCE THAT WE WILL BE TARGETED.
YOU THINK SO?
PIDER
SEE? IT'S JUST LIKE A DATE.
OOH
HEY HAND-SOME!
SMOOCH
EWWW
!!
POW
WHAT ARE YOU DOING?
THIS ISN'T THE PLACE!

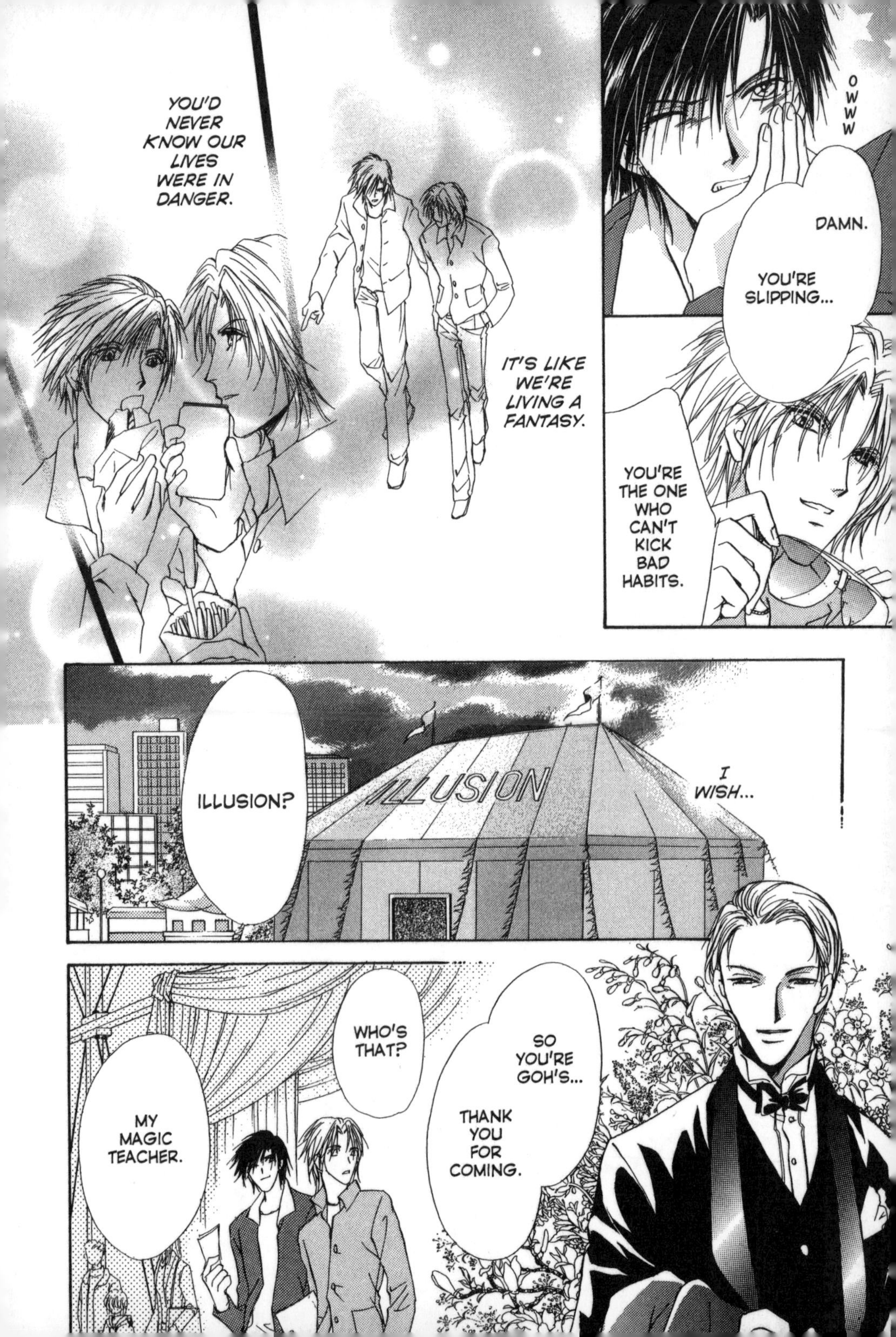
OWWW
DAMN.
YOU'RE SLIPPING...
YOU'RE THE ONE WHO CAN'T KICK BAD HABITS.
YOU'D NEVER KNOW OUR LIVES WERE IN DANGER.
IT'S LIKE WE'RE LIVING A FANTASY.
I WISH...
ILLUSION
ILLUSION?
SO YOU'RE GOH'S...
THANK YOU FOR COMING.
WHO'S THAT?
MY MAGIC TEACHER.

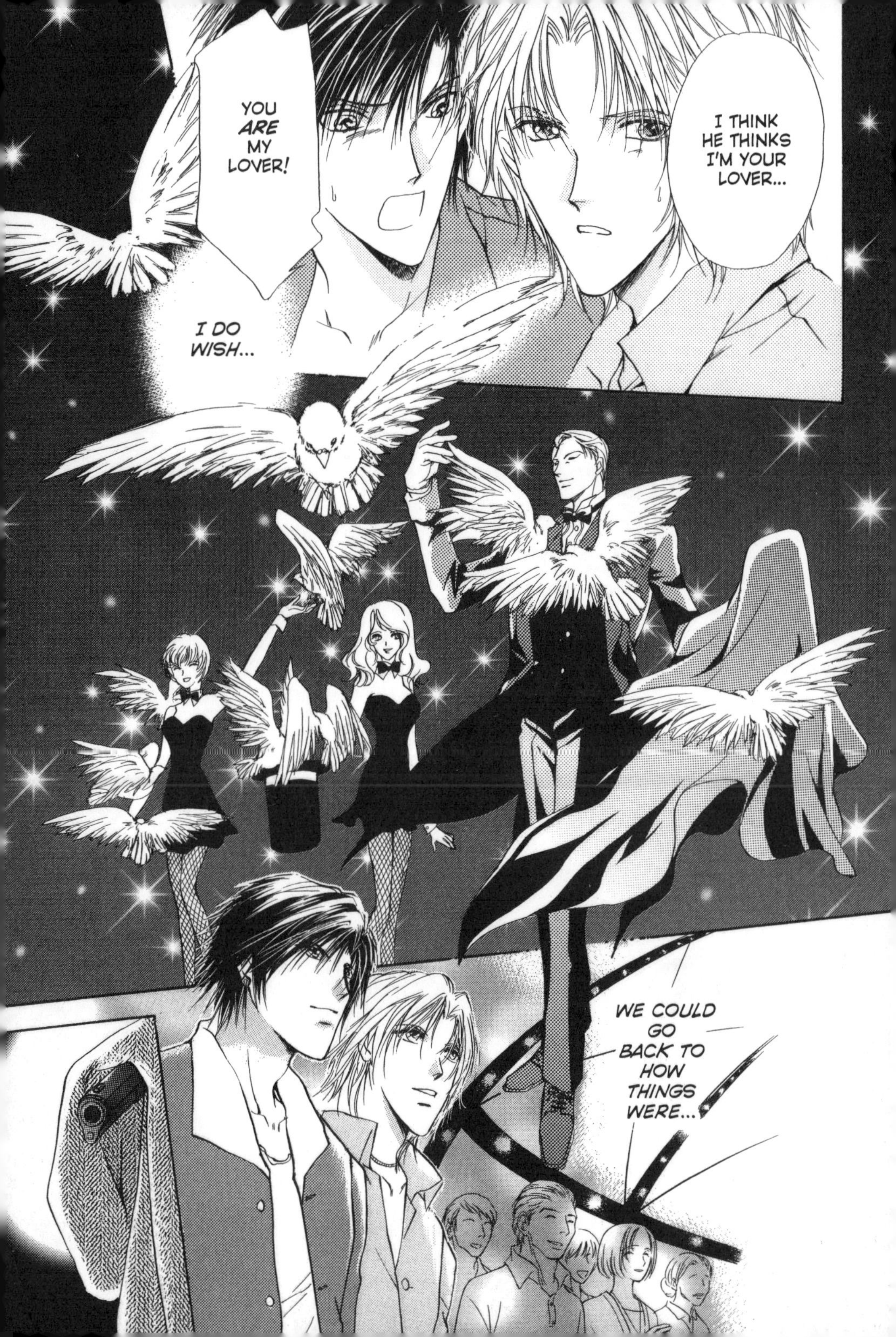
I THINK HE THINKS I'M YOUR LOVER...
YOU *ARE* MY LOVER!
I DO WISH...
WE COULD GO BACK TO HOW THINGS WERE...

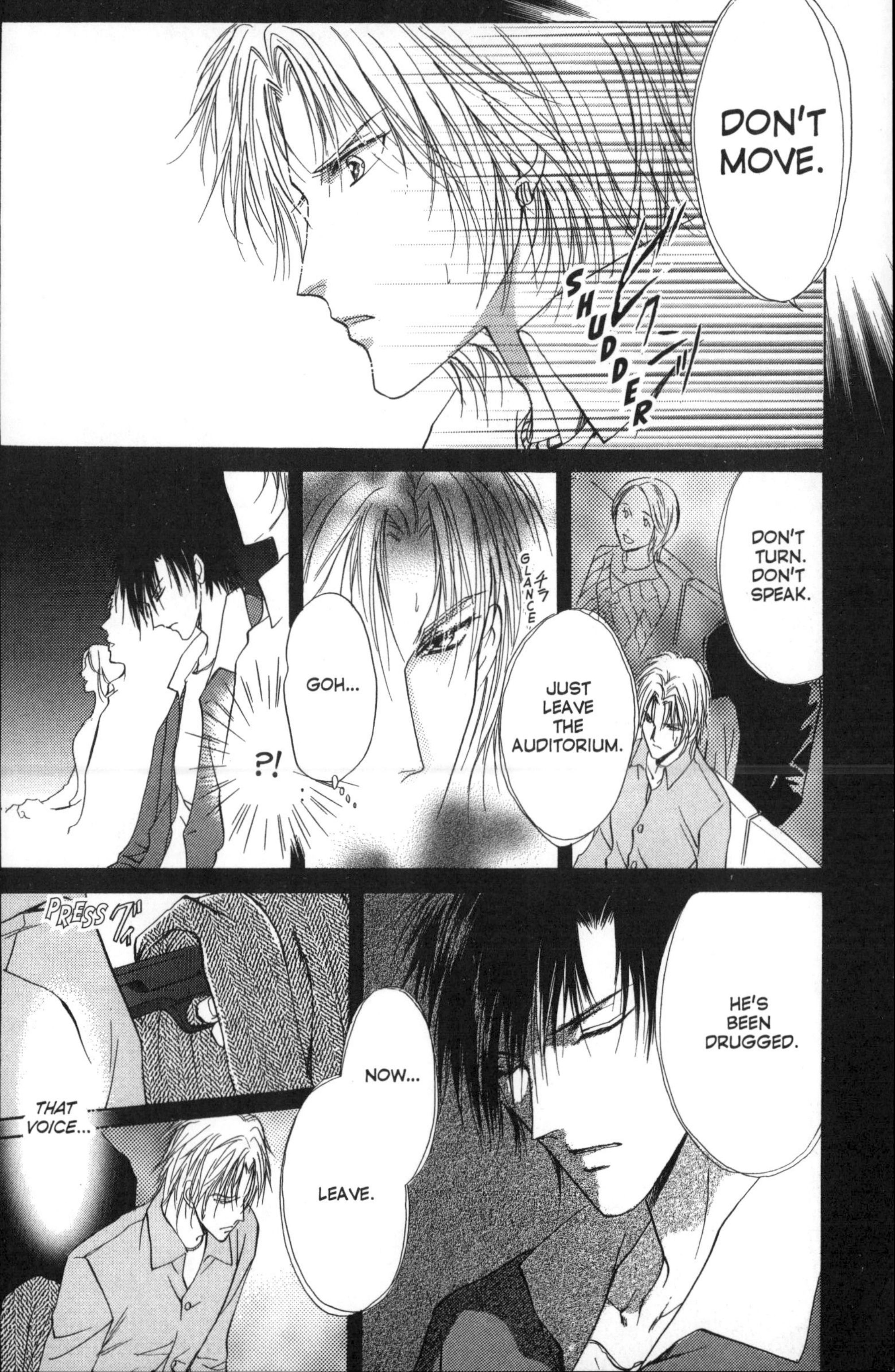
DON'T MOVE.
SHUDDER
DON'T TURN. DON'T SPEAK.
JUST LEAVE THE AUDITORIUM.
GLANCE
GOH...
?!
HE'S BEEN DRUGGED.
NOW...
LEAVE.
PRESS
THAT VOICE...

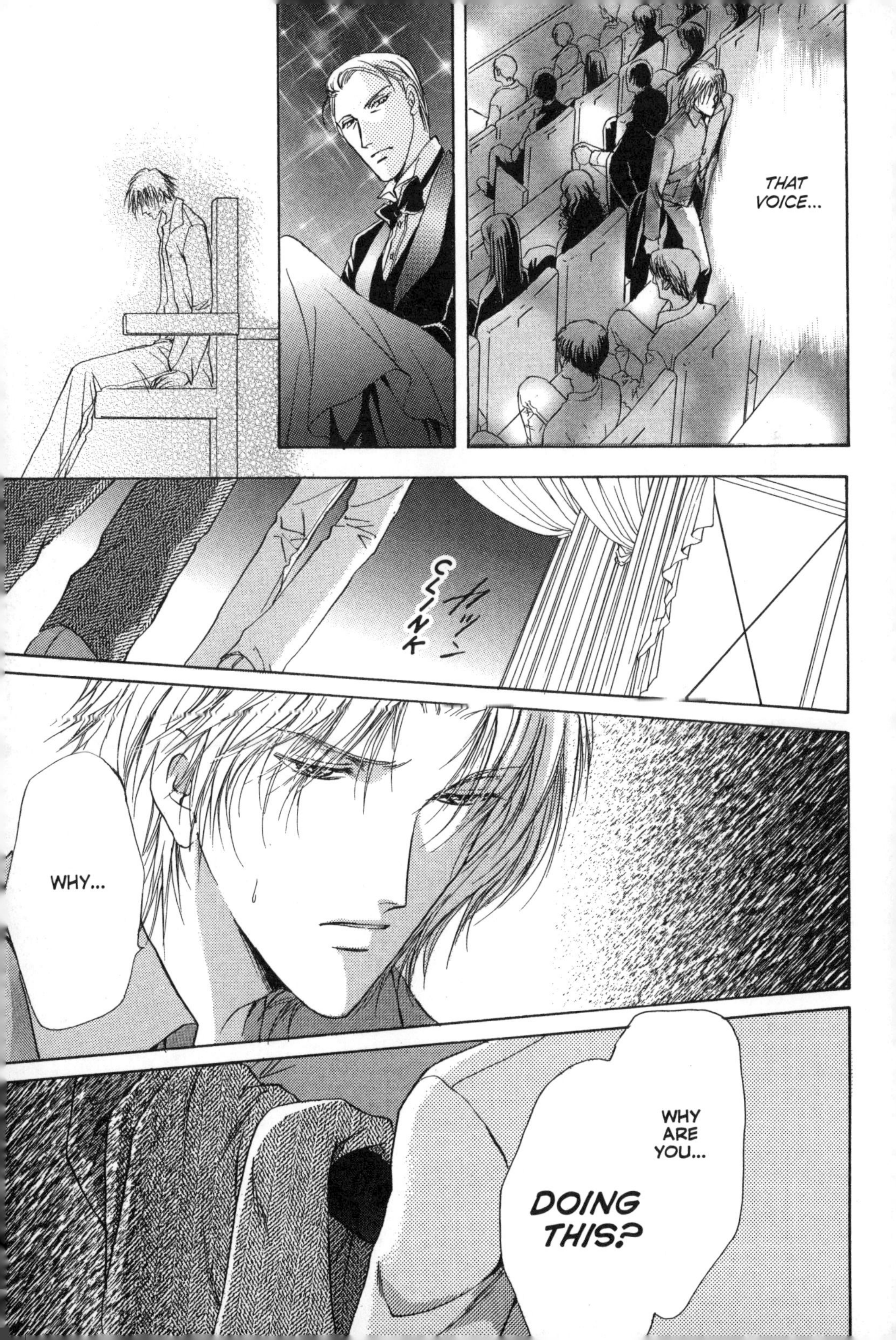
THAT VOICE...
CLINK
WHY...
WHY ARE YOU...
DOING THIS?

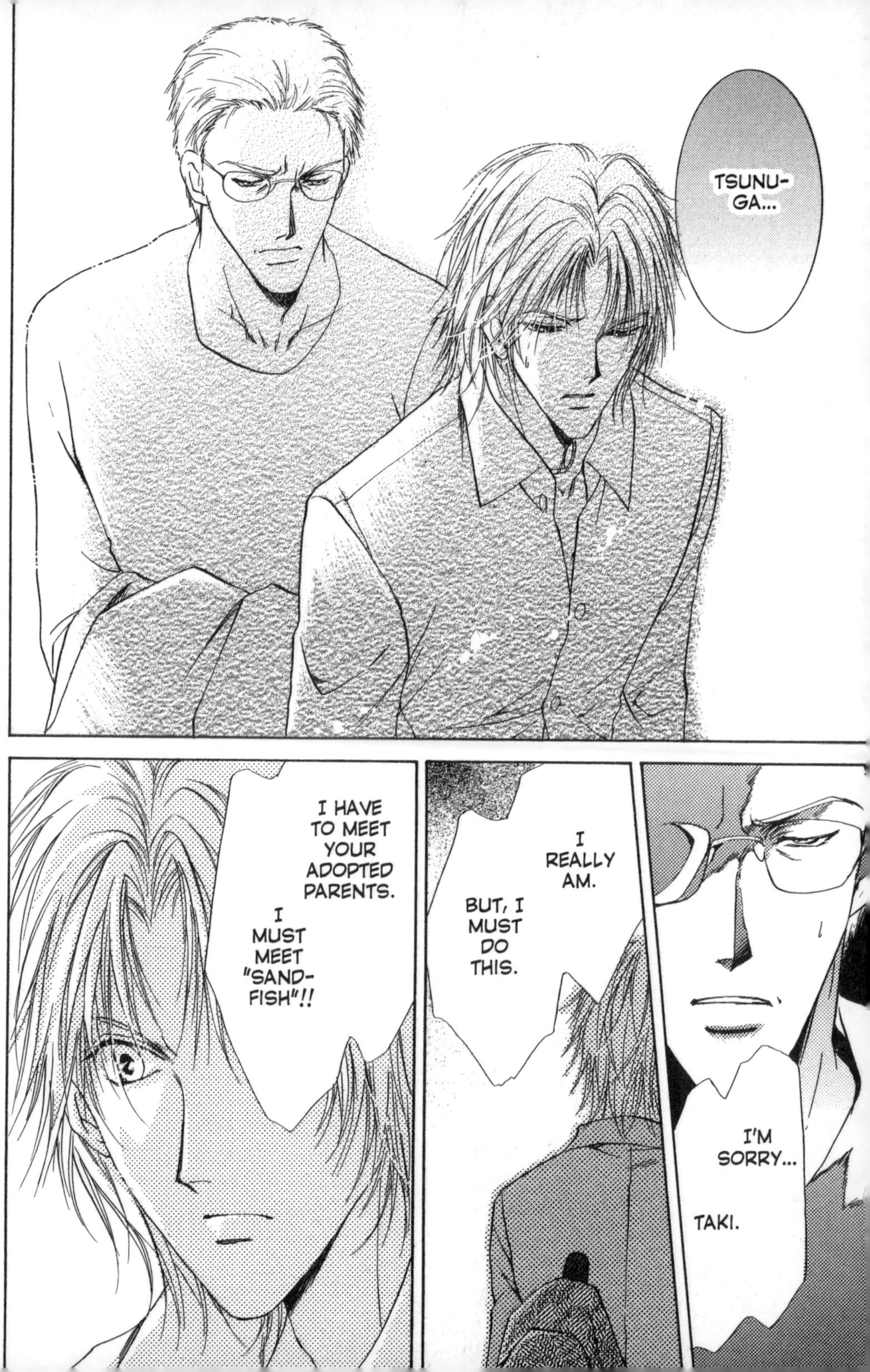
TSUNU-GA...
I'M SORRY...
TAKI.
I REALLY AM.
BUT, I MUST DO THIS.
I HAVE TO MEET YOUR ADOPTED PARENTS.
I MUST MEET "SAND-FISH"!!

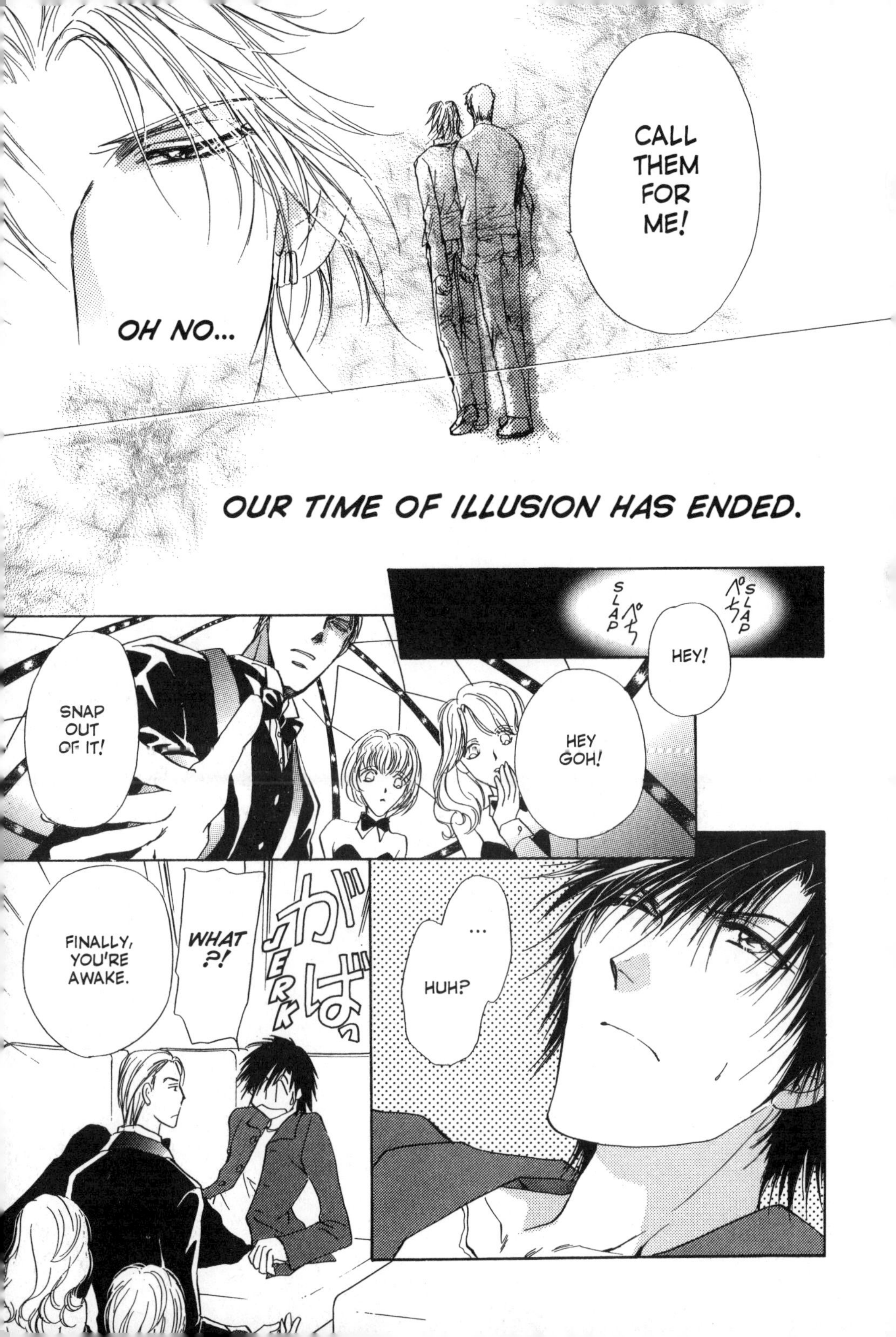
CALL THEM FOR ME!
OH NO...
OUR TIME OF ILLUSION HAS ENDED.
SLAP ぺち
SLAP ぺち
HEY!
HEY GOH!
SNAP OUT OF IT!
...
HUH?
JERK
がばっ
WHAT?!
FINALLY, YOU'RE AWAKE.

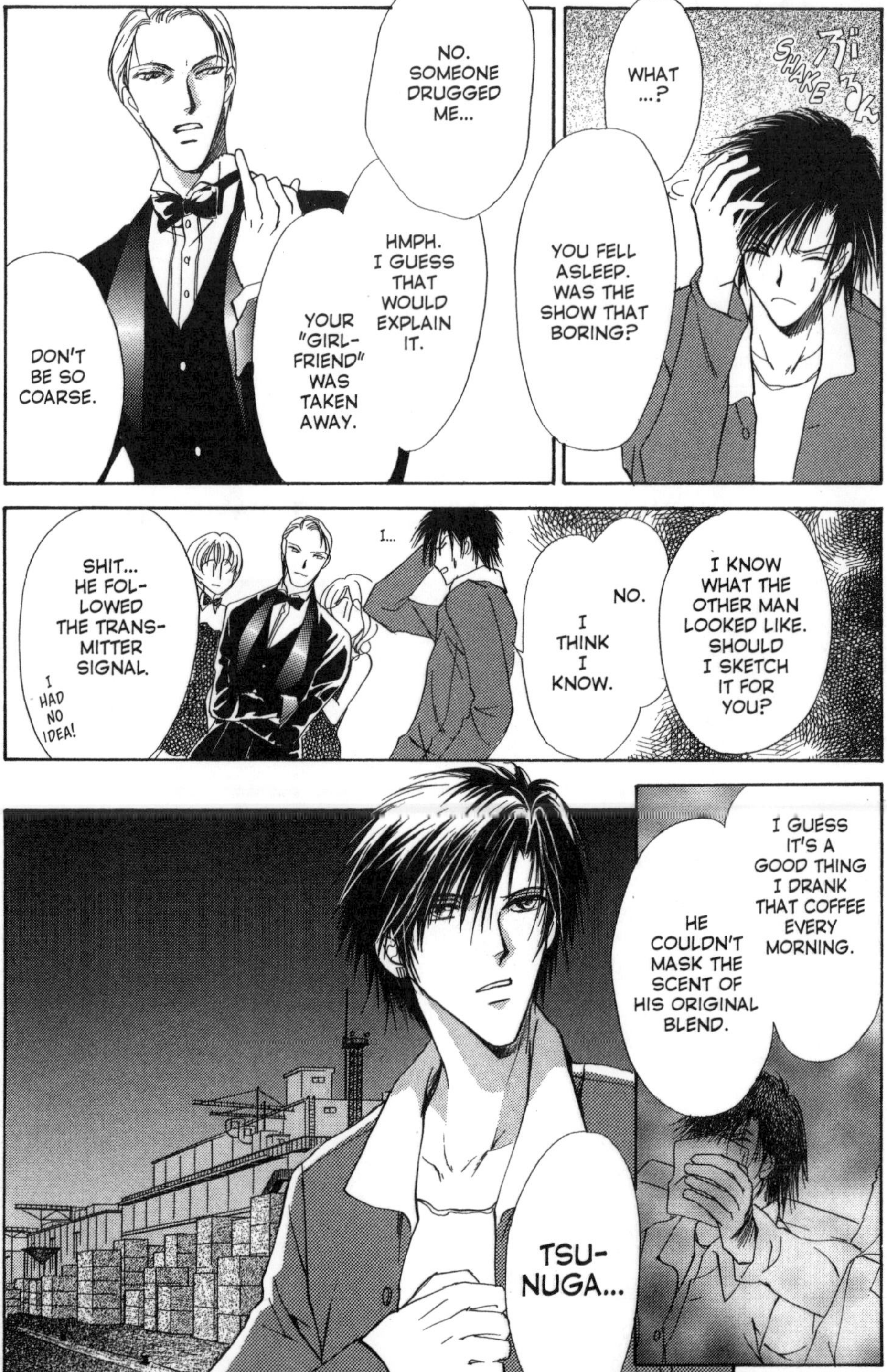
SHAKE
WHAT ...?
YOU FELL ASLEEP. WAS THE SHOW THAT BORING?
NO. SOMEONE DRUGGED ME...
HMPH. I GUESS THAT WOULD EXPLAIN IT.
YOUR "GIRL-FRIEND" WAS TAKEN AWAY.
DON'T BE SO COARSE.
I KNOW WHAT THE OTHER MAN LOOKED LIKE. SHOULD I SKETCH IT FOR YOU?
NO.
I THINK I KNOW.
I...
SHIT... HE FOL-LOWED THE TRANS-MITTER SIGNAL.
I HAD NO IDEA!
I GUESS IT'S A GOOD THING I DRANK THAT COFFEE EVERY MORNING.
HE COULDN'T MASK THE SCENT OF HIS ORIGINAL BLEND.
TSU-NUGA...

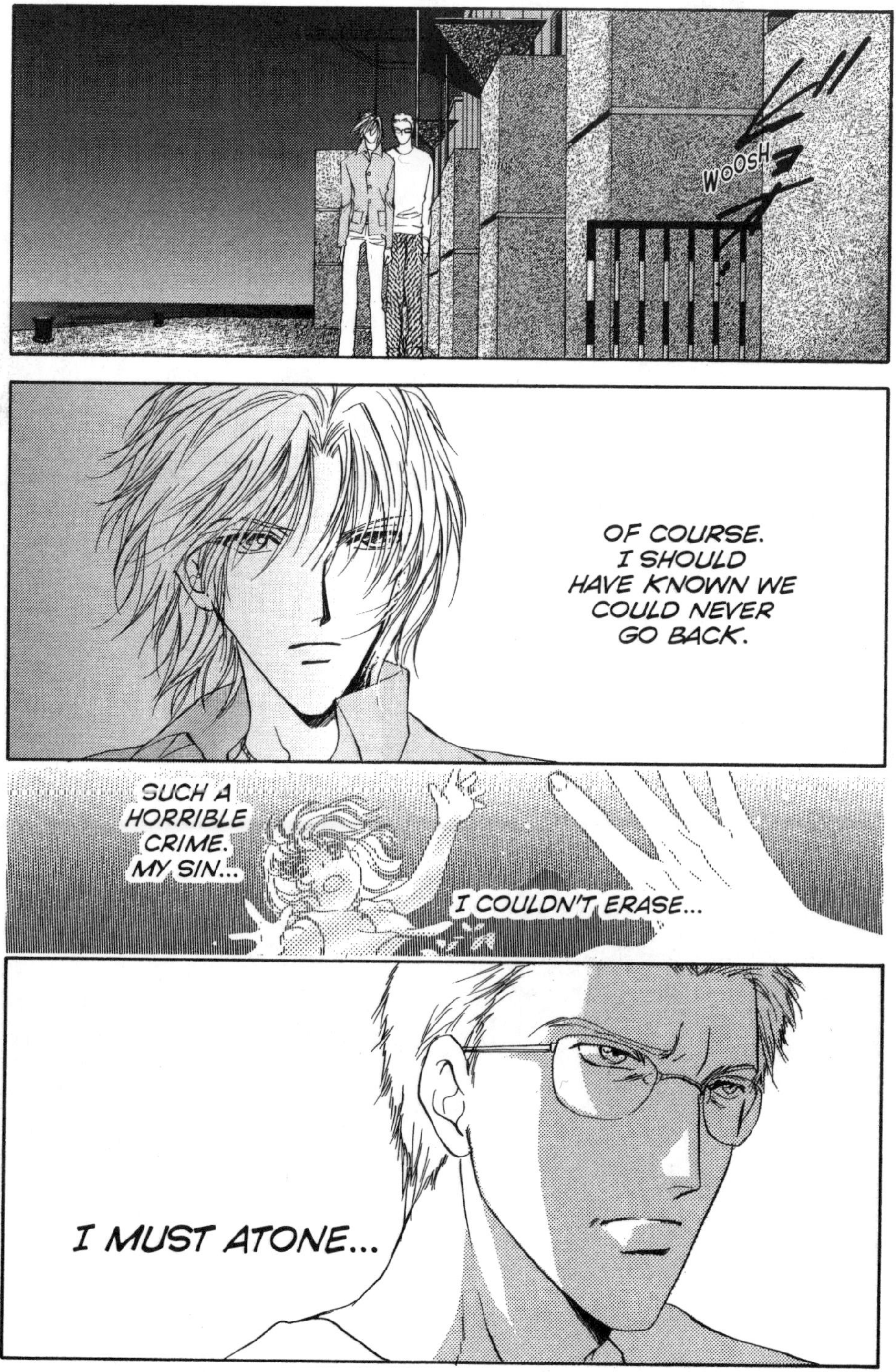
WOOSH
OF COURSE. I SHOULD HAVE KNOWN WE COULD NEVER GO BACK.
SUCH A HORRIBLE CRIME. MY SIN...
I COULDN'T ERASE...
I MUST ATONE...

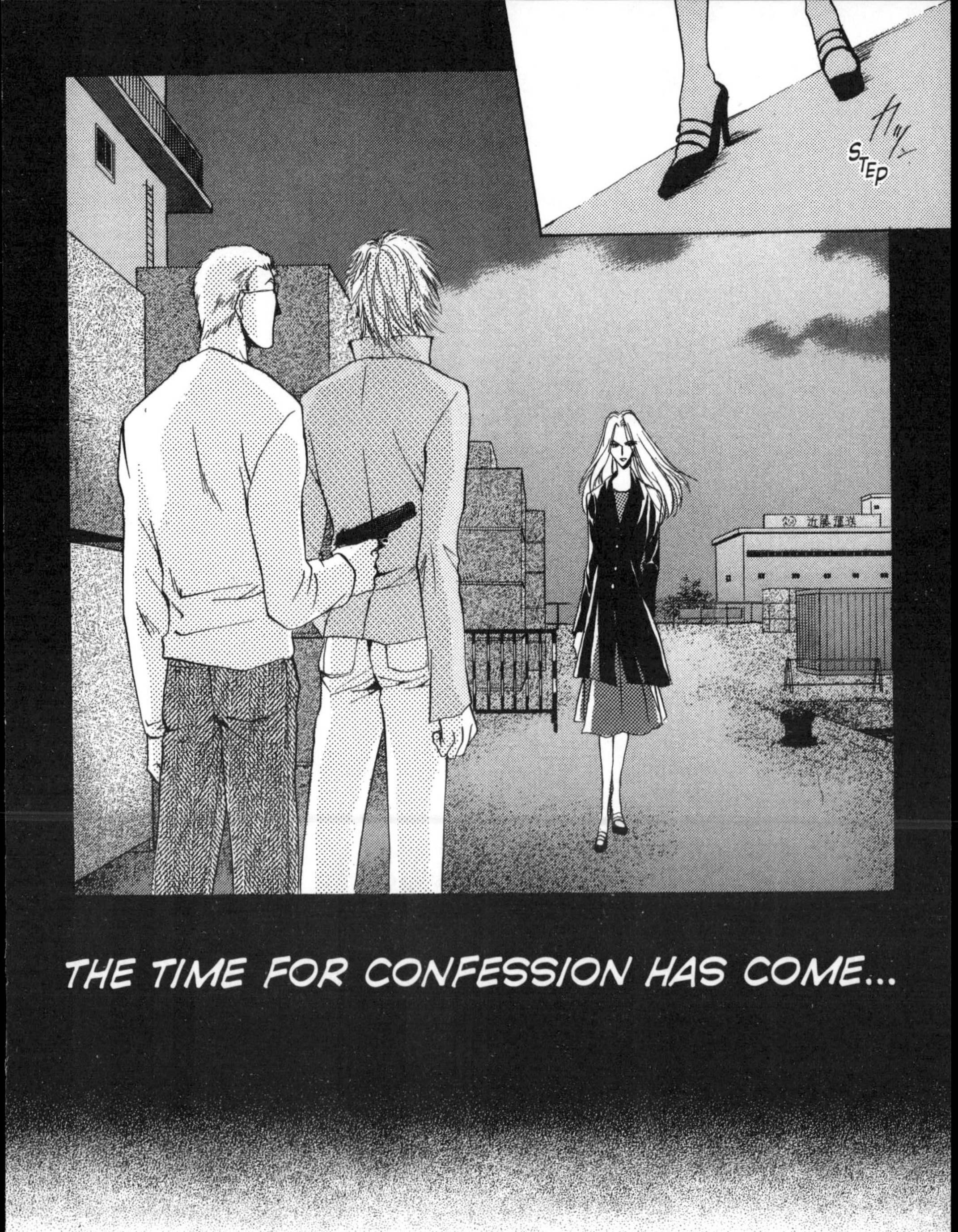
STEP

THE TIME FOR CONFESSION HAS COME...

YELLOW ACT.15/END

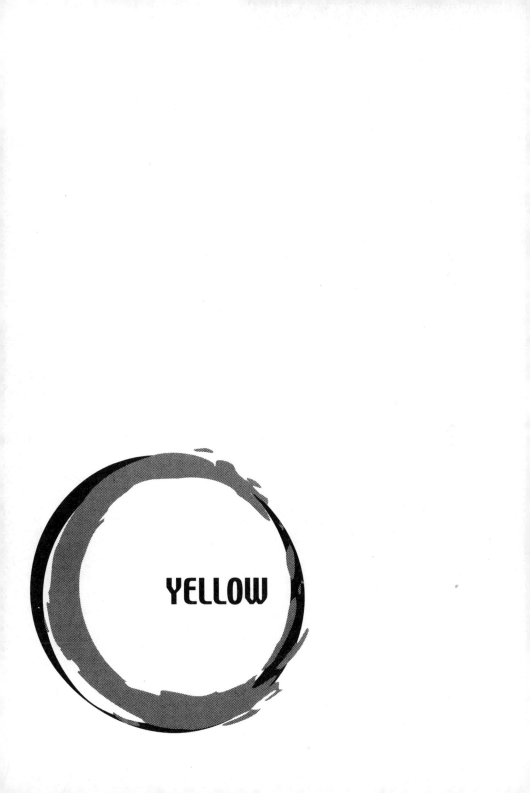

YELLOW

YELLOW

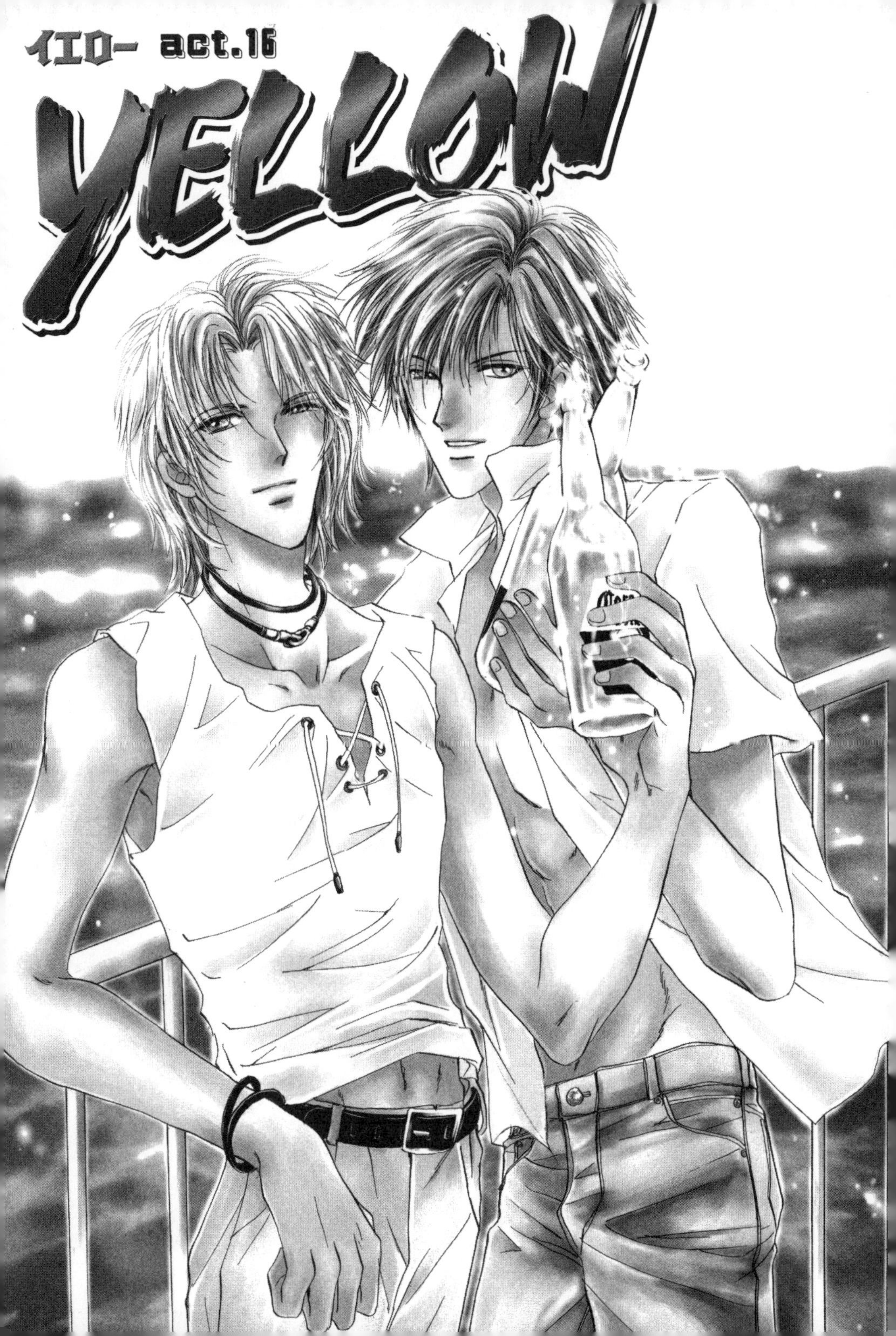
イエロー act.16
YELLOW

YELLOW

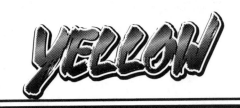

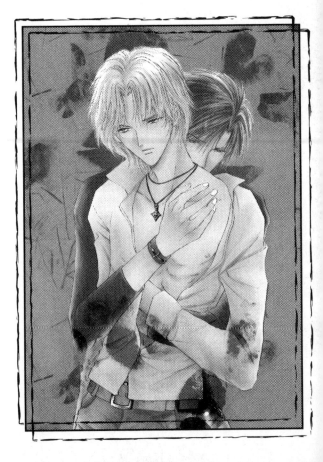

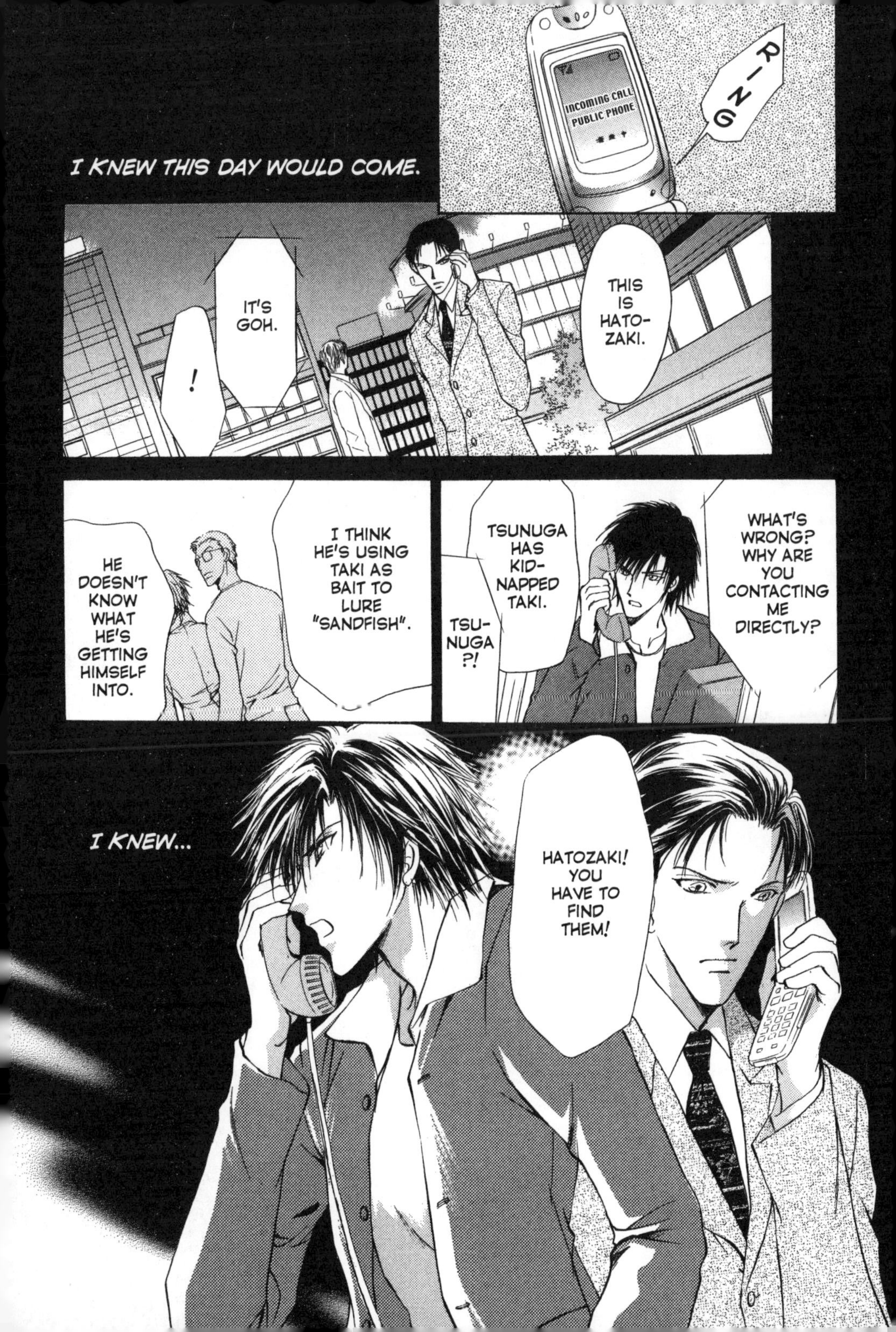
INCOMING CALL
PUBLIC PHONE
RING
I KNEW THIS DAY WOULD COME.
THIS IS HATO-ZAKI.
IT'S GOH.
!
WHAT'S WRONG? WHY ARE YOU CONTACTING ME DIRECTLY?
TSUNUGA HAS KID-NAPPED TAKI.
TSU-NUGA ?!
I THINK HE'S USING TAKI AS BAIT TO LURE "SANDFISH".
HE DOESN'T KNOW WHAT HE'S GETTING HIMSELF INTO.
HATOZAKI! YOU HAVE TO FIND THEM!
I KNEW...

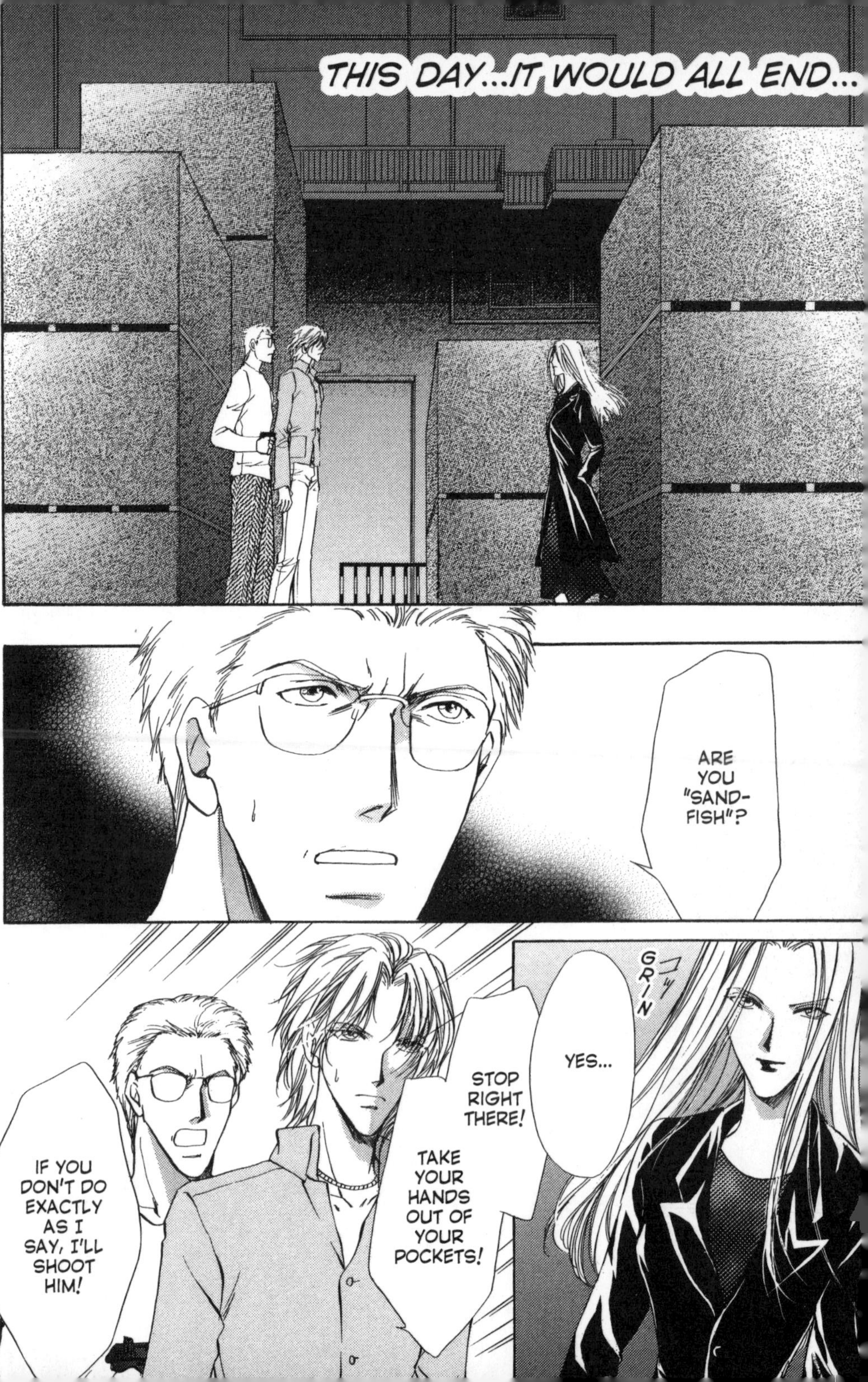
THIS DAY...IT WOULD ALL END...
ARE YOU "SAND-FISH"?
GRIN
YES...
STOP RIGHT THERE!
TAKE YOUR HANDS OUT OF YOUR POCKETS!
IF YOU DON'T DO EXACTLY AS I SAY, I'LL SHOOT HIM!

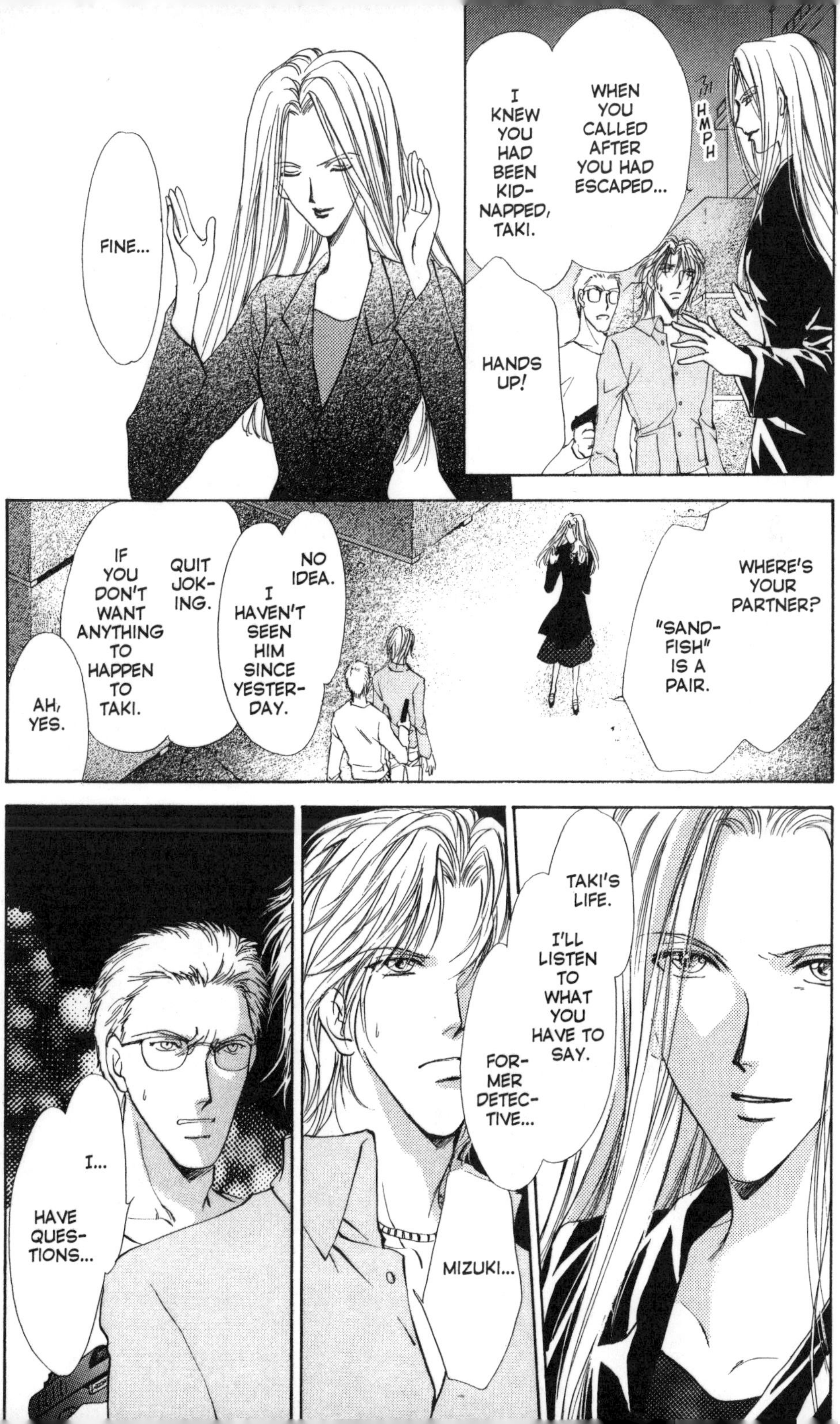
HMPH
WHEN YOU CALLED AFTER YOU HAD ESCAPED...
I KNEW YOU HAD BEEN KID-NAPPED, TAKI.
HANDS UP!
FINE...
WHERE'S YOUR PARTNER?
"SAND-FISH" IS A PAIR.
NO IDEA.
I HAVEN'T SEEN HIM SINCE YESTER-DAY.
QUIT JOK-ING.
IF YOU DON'T WANT ANYTHING TO HAPPEN TO TAKI.
AH, YES.
TAKI'S LIFE.
I'LL LISTEN TO WHAT YOU HAVE TO SAY.
FOR-MER DETEC-TIVE...
MIZUKI...
I...
HAVE QUES-TIONS...

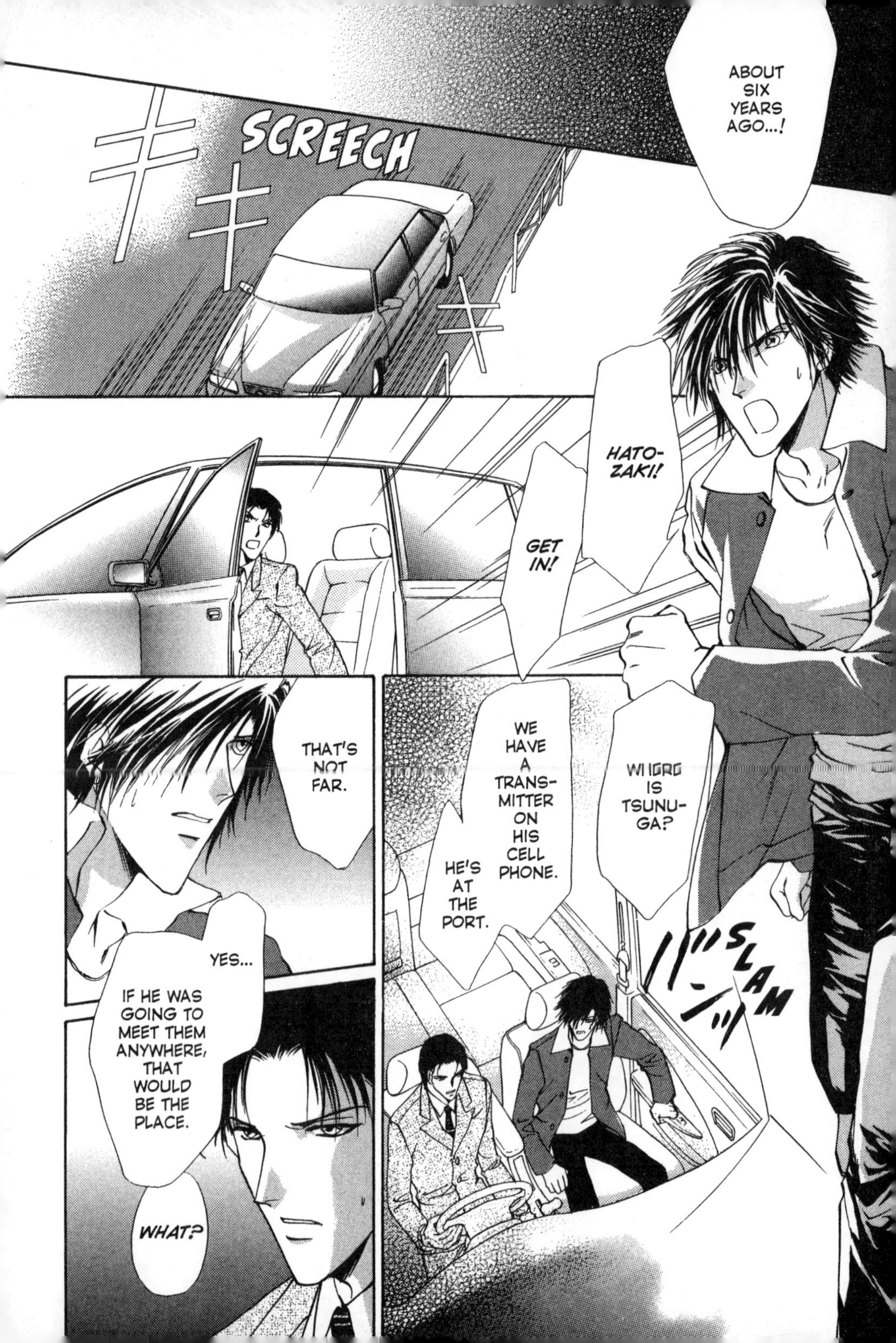
ABOUT SIX YEARS AGO...!
SCREECH
HATO-ZAKI!
GET IN!
WHERE IS TSUNUGA?
WE HAVE A TRANSMITTER ON HIS CELL PHONE.
HE'S AT THE PORT.
SLAM
THAT'S NOT FAR.
YES...
IF HE WAS GOING TO MEET THEM ANYWHERE, THAT WOULD BE THE PLACE.
WHAT?

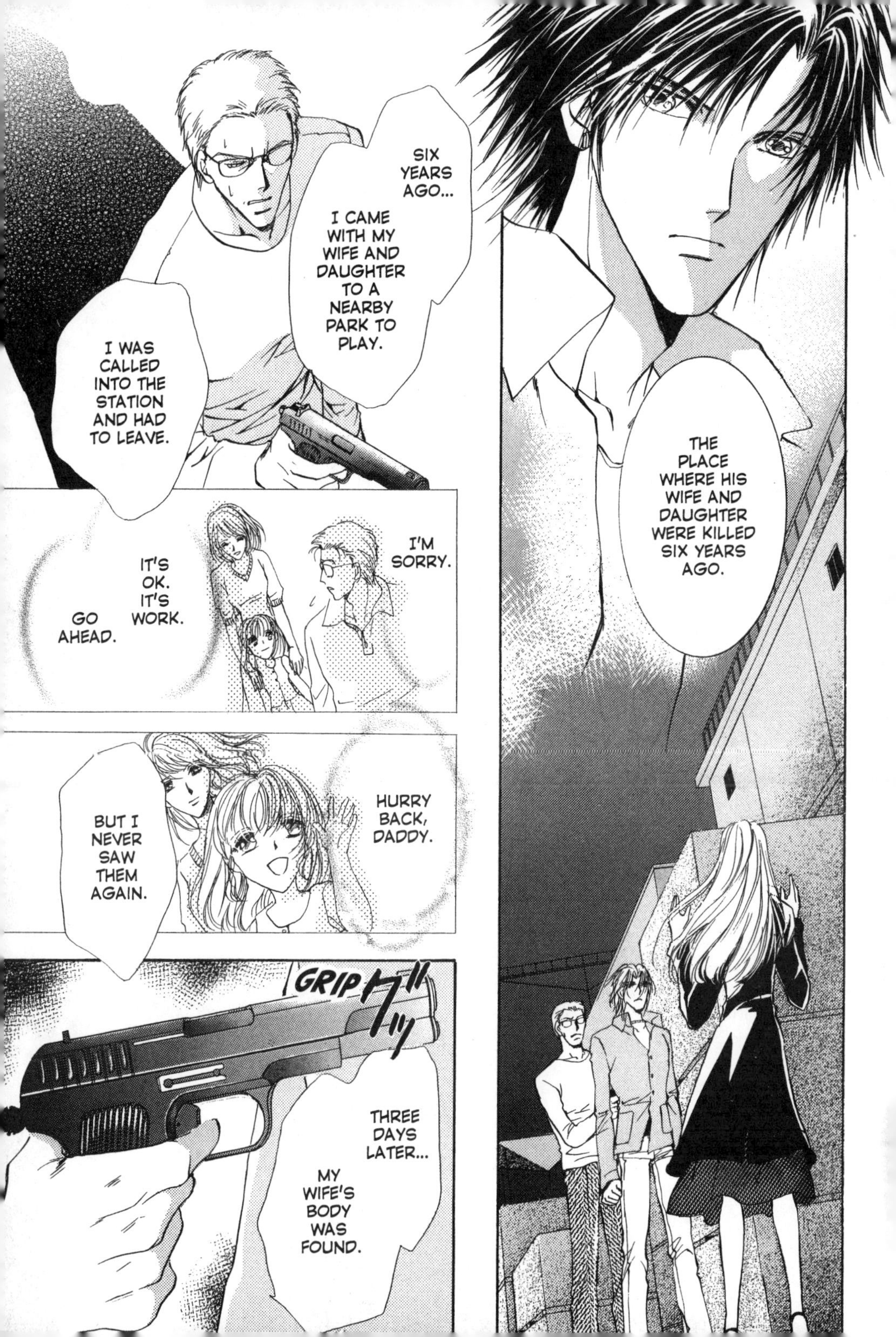
THE PLACE WHERE HIS WIFE AND DAUGHTER WERE KILLED SIX YEARS AGO.
SIX YEARS AGO...
I CAME WITH MY WIFE AND DAUGHTER TO A NEARBY PARK TO PLAY.
I WAS CALLED INTO THE STATION AND HAD TO LEAVE.
I'M SORRY.
IT'S OK. IT'S WORK.
GO AHEAD.
HURRY BACK, DADDY.
BUT I NEVER SAW THEM AGAIN.
GRIP
THREE DAYS LATER...
MY WIFE'S BODY WAS FOUND.

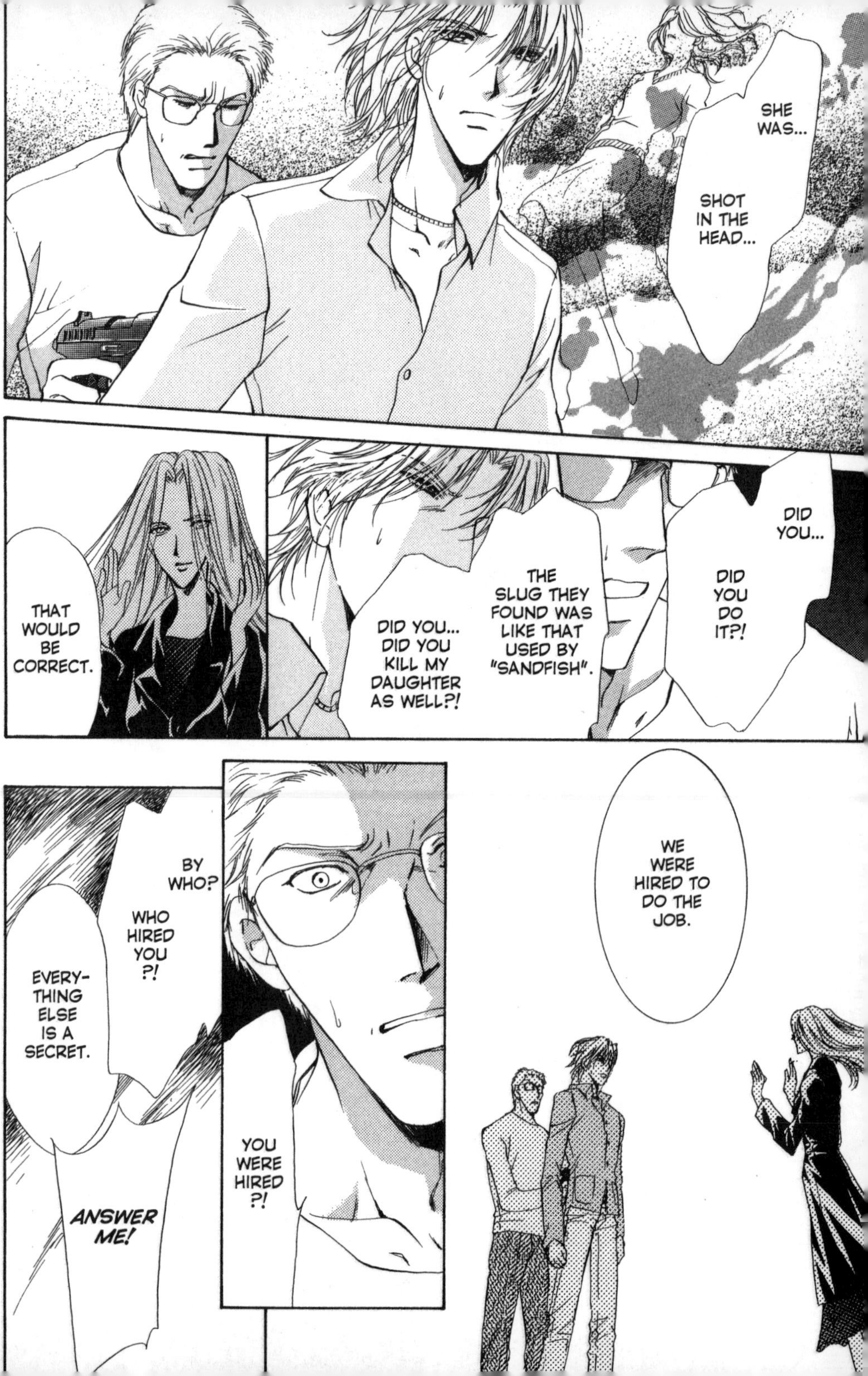
SHE WAS...
SHOT IN THE HEAD...
DID YOU...
DID YOU DO IT?!
THE SLUG THEY FOUND WAS LIKE THAT USED BY "SANDFISH".
DID YOU... DID YOU KILL MY DAUGHTER AS WELL?!
THAT WOULD BE CORRECT.
WE WERE HIRED TO DO THE JOB.
YOU WERE HIRED?!
BY WHO?
WHO HIRED YOU?!
EVERY-THING ELSE IS A SECRET.
ANSWER ME!

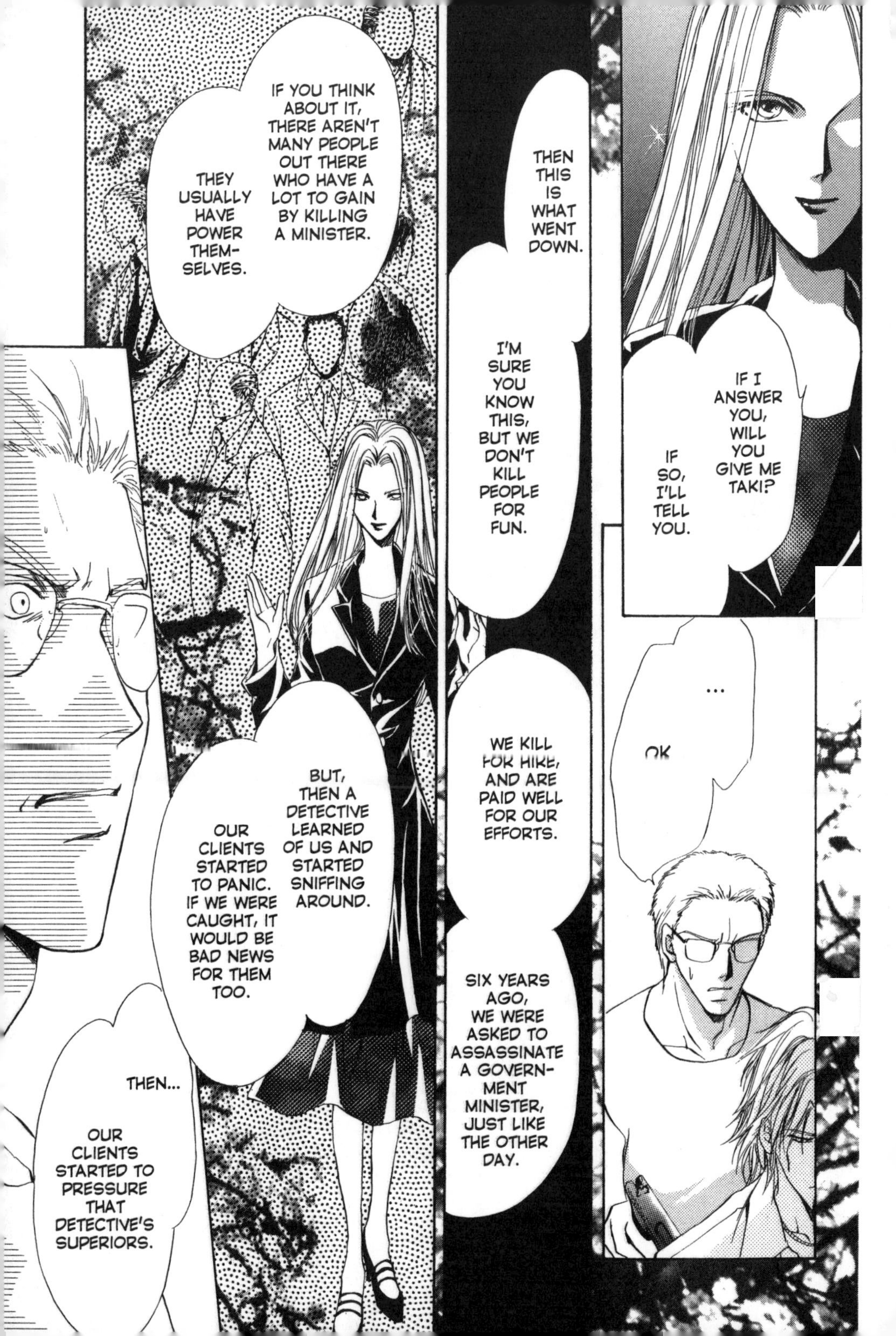
IF I ANSWER YOU, WILL YOU GIVE ME TAKI?
IF SO, I'LL TELL YOU.
...
OK
THEN THIS IS WHAT WENT DOWN.
I'M SURE YOU KNOW THIS, BUT WE DON'T KILL PEOPLE FOR FUN.
WE KILL FOR HIRE, AND ARE PAID WELL FOR OUR EFFORTS.
SIX YEARS AGO, WE WERE ASKED TO ASSASSINATE A GOVERNMENT MINISTER, JUST LIKE THE OTHER DAY.
IF YOU THINK ABOUT IT, THERE AREN'T MANY PEOPLE OUT THERE WHO HAVE A LOT TO GAIN BY KILLING A MINISTER.
THEY USUALLY HAVE POWER THEMSELVES.
BUT, THEN A DETECTIVE LEARNED OF US AND STARTED SNIFFING AROUND.
OUR CLIENTS STARTED TO PANIC. IF WE WERE CAUGHT, IT WOULD BE BAD NEWS FOR THEM TOO.
THEN...
OUR CLIENTS STARTED TO PRESSURE THAT DETECTIVE'S SUPERIORS.

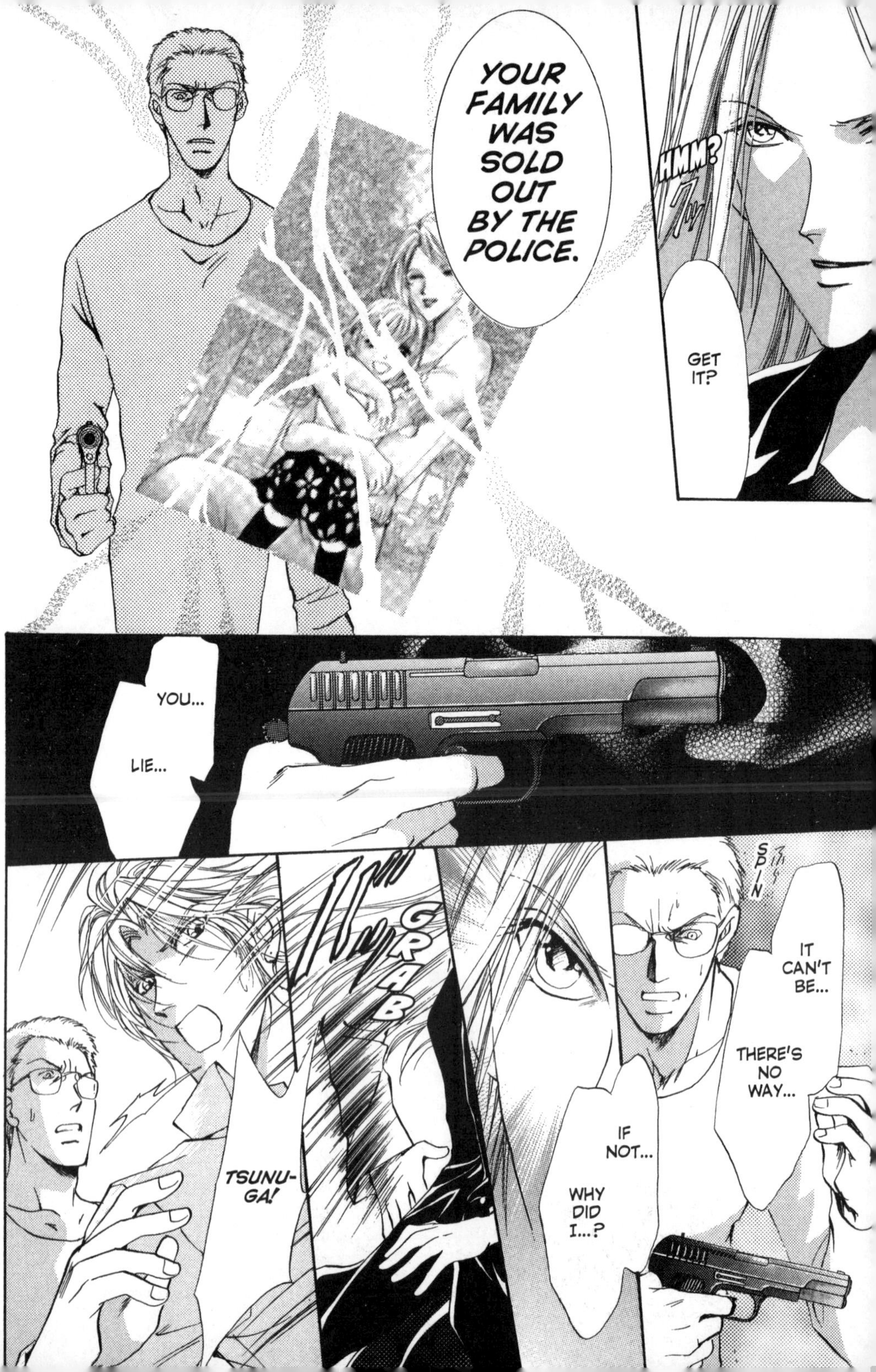
HMM?
GET IT?
YOUR FAMILY WAS SOLD OUT BY THE POLICE.
YOU...
LIE...
SPIN
IT CAN'T BE...
THERE'S NO WAY...
IF NOT...
WHY DID I...?
GRAB
TSUNUGA!

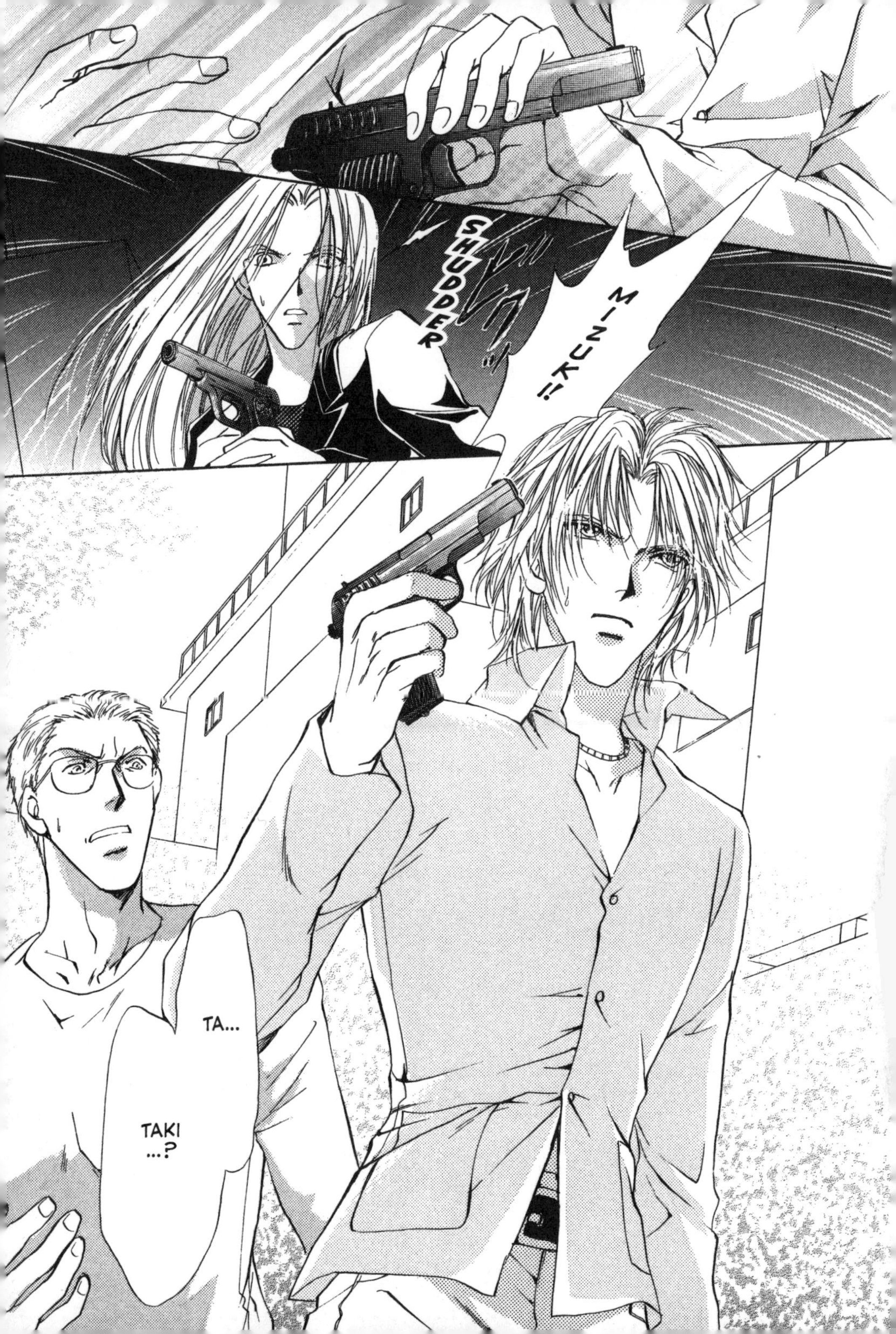
MIZUKI!!
SHUDDER
TA...
TAKI ...?

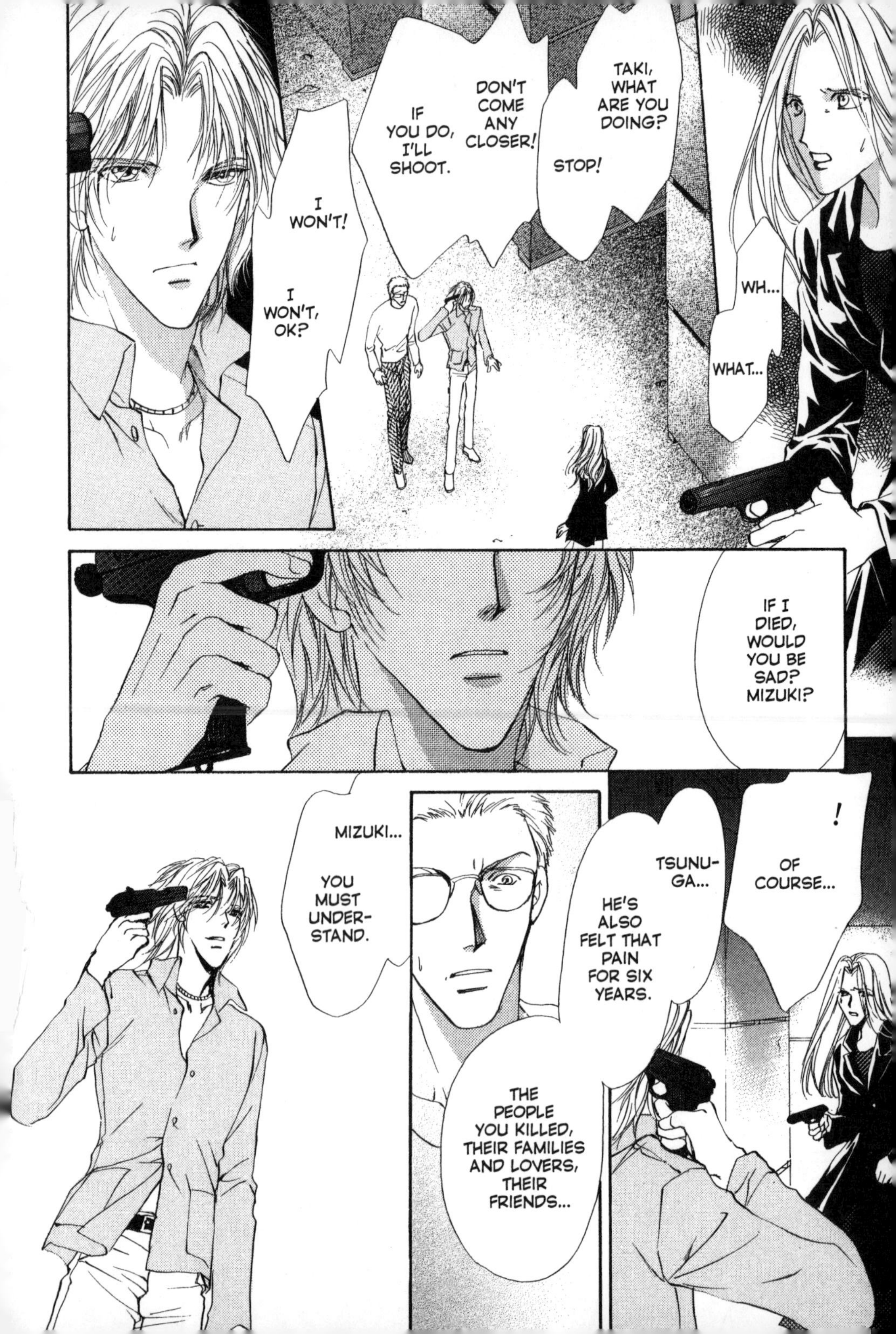
TAKI, WHAT ARE YOU DOING?
STOP!
WH...
WHAT...
DON'T COME ANY CLOSER!
IF YOU DO, I'LL SHOOT.
I WON'T!
I WON'T, OK?
IF I DIED, WOULD YOU BE SAD? MIZUKI?
!
OF COURSE...
TSUNUGA...
HE'S ALSO FELT THAT PAIN FOR SIX YEARS.
THE PEOPLE YOU KILLED, THEIR FAMILIES AND LOVERS, THEIR FRIENDS...
MIZUKI...
YOU MUST UNDER-STAND.

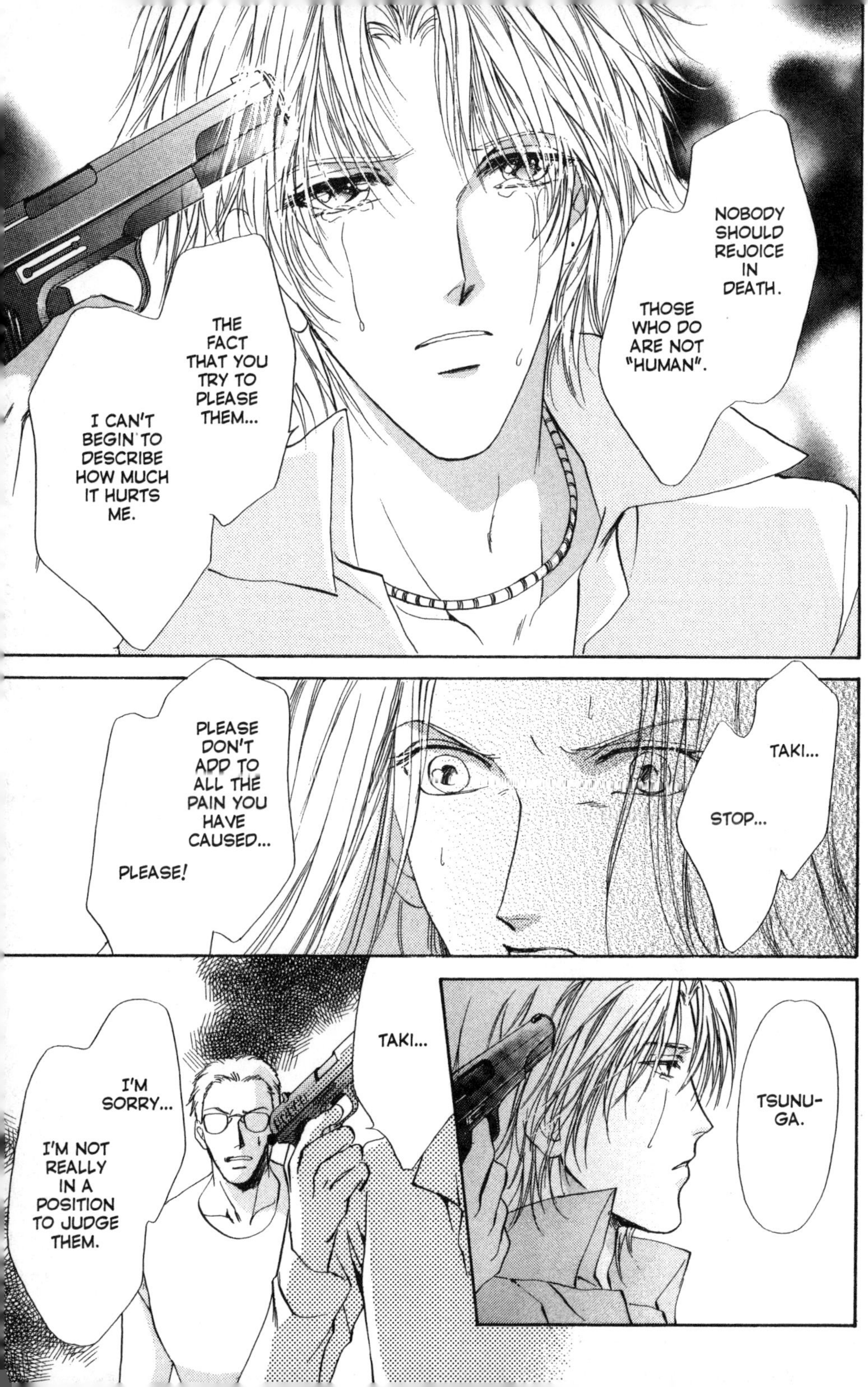
NOBODY SHOULD REJOICE IN DEATH.
THOSE WHO DO ARE NOT "HUMAN".
THE FACT THAT YOU TRY TO PLEASE THEM...
I CAN'T BEGIN TO DESCRIBE HOW MUCH IT HURTS ME.
TAKI...
STOP...
PLEASE DON'T ADD TO ALL THE PAIN YOU HAVE CAUSED...
PLEASE!
TSUNUGA.
TAKI...
I'M SORRY...
I'M NOT REALLY IN A POSITION TO JUDGE THEM.

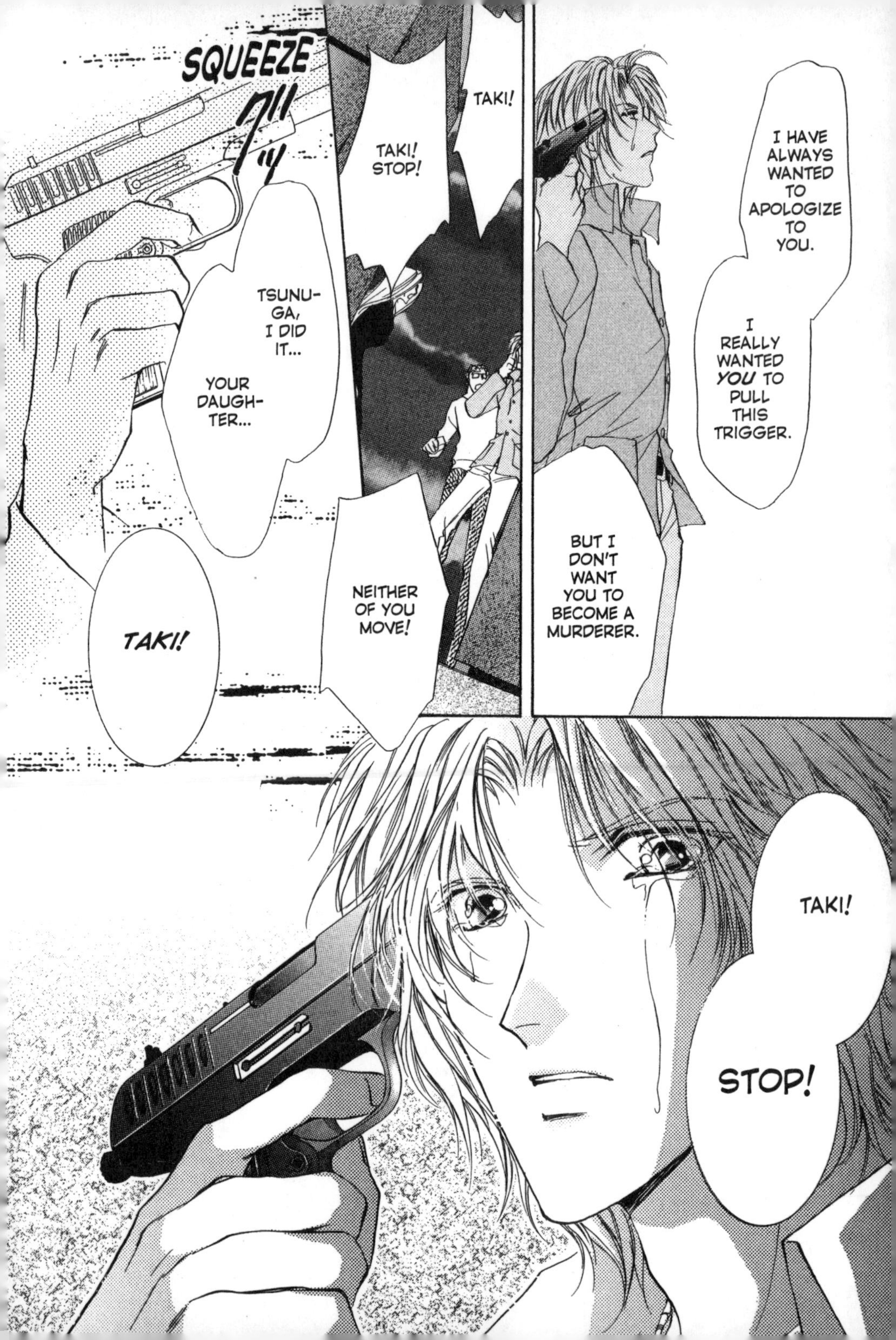
I HAVE ALWAYS WANTED TO APOLOGIZE TO YOU.
I REALLY WANTED *YOU* TO PULL THIS TRIGGER.
BUT I DON'T WANT YOU TO BECOME A MURDERER.
TAKI!
TAKI! STOP!
NEITHER OF YOU MOVE!
SQUEEZE
TSUNU-GA, I DID IT...
YOUR DAUGH-TER...
TAKI!
TAKI!
STOP!

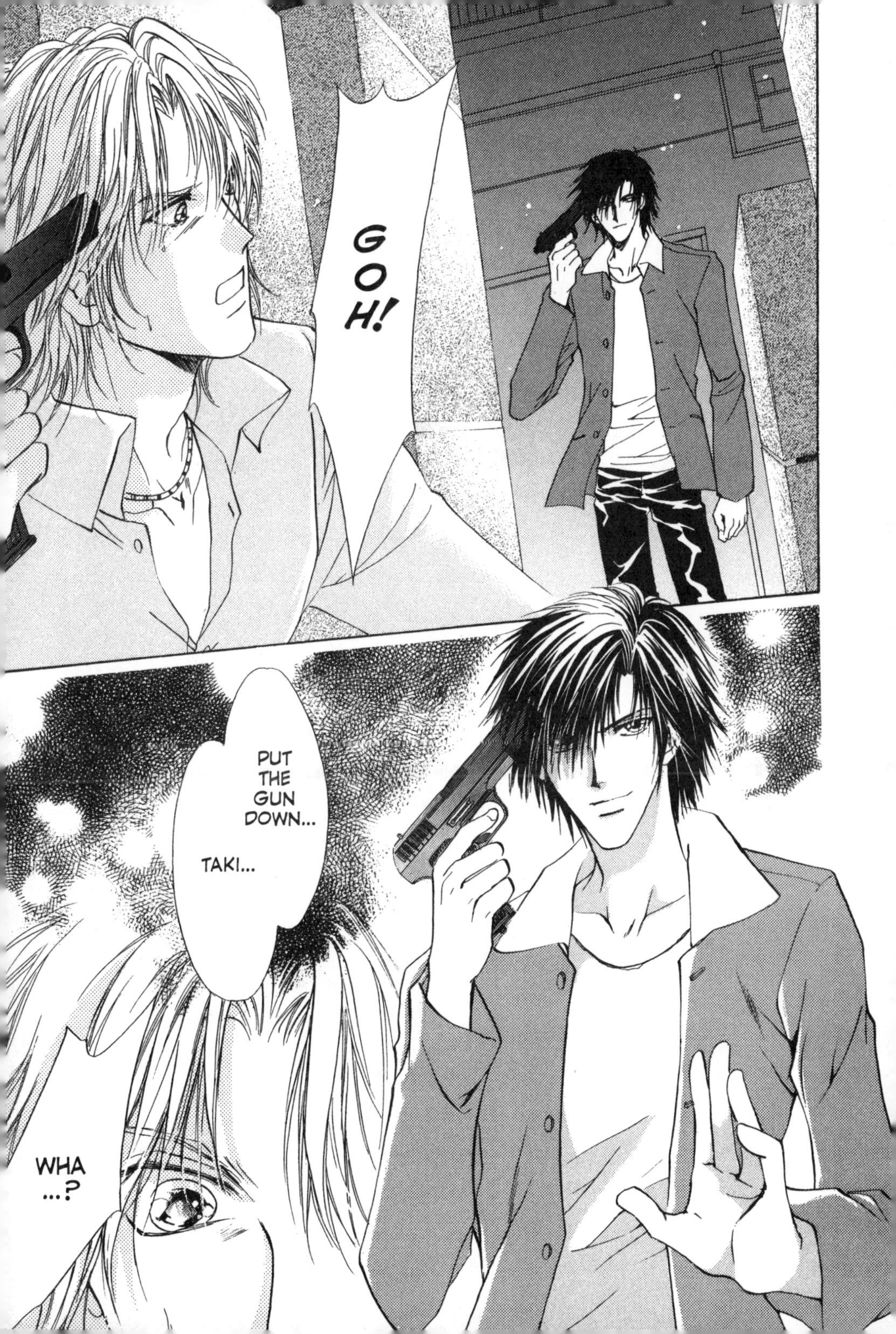
GOH!
PUT THE GUN DOWN...
TAKI...
WHA ...?

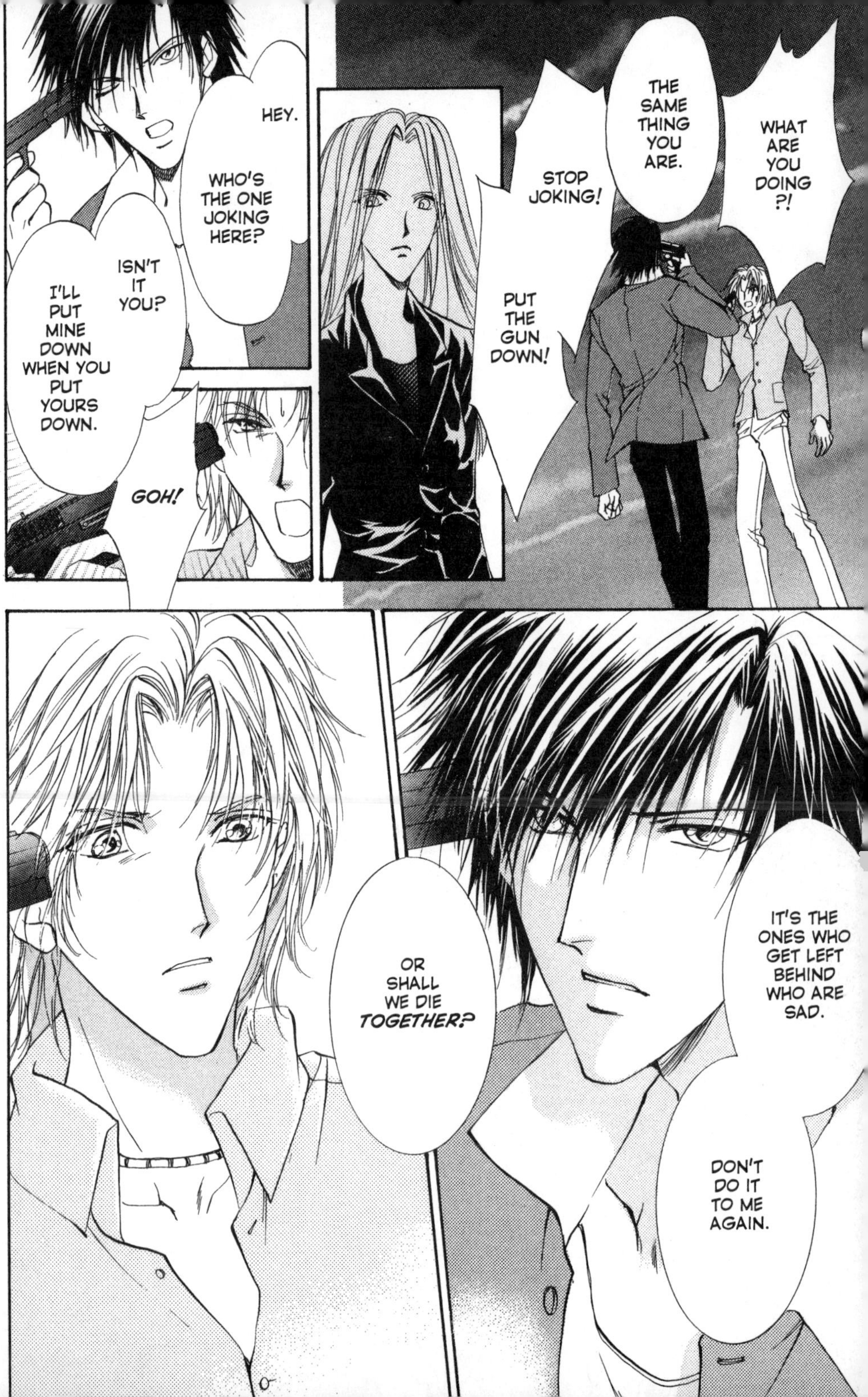
WHAT ARE YOU DOING?!
THE SAME THING YOU ARE.
STOP JOKING!
PUT THE GUN DOWN!
HEY.
WHO'S THE ONE JOKING HERE?
ISN'T IT YOU?
I'LL PUT MINE DOWN WHEN YOU PUT YOURS DOWN.
GOH!
IT'S THE ONES WHO GET LEFT BEHIND WHO ARE SAD.
DON'T DO IT TO ME AGAIN.
OR SHALL WE DIE *TOGETHER?*

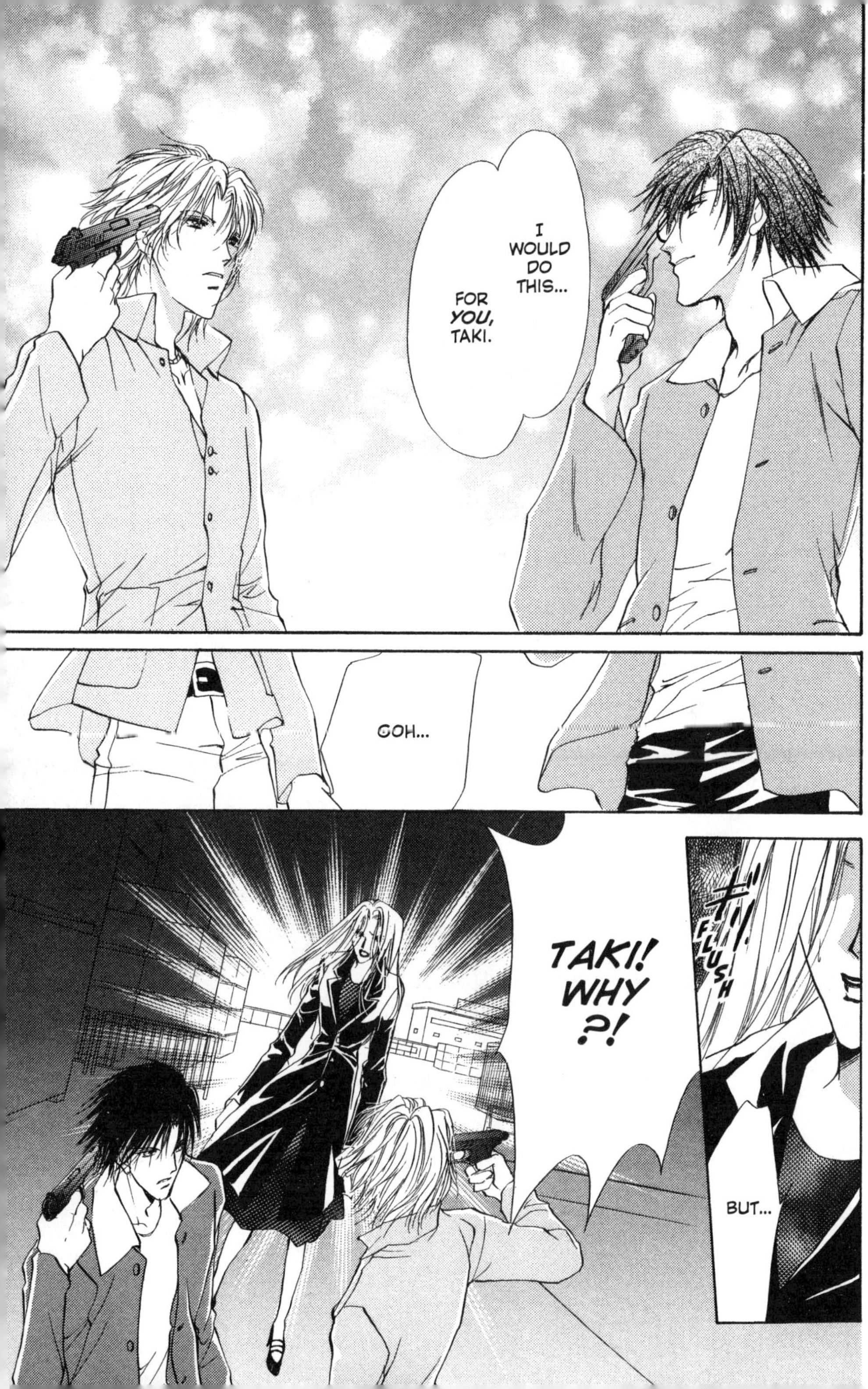
I WOULD DO THIS...
FOR YOU, TAKI.
GOH...
FLUSH
BUT...
TAKI! WHY?!

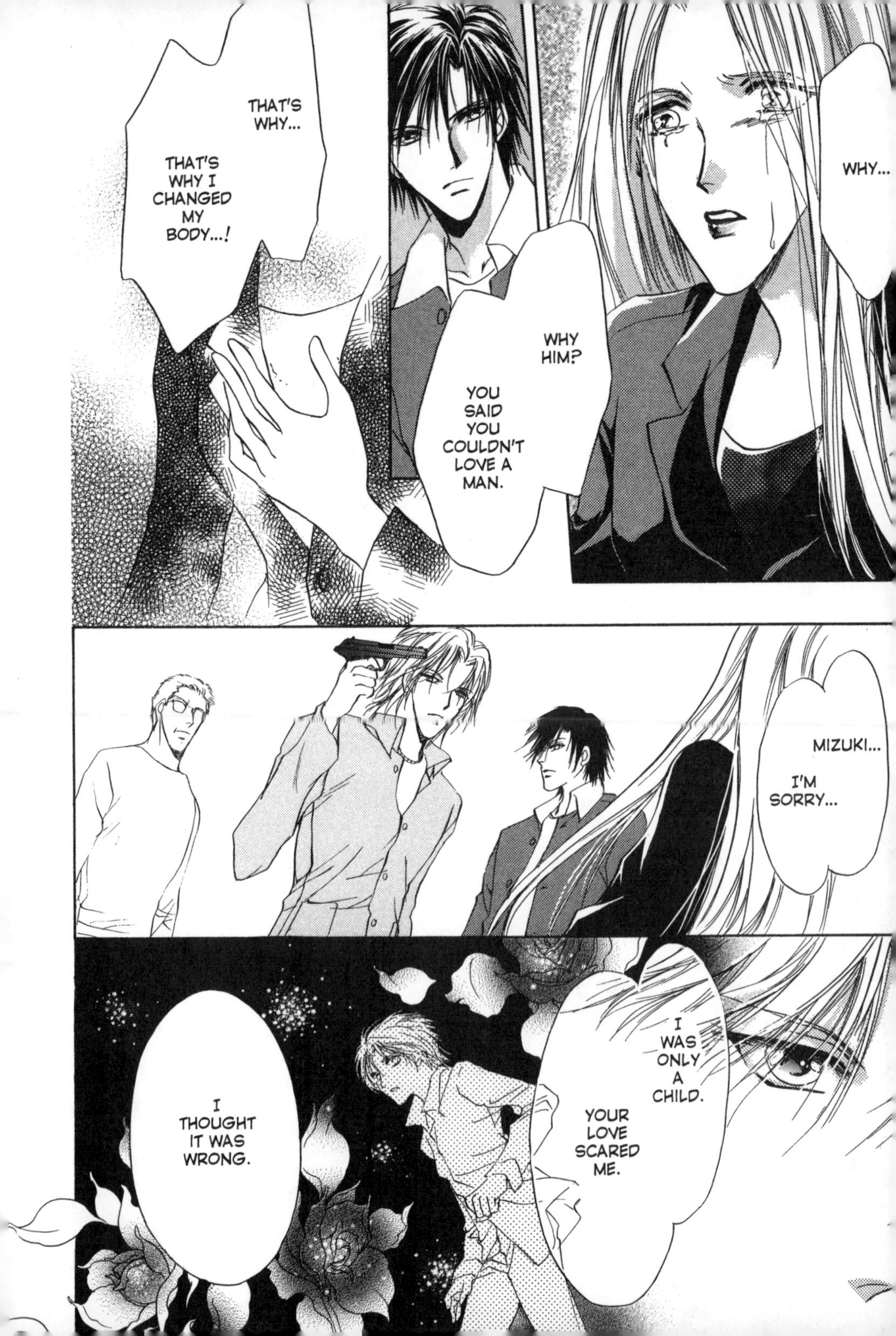
WHY...
WHY HIM?
YOU SAID YOU COULDN'T LOVE A MAN.
THAT'S WHY...
THAT'S WHY I CHANGED MY BODY...!
MIZUKI...
I'M SORRY...
I WAS ONLY A CHILD.
YOUR LOVE SCARED ME.
I THOUGHT IT WAS WRONG.

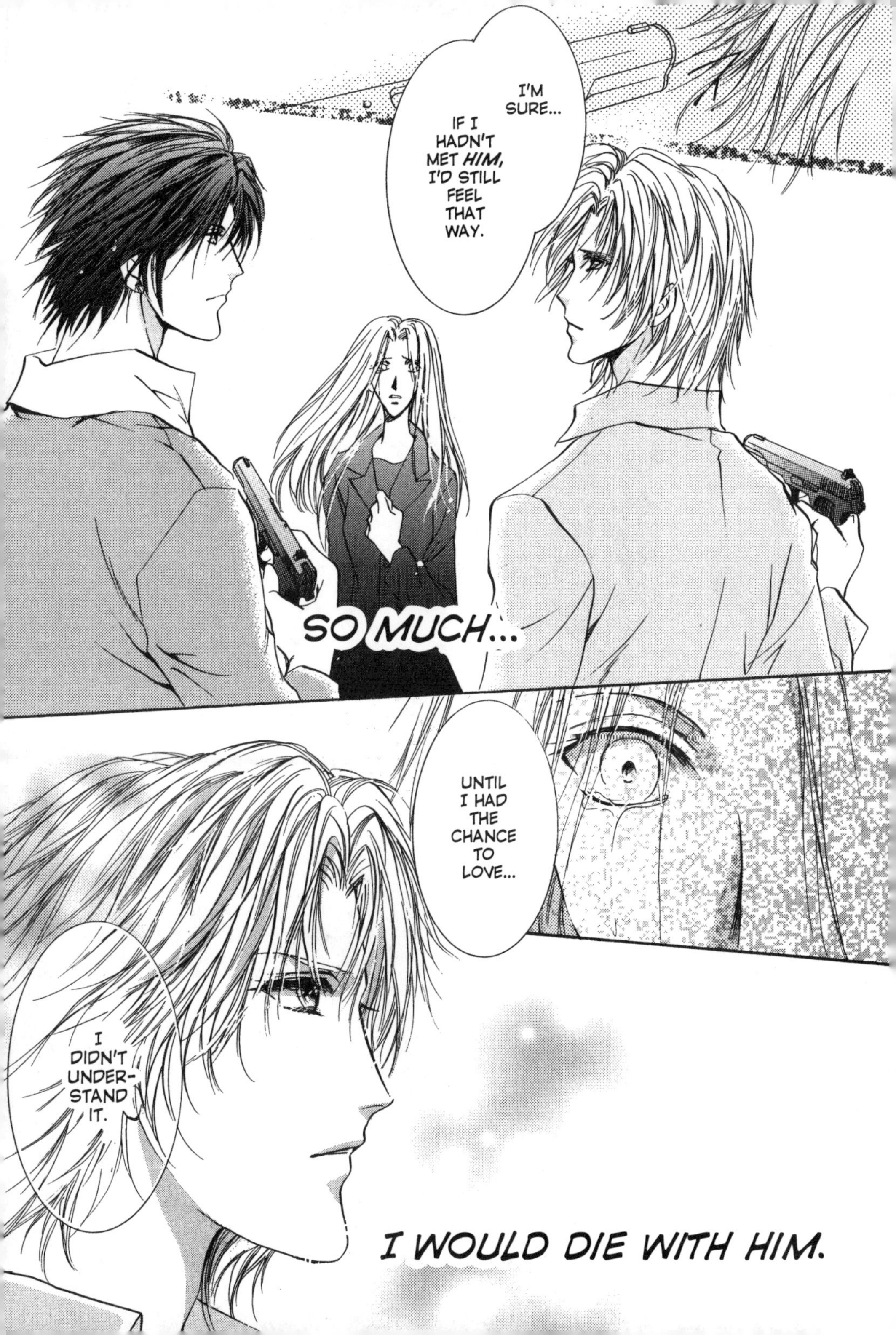
I'M SURE... IF I HADN'T MET *HIM*, I'D STILL FEEL THAT WAY.
SO MUCH...
UNTIL I HAD THE CHANCE TO LOVE...
I DIDN'T UNDER-STAND IT.
I WOULD DIE WITH HIM.

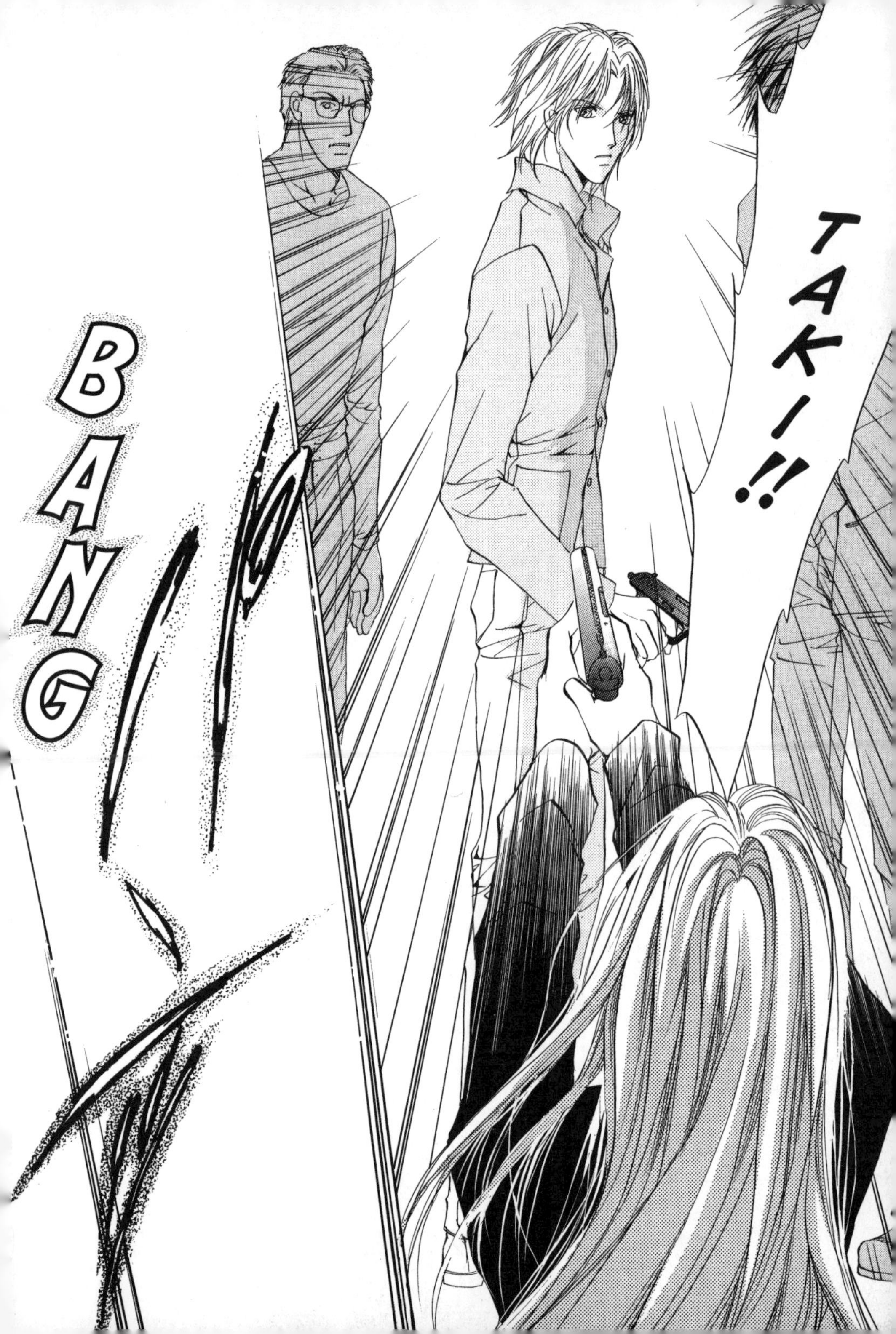
TAKI!!
BANG

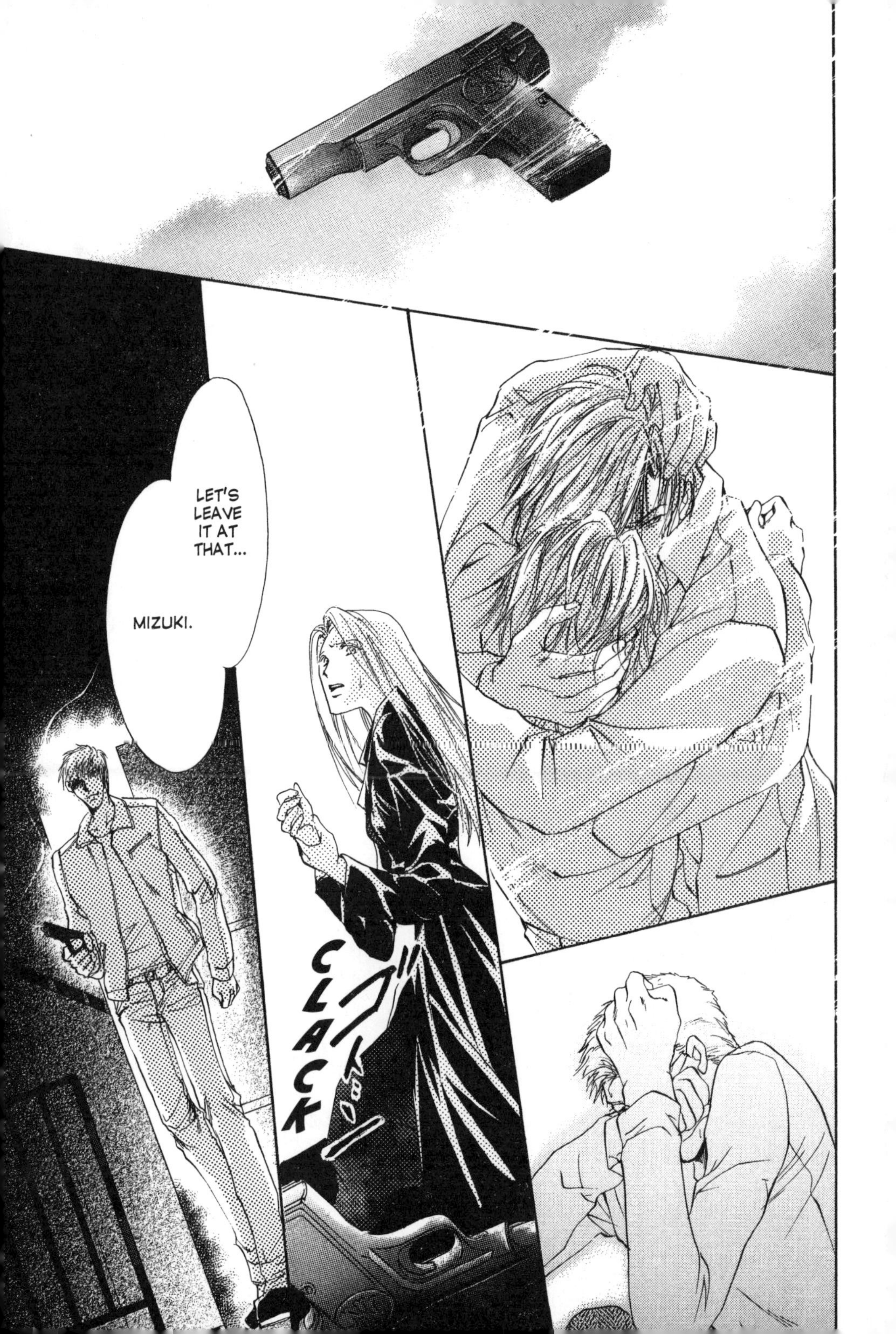
LET'S LEAVE IT AT THAT...
MIZUKI.
CLACK

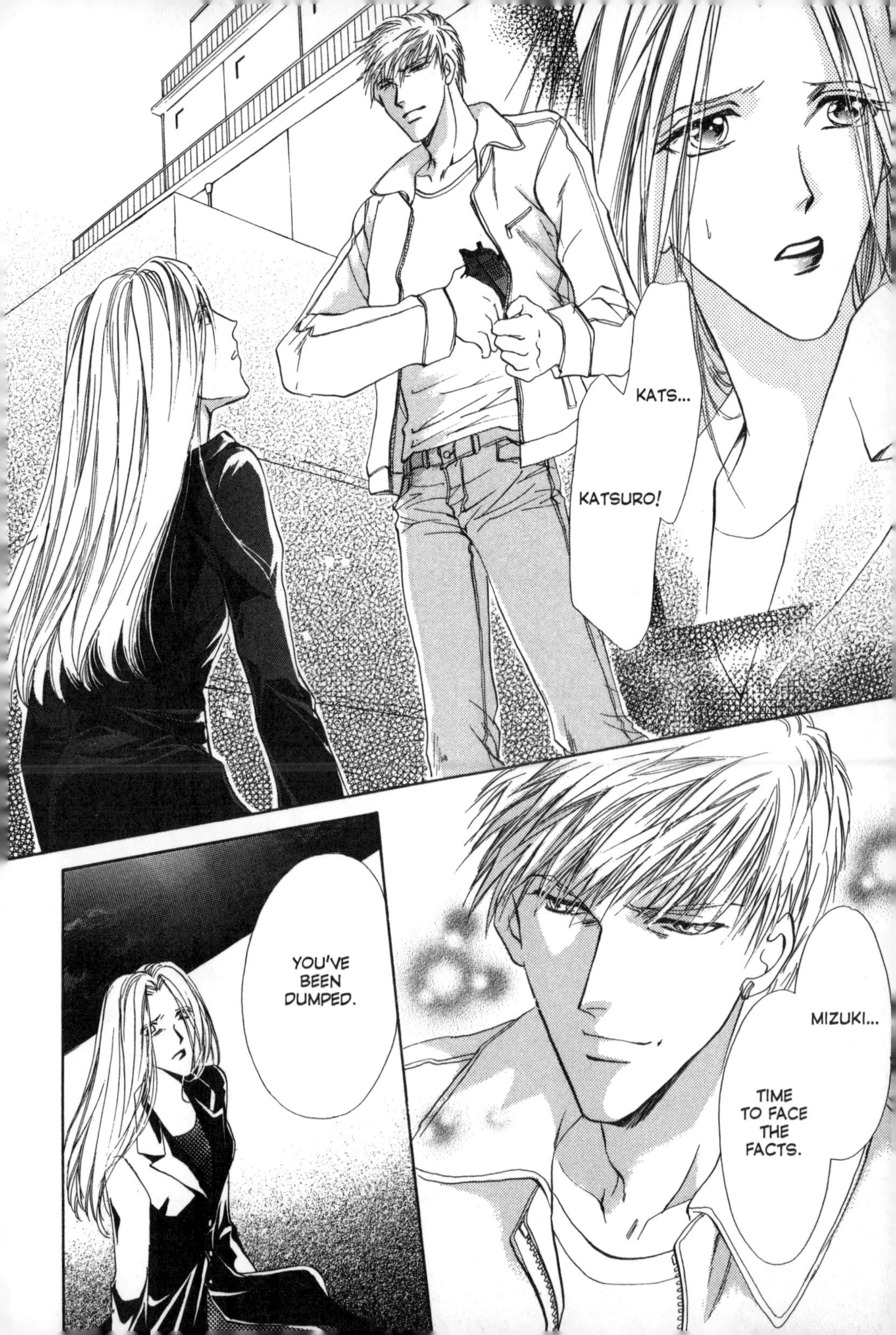
KATS...
KATSURO!
MIZUKI...
TIME TO FACE THE FACTS.
YOU'VE BEEN DUMPED.

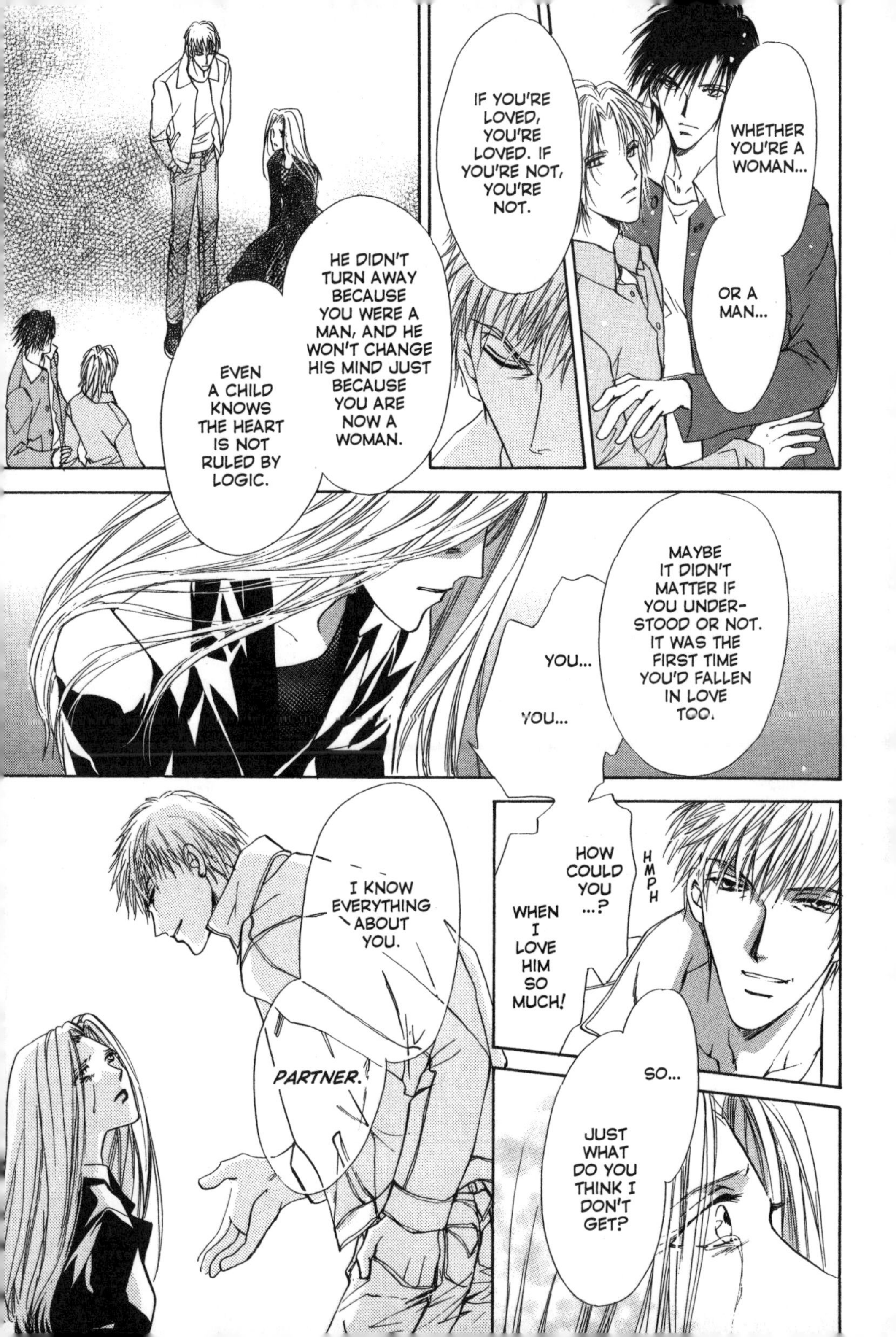
WHETHER YOU'RE A WOMAN...
OR A MAN...
IF YOU'RE LOVED, YOU'RE LOVED. IF YOU'RE NOT, YOU'RE NOT.
HE DIDN'T TURN AWAY BECAUSE YOU WERE A MAN, AND HE WON'T CHANGE HIS MIND JUST BECAUSE YOU ARE NOW A WOMAN.
EVEN A CHILD KNOWS THE HEART IS NOT RULED BY LOGIC.
MAYBE IT DIDN'T MATTER IF YOU UNDERSTOOD OR NOT. IT WAS THE FIRST TIME YOU'D FALLEN IN LOVE TOO.
YOU...
YOU...
HMPH
HOW COULD YOU ...?
WHEN I LOVE HIM SO MUCH!
SO...
JUST WHAT DO YOU THINK I DON'T GET?
I KNOW EVERYTHING ABOUT YOU.
PARTNER.

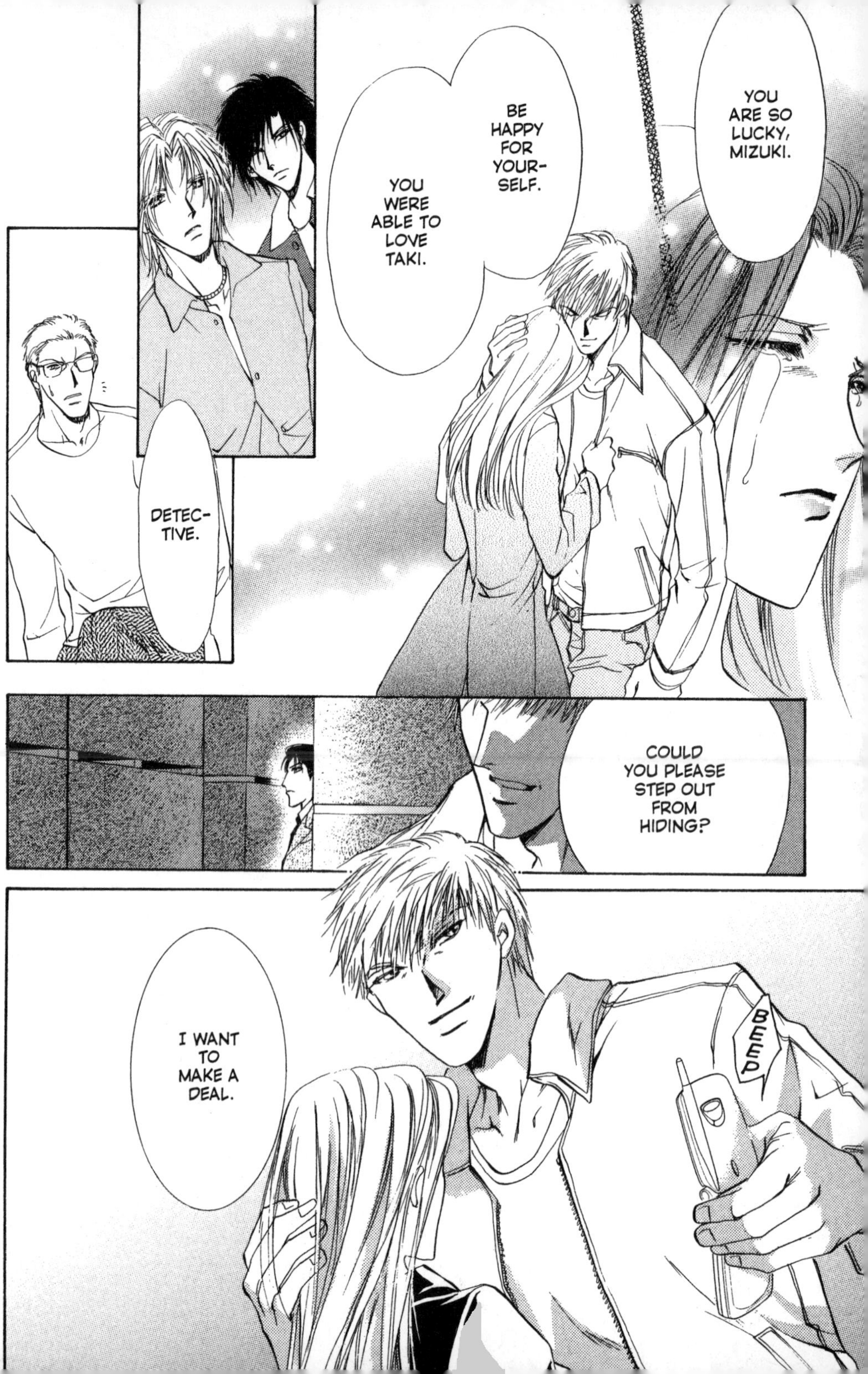
YOU ARE SO LUCKY, MIZUKI.
BE HAPPY FOR YOUR-SELF.
YOU WERE ABLE TO LOVE TAKI.
DETEC-TIVE.
COULD YOU PLEASE STEP OUT FROM HIDING?
BEEP
I WANT TO MAKE A DEAL.

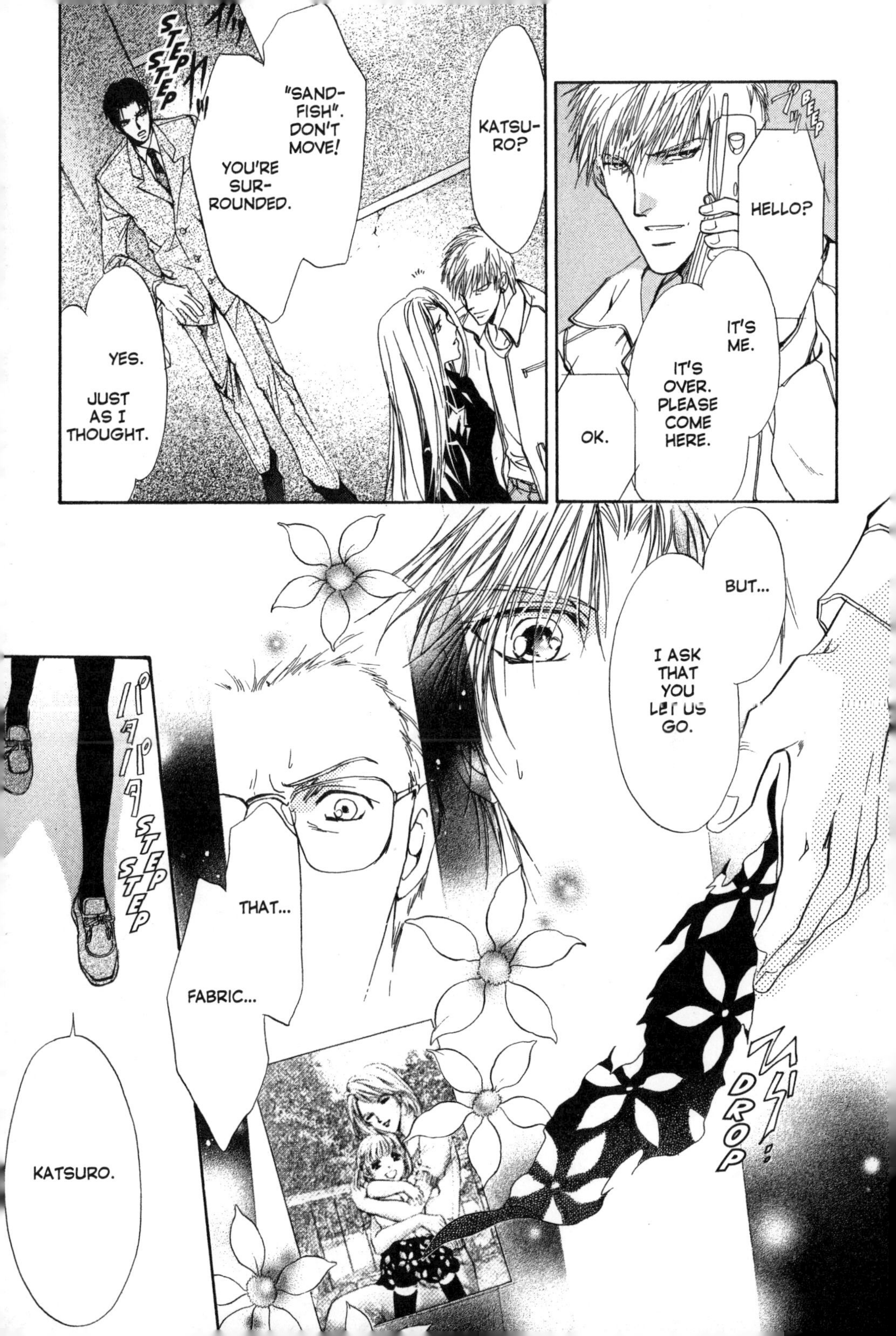
BEEP
HELLO?
IT'S ME.
IT'S OVER. PLEASE COME HERE.
OK.
KATSU-RO?
"SAND-FISH". DON'T MOVE!
YOU'RE SUR-ROUNDED.
STEP STEP
YES.
JUST AS I THOUGHT.
BUT...
I ASK THAT YOU LET US GO.
DROP
THAT...
FABRIC...
STEP STEP
KATSURO.

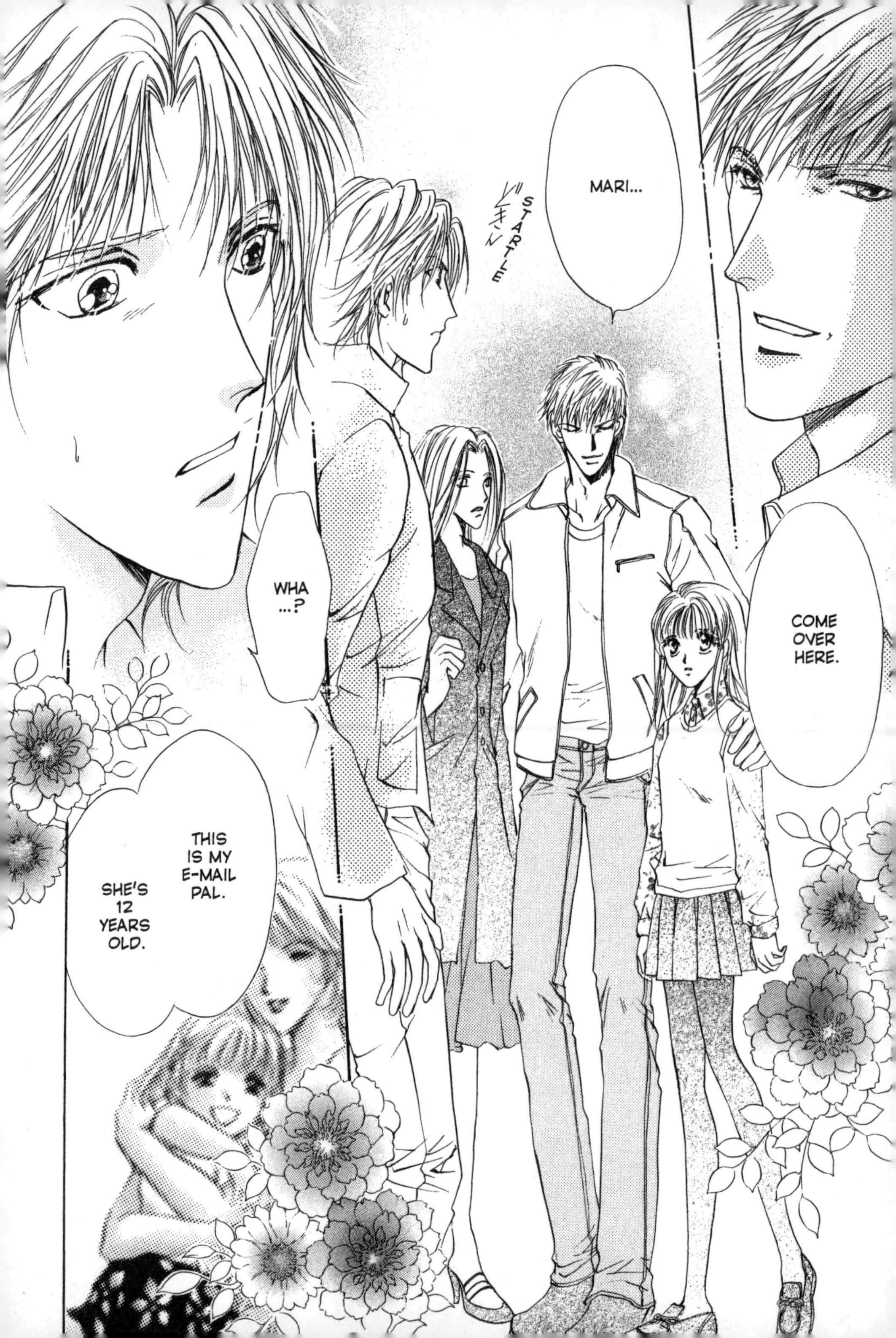
MARI...
COME OVER HERE.
STARTLE
WHA ...?
THIS IS MY E-MAIL PAL.
SHE'S 12 YEARS OLD.

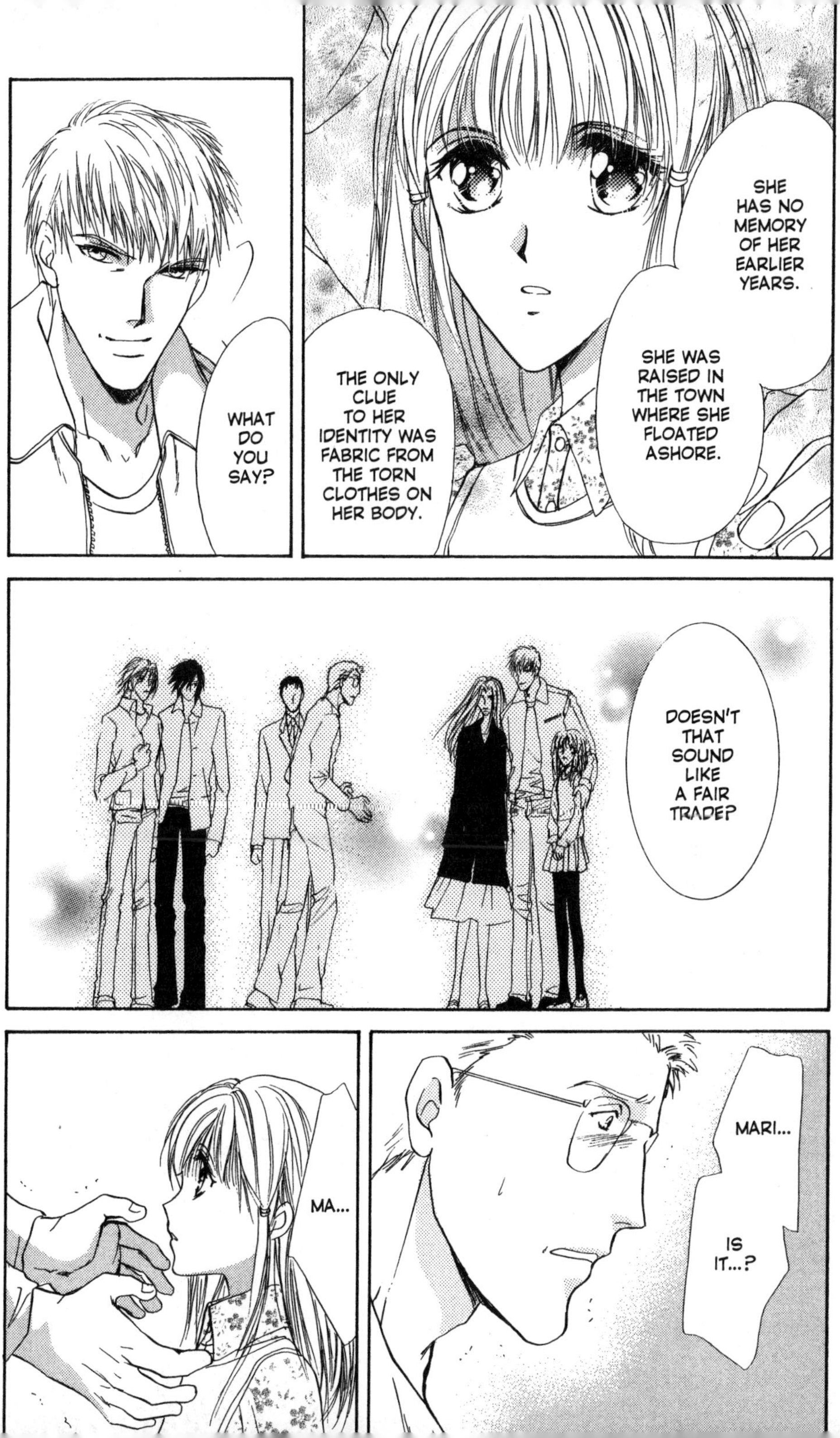
SHE HAS NO MEMORY OF HER EARLIER YEARS.
SHE WAS RAISED IN THE TOWN WHERE SHE FLOATED ASHORE.
THE ONLY CLUE TO HER IDENTITY WAS FABRIC FROM THE TORN CLOTHES ON HER BODY.
WHAT DO YOU SAY?
DOESN'T THAT SOUND LIKE A FAIR TRADE?
MARI...
IS IT...?
MA...

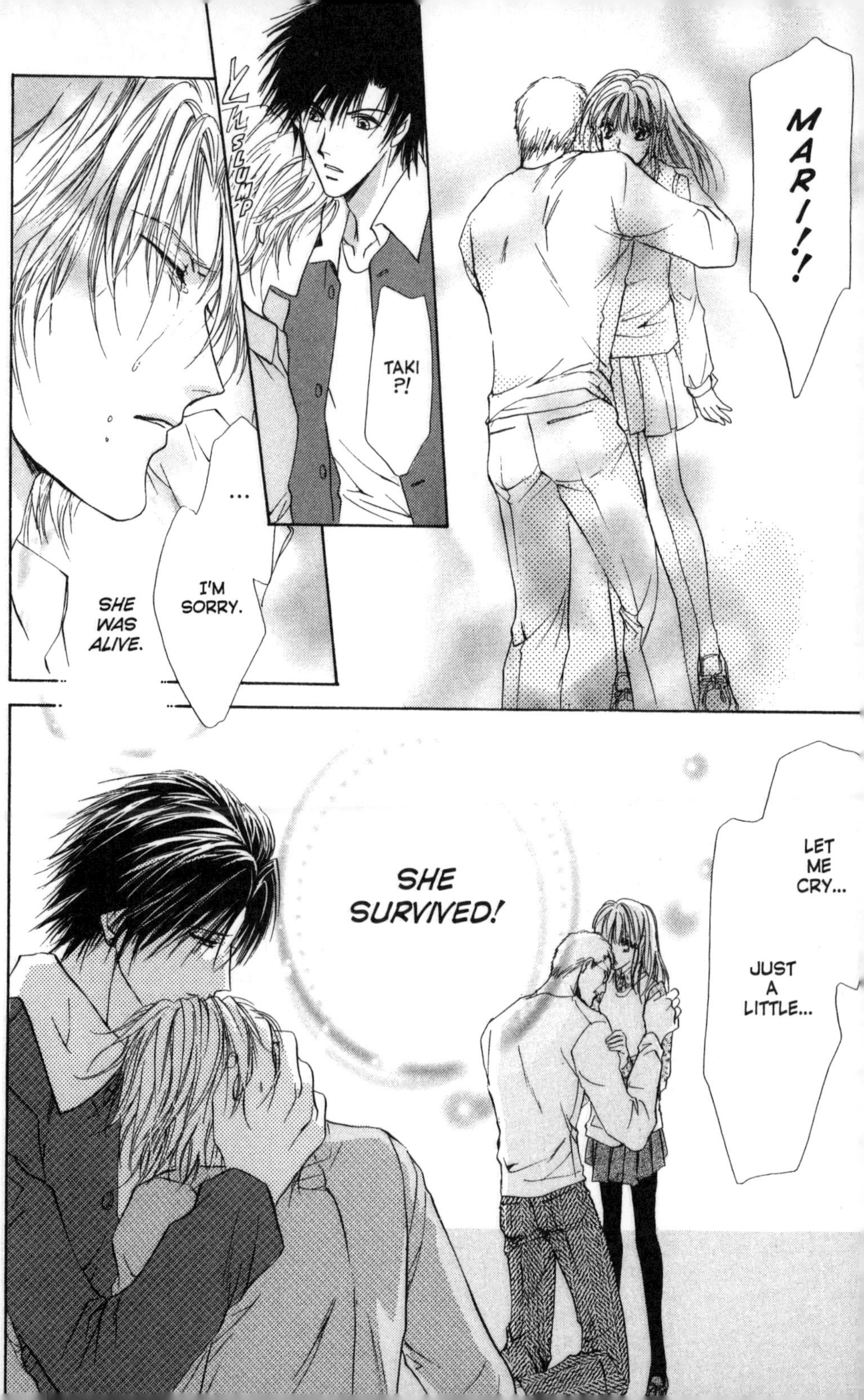
MARI!!
SLUMP
TAKI ?!
...
I'M SORRY.
SHE WAS ALIVE.
LET ME CRY...
JUST A LITTLE...
SHE SURVIVED!

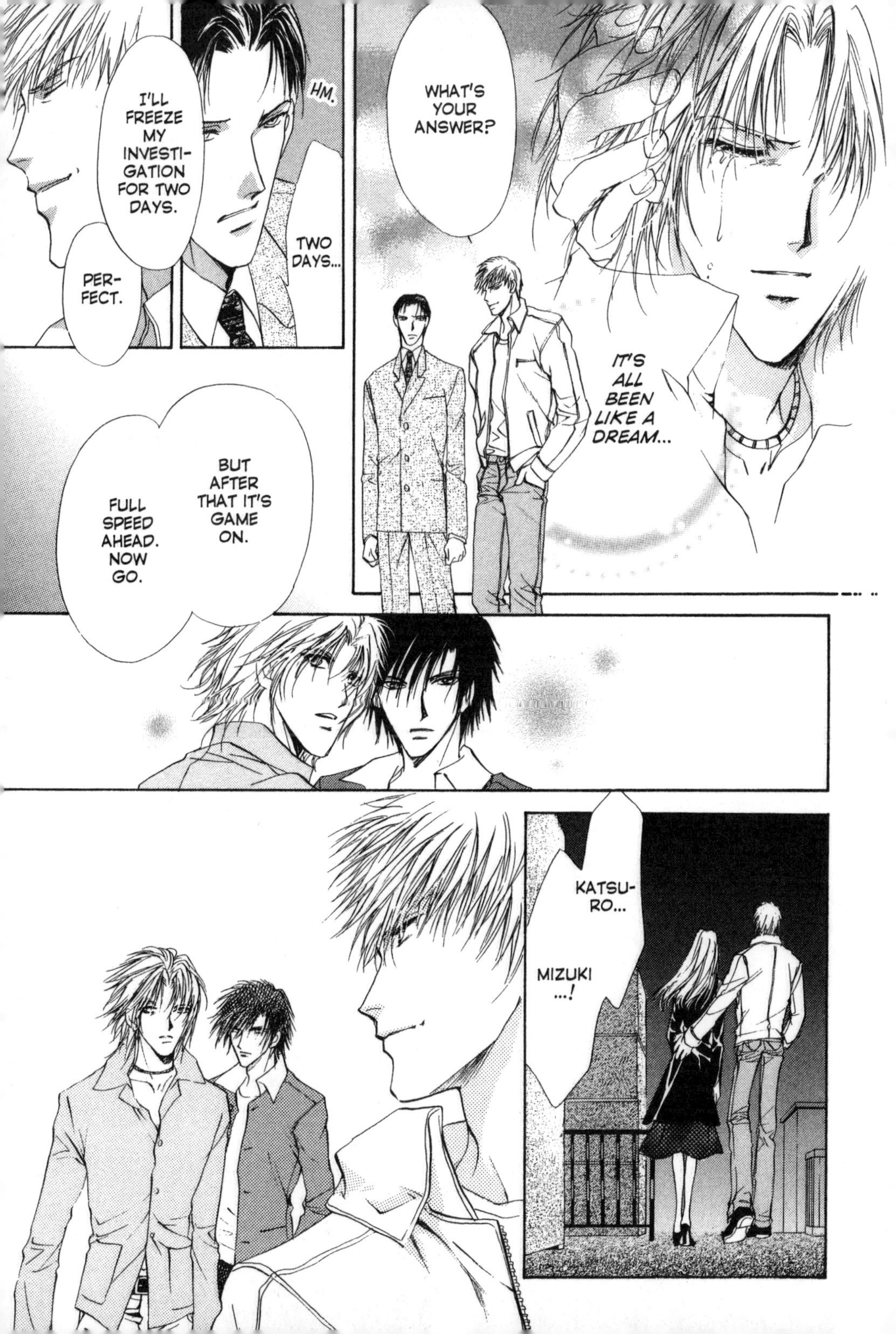

IT'S ALL BEEN LIKE A DREAM...
WHAT'S YOUR ANSWER?
HM.
TWO DAYS...
I'LL FREEZE MY INVESTIGATION FOR TWO DAYS.
PER-FECT.
BUT AFTER THAT IT'S GAME ON.
FULL SPEED AHEAD. NOW GO.
KATSU-RO...
MIZUKI ...!

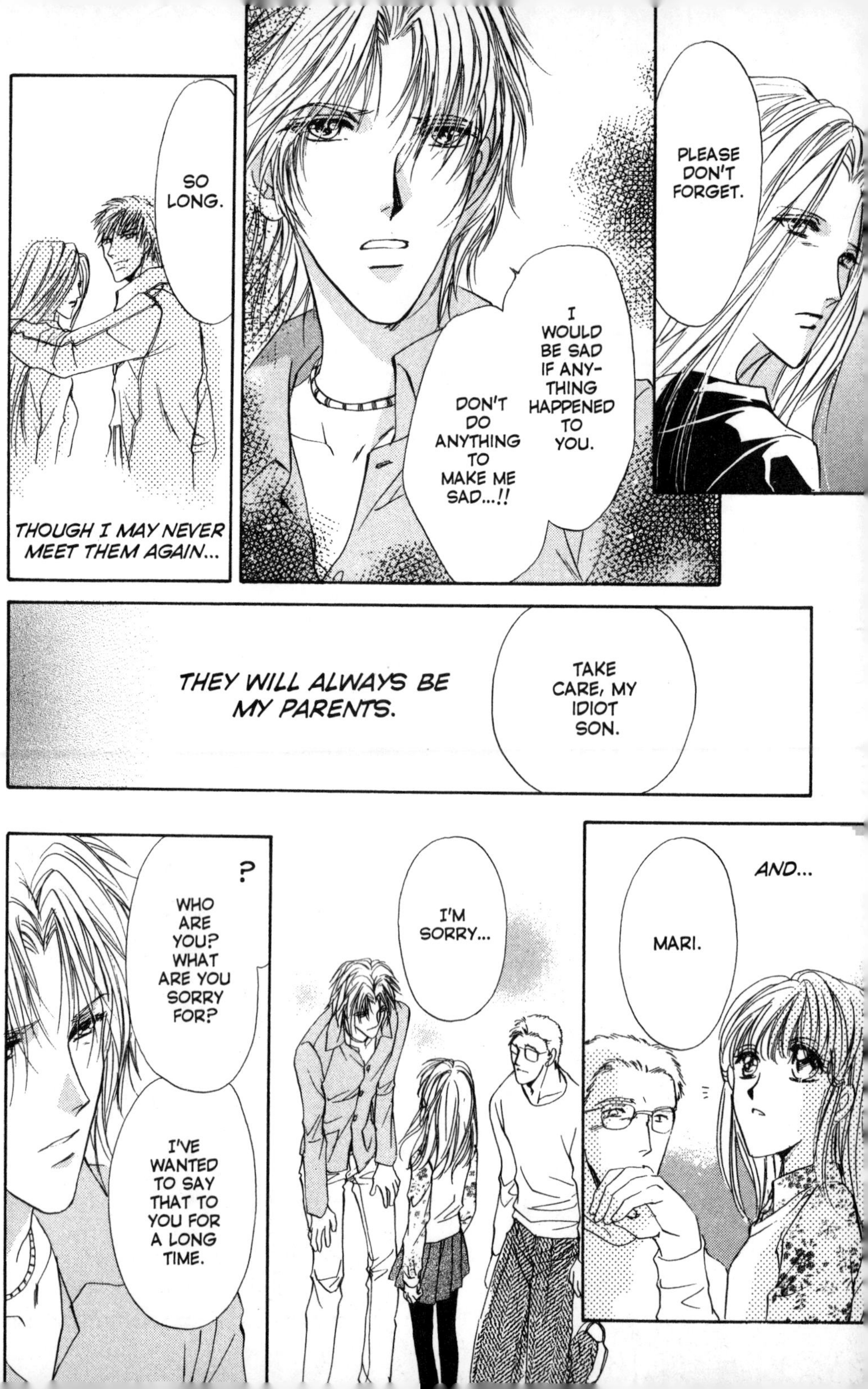
PLEASE DON'T FORGET.
I WOULD BE SAD IF ANY-THING HAPPENED TO YOU.
DON'T DO ANYTHING TO MAKE ME SAD...!!
SO LONG.
THOUGH I MAY NEVER MEET THEM AGAIN...
TAKE CARE, MY IDIOT SON.
THEY WILL ALWAYS BE MY PARENTS.
AND...
MARI.
I'M SORRY...
?
WHO ARE YOU? WHAT ARE YOU SORRY FOR?
I'VE WANTED TO SAY THAT TO YOU FOR A LONG TIME.

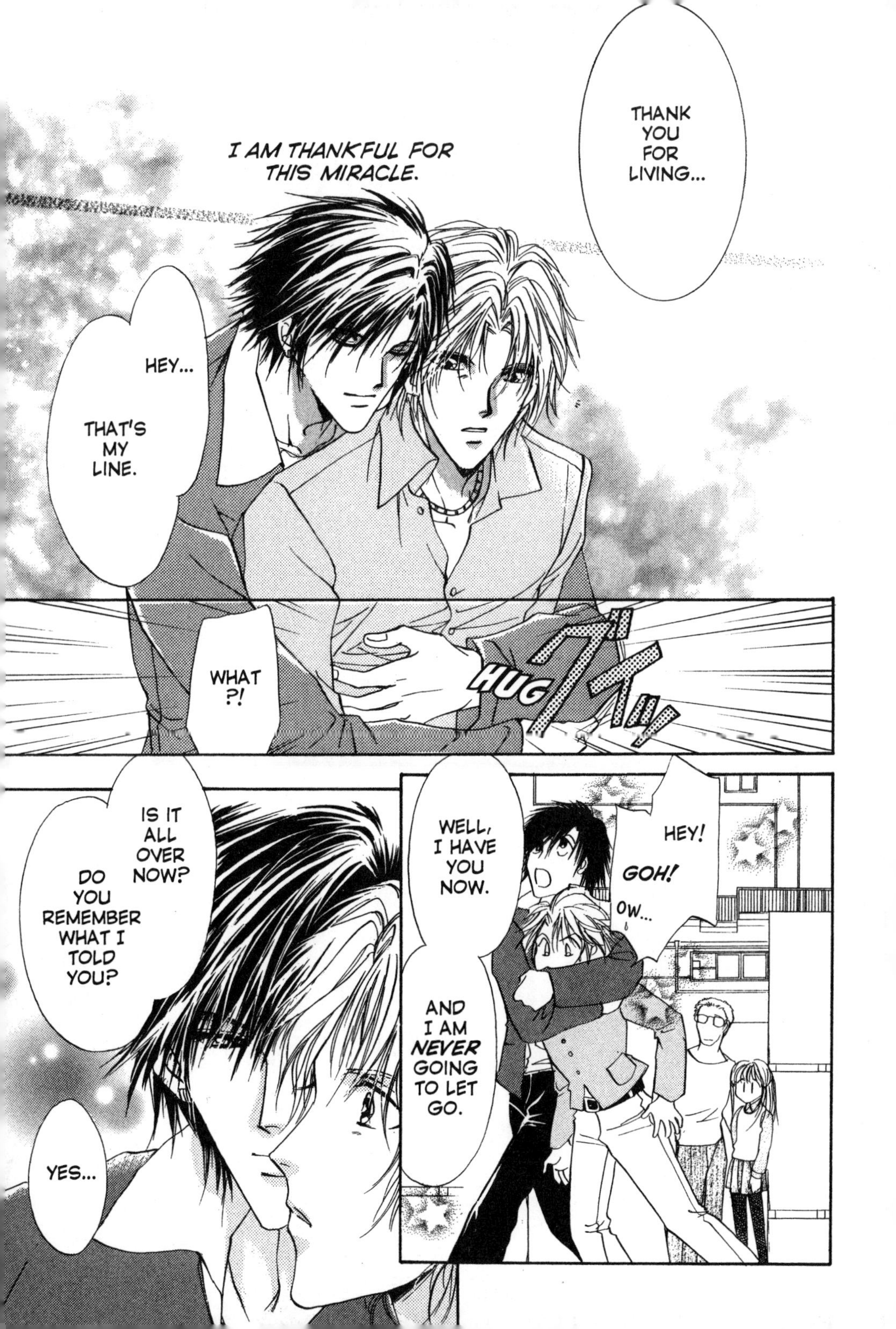
THANK YOU FOR LIVING...
I AM THANKFUL FOR THIS MIRACLE.
HEY...
THAT'S MY LINE.
HUG
WHAT ?!
HEY!
GOH!
OW...
WELL, I HAVE YOU NOW.
AND I AM *NEVER* GOING TO LET GO.
IS IT ALL OVER NOW?
DO YOU REMEMBER WHAT I TOLD YOU?
YES...

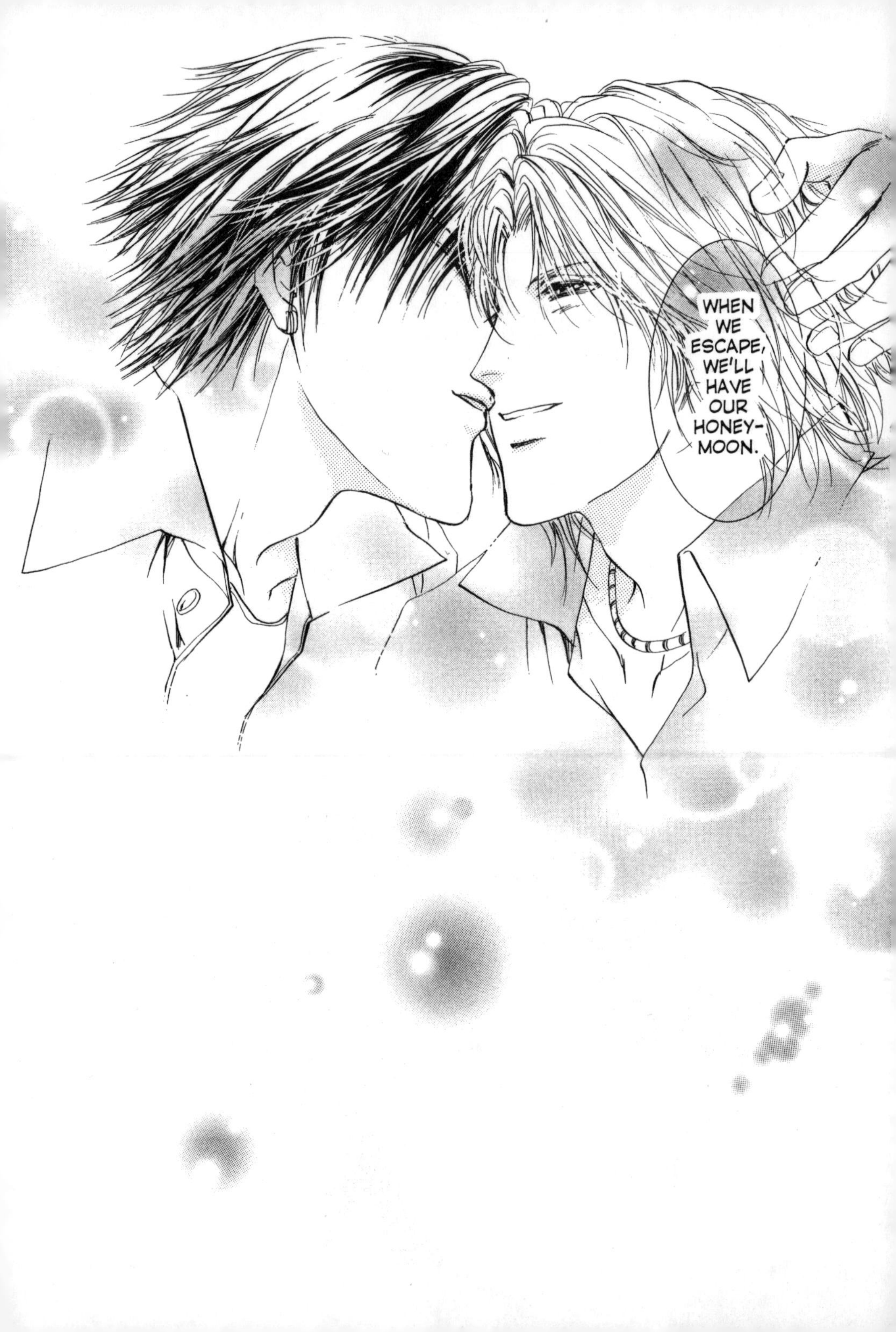
WHEN WE ESCAPE, WE'LL HAVE OUR HONEY-MOON.

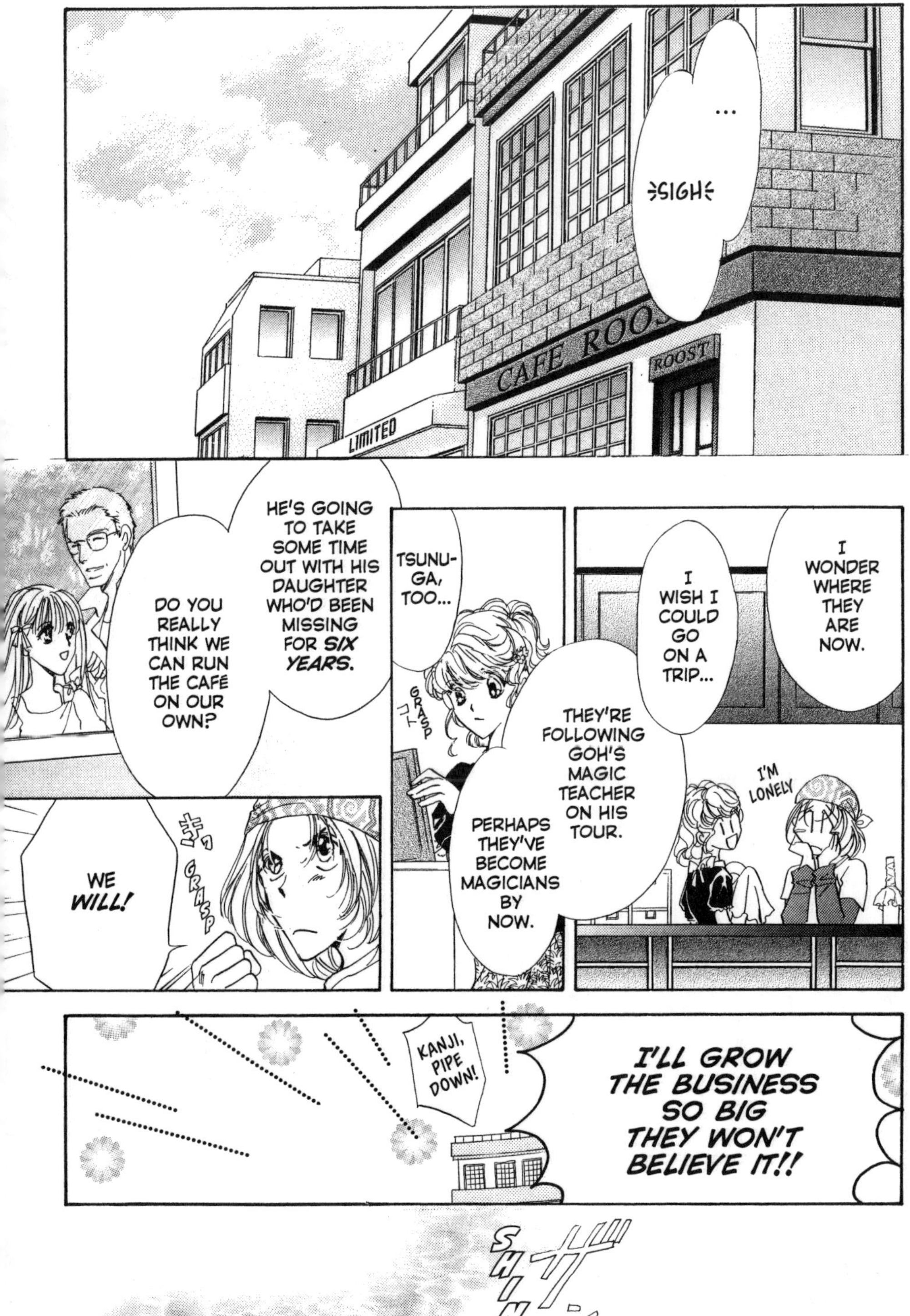
...
SIGH
CAFE ROOST
ROOST
LIMITED
I WONDER WHERE THEY ARE NOW.
I WISH I COULD GO ON A TRIP...
I'M LONELY
TSUNU-GA, TOO...
GRASP
THEY'RE FOLLOWING GOH'S MAGIC TEACHER ON HIS TOUR.
PERHAPS THEY'VE BECOME MAGICIANS BY NOW.
HE'S GOING TO TAKE SOME TIME OUT WITH HIS DAUGHTER WHO'D BEEN MISSING FOR **SIX YEARS**.
DO YOU REALLY THINK WE CAN RUN THE CAFÉ ON OUR OWN?
GRASP
WE **WILL!**
I'LL GROW THE BUSINESS SO BIG THEY WON'T BELIEVE IT!!
KANJI, PIPE DOWN!
SHINE

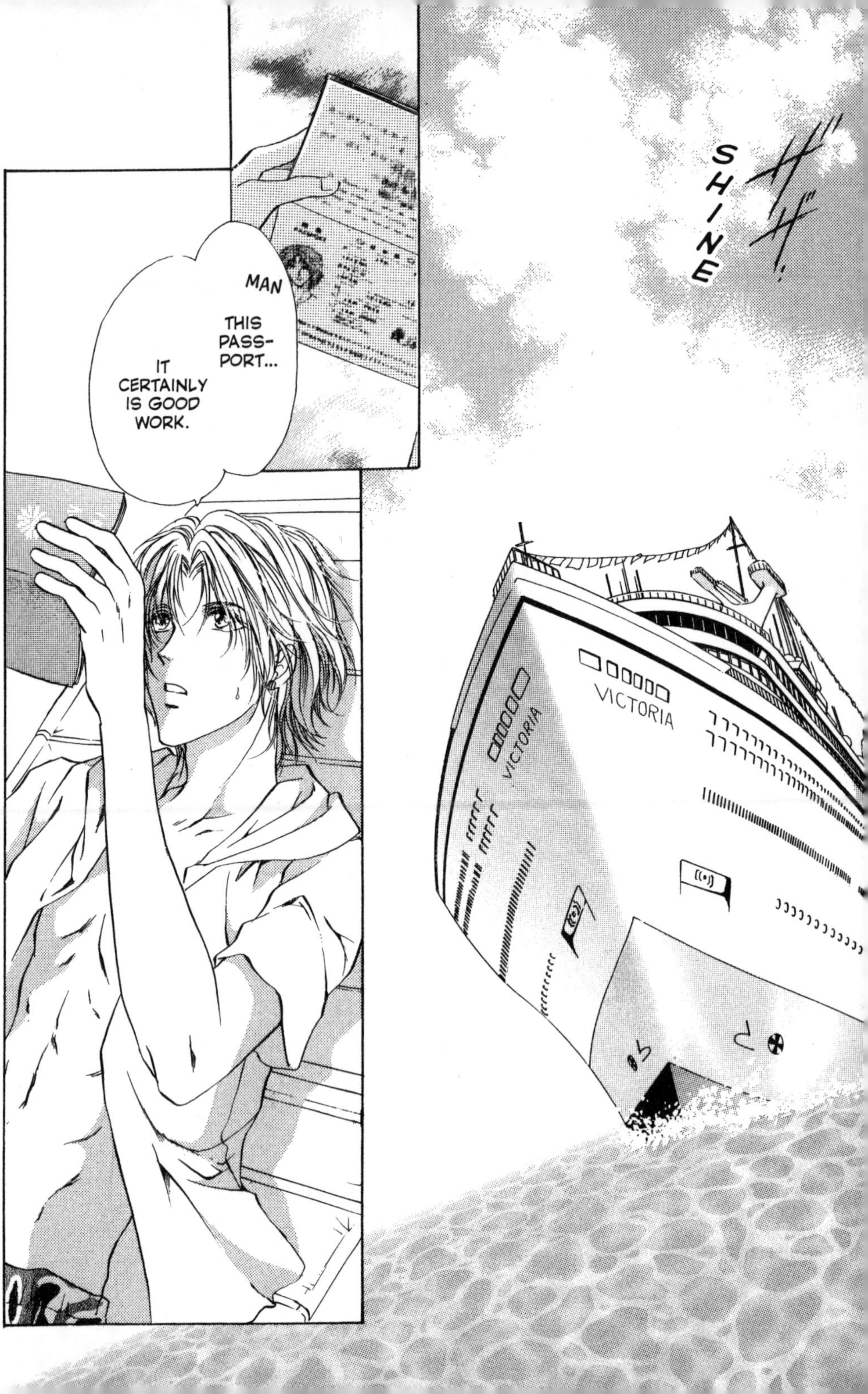
SHINE
VICTORIA
VICTORIA
MAN
THIS PASSPORT...
IT CERTAINLY IS GOOD WORK.

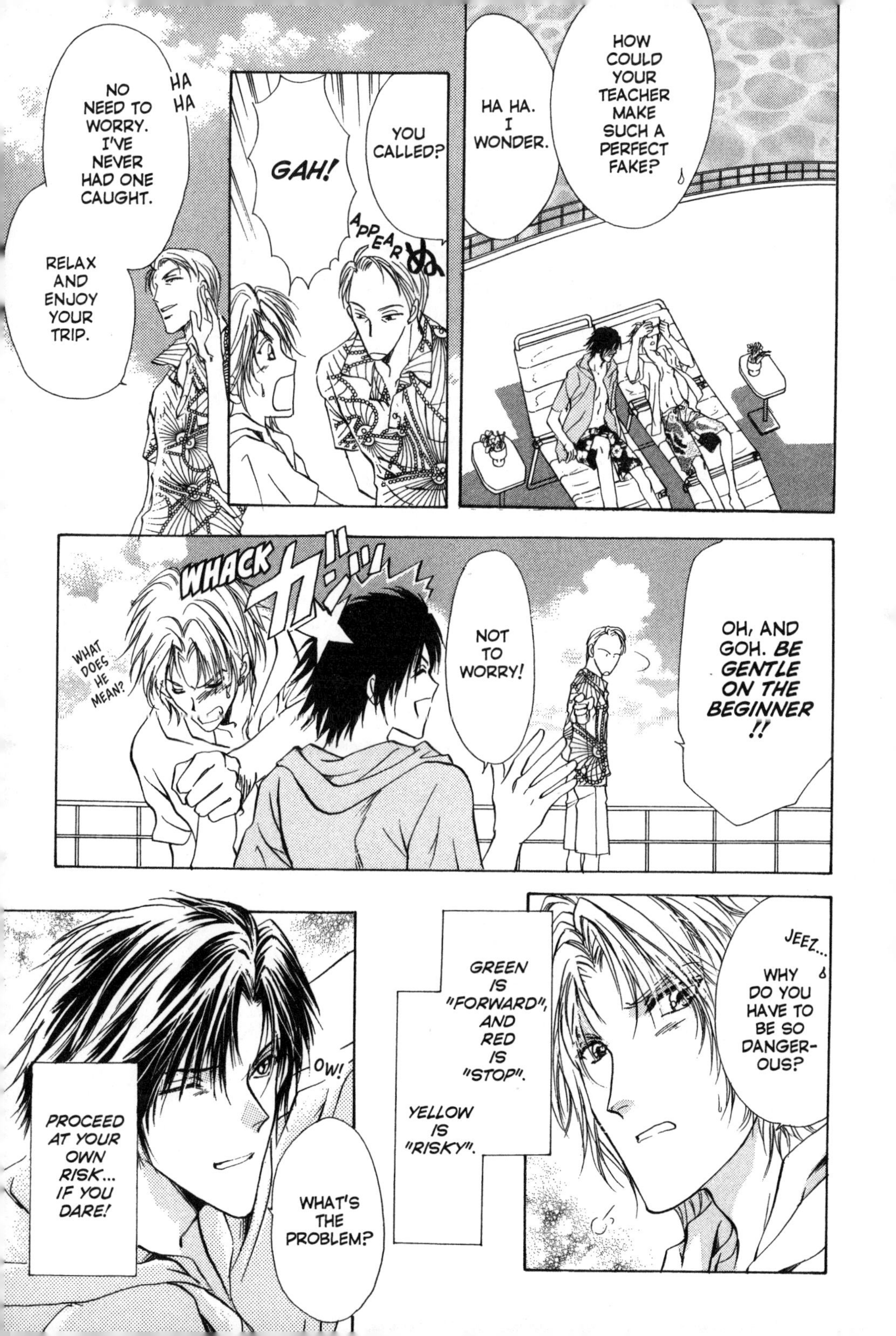
HOW COULD YOUR TEACHER MAKE SUCH A PERFECT FAKE?
HA HA. I WONDER.
YOU CALLED?
APPEAR
GAH!
HA HA
NO NEED TO WORRY. I'VE NEVER HAD ONE CAUGHT.
RELAX AND ENJOY YOUR TRIP.
OH, AND GOH. BE GENTLE ON THE BEGINNER!!
NOT TO WORRY!
WHACK
WHAT DOES HE MEAN?
JEEZ...
WHY DO YOU HAVE TO BE SO DANGER-OUS?
GREEN IS "FORWARD", AND RED IS "STOP".
YELLOW IS "RISKY".
WHAT'S THE PROBLEM?
OW!
PROCEED AT YOUR OWN RISK... IF YOU DARE!

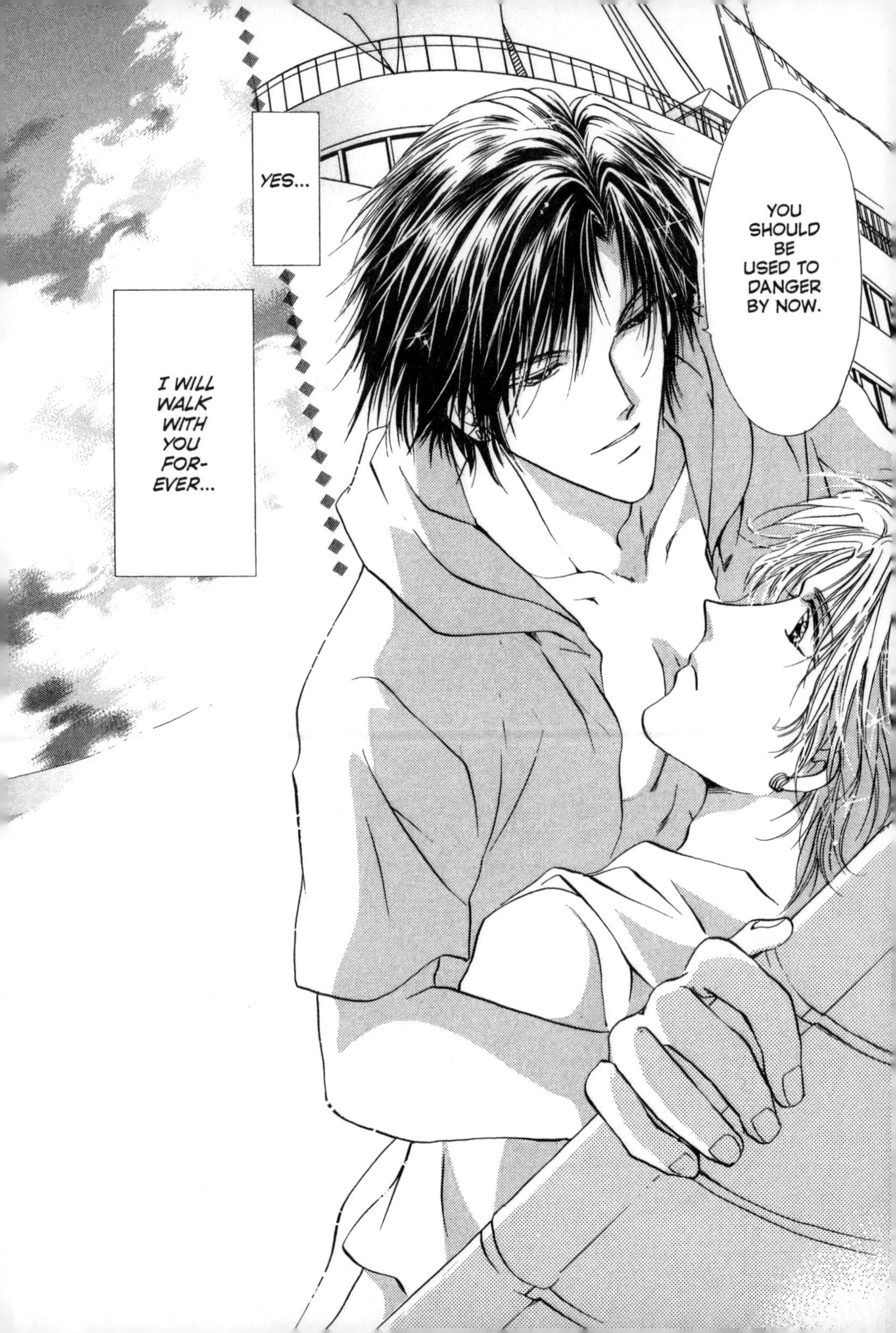
YOU SHOULD BE USED TO DANGER BY NOW.
YES...
I WILL WALK WITH YOU FOR-EVER...

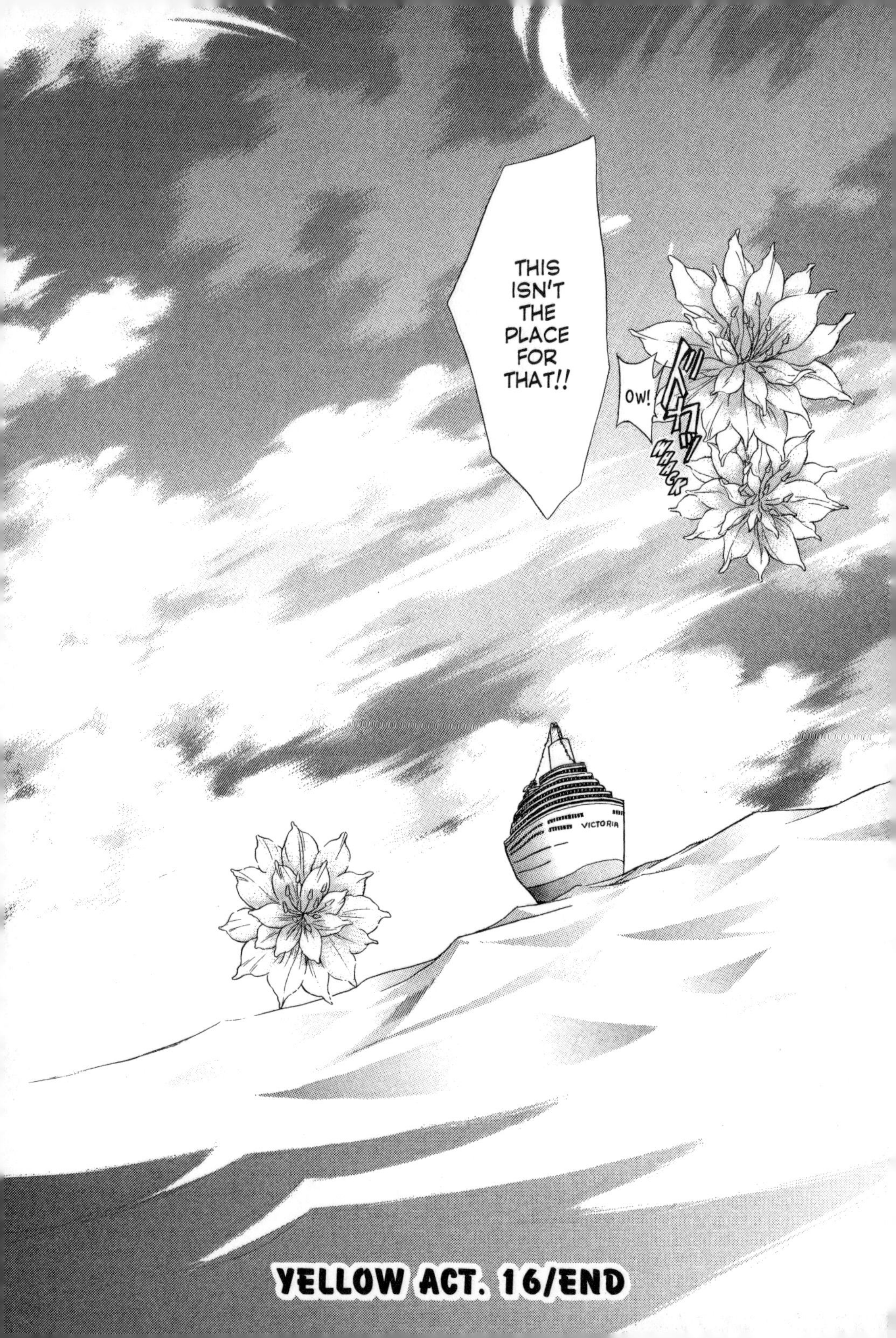
THIS ISN'T THE PLACE FOR THAT!!
OW!
WHACK
VICTORIA
YELLOW ACT. 16/END

YELLOW

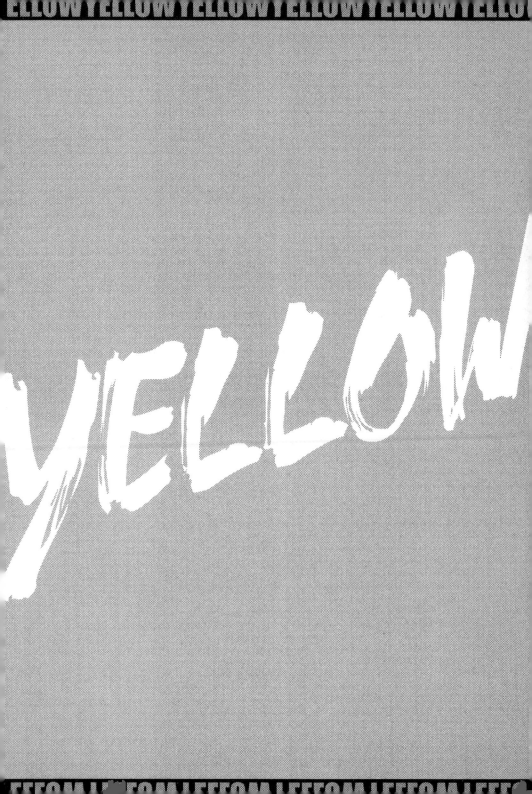

ハニー ムーン
HONEY & MOON

— ROME —

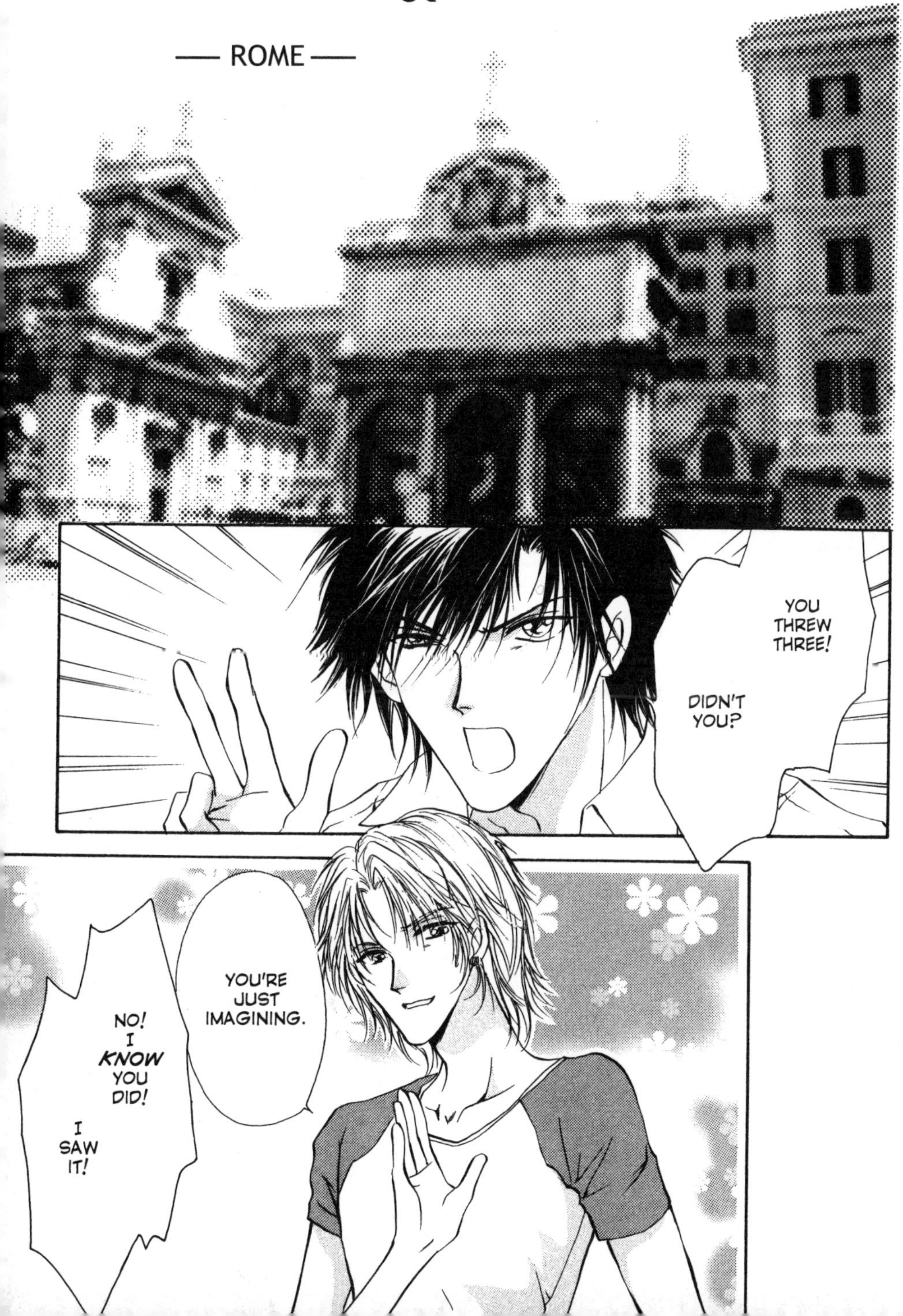

YOU THREW THREE!
DIDN'T YOU?
YOU'RE JUST IMAGINING.
NO! I ***KNOW*** YOU DID!
I SAW IT!

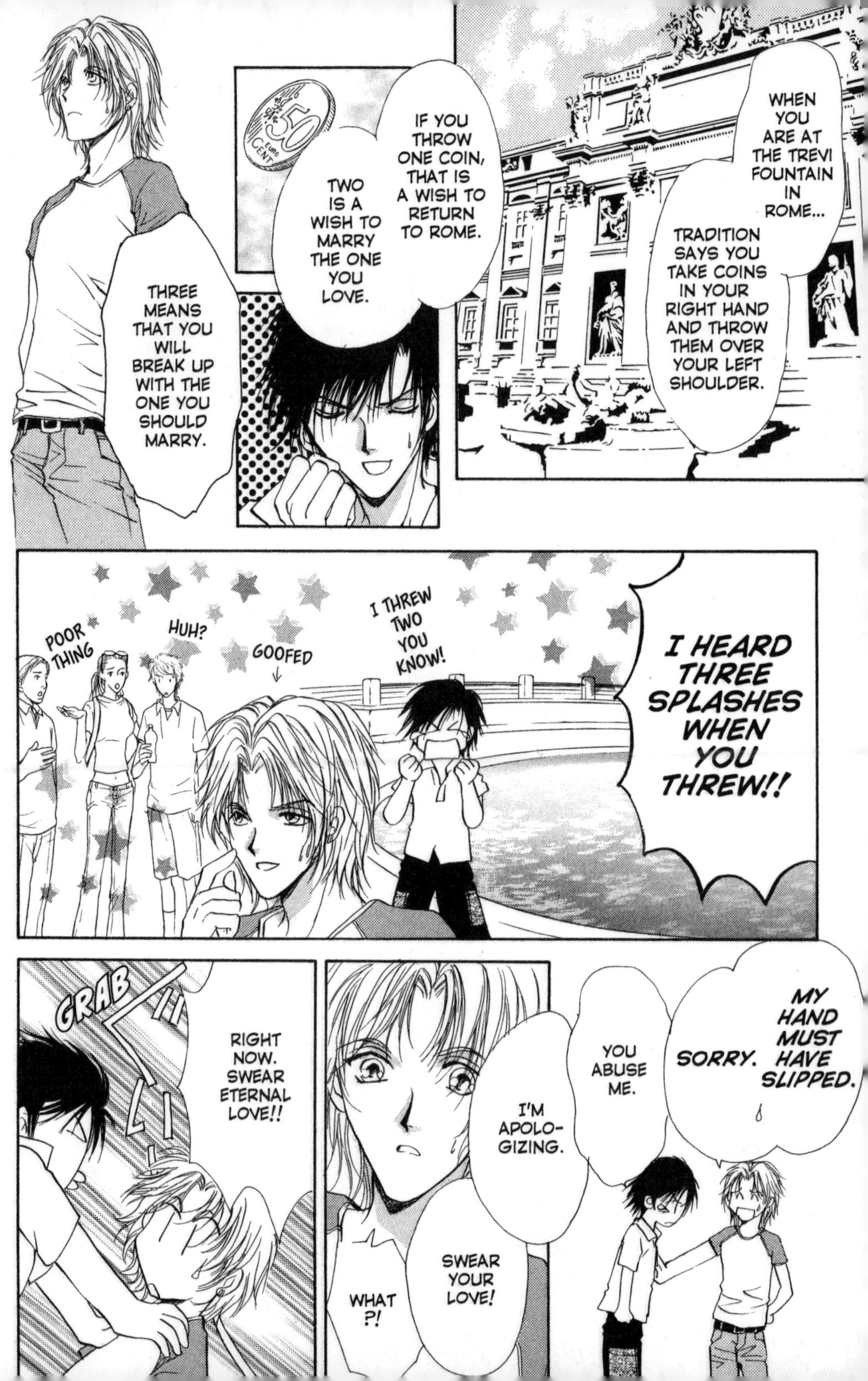
WHEN YOU ARE AT THE TREVI FOUNTAIN IN ROME...
TRADITION SAYS YOU TAKE COINS IN YOUR RIGHT HAND AND THROW THEM OVER YOUR LEFT SHOULDER.
IF YOU THROW ONE COIN, THAT IS A WISH TO RETURN TO ROME.
TWO IS A WISH TO MARRY THE ONE YOU LOVE.
THREE MEANS THAT YOU WILL BREAK UP WITH THE ONE YOU SHOULD MARRY.
I HEARD THREE SPLASHES WHEN YOU THREW!!
I THREW TWO YOU KNOW!
GOOFED
HUH?
POOR THING
MY HAND MUST HAVE SLIPPED.
SORRY.
YOU ABUSE ME.
I'M APOLO-GIZING.
SWEAR YOUR LOVE!
WHAT ?!
RIGHT NOW. SWEAR ETERNAL LOVE!!
GRAB

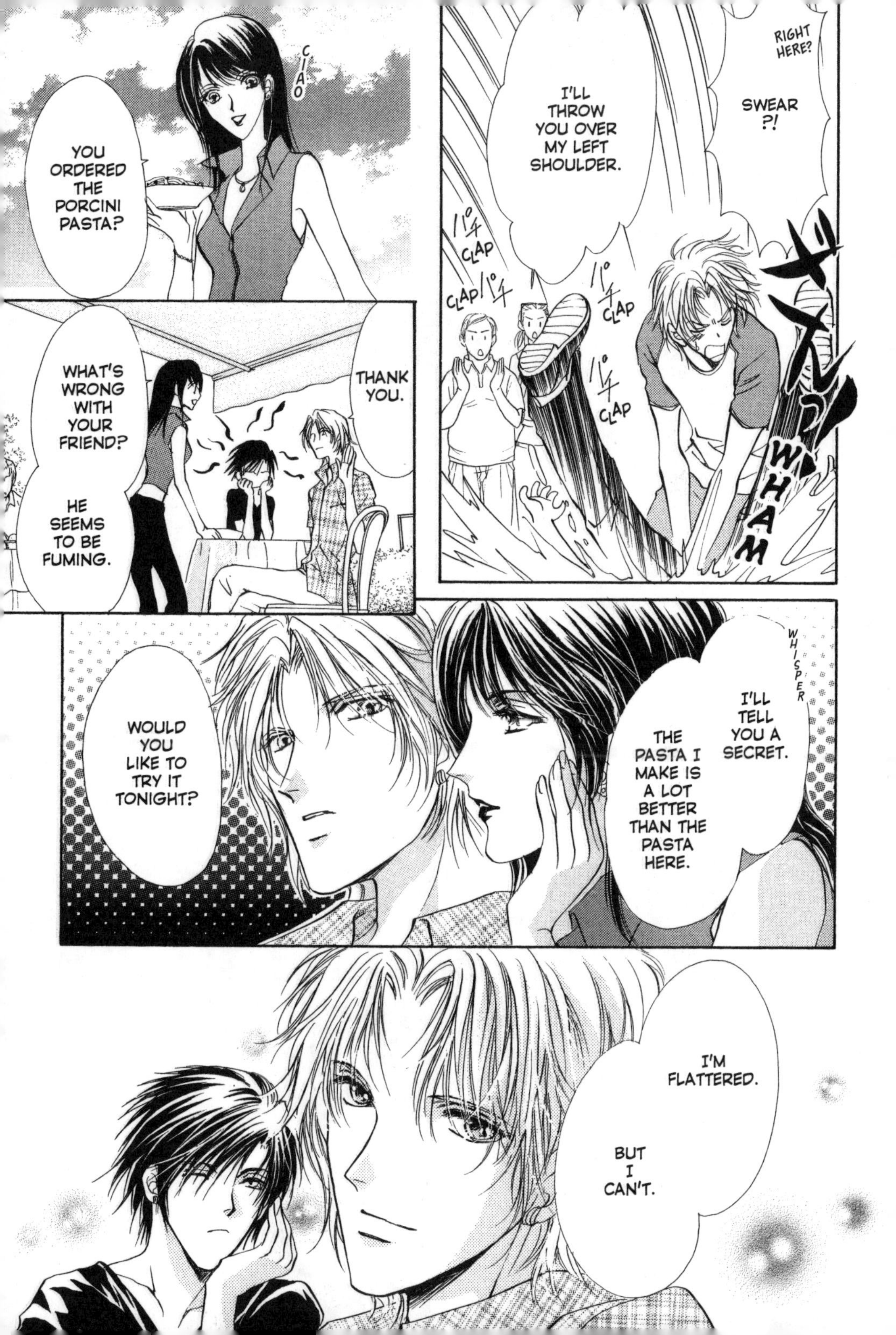
RIGHT HERE?
SWEAR ?!
I'LL THROW YOU OVER MY LEFT SHOULDER.
パチ CLAP
パチ CLAP
CLAP パチ
パチ CLAP
WHAM
CIAO
YOU ORDERED THE PORCINI PASTA?
THANK YOU.
WHAT'S WRONG WITH YOUR FRIEND?
HE SEEMS TO BE FUMING.
WHISPER
I'LL TELL YOU A SECRET.
THE PASTA I MAKE IS A LOT BETTER THAN THE PASTA HERE.
WOULD YOU LIKE TO TRY IT TONIGHT?
I'M FLATTERED.
BUT I CAN'T.

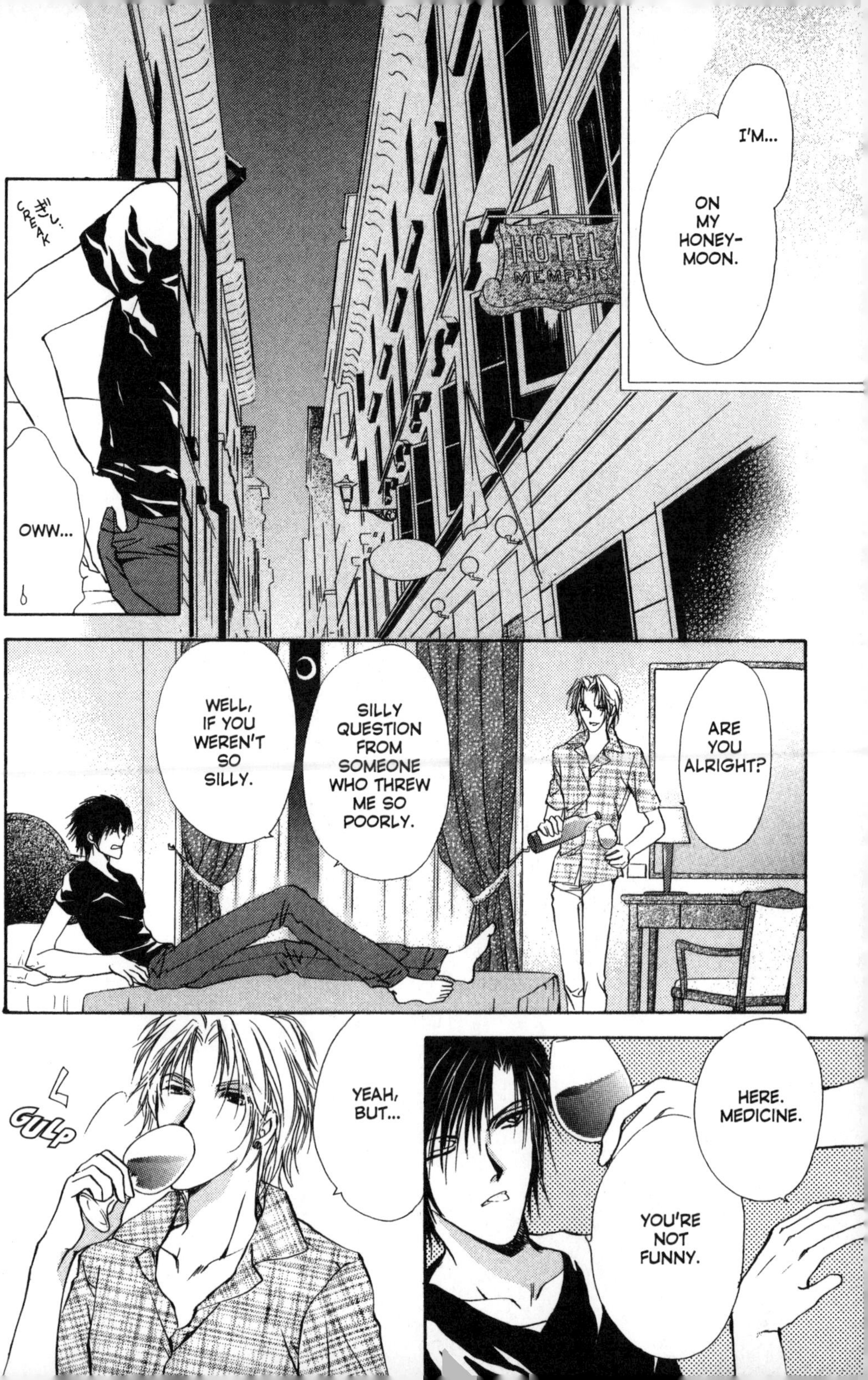
I'M...
ON MY HONEY-MOON.
HOTEL MEMPHIS
CREAK
OWW...
ARE YOU ALRIGHT?
SILLY QUESTION FROM SOMEONE WHO THREW ME SO POORLY.
WELL, IF YOU WEREN'T SO SILLY.
HERE. MEDICINE.
YOU'RE NOT FUNNY.
YEAH, BUT...
GULP

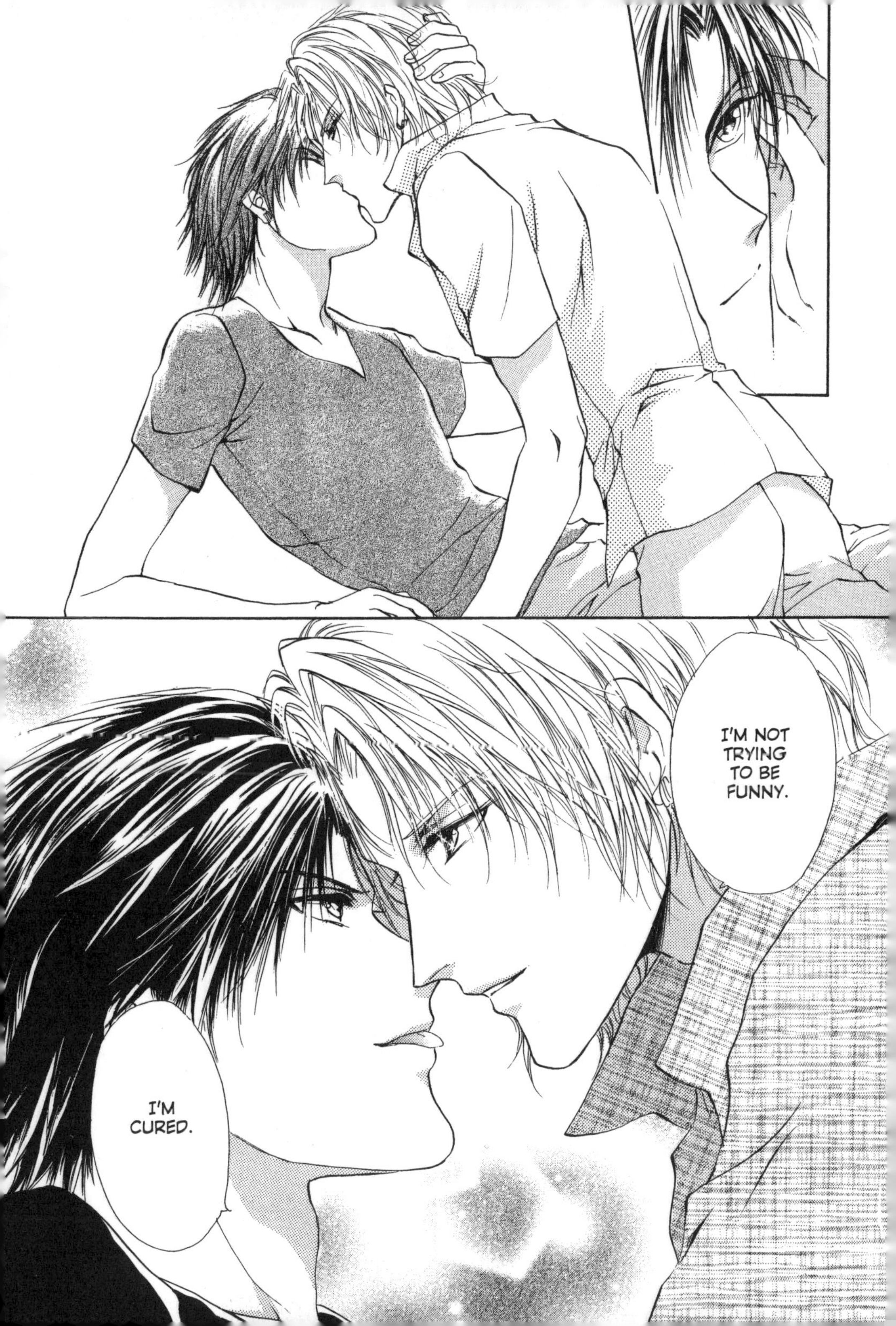
I'M NOT TRYING TO BE FUNNY.
I'M CURED.

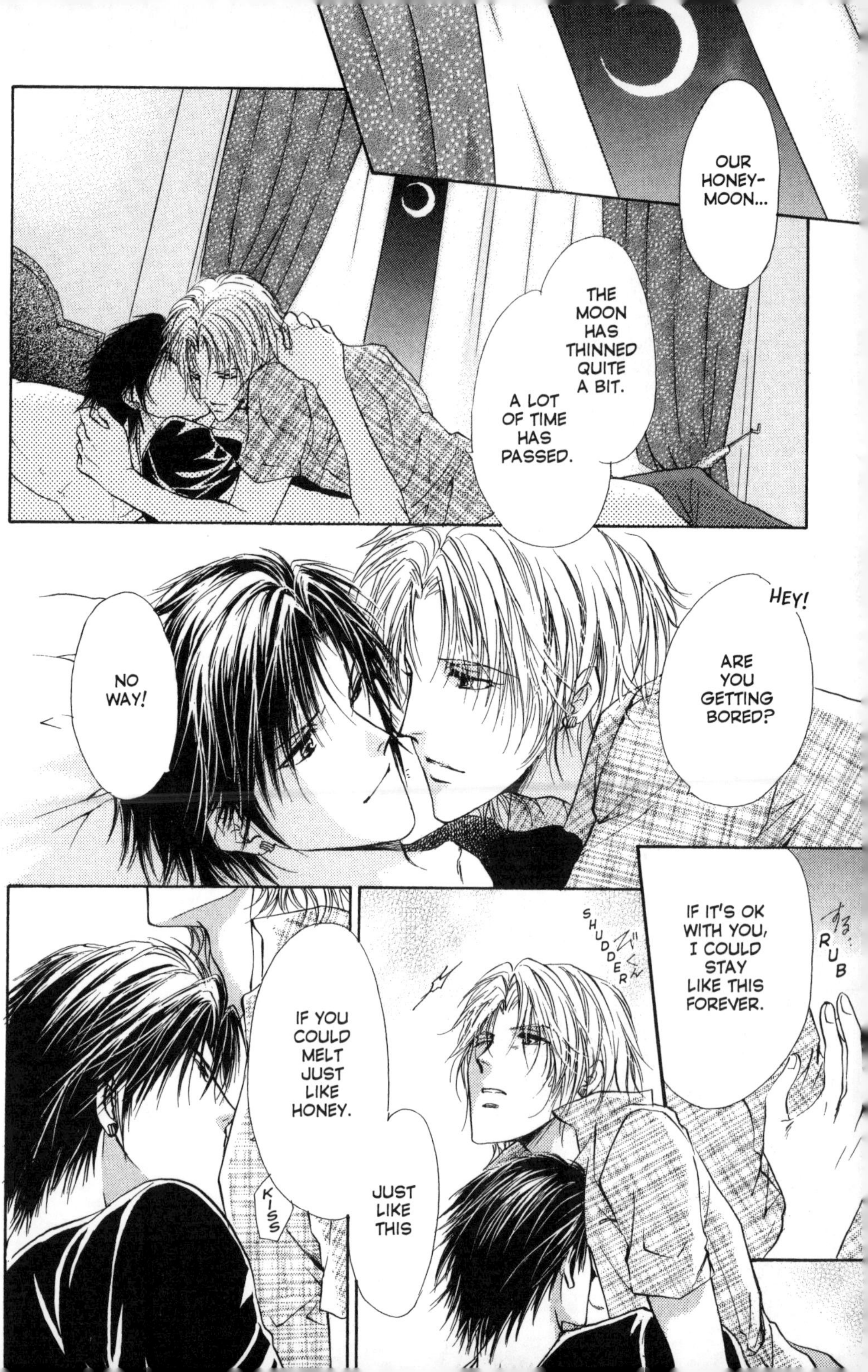
OUR HONEY-MOON...
THE MOON HAS THINNED QUITE A BIT.
A LOT OF TIME HAS PASSED.
HEY!
ARE YOU GETTING BORED?
NO WAY!
RUB
IF IT'S OK WITH YOU, I COULD STAY LIKE THIS FOREVER.
SHUDDER
IF YOU COULD MELT JUST LIKE HONEY.
JUST LIKE THIS
KISS

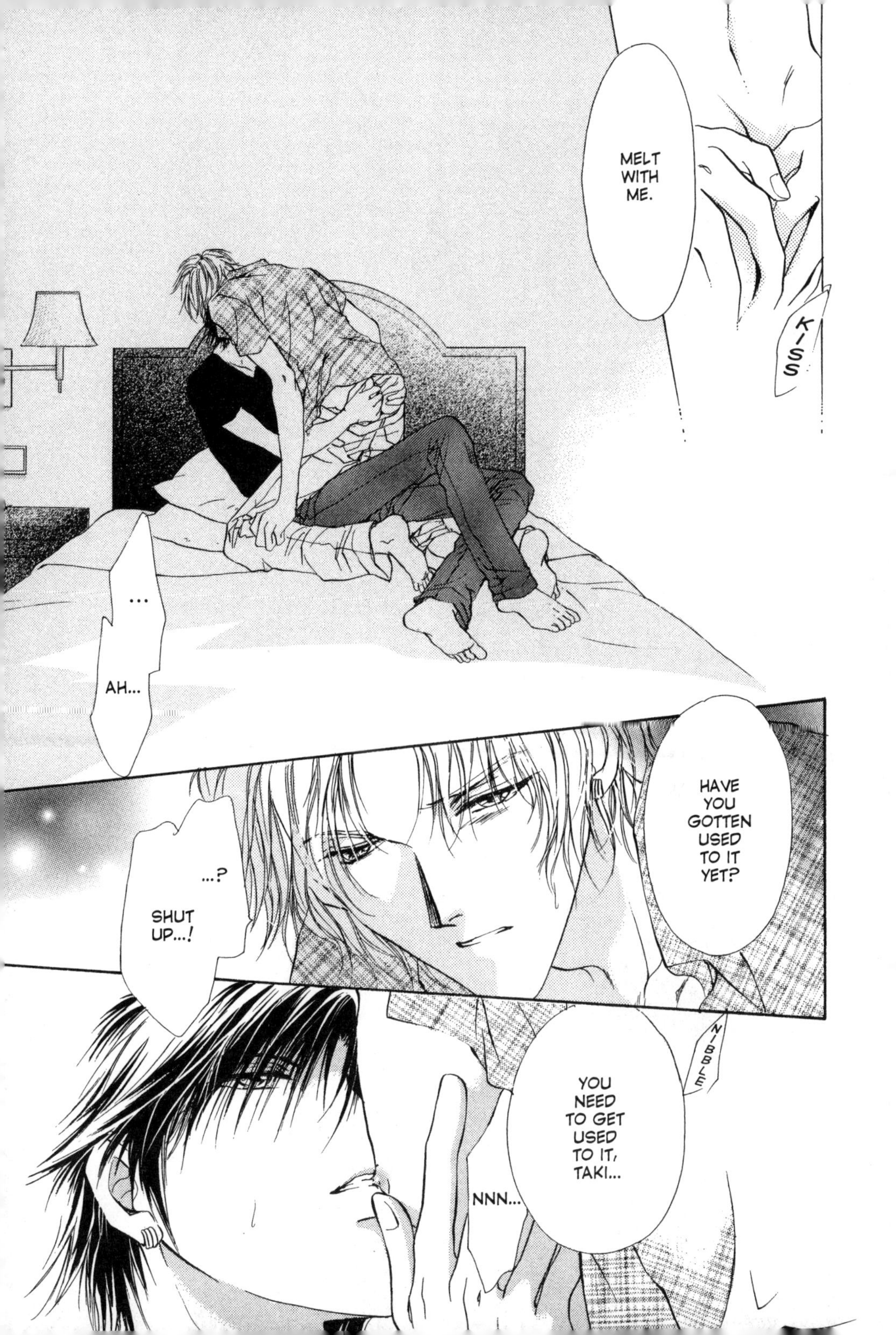
MELT WITH ME.
KISS
...
AH...
HAVE YOU GOTTEN USED TO IT YET?
...?
SHUT UP...!
NIBBLE
YOU NEED TO GET USED TO IT, TAKI...
NNN...

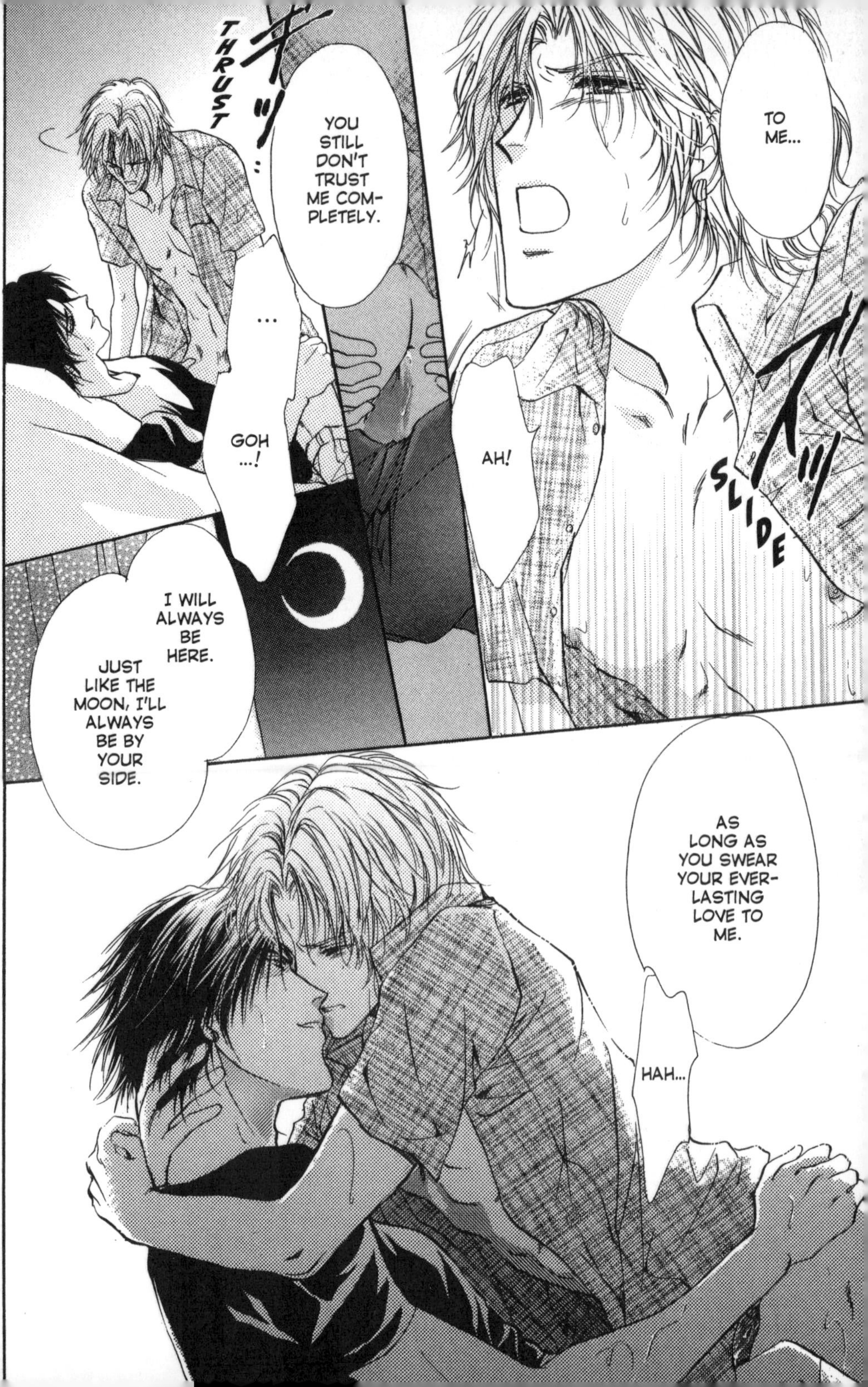
TO ME...
SLIDE
AH!
YOU STILL DON'T TRUST ME COM-PLETELY.
THRUST
...
GOH ...!
I WILL ALWAYS BE HERE.
JUST LIKE THE MOON, I'LL ALWAYS BE BY YOUR SIDE.
AS LONG AS YOU SWEAR YOUR EVER-LASTING LOVE TO ME.
HAH...

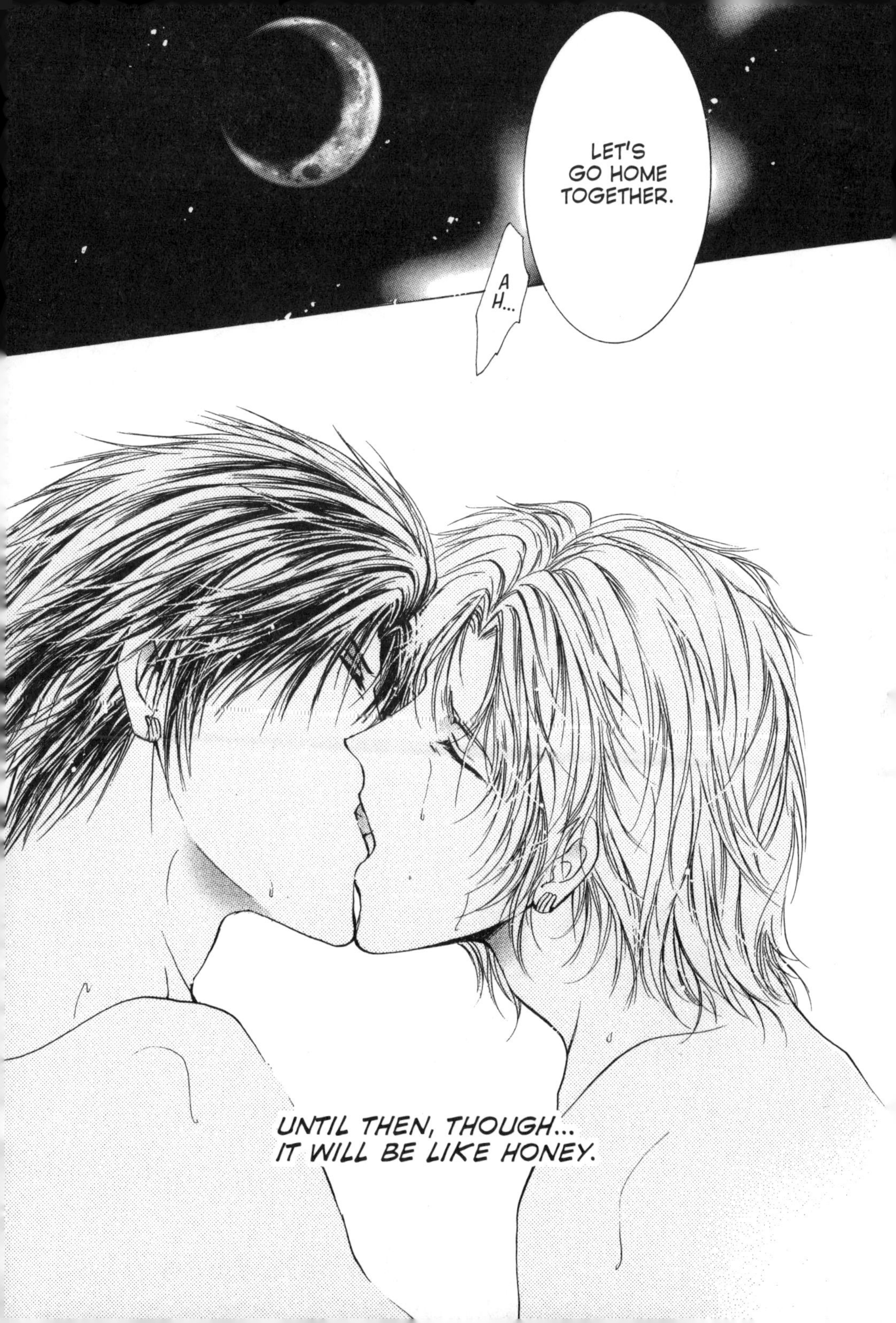
LET'S GO HOME TOGETHER.
AH...
UNTIL THEN, THOUGH...
IT WILL BE LIKE HONEY.

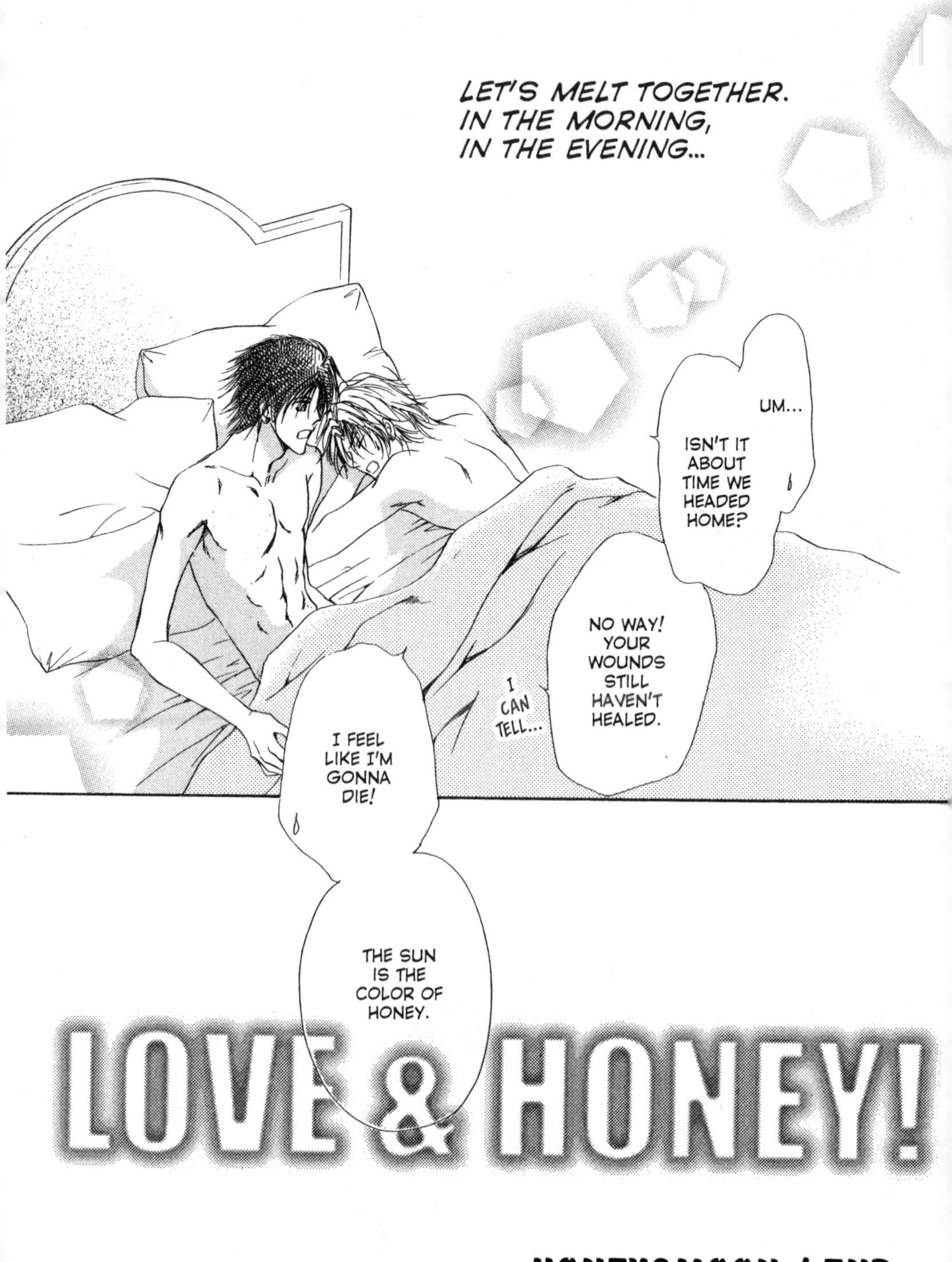
LET'S MELT TOGETHER. IN THE MORNING, IN THE EVENING...
UM...
ISN'T IT ABOUT TIME WE HEADED HOME?
NO WAY! YOUR WOUNDS STILL HAVEN'T HEALED.
I CAN TELL...
I FEEL LIKE I'M GONNA DIE!
THE SUN IS THE COLOR OF HONEY.
LOVE & HONEY!

HONEY&MOON / END

POSTSCRIPT.

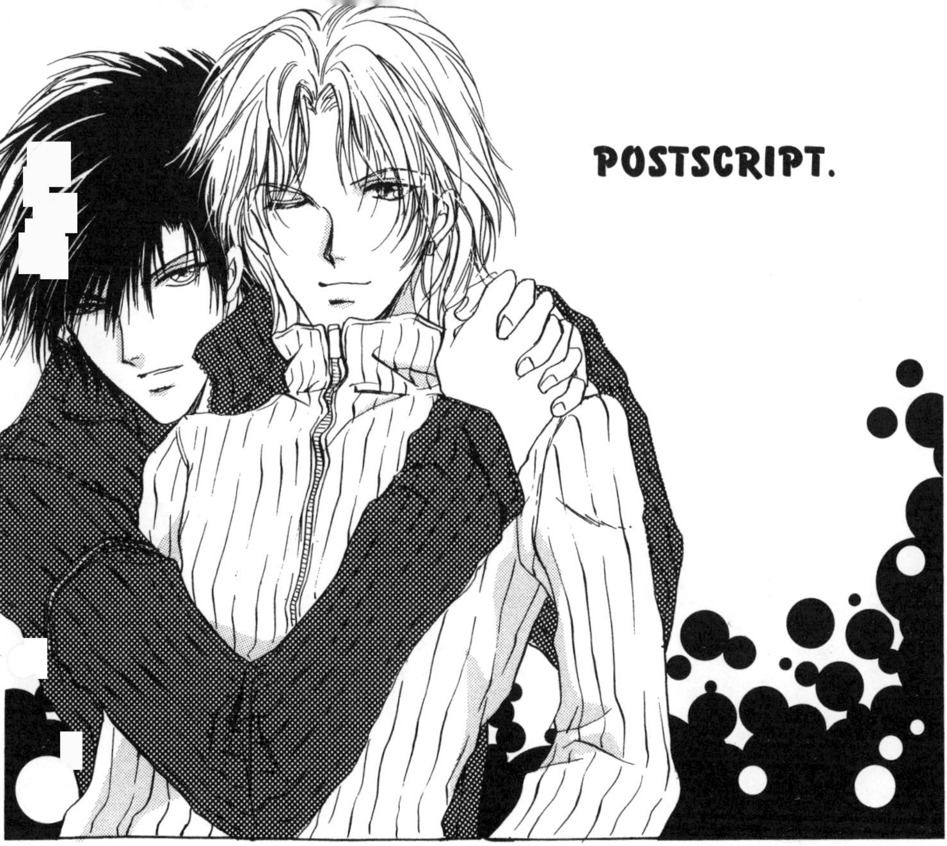

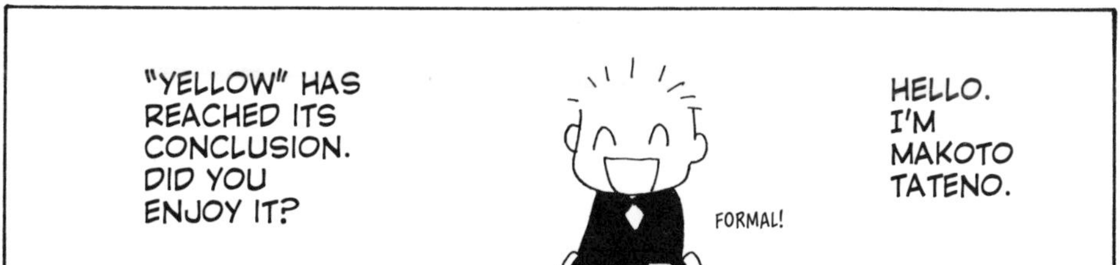

HELLO. I'M MAKOTO TATENO.
FORMAL!
"YELLOW" HAS REACHED ITS CONCLUSION. DID YOU ENJOY IT?

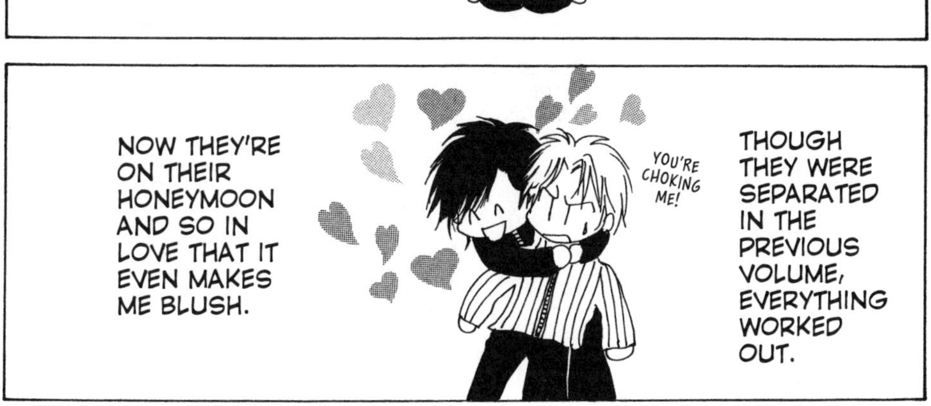

THOUGH THEY WERE SEPARATED IN THE PREVIOUS VOLUME, EVERYTHING WORKED OUT.
YOU'RE CHOKING ME!
NOW THEY'RE ON THEIR HONEYMOON AND SO IN LOVE THAT IT EVEN MAKES ME BLUSH.

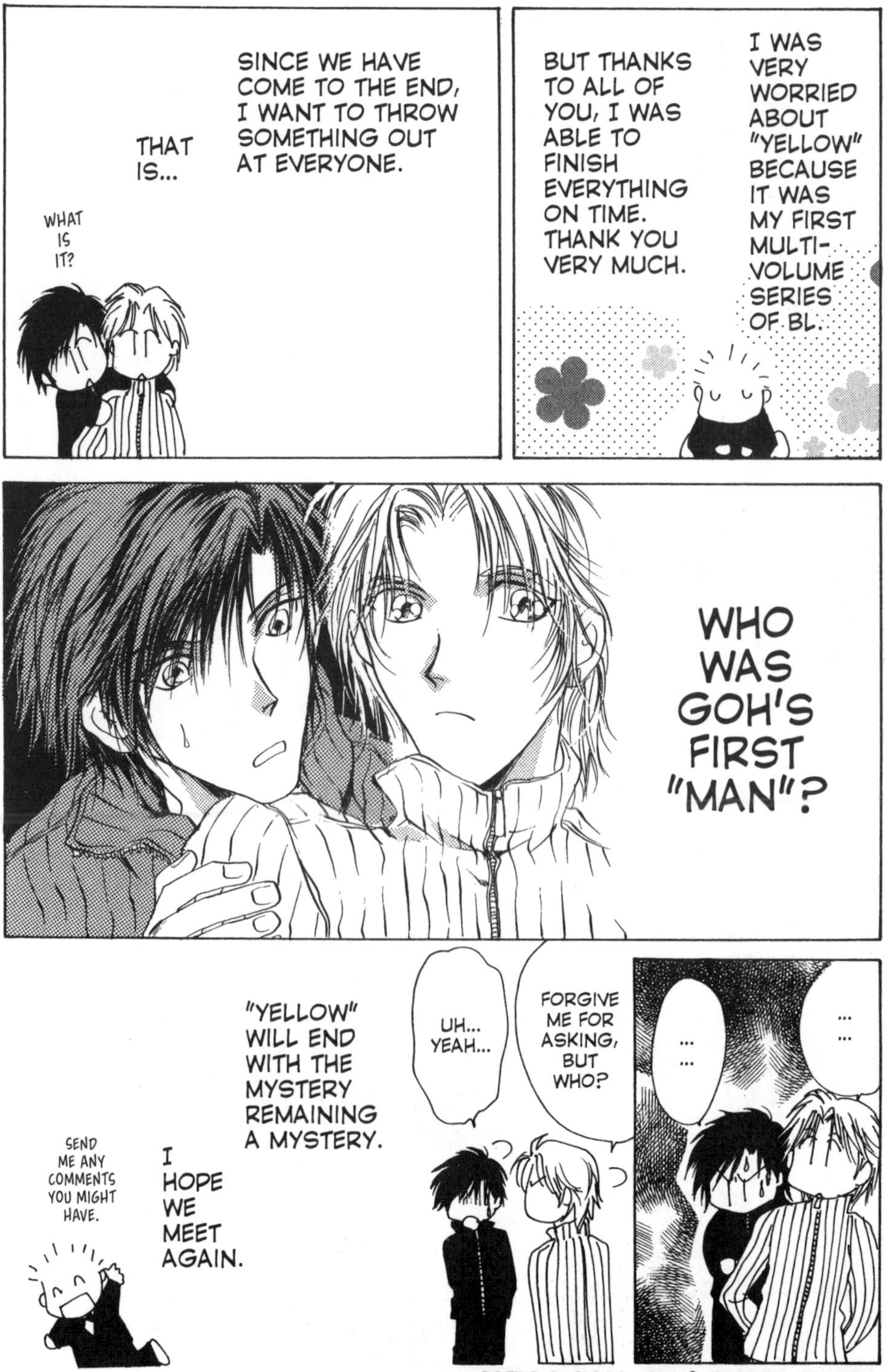
I WAS VERY WORRIED ABOUT "YELLOW" BECAUSE IT WAS MY FIRST MULTI-VOLUME SERIES OF BL.
BUT THANKS TO ALL OF YOU, I WAS ABLE TO FINISH EVERYTHING ON TIME. THANK YOU VERY MUCH.
SINCE WE HAVE COME TO THE END, I WANT TO THROW SOMETHING OUT AT EVERYONE.
THAT IS...
WHAT IS IT?
WHO WAS GOH'S FIRST "MAN"?
... ...
... ...
FORGIVE ME FOR ASKING, BUT WHO?
UH... YEAH...
"YELLOW" WILL END WITH THE MYSTERY REMAINING A MYSTERY.
I HOPE WE MEET AGAIN.
SEND ME ANY COMMENTS YOU MIGHT HAVE.

YELLOW 4 / THE END

Written and Illustrated by
You Higuri

A desperate search…

*In the garden of the
sacred beast…*

Gorgeous
Carat Galaxy

*Danger awaits those
who dare to enter.*

ISBN# 1-56970-903-3 $12.95

Gorgeous Carat Galaxy © You Higur 2004. Originally published
in Japan in 2004 by GENTOSHA Comics Inc., Tokyo.

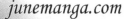

June™

junemanga.com

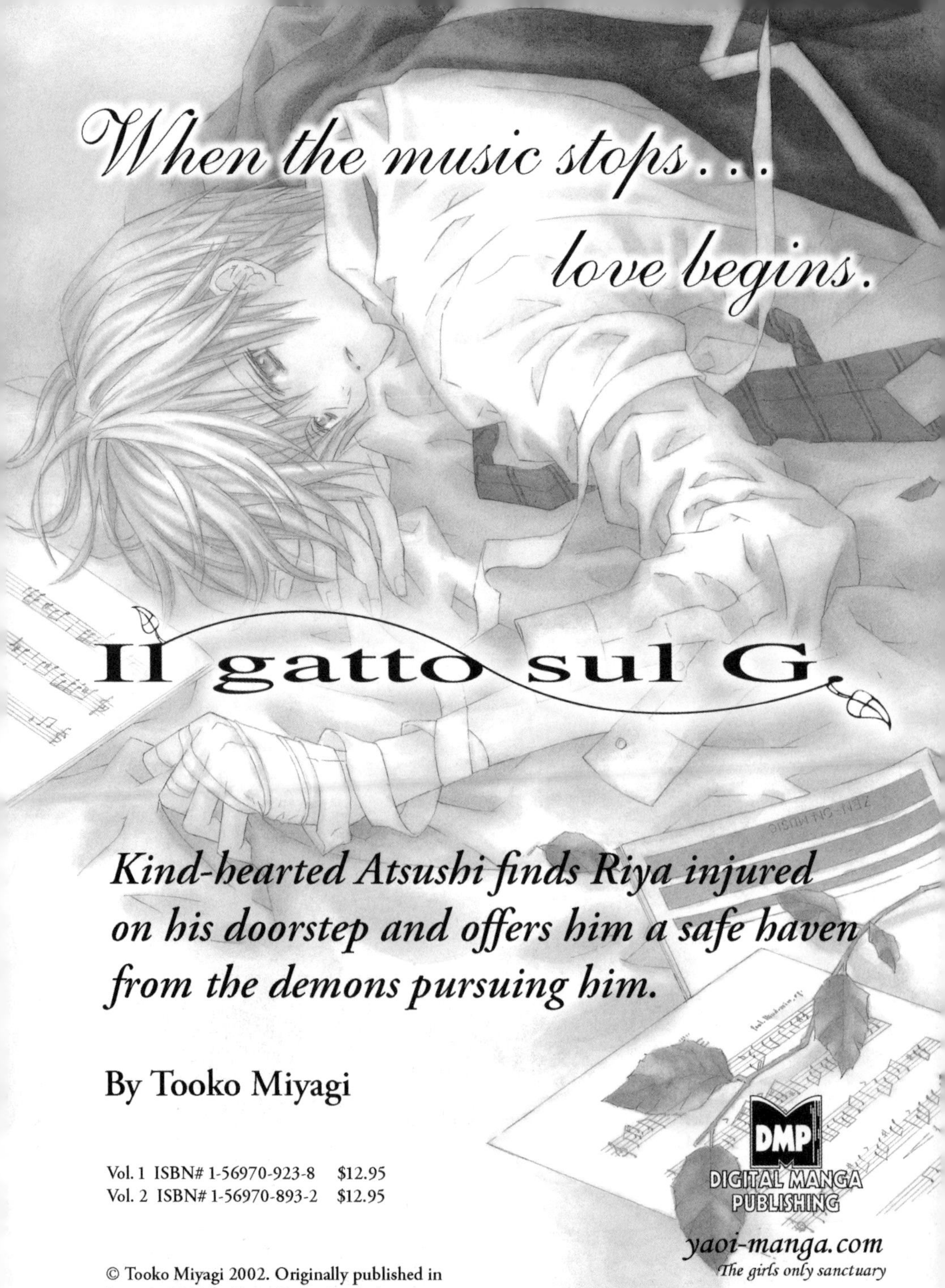
When the music stops . . .
love begins.
Il gatto sul G
Kind-hearted Atsushi finds Riya injured on his doorstep and offers him a safe haven from the demons pursuing him.
ZEN-ON MUSIC

MY ONLY KING
Created by Lily Hoshino
"The Queen of Yaoi"
Royalty appears in many forms...
DMP
DIGITAL MANGA PUBLISHING
© Lily Hoshino 2004. Originally published in Japan in 2004 by Kousai Shobou Co., Ltd.
By Lily Hoshino
ISBN: 1-56970-911-4 $12.95
yaoi-manga.com
The girls only sanctuary

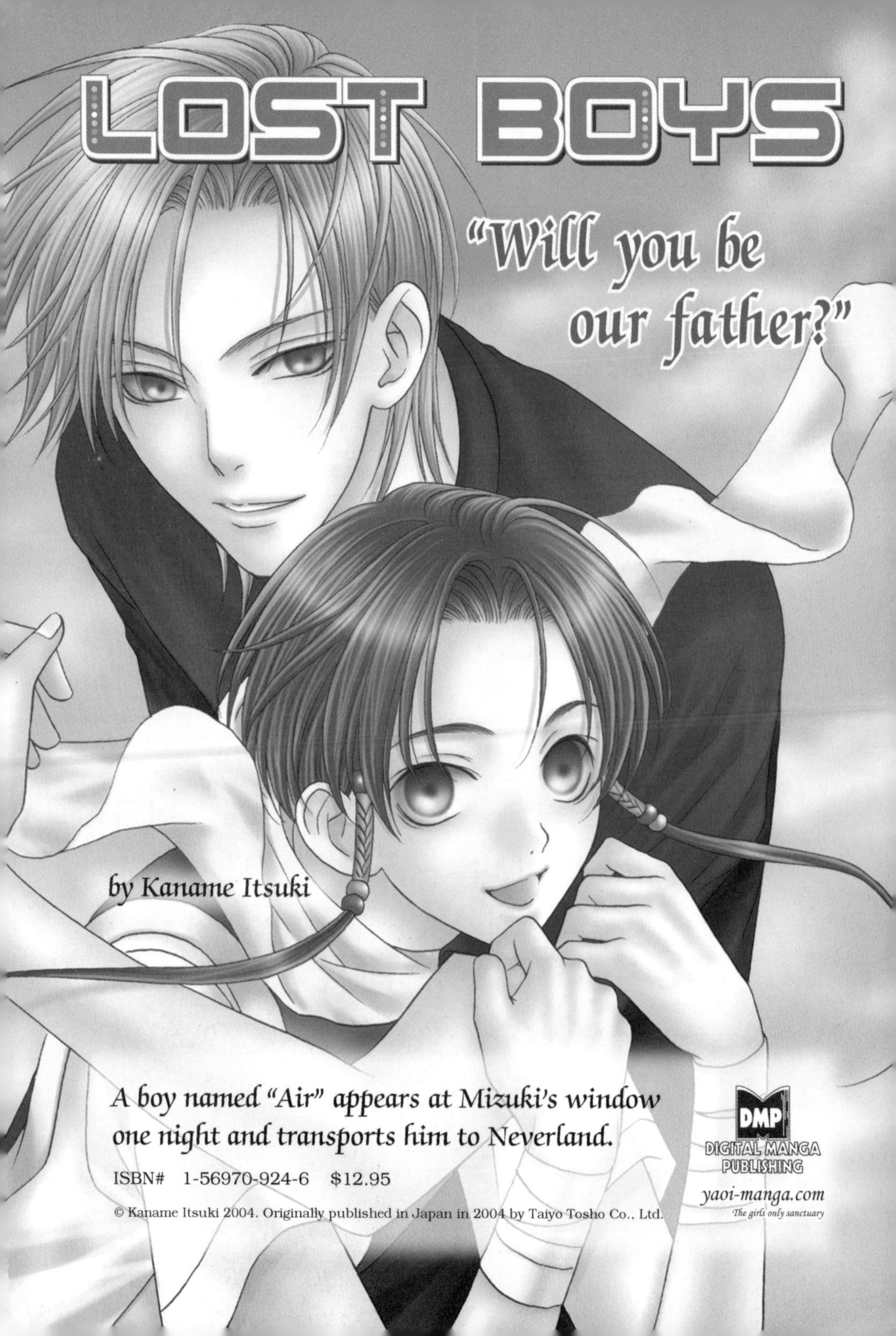
LOST BOYS
"Will you be our father?"
by Kaname Itsuki
A boy named "Air" appears at Mizuki's window one night and transports him to Neverland.
ISBN# 1-56970-924-6 $12.95
© Kaname Itsuki 2004. Originally published in Japan in 2004 by Taiyo Tosho Co., Ltd.
DMP
DIGITAL MANGA PUBLISHING
yaoi-manga.com
The girls only sanctuary

SAME CELL ORGANISM

by Sumomo Yumeka

Different... yet alike...

How can two people be so completely different from one another, yet be so in tune with love?

June
by
DMP

junemanga.com

ISBN: 1-56970-926-2   **$12.95**

Same-Cell Organism/Dousaibou Seibutsu © Sumomo Yumeka 2001.
Originally published in Japan in 2001 by Taiyo Tosho Co., Ltd.

You & Harujion

by Keiko Kinoshita

All is lost . . .

Haru has just lost his father,
Yakuza-esque creditors are
coming to collect on his
father's debts, and the
bank has foreclosed
the mortgage on
the house. . .

When things go from bad to worse,
in steps Yuuji Senoh. . .

**DIGITAL MANGA
PUBLISHING**

yaoi-manga.com
The girls only sanctuary

ISBN# 1-56970-925-4 $12.95

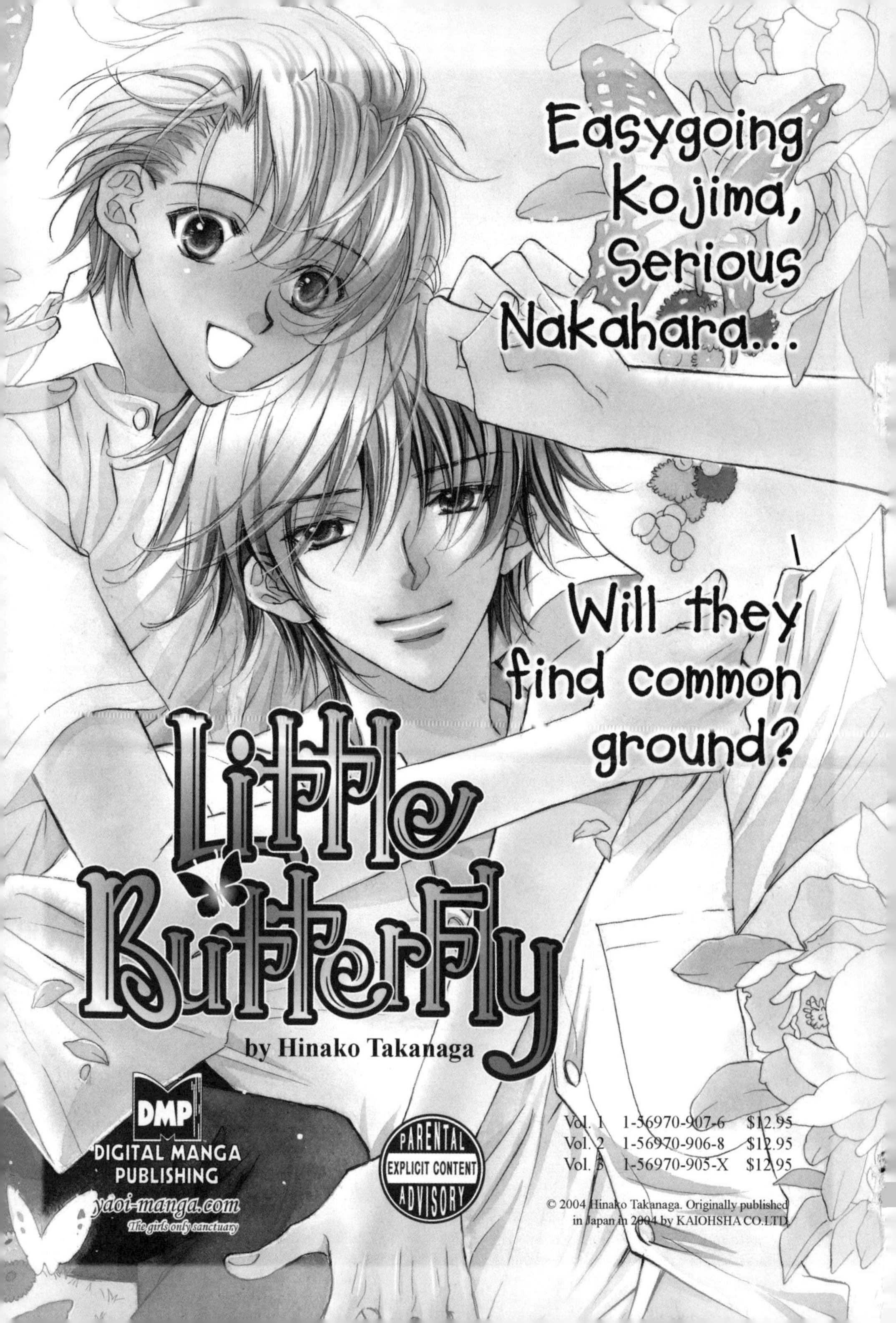
Easygoing Kojima, Serious Nakahara...
Will they find common ground?
Little Butterfly
by Hinako Takanaga
DMP
DIGITAL MANGA PUBLISHING
yaoi-manga.com
The girls only sanctuary
PARENTAL EXPLICIT CONTENT ADVISORY
Vol. 1 1-56970-907-6 $12.95
Vol. 2 1-56970-906-8 $12.95
Vol. 3 1-56970-905-X $12.95
© 2004 Hinako Takanaga. Originally published in Japan in 2004 by KAIOHSHA CO.LTD.

This is the back of the book!
Start from the other side.

NATIVE MANGA
readers read manga from *right to left*.

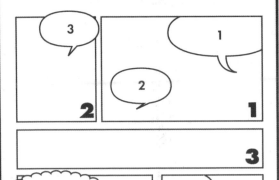

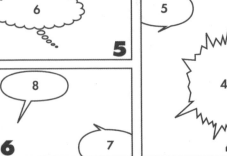

If you run into our *Native Manga* logo on any of our books... you'll know that this manga is published in it's true original native Japanese right to left reading format, as it was intended. Turn to the other side of the book and start reading from right to left, top to bottom.

Follow the diagram to see how its done. *Surf's Up!*

NATIVE MANGA
READ RIGHT TO LEFT